Coercion, Contract, and Free Labor in the Nineteenth Century

This book presents a fundamental reassessment of the nature of wage labor in the nineteenth century, focusing on the common use of penal sanctions in England to enforce wage labor agreements. Professor Steinfeld argues that wage workers were not employees at will but were often bound to their employment by enforceable labor agreements, which employers used whenever available to manage their labor costs and supply. In the northern United States, where employers normally could not use penal sanctions, the common law made other contract remedies available, also placing employers in a position to enforce labor agreements. Modern free wage labor only came into being late in the nineteenth century, as a result of reform legislation that restricted the contract remedies employers could legally use.

Robert J. Steinfeld is a Professor of Law at the School of Law, State University of New York at Buffalo. He is the author of *The Invention of Free Labor* (1991) and numerous essays on labor history and forms of free and coerced labor. Professor Steinfeld has written for *Stanford Law Review*, *William and Mary Quarterly*, *Law and History Review*, and *American Historical Review*. He has been a Langdell Fellow at Harvard Law School and a National Endowment for the Humanities Fellow.

CAMBRIDGE HISTORICAL STUDIES IN AMERICAN LAW AND SOCIETY

Editor

Christopher Tomlins *American Bar Foundation*

Coercion, Contract, and Free Labor in the Nineteenth Century

Robert J. Steinfeld

State University of New York at Buffalo

CAMBRIDGE
UNIVERSITY PRESS

PUBLISHED BY THE PRESS SYNDICATE OF THE UNIVERSITY OF CAMBRIDGE
The Pitt Building, Trumpington Street, Cambridge, United Kingdom

CAMBRIDGE UNIVERSITY PRESS
The Edinburgh Building, Cambridge CB2 2RU, UK
40 West 20th Street, New York, NY 10011-4211, USA
10 Stamford Road, Oakleigh, VIC 3166, Australia
Ruiz de Alarcón 13, 28014 Madrid, Spain
Dock House, The Waterfront, Cape Town 8001, South Africa

http://www.cambridge.org

First published 2001

Printed in the United States of America

Typeface Baskerville 10/12   *System* Corel Ventura Publisher [PBC]

A catalog record for this book is available from the British Library.

Library of Congress Cataloging in Publication Data
Steinfeld, Robert J.
Coercion, contract, and free labor in the nineteenth century / Robert J. Steinfeld.
        p.   cm.
Includes bibliographical references.
ISBN 0-521-77630-1 (hb)
1. Labor contract – Great Britain – Criminal provisions – History.
2. Forced labor – Law and legislation – Great Britain– History.
4. Forced labor – Law and legislation – United States – History.
I. Title. II. Series.
K1765.S74 2000
331.117094209034 – dc21   00-020963
                                                        CIP

ISBN 0 521 77360 1 hardback
ISBN 0 521 77400 4 paperback

For Jenny, Noah, and Ezra
and
for my father

Contents

List of Illustrations

FIGURES

TABLES

Acknowledgments

This book would not have been possible without the aid, encouragement, and advice of numerous people. I would like especially to thank Stan Engerman and Fred Konefsky for reading and commenting on multiple drafts of the manuscript. The work has benefited enormously from their generous advice and criticism. Markus Dubber helped me to see the visual possibilities for presenting statistical data. Gillian Hamilton was kind enough to alert me to some of the problems associated with relating unemployment to prosecution rates. I also owe large debts of gratitude to Guyora Binder, the late Betsy Clark, Seymour Drescher, Eric Foner, Morton ·Horwitz, Linda Kerber, Jan Lucassen, John Munro, David Seipp, Reva Siegel, and Lea Vander Velde for taking the time to comment on the manuscript at earlier stages. I'd like to give special thanks to Chris Thomlins for his support and for his many useful suggestions as this manuscript grew from a long article into a book. I would like to thank the participants in the Boston University Legal History Forum, the Buffalo Law School Faculty Forum, the Yale Legal History Workshop, and the University of Toronto Economic History Workshop for their many useful criticisms and suggestions. Finally, I would like to thank Frank Smith for all his efforts and for his wise advice in seeing this project through from manuscript to final production. None of the above are responsible for the remaining errors.

Introduction

Free Wage Labor in the History of the West

This is a book about the history of free wage labor. It argues that that history needs to be radically revised. We think of wage labor as having always been free and take for granted that in the eighteenth and nineteenth centuries, as today, wage workers enjoyed rights to work for whom they wished and to leave a job whenever they wished. Their lot may not always have been an easy one economically, but they could not be physically forced to perform labor as unfree workers could.

This picture of free wage labor was first developed as part of a larger rethinking of European history undertaken during the Scottish Enlightenment. The new history sought to depict change as unfolding in stages, with the latest stage representing a decisive rupture with the past. Each historical stage possessed its own distinctive form of social and economic organization that included a distinctive labor type. The feudalism of the Middle Ages, for example, was defined in part by the use of a particular form of labor, serfdom. When feudalism began to give way to a mercantilist version of market society, new forms of labor began to replace serfdom. In mercantilism, markets were heavily regulated, as was the wage labor used in these markets. Over time, however, state regulation was relaxed, and by the nineteenth century, free market society, with its characteristic labor type, free wage labor, had triumphed almost completely. In general, the movement from feudalism to free market society brought greater and greater freedoms to more and more people. Unfree serf labor gave way to regulated wage labor and finally to free wage labor as part of this larger historical process.

This narrative, which hardly anyone accepts in this form any longer, has nevertheless left its stamp on what we think wage labor must have been like in the eighteenth and nineteenth centuries. At its core this understanding harbors a set of assumptions about labor contracts. What was crucial in making free wage labor *free* was that wage workers were never forced to perform their labor agreements. If their agreements had been enforced against them wage work would have looked a lot more like unfree contract labor. There were at least two different reasons that wage labor agreements were not enforced against workers according to this story. First, wage workers normally served under agreements that were

1

terminable at will. Agreements terminable at will left workers free to come and go without fear that an employer could resort to law to try to coerce them into staying. Indeed, for some commentators, serving at will has become part of the very definition of wage work. If one does not serve at will but is entangled in an enforceable labor contract, that person is by definition not a wage worker.[1]

But even when workers served under agreements not terminable at will, employers did not enforce these agreements against them because they did not possess an effective legal remedy for doing so. The only remedy employers are generally thought to have enjoyed for breach of contract was money damages. As a practical matter this remedy was useless against wage workers. A contract suit for damages was often more costly than the sum at stake and could never be expected to yield a satisfactory payoff to an employer. Damage judgments secured against people who were propertyless and presumed to be mobile were not worth the paper they were written on. Even worse, damage judgments normally did not include consequential damages, such as the value of lost production, which might be the most important part of the actual damages suffered by an employer when a worker suddenly left. For most employers in most wage labor cases, a contract suit was not even worth thinking about. In effect, then, even where wage workers served under contracts the legal system failed to provide employers with an effective remedy to enforce those agreements.

Ironically, according to the conventional wisdom, the freedom from strict contract enforcement, which was the core freedom of wage workers, was perfectly acceptable to employers. They didn't need to enforce labor contracts against workers and didn't want to. They could rely on the dull compulsion of economic relations to secure all the labor they needed at prices they were willing to pay. Only in places where labor was in chronically short supply and land was abundant would employers even have been interested in trying to compel the performance of labor.[2] By the nineteenth century, this kind of labor scarcity was only a problem in the colonial agricultural periphery of an expanding capitalist universe. There, un-

---

[1] For an example of this viewpoint, see Robert Miles, *Capitalism and Unfree Labour, Anomaly or Necessity?* (London, 1987), 28–33.

[2] Evsey D. Domar, "The Causes of Slavery or Serfdom: A Hypothesis," *Journal of Economic History* 30 (March 1970). Domar's theory has been very influential since the 1970s. At the turn of the twentieth century Herman Nieboer, in *Slavery as an Industrial System* (The Hague, 1910), presented a similar though cruder version of the same theory. Domar's argument is less mechanical than the short description in the text implies. He explicitly acknowledged, for example, that the existence of unfree labor also depended on political variables and that it could occur even where labor was abundant relative to available land. But the short statement in the text accurately portrays the main proposition for which Domar's argument is normally taken to stand.

free slaves and contract workers *were* indeed used. In the metropolis, where labor was abundant, employers simply had no need to resort to legal compulsion. In fact, legal compulsion would have been counterproductive. Where labor was abundant employers found that free wage labor was cheaper to use than slave or indentured labor. In these situations, the movement from unfree to free labor was a natural part of the development of market relations between employers and employed. Employers were only too eager to drop compulsion and to replace unfree workers with free wage workers whenever the opportunity presented itself.[3] The absence of an effective legal means of enforcing labor agreements and the prevalence of employment at will, it is thought, served the interests of employers in fully developed free markets. They would not have wanted or needed strict contract enforcement because the dull compulsion of economic relations represented a far better means for extracting labor services.[4]

By contrast, in the agricultural periphery where labor markets were thin or nonexistent, employers needed to be able to enforce labor agreements and naturally were able to do so. There, contract workers were entangled in enforceable labor agreements in ways that the free wage workers of the metropolis were not. Employers of contract labor were able to

---

[3] Gary Nash and Sharon Salinger make arguments of this kind in explaining why indentured servants and slaves came to make up a smaller and smaller percentage of the labor force in Pennsylvania after the American Revolution. Gary Nash, *The Urban Crucible: Social Change, Political Consciousness, and the Origins of the American Revolution* (Cambridge, Mass., 1979), 320; Sharon Salinger, *"To Serve Well and Faithfully," Labor and Indentured Servants in Pennsylvania, 1682–1800* (Cambridge, Mass., 1987), 149–52. Christopher Whatley makes a similar argument to explain employer support for the abolition of serfdom among Scottish coal miners in the last quarter of the eighteenth century. Christopher Whatley, "'The Fettering Bonds of Brotherhood': Combination and Labour Relations in the Scottish Coal-Mining Industry, c. 1690–1775," *Social History* 12 (May 1987). Arguments like these, about the economic superiority of free labor for employers, date back at least to the eighteenth century. See, for example, Adam Smith, *An Inquiry into the Nature and Causes of the Wealth of Nations,* ed. Edwin Cannan (Chicago, Ill., 1976), I:90, 411–12.

[4] For an early version of this argument, see Joseph Townsend, "A Dissertation on the Poor Laws" in *A Select Collection of Scarce and Valuable Economical Tracts,* ed. J. R. McCulloch (London, 1859), 404, quoted in David Brion Davis, *The Problem of Slavery in the Age of Revolution, 1770–1823* (Ithaca, N.Y., 1975), 358–59, and in Karl Polanyi, *The Great Transformation: The Political and Economic Origins of Our Time* (Boston, 1957), 113–14. Townsend wrote: "Legal constraint is attended with much trouble, violence and noise; creates ill will, and never can be productive of good and acceptable service: whereas hunger is not only peaceable, silent, unremitting pressure, but, as the most natural motive to industry and labor, it calls forth the most powerful exertions; and, when satisfied by the free bounty of another, lays lasting and sure foundations for good will and gratitude. The slave must be compelled to work but the free man should be left to his own judgment, and discretion; should be protected in the full enjoyment of his own, be it much or little; and punished when he invades his neighbor's property."

enforce labor agreements because they had available various nonpecuniary remedies, such as incarceration and corporal punishment, to compel workers to perform those agreements. It is precisely the use of these nonpecuniary pressures to compel work (those that involve physical violence or deprivation of bodily liberty) that define for us what makes a form of labor unfree.[5] Because such nonpecuniary pressures were also used in slavery, today we frequently link slavery and contract labor as forms of "unfree labor." By contrast, the freedom of free wage workers lay first of all in a freedom from nonpecuniary imposition. Wage workers were exposed at times to severe pecuniary pressures (those that involve deprivation of income or property), but never to nonpecuniary pressures to work. If they had been exposed to the latter we would not consider them free workers. These basic assumptions about the history of labor are inscribed in the modern diagram of the historical forms of labor we carry around in our heads:[6]

free	unfree
wage labor	slave
artisanal	serf
free tenantry	indentured labor
	contract labor
	peonage

It is widely believed that the contract practices of free wage labor represented the norm in the Anglo-American and European worlds. The strict enforcement of contract labor agreements through nonpecuniary pressures represented a clear deviation from this norm, made necessary by the extraordinary labor shortages of the agricultural periphery. In part the contractual practices of wage labor are viewed as the norm because the *normal* mode of enforcing contracts in Anglo-American law is thought to have been money damages. Anglo-American law never permitted the specific enforcement of personal service agreements. It is also widely believed among historians and lawyers, at least in the United States, that it also

---

[5] Anthony Kronman, "Paternalism and the Law of Contracts," *Yale Law Journal* 92 (April 1983): 778–79.

[6] This diagram is based on one presented in Jan Lucassen, "Free and Unfree Labour before the Twentieth Century: A Brief Overview," in *Free and Unfree Labour: The Debate Continues,* ed. Tom Brass and Marcel van der Linden (Berne, Switz., 1997), 46. Lucassen's diagram further divides labor into *independent* and *dependent.* Although I would describe the assumptions underlying this diagram as being dominant, it is certainly the case that not everyone subscribes to them. Several historians have begun to question this binary opposition. See in particular Paul Craven and Douglas Hay, "The Criminalization of 'Free' Labour: Master and Servant in Comparative Perspective," *Slavery and Abolition* 15 (August 1994): 72; and David Eltis, "Labour and Coercion in the English Atlantic World from the Seventeenth to the Early Twentieth Century," *Slavery and Abolition* 14 (April 1993): 207.

never authorized criminal penalties to enforce labor agreements.[7] The differing contract practices of wage labor and contract labor are viewed as having been inseparable from the forms of labor themselves, in effect timeless features of two distinct species of labor. Wherever contract labor was used one set of contract practices is thought to have been in effect. Wherever wage labor was used the other set was.

It is a little surprising that these conceptions about historical wage labor have survived to the present. For one thing, there is now a small literature showing that English wage workers had been punished criminally during the nineteenth century for breaking their labor agreements. Until recently, however, that handful of historians who had written about the English Master and Servant acts tended to treat them as anomalous. Rather than use the existence of criminal sanctions to reassess the traditional wisdom about wage labor, these historians tended to use the traditional wisdom to assess the historical significance of criminal sanctions. Of the more than 700 pages the Webbs devoted to *The History of Trade Unionism*, they devoted fewer than ten pages to a discussion of the Master and Servant acts. Indeed, they dismissed as "somewhat exaggerated" the view of one nineteenth-century writer that the Master and Servant acts played a more important role in oppressing working people than the Combination acts.[8] In the 1950s, Daphne Simon wrote the modern classic on the Master and Servant acts, but her main argument was that by the nineteenth century these acts embodied practices that were outdated. In effect penal sanctions were a relic of feudalism, reflecting the primitive labor practices of an earlier stage of historical development that had inexplicably survived into the nineteenth century; they were really no part of modern wage labor. Genuinely modern business, as represented by the large cotton mills, had no need for this kind of compulsion and did not use it.[9] More recently a number of historians have written short pieces on the Master and Servant

---

[7] The American South following the Civil War is normally thought to have been the one major exception and a striking anomaly in the Anglo-American legal universe. See Benno C. Schmidt, Jr., "Principle and Prejudice: The Supreme Court and Race in the Progressive Era. Part 2: The Peonage Cases," *Columbia Law Review* 82 (1982): 705.

[8] Sidney Webb and Beatrice Webb, *The History of Trade Unionism* (London, 1956), 250 n. 2. Douglas Hay and Paul Craven have recently collected evidence that tends to support the view that the Master and Servant acts were indeed more important in oppressing working people than the Combination acts. "Master and Servant in England and the Empire: A Comparative Study," *Labour/Le Travail* 31 (Spring 1993): 176. ("There is a very large literature on the statutes against 'combination' in England during this period, but contemporary argument that employers used master and servant more often is amply borne out by our preliminary findings: in one English county, 130 men and women were imprisoned under master and servant for every one imprisoned for combination.")

[9] Daphne Simon, "Master and Servant," in *Democracy and the Labour Movement: Essays in Honour of Dona Torr*, ed. John Saville (London, 1954), 191–95.

acts,[10] some of them flatly rejecting Simon's contention that penal sanctions were a feudal relic by the nineteenth century. They have shown just how central criminal sanctions were to the practice of English wage labor of the period.[11] For the most part, however, these writers have failed to use the fact of criminal sanctions to try to begin to rethink the larger narrative of free wage labor.[12] As a result, the history of criminal sanctions has remained a particular history, an interesting sidelight that has not become part of any larger account of the history of wage labor. Meanwhile, the traditional view of free wage labor as a natural feature of free markets has continued to shape our understanding of the fundamental nature of wage labor in the nineteenth century.

There is a second reason that it is a little surprising that the narrative of free wage labor has survived. In the 1970s, two economic historians, Robert Fogel and Stanley Engerman, produced a devastating critique of its underlying economic logic. In their study of antebellum slavery, *Time on the Cross*,[13] they showed, in effect, that nonpecuniary compulsion was not economically inferior to pecuniary pressure as a means for extracting labor services efficiently and at low cost. They demonstrated that slaves in the antebellum South produced certain agricultural crops more efficiently than free northern agricultural workers, but perhaps more important, they also demonstrated that slaves performed artisanal and industrial work in urban settings at least as efficiently as northern free labor. Com-

[10] See, for example, D. C. Woods, "The Operation of the Master and Servants Act in the Black Country, 1858–1875," *Midland History* 7 (1982); M. R. Freedland, *The Contract of Employment* (Oxford, 1976); John Orth, *Combination and Conspiracy: A Legal History of Trade Unionism, 1721–1906* (Oxford, 1991); and David Galenson, "The Rise of Free Labor: Economic Change and the Enforcement of Service Contracts in England, 1351–1875," in *Capitalism in Context: Essays on Economic Development and Cultural Change in Honor of R. M. Hartwell*, ed. John A. James and Mark Thomas (Chicago, Ill., 1994), 114–37.

[11] See, for example, Woods in "Operation of the Master and Servants Act in the Black Country," 109–13; and Douglas Hay, "Penal Sanctions, Masters, and Servants" (Unpublished manuscript, 1990), 3–5, and "Masters, Servants, Justices and Judges" (Unpublished manuscript, 1988). Paul Craven and Adrian Merritt have taken similar positions with regard to nineteenth-century master/servant law in Canada and Australia. Paul Craven, "The Law of Master and Servant in Mid-Nineteenth-Century Ontario," in *Essays in the History of Canadian Law*, ed. David Flaherty (Toronto, 1981), I:175–211, especially 204; and Adrian Merritt, "The Historical Role of Law in the Regulation of Employment – Abstentionist or Interventionist?" *Australian Journal of Law & Society* 1 (1982).

[12] Douglas Hay is an exception. In "Penal Sanctions, Masters, and Servants," 3–5, and in "Masters, Servants, Justices and Judges," he began to reassess the larger significance of penal sanctions for nineteenth-century wage labor, arguing that criminal prosecutions for contract breaches became more common with the onset of the Industrial Revolution. See also Craven and Hay, "Criminalization of 'Free' Labour,"; and Eltis, "Labour and Coercion in the English Atlantic."

[13] Robert Fogel and Stanley Engerman, *Time on the Cross: The Economics of American Negro Slavery* (Boston, 1974).

pulsion worked well, seemingly, not only in primitive agriculture but also in skilled urban crafts. Indeed it seemed pretty clear as a result of their work that nonpecuniary pressures could be used as an effective substitute for pecuniary pressures in extracting labor, even skilled urban artisanal and industrial labor.

Fogel and Engerman also found that southern slave masters felt perfectly comfortable using both kinds of pressure together. They whipped their slaves but also often offered them pecuniary inducements. Their aim was to create an optimum mix of incentives to drive slaves to work harder. Slavery was a form of coerced labor, but that did not preclude masters from using both pecuniary and nonpecuniary pressures to push slave workers toward greater productivity. Fogel and Engerman's work discredited the notion that pecuniary and nonpecuniary pressures could not be effectively substituted for one another. They showed that nonpecuniary pressures could be used to extract skilled work efficiently. Beyond that they also demonstrated that it had not been necessary to choose one kind of pressure to the exclusion of the other. The two types of pressure could be used in tandem in any combination employers found advantageous. The obvious question raised by these insights is that if it was economically rational for slave masters to use nonpecuniary pressures to improve the efficiency of slave labor, might it not also have been economically rational for employers of wage labor to use nonpecuniary pressures for similar purposes? Might not the nonpecuniary penal sanctions actually used by employers of wage labor in nineteenth-century England have constituted an important part of their economic strategy for making wage labor more efficient?

We tend not to make these kinds of connections because we shrink from making direct comparisons between wage labor and slavery. Yet since the 1970s our picture of slavery has changed. The dynamics of slavery have begun to look a little more like the dynamics of wage labor. For one thing, historians now tend to see slavery as a negotiated relationship.[14] One of the sources of power slaves possessed came from their ability to withdraw labor at crucial moments in the production process. In numerous instances individual slaves ran away for short periods just when their labor was desperately needed. In other cases they ran away at times when masters were making excessive demands on them. In some cases slaves were even known to withdraw their labor collectively, to strike, as it were.[15] Although slaves often paid dearly for withdrawing their labor, the continued willingness of some slaves to do so presented a cautionary tale

---

[14] Ira Berlin, *Many Thousands Gone: The First Two Centuries of Slavery in North America* (Cambridge, Mass., 1998).

[15] See Mary Turner, ed., *From Chattel Slaves to Wage Slaves: The Dynamics of Labour Bargaining in the Americas* (Bloomington, Ind., 1995).

for masters. To keep to a minimum the value of lost production as well as replacement costs, masters could make concessions to slaves, increase punishments, or both. Slaves also possessed other sources of power. They could work more slowly than they were capable of, perform work badly, or both. Masters could respond to the effort problem by increasing supervision, but that was always imperfect and costly. To reduce agency costs (the combined costs of shirking and supervision) as much as possible, masters again could make concessions to slaves, try to intensify punishments, or both.

This changed picture of slavery reveals that slavery shared certain basic dynamics with wage labor. Both were negotiated relationships in which labor's ultimate sources of power were similar: the power to withdraw labor and the power to work less hard or well than was possible. The other side of this coin is that employers of labor in both relationships faced certain similar basic problems. In both situations, a sudden loss of labor could result in costly lost production. More frequently, employers had to develop strategies to deal with effort problems.

Our picture of wage labor has changed much less than our picture of slavery. Might the nonpecuniary criminal sanctions used against wage workers in nineteenth-century England indicate not only that slavery shared certain characteristics with wage labor but also that wage labor shared certain characteristics with slavery? In particular, both slavery and wage labor seem to have shared the use of nonpecuniary pressure in certain situations to address certain basic labor problems.

I do not want to be misunderstood. This is not an argument that wage labor was a form of slavery. It was not. I am arguing rather that it is necessary to begin thinking about the different forms of the labor relationship differently. We have to give up the idea that so-called free and coerced labor inhabited completely separate universes and try to understand both in terms of a common framework. We should recognize that employers of all forms of labor confronted certain basic problems that derived from the ability of workers to thwart their economic objectives and that employers of all forms of labor, *including wage labor,* found nonpecuniary pressures useful in trying to deal with these problems. What was different about the different forms of labor was the harshness and comprehensiveness of the pressures that the state permitted employers to bring to bear. Also different were the measures the state permitted workers to take for self-protection and the political power that was given them to participate in the formulation of the basic rules that were to govern these relationships. As vast as these differences undoubtedly were, they should be understood as establishing the terms of labor along a very broad continuum rather than as a binary opposition.

The following history of wage labor in England and the United States focuses on the enforcement of labor contracts. In England, which possessed one of the most advanced economies of the nineteenth century, wage work did not conform to its image as employment at will. Wage workers commonly served under agreements that could *not* be terminated at will, and employers commonly sought to have those agreements enforced against them. They could do so because English law gave employers effective remedies for breach of contract. English wage workers could be imprisoned at hard labor for failing or refusing to perform their labor agreements. Strict labor contract enforcement through nonpecuniary pressure of this kind was an integral feature of English wage labor in the nineteenth century. The strict enforcement of labor contracts turns out to have been the norm not only in areas of the empire using contract labor but also in the English metropolis. Wage and contract labor were merely variations on a common regime of contract.

Employers of wage labor resorted to this kind of strict contract enforcement to address some of the same problems that employers of contract labor and slavery also attempted to address by using nonpecuniary pressure. In the fully developed wage labor markets of nineteenth-century England, employers had sound economic reasons for wanting to hire wage workers under enforceable agreements and for enforcing those agreements against them. Nonpecuniary pressure served as a useful supplement to the dull compulsion of economic relations in helping employers reduce the cost of and improve the efficiency of wage labor.

Wage labor markets in England came increasingly to be organized around the principle of contract during the nineteenth century. Employers and workers became freer to set the terms of their relationship with one another through agreements. However, many employers of the time believed that for these reforms to work it was essential for them to be able to hold wage workers to their promises, and penal sanctions made it possible for employers to do so. In this respect the criminal enforcement of labor agreements was an integral aspect of the first blossoming of free contract in labor markets. Freedom of contract implied that workers should not be constrained to enter only revocable agreements but should be free to bind their labor irrevocably as well.

The account presented in this book turns the traditional narrative of free labor on its head. It shows that the introduction of free contract and free markets in labor in the nineteenth century did not produce what we in the twentieth century consider free wage labor. It produced a regime that employed nonpecuniary pressures to extract labor from workers, pressures that by twentieth-century standards make the wage work a form of coerced contractual labor. Penal sanctions for labor contract breaches were eliminated in England only as a result of the efforts of organized labor to change state rules governing labor contracts. They did not disappear because employers finally discovered that the dull compulsion of economic relations made them unnecessary. Labor agitated for more than a decade to have the law of labor contracts changed. In 1875, as a result of this campaign, penal sanctions for contract breaches were largely eliminated. Their elimination must be seen as part of the wider campaign mounted in the late nineteenth and early twentieth centuries to pass pro-labor legislation to place restraints on freedom of the market. The 1875 legislation was one of the ways in which freedom of contract was restricted. This legislation, along with other legislative restrictions on freedom of contract such as maximum hours and minimum wages laws, was meant to bolster the position of labor. The origins of modern free wage labor are not to be found in the free contracts in free markets of the first half of the nineteenth century but in the restrictions placed on freedom of contract by the social and economic legislation adopted during the final quarter of the century.

Although the history of wage labor in other countries such as France and Germany was quite different in detail, it followed a surprisingly similar general pattern, beginning with the strict enforcement of wage labor agreements in the nineteenth century. A similar pattern, moreover, is even to be found in the United States, where employers did not normally have available penal sanctions or specific performance to enforce labor agreements. In the nineteenth century, wage workers in the United States, like their English counterparts, commonly did *not* serve under agreements terminable at will. The labor agreements under which they did serve were often enforced against them. Employers could enforce these agreements in the United States because the common law of contract gave them an effective remedy for breach, in this case, a pecuniary remedy. American workers in most states were subject to wage forfeiture for violating their labor agreements during the nineteenth century. A few states changed this rule before 1860 as a result of judicial opinions. Significant numbers of states, however, did not begin to reject it until the 1870s. After 1875, the pace of change accelerated as more and more states passed periodic wage payment laws that required employers to pay wages at regular and increasingly shorter intervals. Over time, changed judicial sentiment, but more importantly this new legislation, gradually eroded the ability of employers to use wage forfeiture legally to enforce labor agreements. As in England, it is primarily to restrictive labor legislation, not to free contract in free markets, that we should trace the origins of modern free wage labor in the United States.

RETHINKING FREE/UNFREE LABOR

One of the basic assumptions underlying the traditional narrative of free labor is that there are two fundamentally different kinds of labor, free and coerced. The two are thought to be opposites of one another, not different in degree but different in kind. The line that naturally divides the two is thought to fall at the point where physical violence or bodily confinement is used to extract labor. Where such pressures are used the resulting labor is considered coerced even if it was originally undertaken voluntarily pursuant to a binding agreement.

In the United States, the Supreme Court began to articulate this position during the first decades of the twentieth century. In 1911, the Court struck down Alabama's false pretenses statute.[16] That statute subjected workers to criminal punishment for fraud if they abandoned a labor contract while they were working out a debt to an employer. The court declared the statute unconstitutional on the ground that it established involuntary servitude by criminally compelling the performance of labor, a thing no state could do under the Thirteenth Amendment, even if the labor had been voluntarily undertaken in the first place:

> *[T]he State could not authorize its constabulary to prevent the servant from escaping* and . . . force him to work out his debt. *But the State could not avail itself of the sanction of the criminal law to supply the compulsion any more than it could use or authorize the use of physical force.*[17] (emphasis added)

In 1944, the Court reiterated this position. In *Pollack v. Williams* it declared:

> *Whatever of social value there may be, and of course it is great, in enforcing contracts* and collection of debts, Congress has put it beyond debate that no indebtedness warrants a suspension of the *right to be free from compulsory service.* This congressional policy means that *no state can make the quitting of work any component of a crime, or make criminal sanctions available for holding unwilling persons to labor.*[18] (emphasis added)

Measured by this standard there can be no question that nineteenth-century English wage labor constituted coerced or unfree labor. Consider the following account of replacement workers brought into the northern English coal fields during the great strike of 1844:

> The agents of Radcliffe Colliery, in the North, by false pretenses brought thirty-two Cornish miners to supplant their old pitmen, and engaged them for twelve months at 4s. per day. . . . After the second fortnight the viewer offered these men 4d. per tub, and they all, with the exception of four, absconded. . . . A reward of £50 was offered for the apprehension of the runaway Cornish men. The Newcastle police captured four of them, brought them to Amble in gigs, together with a *posse* of police. The poor fellows were kept from the Monday night till . . . on the Tuesday night they attempted to make their escape [and were successful]. . . . The others who absconded

---

[16] *Bailey v. Alabama,* 219 U.S. 219 (1911).

[17] Ibid., 243–44.

[18] 322 U.S. 4 (1944), 18; see also *Clyatt v. United States,* 197 U.S. 207 (1905), 215–16.

were arrested by the North Shields police force, and a steam-boat, carrying the police force and the special constables, was sent to bring them to Alnmouth, and thence to Alnwick, to answer for their conduct before the magistrates.[19]

But for certain of the details, this could have been a story set in the American South during the early decades of the twentieth century. There can be no doubt that under the Supreme Court decisions that were rendered to combat these southern practices, the Cornish miners would have been considered unfree workers.

This way of thinking about what constitutes coerced labor has come to seem so natural that it is surprising that anyone could ever have thought differently, but the English in the nineteenth century did. Like us, they believed that labor could be divided into free and coerced, but they drew the distinction between the two differently than we normally do. For the most part, they did not view wage workers as unfree laborers, even though criminal sanctions were generally available to enforce wage work. This view seems to have been shared by many British working men as well. When British workers began to demand reform of the Master and Servant acts in the early 1860s, it was *not* one of their arguments that these acts established "slavery." This is especially surprising given the long English tradition of denouncing all sorts of social and political practices as slavery unfit for freeborn Englishmen.[20] Working men mainly argued that penal sanctions should be eliminated because they subjected the working classes to unequal treatment under law. Employers were not subject to criminal punishment for breaches of their side of labor agreements. For the most part, it seems, the dominant view among the nineteenth-century English was that penal sanctions for contract breaches did not make English wage work unfree labor.

---

[19] Richard Fynes, *The Miners of Northumberland and Durham: A History of Their Social and Political Progress* (1873; reprint Sunderland, England, 1923), 91–93. As the masters had first breached the agreement, the workmen were found to have been justified in leaving.

[20] Indeed, for centuries English workers had denounced the workings of the master and servant laws as a slavery unfit for freeborn Englishmen. In the eighteenth century Daniel Defoe quoted one anonymous worker as saying to his employer, "I hope you won't take it amiss that I dismiss myself, and from this Minute I am your Servant no longer; and as I am a Free-Born *Englishman*, and no Slave, I live in a Free Nation, and must have my LIBERTY." Daniel Defoe, *The Great Law of Subordination Consider'd: Or, the Insolence and Unsufferable Behavior of Servants in England Duly Enquir'd Into* (London, 1723), 29. For earlier examples, see Robert Steinfeld, *The Invention of Free Labor: The Employment Relation in English and American Law and Culture* (Chapel Hill, N.C., 1991), 95–98. A failed attempt in 1823 to reform master and servant law also drew on this rhetorical tradition. See George White and Gravener Henson, *A Few Remarks on the State of the Laws, at Present in Existence, for Regulating Masters and Work-People, Intended as a Guide for the Consideration of the House, in Their Discussions on the Bill for Repealing Several Acts Relating to Combinations of Workingmen* (1823), 51–53, 108–09, 117. This rhetoric, however, does not seem to have played a public role in the final campaign to repeal criminal sanctions launched in the 1860s.

But English workers *did* sometimes talk as though certain forms of wage work were free and others unfree. When they did, however, they seem to have distinguished the two differently than we do. By the 1870s some were saying that workers hired under long contracts "were bound like slaves to the employers," whereas those serving under short contracts were "free" men.[21] The length of contracted-for service appears to have been the crucial factor separating free from unfree, rather than whether a worker could be compelled to perform a contract through criminal punishment. In the case of wage workers under short contracts, criminal punishment was viewed as nothing more than a contract remedy to enforce certain kinds of voluntary agreements.

At the same time, however, many nineteenth-century working people, in the United States as well as in England, drew the line in still a different way, denouncing all wage labor as coerced labor, whether or not breaches of contract were punishable by imprisonment. On both sides of the Atlantic, it was common to hear wage labor described as "wage slavery."[22] In *The Condition of the Working Class in England*, Friedrich Engels attacked the practice of imprisoning coal miners for breaches of their annual contracts, but he did not single it out for special notice. It was only one among many factors, most of them economic, that contributed to "the enslavement of the miners."[23] In one common view, only the ownership of productive property could make a working person a truly "free" laborer.[24] Even so, "wage slavery" was considered "free labor" by nearly everyone, at least insofar as it stood in contrast to serfdom and real slavery.[25] What seems to have placed wage labor on the free side of the binary opposition for many people in the nineteenth century was that wage laborers possessed the freedom "of removing to some other locality, or of making choice of some other employment."[26]

---

[21] *Wolverhampton Chronicle*, 24 March 1875, quoted in Woods, "Operation of the Master and Servants Act in the Black Country," 103.

[22] For England, see Friedrich Engels, *The Condition of the Working Class in England* (Stanford, Calif., 1968), 93; for the United States, see David Montgomery, *Beyond Equality: Labor and the Radical Republican, 1862–1872* (Urbana, Ill., 1981), 30.

[23] Engels, *Condition of the Working Class in England*, 286.

[24] See Eric Foner, *Free Soil, Free Labor, Free Men: The Ideology of the Republican Party before the Civil War* (New York, 1970), and *Political Ideology in the Age of the Civil War* (New York, 1980); see also William Forbath, "The Ambiguities of Free Labor: Labor and the Law in the Gilded Age," *Wisconsin Law Review* (1985).

[25] See, for example, Karl Marx, *Capital* (Harmondsworth, Eng., 1976), I:272–73, 874–75, 908–9; see also Karl Marx, *Grundrisse* (Harmondsworth, Eng., 1973), 464–65, 507.

[26] Fynes, *Miners of Northumberland and Durham*, 144, contrasting the serfdom of eighteenth-century Scottish colliers with the freedom of ordinary British wage workers. Fynes was a nineteenth-century English coal miner who worked at a time when miners could still be criminally punished for breaching labor agreements. For a similar, present-day view, see Miles, *Capitalism and Unfree Labour*, 25. ("The freedom of the wage labourer is grounded in an ability to decide whether, and to whom, his or her labour power will be sold.")

What are we to make of these multiple, conflicting ways of drawing the line between two kinds of labor that are supposed to be opposites of one another? For one thing, these conflicting definitions make clear that the line separating free from unfree labor is not natural, but conventional. It is drawn in different ways depending on what kinds of pressures and working conditions are viewed as placing a worker in one category as opposed to the other.[27]

It is possible to draw the line between free and coerced labor in different ways for a number of reasons. Different definitions focus on different aspects of the labor relation, such as length of binding and type of working conditions. To the extent that the distinction has been used to capture the difference between labor that is offered voluntarily and labor that is offered under compulsion, however, there is a good reason that the line has been drawn in different ways at different times. Nearly all forms of labor not performed for sheer pleasure can be characterized as either voluntary or coerced. Robert Hale noted that compulsion in labor relations is of two fundamentally different kinds.[28] The first involves overpowering physical force applied to impart involuntary motion to a person's body, as when a person is carried somewhere bodily against his or her will. However, this kind of physical compulsion is not what we normally mean when we speak about coerced labor. When we speak about most forms of labor compulsion, we are talking about situations in which the compelled party is offered a choice between disagreeable alternatives and chooses the lesser evil.[29]

The latter type of compulsion is present in both slavery and modern free wage labor. In slavery, for example, labor is not normally elicited by directly imparting motion to a slave's limbs through overpowering physical force. It is compelled by forcing slaves to choose between very unpleasant alternatives, such as death, torture, and endless confinement, on the one hand, or back-breaking physical labor on the other. The labor of free wage workers is normally elicited by offering workers a choice, for example, between life on an inadequate welfare stipend or, in the extreme, star-

---

[27] By the 1890s, English elites had developed their own definition of "free labor." "The *Economist* noted in 1891 . . . that 'the general labour controversy is going largely to turn upon the respective rights and duties of free labourers and unionists' – free labourers being defined as all those who wished to make their own independent contract with their employers regardless of the trade-union position." John Saville, "Trade Unions and Free Labour: The Background to the Taff Vale Decision," in *Essays in Labour History,* ed. Asa Briggs and John Saville (London, 1967), 319.

[28] Thomas Hobbes discusses this distinction in *Leviathan* (New York, 1950), chapters 14, 15.

[29] Robert Hale, "Force and the State: A Comparison of 'Political' and 'Economic' Compulsion," *Columbia Law Review* 35 (1935): 149–61; and Robert Hale, *Freedom through Law: Public Control of Private Governing Power* (New York, 1952), 189–96.

vation, on the one hand, and performing more or less unpleasant work for wages on the other. Writing a decade after the principle of less eligibility had been adopted in the Poor Law Reforms of 1834, John Stuart Mill observed

> If the condition of a person receiving [poor] relief is made as eligible as that of the labourer who supports himself by his own exertions . . . [it] would require as its supplement an organized system of compulsion, for governing and setting [people] to work. . . . But if, consistently with guaranteeing all persons against absolute want, the condition of those who are supported by legal charity can be kept considerably less desirable than the condition of those who find support for themselves, none but beneficial consequences can arise.[30]

In the cases of both the slave and the free wage worker, the parties may be said to have been coerced into performing the labor or to have freely chosen the lesser evil. Either characterization is available, which is why some choices among evils can be characterized as voluntary decisions, made because they benefit the choosing party (under the circumstances), whereas other choices among evils can simultaneously be characterized as coerced. From a purely logical standpoint, where the line is drawn is arbitrary. One tradition of thought, for example, portrayed slavery as completely consensual, arising out of an implicit agreement in which the slave voluntarily granted to his master absolute control over his person in exchange for his life.[31]

Needless to say, the choices presented in slavery were normally vastly harsher than the choices presented in free wage labor, so we may rightly say that the degree of coercion in one form is generally vastly greater than in the other, but there are no logical grounds for saying that the performance of labor in one case is coerced and in the other it is voluntary. As a matter of logic we have to say either that both are involuntary in different degrees or that both involve the free choice of a lesser evil. In 1918, Justice Oliver Wendell Holmes pointed out that "[i]t always is for the interest of a party under duress to choose the lesser of two evils. But the fact that a choice was made according to interest [rather than the will being overborne] does not exclude duress. It is the characteristic of duress properly so called."[32] John Dawson, writing several decades later, put the paradox of coercion and consent even more vividly: "[C]ourts ha[ve] been slow to

---

[30] John Stuart Mill, *Collected Works*, vol. III, *Principles of Political Economy with Some of Their Applications to Social Philosophy* (Toronto, 1965), 961.

[31] This tradition sought to justify all forms of slavery, not merely those in which slaves had formally contracted into the condition but also those in which captives had tacitly chosen slavery rather than death.

[32] *Union Pacific Ry. v. Public Service Commission*, 248 U.S. 67 (1918), 70.

realize that the instances of more extreme pressure were precisely those in which the consent expressed was *more* real; the more unpleasant the alternative, the more real the consent to a course which would avoid it."[33] Whether to characterize a choice as being in the interest of a person because it is the better choice under the circumstances or as coercing a person because it only presents a choice among evils is a matter of arbitrarily drawing a line through a continuum of coercive pressures.

The judgment about where to draw a line to separate free from coerced labor turns out not to be a judgment about whether the labor is voluntary or compelled but rather a judgment about what kinds of coercive pressures are legitimate and illegitimate in labor relations. Rather than seeing forms of labor in terms of a binary opposition, it would be more accurate to think about labor relations in terms of degrees of coercive pressure that can be brought to bear to elicit labor. These coercive pressures all take a similar form. One person is placed in a position to force another person to choose between labor and other alternatives that are more disagreeable than the labor itself. The judgment about which kinds of forced choices to allow and which to prohibit would then have to be made on explicitly moral or political grounds rather than in terms of a natural distinction between two entirely different species of labor.

In modern law this line has normally been drawn between pecuniary and nonpecuniary disagreeable alternatives to labor. The same United States Supreme Court that ruled that nonpecuniary criminal penalties for labor contract breaches produced coerced labor also ruled that pecuniary remedies for contract breaches did not. In *Bailey v. Alabama* the court contended that

> A clear distinction exists between peonage and the voluntary performance of labor. . . . In the latter case the debtor, though contracting to pay his indebtedness by labor or service, and *subject like any other contractor to an action for damages for breach of that contract, can elect at any time to break it, and no law or force compels performance or a continuance of the service.*[34] (emphasis added)

According to this, the modern view, labor is divided into free and coerced based on whether a labor contract is enforced through a pecuniary or a nonpecuniary legal remedy. Nonpecuniary legal remedies produce compulsory labor however mild they may be (a day under detention); pecuniary remedies produce free labor. One is considered legal compulsion,

---

[33] John Dawson, "Economic Duress – An Essay in Perspective," *Michigan Law Review* 45 (January 1947): 267. On the failure of efforts to develop objective criteria to distinguish "threats" from "offers," see Michael J. Trebilcock, *The Limits of Freedom of Contract* (Cambridge, Mass., 1993), 78–81; see also Robert Hale, "Coercion and Distribution in a Supposedly Non-Coercive State," *Political Science Quarterly* 38 (1923).

[34] *Bailey v. Alabama*, 219 U.S. 219 (1911), 243–44.

the other not, although it is also a legal remedy creating pressures to perform labor.

The problem with this position is that all legal remedies for breaches of labor contracts can coerce the performance of labor under certain circumstances. This is as true of pecuniary remedies as of nonpecuniary ones. In his dissent in *Bailey v. Alabama,* Justice Oliver Wendell Holmes pointed out that "any legal liability for breach of contract is a disagreeable consequence which tends to make the contractor do as he said he would."[35] Robert Hale observed that

> in the case of a solvent person, the motive for performing [a contract] might often be the desire to escape pecuniary liability. If such desire is strong enough to make him render the services stipulated in his contract, then the law does compel performance and enforce the labor.[36]

It is pretty obvious, on the other hand, that certain pecuniary remedies, such as ordinary money damages, do not in most cases create very much pressure for a wage worker to perform his agreement.[37] But money damages is not the only pecuniary remedy that may be available to employers for contract breaches. Other pecuniary remedies can erect alternatives to performance that may be as disagreeable as the short term of confinement to which English workers could be sentenced under the Master and Servant acts.

Under a nineteenth-century American common law rule, workers could forfeit all their back wages if they failed faithfully to perform their labor agreements.[38] Where an employer withheld wages, this rule forced a worker to choose between staying at work and forfeiting accumulated pay. It is incorrect to think of such a choice merely as one between pecuniary loss and performance. Often, pecuniary loss could involve substantially reduced life circumstances. The real choice facing a working person in such a situation might well have been between continued labor and possible loss of home or of ability to feed a family. In the twentieth century, it began to be acknowledged in international law circles that

---

[35] Ibid., 246.

[36] Hale, *Freedom through Law,* 191.

[37] Christopher T. Wonnell, "The Contractual Disempowerment of Employees," *Stanford Law Review* 46 (November 1993): 91–92.

[38] Nearly all states had such a rule during the first half of the nineteenth century. See Wythe Holt, "Recovery by the Worker Who Quits," *Wisconsin Law Review* (1986); and Peter Karsten, "'Bottomed on Justice': A Reappraisal of Critical Legal Studies Scholarship Concerning Breaches of Labor Contracts by Quitting or Firing in Britain and the U.S., 1630–1880," *American Journal of Legal History* 34 (1990). A similar English rule had a longer history. See Steinfeld, *Invention of Free Labor,* 240–42.

in certain circumstances conditions analogous to forced or compulsory labour may arise as a consequence of the method of payment to the worker whereby his employer defers payment to a given date or postpones payment after the agreed date, thereby depriving the worker of a genuine possibility of terminating his employment.[39]

Sweeping negative injunctions to abstain from all employment other than that contracted for enforces performance of service by making the possible alternative starvation or life on welfare. A negative injunction to abstain from one particular line of work in which a worker is particularly skilled enforces performance by making the alternative to performance much less remunerative work. Different pecuniary remedies for contract breach may operate with different degrees of coerciveness depending on how disagreeable the alternatives to performance they erect are. Certain pecuniary remedies may be quite severe, others much less severe, but severe pecuniary remedies may rival a short imprisonment in their coerciveness. Yet according to modern views, pecuniary remedies for breaches of labor contracts, even many severe pecuniary remedies, do not produce coerced labor, whereas nonpecuniary remedies, even mild ones, invariably do.[40]

Not only does the distinction between free and coerced labor based on kinds of pressure used to extract labor make little sense, it also serves to obscure the fact that severe pecuniary remedies can be used to accomplish certain of the same objectives that nonpecuniary remedies can. It serves to obscure that the two kinds of pressure are in fact commensurable and partially substitutable. In the United States, the use of severe pecuniary remedies such as wage forfeiture made it possible for employers to use contracts in wage labor to accomplish many of the economic objectives that

---

[39] International Labour Conference, *Forced Labor*, Report IV (2) (Fortieth Session, Geneva, 1957), 28.

[40] A recent article notes that the difference between "liability" and "property" rules is not necessarily a difference in the types of remedies available to plaintiffs, but in the severity of the sanctions to which defendants are exposed. Property rules are supported by sanctions that are severe enough to deter all nonconsensual takings. Pecuniary sanctions, if they are severe enough, can serve this goal as well as other types of remedies. Liability rules also deter takings, but in a narrower range of circumstances. The binary scheme liability/property rule is badly equipped to deal with degrees of severity, much as the free/unfree distinction is. How precisely do we go about determining whether a contract remedy such as losing all back wages is more or less severe than a fourteen-day prison term? As a practical matter, does it fall on the "property" or on the "liability" side? See Ian Ayres and Eric Talley, "Solomonic Bargaining: Dividing a Legal Entitlement to Facilitate Coasean Trade," *The Yale Law Journal* 104 (1995): 1036, 1041, and n. 35 citing David D. Haddock et al., "An Ordinary Economic Rationale for Extraordinary Legal Sanctions," *Cal. L. Rev.* 78 (1990): 133. (Property rule damages are defined as those that "would reduce to zero the expected gain available to the defendant from the injurious activity, leaving no incentive for him to attempt the activity in the first place.")

English employers sought to accomplish through the use of nonpecuniary pressures. Contracts and contract enforcement were integral aspects of nineteenth-century American wage labor just as they were of nineteenth-century English wage labor precisely because pecuniary and nonpecuniary remedies for contract breaches could serve as partial substitutes for one another.

Today, in cases in which wage workers are not subject to contractual liability but to a different kind of pecuniary pressure, the ordinary economic pressures of a market society, we classify these workers as free. Two implicit assumptions are usually made about economic pressure. First, it is supposed to have a different source and different characteristics than nonpecuniary pressure typically does. Law is supposed to be the main source of the nonpecuniary pressure used in unfree labor. It is law, normally, that authorizes or permits individuals and state officials to use physical violence or confinement to extract labor. By contrast, market forces are supposed to be the source of economic pressure and to operate impersonally and indirectly. They are supposed to exert pressure only in the way nature exerts pressure: If you do not work you starve. No one controls market forces. By contrast, law is manufactured and controlled by people. Second, these different kinds of pressure are supposed to operate with radically different degrees of harshness. Physical violence and imprisonment are viewed as much severer than economic pressures.

The simple opposition, economic (pecuniary) versus legal (nonpecuniary) coercion, which places labor subject to one in one category and labor subject to the other in an opposite category, operates to obscure the common sources and characteristics of the two. Economic coercion always has its source in a set of legal rights, privileges, and powers that place one person in a position to force another person to choose between labor and some more disagreeable alternative to the labor, just as so-called legal compulsion does. The exercise of economic power is also quite personal and direct. Consider economic coercion in the bargaining relationship between employers and employees. Robert Hale showed that law was the ultimate source of an employer's power to force a worker to choose between wage work and a more disagreeable alternative to work. His argument is worth quoting at length:

> The owner [of private property] can remove the legal duty under which the non-owner labors [not to consume or otherwise use that property]. He can remove it, or keep it in force, at his discretion. To keep it in force may or may not have unpleasant consequences to the non-owner – consequences which spring from the law's creation of a legal duty. To avoid these consequences, the non-owner may be willing to obey the will of the owner, provided that the obedience is not in itself more unpleasant than the consequences to be avoided. Such

obedience may take the trivial form of paying five cents for legal permission to eat a particular bag of peanuts, or it may take the more
significant form of working for [a factory] owner at disagreeable toil
for a slight wage. In either case the conduct is motivated . . . by a desire to escape a more disagreeable alternative. . . . In the case of the
labor what would be the consequence of refusal to comply with the
owner's terms? It would be either absence of wages, or obedience to
the terms of some other employer. . . . Suppose, now, the worker
were to refuse to yield to the coercion of any employer, but were to
choose instead to remain under the legal duty to abstain from the use
of any of the money which anyone owns. He must eat. While there
is no law against eating in the abstract, there is a law which forbids
him to eat any of the food which actually exists in the community –
and that law is the law of property. It can be lifted as to any specific
food at the discretion of its owner, but if the owners unanimously refuse to lift the prohibition, the non-owner will starve unless he can
himself produce food. And there is every likelihood that the owners
will be unanimous in refusing, if he has no money. . . . Unless, then,
the non-owner can produce his own food, the law compels him to
starve if he has not wages, and compels him to go without wages unless he obeys the behests of some employer. It is the law that coerces
him into wage-work under penalty of starvation – unless he can produce food. Can he? Here again there is no law to prevent the production of food in the abstract; but in every settled country there is a law
which forbids him to cultivate any particular piece of ground unless
he happens to be an owner. This again is the law of property. And
this again will not be likely to be lifted unless he already has money.
That way of escape from the law-made dilemma of starvation or obedience is closed to him. . . . In short, if he be not a property owner,
the law which forbids him to produce with any of the existing equipment, and the law which forbids him to eat any of the existing food,
will be lifted *only* in case he works for an employer. It is the law of
property which coerces people into working for factory owners.[41]
(emphasis original)

So-called economic coercion is an artifact of law, not of nature. Organized
markets and economic coercion within markets have their origins in an
act of the state to restrict liberty, the liberty to use and consume resources,
by establishing the law of private property.

There is, however, a crucial respect in which economic compulsion dif-
fers from what we normally think of as legal compulsion. Legal compulsion normally confronts a party with a narrow set of unpleasant alternatives from which to choose. The choices, for example, might be between

---

[41] Hale, "Coercion and Distribution in a Supposedly Non-Coercive State," 472–73.

confinement at hard labor, becoming a fugitive from justice, or remaining at work, as they were in the case of one of the main legal remedies used to enforce nineteenth-century English wage labor agreements. In most cases of economic compulsion, the universe of alternatives is, at least in theory, much wider. A worker thinking about leaving an employer can try to find another employer, apply for food stamps and Section 8 housing, open a small business repairing cars in the back yard, homestead in Alaska, move to Georgia where there are more jobs, emigrate to Australia, go back to school to retrain, join the army, move in with relatives, play guitar in the subway, and so forth. What is different about economic compulsion is that it is often difficult to evaluate the universe of alternatives that an individual faces. If all the above options are unfeasible, as they often are, and if unemployment is high, the real choices may be much narrower: remain at work and follow orders, apply for welfare, become homeless. The degree of coercion operating in this situation may be as great as the degree of coercion operating when the threat is a mere fourteen-day sentence in the house of correction. On the other hand, if Australia is desperate for workers and is willing to subsidize passage, provide housing, and guarantee a good paying job, and the unemployment rate in the United States is 2 percent, then the degree of coercion operating in this situation may be practically nonexistent.[42] Therefore it is difficult to characterize this worker's situation in the abstract, because the feasibility and unpleasantness of all the potential alternatives involve highly context-specific information. It is difficult even to compile a definitive list of what all the "real" options may or may not be. It is much easier to evaluate degrees of coercion when the alternatives confronting a party are clearly defined and strictly circumscribed. This is why economic coercion is such a slippery and contestable concept.

---

[42] "From 1840 to 1878 the Colonial Land and Emigration Board in Great Britain selected residents of the British Isles for free or assisted passage to colonies in Australia. Over 350,000 Europeans received passages assisted by the governments of Australia, New Zealand, southern Africa, and other British colonies. The governments of underpopulated lands such as Canada also subsidized passages for British citizens and other Europeans. . . . The provincial government of Sao Paulo, Brazil, similarly underwrote the recruitment of over 800,000 Europeans mostly from Italy, in the decades before 1907. Overall about 10 percent of European migrants in the nineteenth century traveled under government subsidy." David Northrup, *Indentured Labor in the Age of Imperialism, 1834–1922* (Cambridge, 1995), 8–9. Subsidized passage was not always an attractive alternative, however, because in many cases immigrants had to sign multiyear labor contracts to repay transportation expenses. Nevertheless, British labor was quite aware that there was a relationship between easy emigration and their bargaining position. From the mid-1840s to the mid-1850s "an Emigration Fund becomes a constant feature of many of the large [workingmen's] societies, to be abandoned only when it was discovered that the few thousands of pounds which could be afforded for this purpose produced no visible effect in diminishing surplus labour." Webb and Webb, *History of Trade Unionism*, 201.

But this difference does not make economic coercion natural.[43] The background conditions that constitute the options available to individuals and determine the degree of economic pressure operating in any situation are pervasively shaped by law.[44] Whether welfare is a good, bad, or impossible option depends on welfare law, eligibility rules, and payment standards.[45] It also depends on how welfare rules are administered.[46] Emigrating to Australia may be difficult or easy depending on Australian immigration rules, but it is only an option because American workers enjoy a background legal privilege of leaving the country whenever they wish to work elsewhere. Alaska may be a better or worse option depending on whether the state government has a homestead program, but it is an option because Americans enjoy a legal privilege of settling in any state in the union. Playing guitar in the subway may be more or less feasible depending on vagrancy rules and their enforcement.[47] Taking another job

---

[43] "Now to say that these [massive inflows of immigrants] were labor market phenomena is not to say that they were natural, inevitable, or beyond debate and evaluation. The scope and terms of labor markets are influenced by a host of public policies, from national immigration and transportation systems to local public schools and social services to state laws governing labor contracts. If citizenship means anything at all, the terms by which new persons are admitted into a jurisdiction must be governed by some kind of public policy. This is not merely hypothetical: the antebellum South remained largely untouched by foreign workers, even during periods of strong demand and rising labor costs, because dominant political interests were hostile to immigration." Gavin Wright, "Labor History and Labor Economics," in *The Future of Economic History*, ed. Alexander J. Field (Boston, Mass., 1987), 330.

[44] Duncan Kennedy, "The Stakes of Law, or Hale and Foucault!" *Legal Studies Forum* 15 (1991): 330–34, and "The Role of Law in Economic Thought," *The American University Law Review* 34 (1985): 965–67. See also Barbara Fried, *The Progressive Assault on Laissez Faire: Robert Hale and the First Law and Economics Movement* (Cambridge, Mass., 1998), 17–19.

[45] See, for example, Mill, *Collected Works*, vol. III, *Principles of Political Economy*, Book V, chap. xi, § 13.

[46] During a long strike in the English coal fields in 1844, employers and the local authorities tried to break the strike and force workers back to work by closing off as many of their alternatives as possible: "[T]he workhouses were closed against [the pitmen], their hungry wives, and starving children. Magistrates and clergymen alike gave their sanction and protection to this holy work; and some of them even gave their presence and superintendence to see that there was no breach of the peace in their illegal and unjust orders being executed." Fynes, *Miners of Northumberland and Durham*, 85.

[47] During the long strike mentioned in note 46, "[h]undreds of the men on strike were at this time away in other parts of the country, some of them staying with their friends and relatives, some working in other places with their friends during the strike, whilst many who were travelling the country to collect subscriptions, grouped together in musical bands, met with harsh and unjust treatment. . . . [Ten of these men] were one day playing in the street, the other two being on the alert to receive any donation that might be given them. They never went into any house, nor yet asked any person for anything, but suddenly one of them . . . was taken into custody . . . and charged with begging in the street,

may be a better or worse option depending on how great the demand for labor is. It is only because a worker possesses a background legal privilege of selling or withholding labor in the first place, however, that increased demand for labor can make this a better or worse option. Looking for other work might not be as good an option even when demand for labor is high if immigration restrictions are relaxed or eliminated. If a preparatory course and a license are required to repair other people's automobiles, opening a small shop in one's yard may be more or less feasible. Let's not even mention nuisance law and zoning rules. How desperate workers as a group may be for work depends in good part on how widely property is distributed.[48] Even this situation is conditioned to a great extent by a larger set of taken-for-granted background legal rules. Property is so unevenly distributed in part because inheritance laws make it possible for accumulations of property to be preserved over the generations, and so forth.[49]

Law pervasively conditions the universe of possibilities that determine the degree of economic compulsion individuals confront in all market societies. It has long been recognized that governing elites in certain polities

a charge which the prisoner denied. The magistrates asked him where he came from, and who he was; he told the magistrate that he belonged to the County of Durham, a miner, and out of employ for twelve weeks. The magistrate read the clause in the Act of Parliament, and said he was liable to 28 days, but he would only commit him to the House of Correction for 14 days." Ibid., 101.

[48] "Nothing is more instructive than to trace the fate of the repeated attempts to provide, by legal encouragement, smallholdings for agricultural labourers, which had proved, wherever they were maintained by philanthropic landlords, to be highly beneficial to labourers and the community. The causes of the failure are perhaps best given in Cobbett's language, describing the fatal opposition he encountered in his parish of Bishops Waltham when he attempted, during the post-war slump, to offer each married labourer an acre of waste land on condition that he would enclose it, cultivate it, and live on it: 'Budd said, that to give the labourers a bit of land would make them sacy; ... and Steel said, it would make them demand higher wages.'" Sidney Pollard, "Labour in Great Britain," in Peter Mathias and M. M. Postan, ed., *The Cambridge Economic History of Europe* (Cambridge, 1978), VII, Part I:152 (describing proposals to distribute land to agricultural laboring poor in England during first three decades of the nineteenth century).

[49] On the "artificial" or "positive" nature of the law of inheritance see, for example, William Blackstone, *Commentaries on the Laws of England (1765–1769),* Book II, 10, 12. "The most universal and effectual way, of abandoning property, is by the death of the occupant; when, both the actual possession and intention of keeping possession ceasing, the property, which is founded upon such possession and intention, ought also to cease of course. ... All property must therefore cease upon death, considering men as absolute individuals, and unconnected with civil society. ... Wills therefore and testaments, rights of inheritance and successions, are all of them creatures of the civil or municipal laws, and accordingly are in all respects regulated by them." See also Fried, *Progressive Assault on Laissez Faire,* 99: "[T]he Supreme Court ... in its 1898 decision in *Magoun v. Illinois Trust,* [upheld] a progressive inheritance tax against an equal protection claim, on the ground that since inheritance itself was a special privilege conferred by the state, the state was free to condition it as it saw fit."

self-consciously used restrictions on property ownership and enforcement of vagrancy legislation to drive workers into wage labor, as, for example, in South Africa. What is true about these extreme cases is that in these situations law-conditioned (created) economic compulsion could produce outcomes very similar to those achievable under slave regimes of direct legal compulsion.[50] But in all market societies, an extensive set of background legal rules establishes to a significant degree the real alternatives working people have available, as they decide whether to enter or to remain at a job. In most market societies, these numerous background rules are not adopted to promote a single end. They are put in place for many different reasons. Regardless of the reasons for their adoption, however, they affect the universe of possibilities open to working people, creating a systematic field of effects. "To govern," Michel Foucault has written, "is to structure the possible field of action of others."[51] In many cases, at least certain of these rules have consciously been adopted with an eye toward inducing laboring people to enter into or remain in wage work. Because these rules can differ significantly in detail from country to country, the magnitude of the pressures facing ordinary people to enter into a particular laboring relationship or to remain in such a relationship can be quite different in different free market societies.

These background rules are far from being the only legal rules that condition the degree of economic compulsion to which working people may be exposed in free markets. Legal rules governing what behavior is permissible and impermissible in market bargaining play as important a role in so-called economic pressure as the background rules we have thus far been discussing. In free markets, the state must always decide which bargaining tactics will be permitted and which prohibited. It simply has no choice. The legal system will always be confronted with claims that some action of a bargaining party has injured another party. If workers are given the privilege of freely combining to withhold their labor, employers may enjoy less coercive power because workers have been granted legal permission to injure them through certain forms of activity. If workers are permitted to mount secondary boycotts, employers may have less power still, because workers have been granted legal permission to injure them through other activity. If employers may not replace workers who go out on strike because workers have been granted property rights in their jobs, they may enjoy even less coercive power. On the other hand, if

---

[50] "While individuals maintained legal property rights in themselves, controls over land and capital led to economic outcomes resembling those when property rights in persons belonged to others." Stanley Engerman, "Coerced and Free Labor: Property Rights and the Development of the Labor Force," *Explorations in Economic History* 29 (January 1992): 18.

[51] Michel Foucault, "The Subject and Power," in *Michel Foucault: Beyond Structuralism and Hermeneutics,* ed. Hubert L. Dreyfus and Paul Rabinow (Chicago, Ill., 1982), 220.

employers possess the legal privilege of combining to negotiate with work-ers, they may enjoy more power vis-à-vis employees, and so forth. Change one or two rules and you may change the degree of compulsion in one direction slightly. Change all the rules in favor of one party and you may change the degree of compulsion radically. There are numerous possible ways in which free market bargaining relationships can be legally constructed, all of them placing the parties in different positions to coerce one another.[52] When we take a close look at economic and legal coercion, the sharp distinction that is normally drawn between the two dissolves into a complex account of the numerous ways in which economic as well as legal pressure is constituted by law.

The second assumption that justifies the view that labor subject to eco-nomic pressure is free but labor subject to (nonpecuniary) legal pressure is unfree is that economic pressure operates less harshly than (nonpe-cuniary) legal pressure. Modern American constitutional law certainly seems to rely on a scale of pressures arranged abstractly by type. Eco-nomic pressure is placed at one end as mild, and physical coercion and imprisonment are placed at the other as severe. But does this scale make sense? Can economic (pecuniary) coercion never be as severe as nonpe-cuniary coercion? Depending on precise circumstances, it seems pretty clear, physical confinement may or may not be more disagreeable than so-called economic threats. The threat of starvation may certainly operate more powerfully than a short term of confinement. English wage workers sometimes chose to serve a short sentence in the house of correction rather than forego the opportunity to earn higher wages by changing em-ployers. A good way of thinking about the potential severity of economic compulsion is to consider what people have sometimes been willing to do to escape an economic threat such as starvation or Third World poverty. They have been willing to enslave themselves, indent themselves for long periods of time, and risk their lives crossing borders. All these alternatives must have seemed less disagreeable than the economic threats they faced.

It is apparent that there can be numerous degrees of economic pressure, ranging from very severe to mild, just as there can be numerous degrees of legal pressure. Rather than think about compulsion in labor relations in terms of a scale arranged according to abstract types of pressure, it would be more accurate to begin thinking in terms of a combined pecuniary/non-pecuniary scale of coercive pressures running from severe to mild. This would help us to see that the various kinds of pressures used in labor rela-tions are commensurable, differing mainly in degree, and that economic pressures and nonpecuniary legal pressures can be substituted for one an-other in many cases and used interchangeably to accomplish similar goals.

---

[52] The preceding paragraph draws heavily from Kennedy, "The Stakes of Law, or Hale and Foucault!" and Kennedy, "Role of Law in Economic Thought."

CONCLUSION

Where the opposition free/coerced labor is used, we have to see the line drawn between the two as a matter of convention. Practically all labor is elicited by confronting workers with a choice between work and a set of more or less disagreeable alternatives to work. We may rightly say that the degree of compulsion operating in these different choices is greater or lesser, but there are no logical grounds for saying that the performance of labor in one case is coerced and in the other it is voluntary. In the following chapters I attempt to explain how the lines that divide labor into free and coerced came to be drawn. How did certain kinds of difficult choices one person can force another person to make come to be seen as coercing labor, whereas other kinds of difficult choices came to be seen as giving rise to voluntary labor? Most nineteenth-century English people considered wage workers free despite the fact that their labor could be extracted by forcing them to choose between confinement at hard labor and the continued performance of services. Today, the decision of a worker to remain in a job because he or she faced confinement at hard labor would be viewed and treated in law as a coerced decision in which the continued service was involuntary. On the other hand, the decision of a worker to remain in a job because he or she faced forfeiture of back wages or a negative injunction would still not be considered a coerced decision. Nor would the decision of a worker to accept an employer's offer of a disagreeable job at low wages because he or she did not qualify for welfare and might face hunger and homelessness if he or she refused. It must be one of our tasks to try to understand how confinement at hard labor came to be treated and characterized differently than wage forfeiture and negative injunctions.

The conventional narrative of free labor continues to rest on the assumption that labor falls into discrete, discontinuous types – wage labor, contract labor, indentured servitude, serfdom, slavery – each having its own natural set of characteristics that define it as either free or unfree. In the following chapters I examine the practice of contract labor in the northern United States and wage labor in England to test whether this way of thinking about labor relations can stand up to historical scrutiny.

PART ONE

American Contract Labor and English Wage Labor

The Uses of Pecuniary and Nonpecuniary Pressure

1

"Free" Contract Labor in the United States

An Anti-essentialist View of Labor Types I

Although the main concern of this book is wage labor in the nineteenth century, I want to begin by approaching the subject through the back door, as it were. The conventional view is that wage labor is one of a small number of standard labor types. Each form of labor is thought to possess its own timeless characteristics. Freedom from physical or other nonpecuniary forms of coercion is considered to be wage labor's most notable characteristic. Imported contract labor represents another of these standard types. Its most salient feature, however, is thought to be that it is compelled by threats of confinement or corporal punishment. In this chapter I ask whether, as a matter of historical practice, contract labor has always been unfree in the sense that it has been enforced through nonpecuniary threats. If it has sometimes been "free" labor in the sense that only pecuniary sanctions have been available to employers, this would raise difficulties for the assumption that a particular labor "type" is invariably either "free" or "unfree." It would also make necessary a revision of the view that the history of labor should be understood in terms of fixed types used only at particular stages of social and economic development.

Until about 1830 the American experience with imported labor conformed to the conventional wisdom. Throughout the seventeenth and eighteenth centuries land was readily available in the American colonies, and hired labor was expensive and difficult to retain. During this time, Americans did import large numbers of unfree workers (indentured servants and slaves) to satisfy their labor needs.

After the American Revolution, however, important changes began to take place in American life. During the early years of the nineteenth century, Congress closed the slave trade to Americans. Until 1820, however, Americans continued to import large numbers of indentured servants and contract laborers whenever the international situation permitted it.[1] But

---

[1] See Louis P. Hennighausen, *History of the German Society of Maryland* (Baltimore, Md., 1909), 56–57; and Farley Grubb, "The Disappearance of European Immigrant Servitude in the United States: An Economic Analysis of Market Collapse, 1785–1835" (Unpublished manuscript, September 1988), 7–8.

in 1820 the market in imported servants collapsed.[2] Thereafter, between 1820 and 1830, relatively few adult white servants were imported, and after the early 1830s, none were.[3] By the end of the 1830s servants who had been imported earlier had completed their terms of service, and adult white European servitude simply disappeared. From the perspective of the conventional wisdom, these changes were to be expected. By the time indentured servitude disappeared, the United States had become home to a permanent pool of propertyless wage workers.

What does pose a challenge to the conventional wisdom, however, is the American experience with contract labor in the decades after 1830. The disappearance of indentured servitude did not mark the end of the importation of European workers. Throughout the late 1830s, 1840s, and 1850s, American employers continued to import small numbers of European contract workers. For the most part, they brought over workers who had been trained on the advanced British manufacturing equipment of the period. American entrepreneurs were struggling to establish a factory system that could rival Britain's, and there was simply no good substitute for these workers.[4] Before 1850, imported British mechanics generally signed two- or three-year contracts, but some of them bound themselves for as long as five or six years.[5] Normally, their contracts called for the regular payment of wages from which transportation debts were to be deducted. In the case of especially valuable workers, however, transportation loans were sometimes forgiven altogether.

The Civil War changed this relatively stable situation by precipitating a labor crisis in the North. Over the first few years of the war demand for northern factory goods rose sharply at the same time that large numbers of factory workers left their jobs to take up arms. Tight domestic labor markets created an opportunity for labor recruiters. Several groups of recruiters approached Congress to request legislation to make it easier to import foreign workers. In 1864 Congress responded by passing "An Act to Encourage Immigration."[6]

American importers of contract labor, of course, wanted very much to be able to hold workers to their agreements. They realized that if they could not enforce contracts, they stood to lose not only their transportation advances but also any hope of solving their labor problems with foreign labor. The original "Act to Encourage Immigration" established new remedies for contract breach beyond those available at common law. Un-

---

[2] Grubb, "Disappearance of European Immigrant Servitude in the United States," 12–13.

[3] Ibid.

[4] Charlotte Erickson, *American Industry and the European Immigrant, 1860–1885* (Cambridge, Mass., 1957), 4–6.

[5] Ibid.

[6] *An Act to Encourage Immigration, U.S. Statutes at Large,* 13(1864):385–87.

der this legislation importers of contract labor could place a lien on land
or other property a breaching immigrant might later acquire.[7] The problem was that many immigrants were urban workers with no interest in
farming and would never acquire enough land or other property to make
a suit worthwhile.

The associations that had originally lobbied Congress began to com-
plain that the contract remedies in the act were inadequate. They asked
Congress to amend the act to make absconding workers liable for double
the unpaid balance of money owed to employers and to make workers'
future wages subject to the debt. They further proposed that new employers of absconding workers who refused to dismiss a worker be made responsible for the unpaid balance of the debt. Undoubtedly, these would
have been effective contract enforcement devices, but Congress refused to
adopt them. However, one state, Connecticut, did.[8]

From the perspective of the conventional wisdom, the shocking part of
this story is that from the 1830s on, contract workers were imported into
the United States not as unfree workers, but as free workers. American
contract workers could not be imprisoned for breaching their agreements,
nor could they be ordered specifically to perform them. Even during the
Civil War, at a time of great need, Congress only agreed to add a set of
relatively trivial contract remedies to those existing at common law. More
surprising, apparently none of the groups that had lobbied Congress for
harsher remedies ever asked Congress to amend the act to establish criminal penalties for contract breaches. Indeed, in 1868, Congress repealed
the "Act to Encourage Immigration" altogether, leaving employers in most
states to their common law remedies. Until 1885 and the passage of the
Foran Act, however, Congress did not prohibit the importation of contract
workers, and in the years following the Civil War several American employers continued to import foreign workers.[9] How were these employers
able to manage, given that they could neither invoke criminal sanctions
nor secure decrees of specific performance to enforce labor contracts?

The Amoskeag mills began to import contract workers after the war
for several reasons. The most important was that they could not secure
enough labor domestically. The mills were located away from large cities,
and although the company tried to induce workers to move to the mills
by advertising premium wages in newspapers throughout the region, they
never succeeded in securing enough workers to keep the mills running at

---

[7] The account in this paragraph is drawn from Erickson, *American Industry and the European
Immigrant,* 3–30.

[8] Ibid., 28–29.

[9] Ibid., 32–148. Indeed, contract workers continued to be imported, illegally, long after the
Foran Act was passed. See Gunther Peck, "Reinventing Free Labor: Immigrant Padrones
and Contract Laborers in North America, 1885–1925," *The Journal of American History* 83
(December 1996).

full capacity.[10] Meanwhile, the board of directors decided that the company's future lay in producing fancy ginghams. The problem was that few American weavers possessed the skills to produce this fine grade of cloth.[11] To solve both problems the board undertook to import a group of Scottish weavers. The weavers arrived the next year, committed to serve under one-year contracts. These contracts authorized the company to deduct an amount from wages each month to recover transportation expenses.

The company did not rely primarily on common law contract remedies to enforce these agreements. The contracts were written to include a number of provisions that placed the mills in a good position to pressure immigrants into serving out their terms of service. Upon their arrival in New York, immigrants were obligated under the contract to turn their baggage over to the company for transportation to New Hampshire. Company employees escorted the immigrants during the journey. Groups of immigrants from a single town were required to "jointly and severally guarantee the performance" of contracts.[12] Should any member of a group breach his or her agreement, other group members might be held liable for the absconding person's debt. Often, the company also required a propertied person in the immigrant's homeland to sign a promissory note "guaranteeing repayment of the passage money should the migrating worker fail to fulfill the contract."[13] The company also retained a debt collector to pursue workers who left owing money.[14] Apparently, these devices worked well enough, because the year after the first group of weavers arrived, the Amoskeag board voted to expand the production of fancy ginghams and to import more weavers. Faced with a breakdown of the domestic wage labor market, the Amoskeag mills turned to imported contract labor and made a success of it, using pecuniary sanctions as a substitute for the nonpecuniary remedies that were unavailable to them.[15]

Other American importers of contract labor, however, did not fare as well. Many contract workers absconded before they repaid their transportation debts. They took jobs with competitors, returned home, or set out on their own. As a result of these kinds of problems the contract labor system never developed into a significant source of labor for American employers.[16]

[10] Daniel Creamer, "Recruiting Contract Laborers for the Amoskeag Mills," *Journal of Economic History* 1 (May 1941): 43–44.

[11] Ibid., 47–48.

[12] Ibid., 46.

[13] Ibid., 49, 53.

[14] Ibid., 55–56.

[15] Ibid., 56.

[16] Erickson, *American Industry and the European Immigrant*, 46–63.

The American experience with contract labor raises several questions about the explanatory logic underlying the narrative of free labor. The conventional view is that employers were faced with an established menu of fixed labor types, some free, some unfree. Economic conditions explain why they chose one type rather than another. Unfree imported contract labor was chosen where wage labor markets had not yet been created or where they had broken down.

It is true that Americans imported contract workers when the domestic wage labor market failed, but after the 1830s American contract labor was "free" labor in the sense that employers could only utilize pecuniary sanctions to enforce contracts. One difficulty with the conventional wisdom is that it reifies labor types, treats them as "things" with a fixed content rather than as social/legal practices that might be constructed in a range of different ways.[17] "Unfreedom" (coercion of labor through threats of corporal punishment or confinement) turns out to have been an accidental rather than an essential feature of contract labor. A given polity might decide to establish criminal sanctions to punish contract breaches, but it might also decide not to. That choice, moreover, was only one of numerous decisions that went into the construction of a labor practice. A hundred similar decisions determined the fine-grained, coercive content of a labor practice along a continuum. The coercive content of any labor relation involved much more than a single yes/no decision about whether to make criminal sanctions available to employers.

As mentioned, certain American employers made a success of contract labor even though they did not enjoy criminal sanctions for contract breaches. They were able to do so in part because the law permitted them to incorporate into immigrants' contracts various pecuniary sanctions to make performance more certain. Suppose for a moment that American

---

[17] The modern picture of slavery also departs from these views about fixed labor types. A number of scholars have recently shown that slavery was constructed in significantly different ways in different places at different times. In the antebellum American South, to take a single example, skilled slaves sometimes lived apart from their masters, rented their own quarters, supplied their own food and clothing, and hired themselves out in local labor markets. They made regular payments back to their masters, in effect renting themselves from their masters. In many ways such slaves lived as free wage workers did but had to contend with the terrible possibility that they might be required to return to their masters. A similar system existed in the Bahamas after 1800. Recent research on slavery suggests that the rigid boundaries that were supposed to separate slavery from other labor "types" were sometimes blurred in practice. Ira Berlin, *Many Thousands Gone: The First Two Centuries of Slavery in North America* (Cambridge, Mass., 1998); Mary Turner, ed., *From Chattel Slaves to Wage Slaves: The Dynamics of Labour Bargaining in the Americas* (Bloomington, Ind., 1995); Paul Craven and Douglas Hay, "The Criminalization of 'Free' Labour: Master and Servant in Comparative Perspective," *Slavery and Abolition* 15 (August 1994); and David Eltis, "Labour and Coercion in the English Atlantic World from the Seventeenth to the Early Twentieth Century," *Slavery and Abolition* 14 (April 1993).

courts had refused to enforce contracts that contained clauses making immigrants jointly and severally liable for breach or had prohibited these kinds of contract clauses altogether. Suppose that they had also prohibited other similarly designed contract provisions. They might have taken these steps on the ground that these measures represented an unwarranted imposition on vulnerable immigrants. Or suppose the opposite, that Congress had responded to the complaints of labor recruiters by adding additional remedies to the "Act to Encourage Immigration." Suppose employers were entitled to double damages for premature departure, could garnishee future wages to collect damage awards, and could hold new employers responsible for transportation debts. A range of different possible practices of contract labor could have been constructed giving employers numerous different degrees of coercive power to enforce contracts.

American experience makes clear that contract labor could be either "free" or "unfree" in the sense that workers serving under contracts could either be subject to nonpecuniary pressures to perform or not. Whether labor used in a particular place, therefore, was "free" or "unfree" depended less on the type of labor than on the rules that governed that labor. It may still be, of course, that economic conditions determined, even if at one remove, whether the labor was free or unfree. It is worth asking, therefore, whether economic circumstances can explain the contract rules that governed American contract labor after the 1830s. In particular, can the economic interests of importers of labor explain these rules? As a group, Americans who imported contract workers were deeply interested in being able to hold contract workers to their agreements. They strove, in numerous ways, to place themselves in a position to pressure workers into performing their contracts. One can only assume that they would have greeted criminal sanctions for contract breach warmly as a powerful addition to their arsenal of coercive devices. Consequently, it doesn't seem plausible to ascribe the contract rules that foreclosed the use of criminal sanctions to the economic interests of importers of labor.

Perhaps these rules can nevertheless be ascribed to the economic interests of the larger group of employers of wage labor. Free wage labor, after all, was the dominant form of labor used in the United States by that time. The formal and informal rules that foreclosed the use of criminal sanctions for contract breaches may merely have reflected the widespread use of free wage labor, which is typically viewed as being incompatible with nonpecuniary forms of coercion. The problem here is that nineteenth-century employers of wage labor in other places felt no hesitation in using criminal sanctions to enforce wage labor agreements, and in fact in many cases believed that they could not get along without them.

Perhaps American contract workers received favorable treatment because they enjoyed a superior bargaining position. They were mainly highly sought-after, skilled workers. Perhaps they were able to bargain for "freedom" with their American employers. Although we can't absolutely foreclose this possibility, there are good reasons for doubting it. First, during the eighteenth century a large number of skilled British workers had been imported as *unfree* workers. Had American demand for imported skilled labor increased so much over the period that workers were now in a position to bargain for freedom, although they had not been able to earlier? Had the supply of skilled workers contracted so drastically? It is not possible to say with complete certainty, but we do know that Americans had always been desperate for skilled labor and were probably at least as desperate during the colonial period, when skilled workers were imported as unfree workers, as afterwards, when they were not.

More important, there is absolutely no evidence to support the idea that the "free" status of these workers was a function of individual bargaining. Contract workers were "free" in the northern states because the law did not authorize criminal sanctions for contract breach, not because "freedom" had been bargained for.

Neither the economic interests of employers nor simple bargaining provide plausible explanations for the contract rules that were in effect in the northern half of the United States. I have offered a detailed account of the development of northern contract rules elsewhere.[18] Suffice it to say that the American contract rules that foreclosed the use of criminal sanctions to enforce labor agreements have to be understood as decisions taken by northern polities through their legal systems to authorize certain kinds of pressures in labor relations, but not others. Local political (including the scope of the suffrage), legal, cultural, and economic conditions all played roles in the adoption and maintenance of these rules. They were a product of a long and complex history of conflict. What emerged from this history was a collective determination in most places in the North, and later in the United States as a whole, to outlaw slavery, and along with it forms of labor directly analogous to slavery.[19] The 1864 "Act to Encourage Immigration" makes clear why criminal sanctions for breach played no part in this legislation. After describing the contract remedies that would henceforth be available to importers of labor, section 2 of the act concluded by declaring: "Nothing herein contained shall be deemed to authorize any contract contravening the Constitution of the United States, or creating in any way the relation of slavery or servitude."[20]

Rules of this kind impose real constraints on economic actors. American importers of contract labor certainly pursued their perceived eco-

---

[18] See Robert Steinfeld, *The Invention of Free Labor: The Employment Relation in English and American Law and Culture* (Chapel Hill, N.C., 1991).

[19] This position was vigorously propounded by the Massachusetts Supreme Judicial Court in 1856. See *Parsons v. Trask, and Others,* 73 Mass. (7 Gray) 473 (1856).

[20] *An Act to Encourage Immigration,* 385–87.

nomic interests, but they did so within a framework of rules (both prohibitions and permissions) put in place by legislatures and courts for a complicated set of reasons. These rules have to be part of any analysis of the economic calculations of employers. Their calculations might have been different, for example, had criminal penalties for breach been available. If they had, perhaps more contract workers would have been imported, and perhaps more employers would have been satisfied with the results. The calculations of employers might also have been different had some of the coercive enforcement mechanisms they were able to substitute for criminal sanctions been prohibited. In that case, perhaps even fewer contract workers would have been imported, and perhaps more employers who imported contract workers would have been unhappy with the results. At a certain point, as greater numbers of coercive enforcement practices were prohibited, it probably would have become totally uneconomic for employers to contemplate importing contract workers.[21]

It is important to understand that it was not just in the United States that economic decisions about contract labor were made within a set of political, legal, and social constraints. Imported slaves might have served the economic purposes of English colonial planters in the middle of the nineteenth century as well as or better than contract workers, but because slavery had been abolished by England in 1833, that simply was no longer a "live" option. Even the turn to contract labor in the English colonies took place only as a result of a legal prohibition combined with a legal permission, the abolition of slavery together with a decision to permit the criminal enforcement of contract labor agreements.[22]

At an earlier time, when slavery itself was permitted in these colonies, employers still made their economic calculations about supplying their labor needs within a set of established "prohibitions" and "permissions." The English poor might have been imported as slaves more cheaply than black Africans, but they were placed off limits as a potential supply of slave labor by existing cultural "prohibitions," while at the same time cultural and legal "permissions" left African labor vulnerable to this kind of exploitation.[23] The economic calculations of employers are always made

---

[21] See Douglass C. North, *Institutions, Institutional Change and Economic Performance* (Cambridge, 1990), for a detailed description of this type of institutional economic analysis.

[22] The British decision to permit contract labor after the abolition of slavery has a complicated political history of its own. See William A. Green, "Emancipation to Indenture: A Question of Imperial Morality," *The Journal of British Studies* 22 (Spring 1983).

[23] David Eltis, "Europeans and the Rise and Fall of African Slavery in the Americas: An Interpretation," *American Historical Review* 98 (December 1993). Much recent work on the abolition of slavery has been devoted to showing that the rules prohibiting this form of labor coercion were not adopted for economic reasons, but were based on collective decisions that such coercive practices simply should not be authorized or permitted. Unfortunately, this scholarship has tended to treat the case of slavery as unique, rather than as

in the context of a dense web of prohibitions *and* permissions, and accounts of these rules have to become an integral part of labor histories if they are to explain not only why a particular form of labor was used in a particular place but also why it contained the particular coercive content it did.

Where rules operate as constraints on economic actors, it is often because they have become so deeply embedded in the law and culture of a place that most economic actors simply take them for granted in their calculations. Such rules, in other words, have become widely accepted ground rules. Other imaginable rules for conducting life appear to most persons no longer to be "live options." At times alternative rules are not even imaginable.[24] Even though American labor recruiters thought that the 1864 "Act to Encourage Immigration" contained inadequate contract enforcement mechanisms, apparently none of those who sought to amend the act ever asked Congress to establish criminal penalties to enforce labor contracts. Nor did any Americans who imported contract workers. Either they could not imagine the possibility of criminal sanctions, or they assumed that kind of practice was simply not a "live option" in the circumstances. Working within this widely accepted background constraint, they sought to create pecuniary substitutes for criminal sanctions. Needless to say, some of these substitutes worked better than others.

It would be wrong, however, to assume that these kinds of rules always operate merely as an unalterable background constraint on economic actors. What does not appear to be a "live option" or even imaginable to many people at one moment in one place may come to be seen as a "live option" again at another time. Ground rules are nearly always subject to challenge and may become the object of political and legal struggle at any time. In the early twentieth century, a number of northern states, including Maine, Michigan, and Minnesota, passed laws to punish criminally as fraud failure to perform labor contracts where advances had been given to a worker.[25] Even where ground rules are not directly challenged, often groups motivated by conflicting ideas and conflicting sets of perceived interests will struggle over their interpretation, testing the limits of a rule in one direction or another. Sometimes these interpretive struggles will yield a partly different set of rules. Not infrequently, individuals will simply ig-

---

one example of a more general process in which societies constantly make decisions about precisely which coercive practices to prohibit, authorize, or permit from among a rich variety of coercive possibilities in all forms of labor relations.

[24] "[T]he weight of tradition, through a process understood only imperfectly, may make it simply *unthinkable* for any agent to violate the current practice, in spite of individual incentives to do so." Alexander J. Field, "Microeconomics, Norms, and Rationality," *Economic Development and Cultural Change* 32 (July 1984): 700–1, quoted in Michael Huberman, *Escape from the Market: Negotiating Work in Lancashire* (Cambridge, 1996), 125.

[25] 1907 Me. Rev. Stat. c. 127; 1903 Mich. Pub. Acts No. 106; 1901 Minn. Laws c. 165.

nore or disobey rules. Sometimes, individuals or groups will try to exploit disjunctions between formal and informal rules, and so forth. On the other hand, sometimes a group will succeed in changing ground rules outright. These multilayered struggles over rules must also be part of labor histories if such histories are to provide an understanding of the subtle and not so subtle changes that can take place over time in the terms on which any particular type of labor is offered.

It seems to have been true that contract labor was mainly used in situations where wage labor markets had not yet been created or where they had broken down, just as the conventional wisdom supposes. However, contract labor turns out not to have been a "thing" with fixed characteristics, one of which was "unfreedom." It turns out to have been a social/legal practice that could be constructed as either "free" or "unfree" labor. Furthermore, the absence or breakdown of a domestic wage labor market does not explain why it was constructed in one way rather than another, because this condition gave rise to both "free" and "unfree" contract labor in different places. To explain why contract labor was constructed as "free" or "unfree" labor, it is necessary to explain the set of formal and informal rules that governed the practice in a particular place. To do this it is necessary to look to politics, law, and culture as well as to economic conditions and interests. Not uncommonly, these kinds of rules operated as a partial constraint on employer interests rather than as a pure expression of those interests. In the case of the northern United States, contract labor was constructed as "free" labor because northern polities had decided that to permit employers to use criminal sanctions to enforce labor contracts would have given them illegitimate coercive power over their workers. This ground rule, however, became a subject of struggle again after the Civil War as southern states adopted criminal sanctions for breaches of labor contracts, and as a few northern states joined them.

In the next few chapters I turn to England to examine more closely the legal condition of wage labor as it existed in the nineteenth-century metropolitan homeland. Measured by comparative wage rates, American labor was in shorter supply than English wage labor throughout the nineteenth century, and land in the United States was cheaper. Given that American wage and contract labor were "free" labor, the conventional wisdom tells us that English wage labor should also have been "free" labor. However, exactly the opposite turns out to have been the case. Where labor was scarcer and land more abundant in the United States, wage labor was "free." Where labor was abundant and land scarce in England, wage labor was, in modern terms, "unfree." The existence of "unfree" wage labor in England for nearly a century after the Industrial Revolution makes necessary a radical revision of the traditional account of the rise of free labor.

2

"Unfree" Wage Labor in Nineteenth-Century England

An Anti-essentialist View of Labor Types II

The history of wage labor in England has often been described as a movement from the statutes of laborers to free contract, from comprehensive state regulation of labor markets to laissez-faire back to comprehensive regulation. This book adopts some of that approach but introduces important modifications. The laissez-faire regime of free contract described in this and later chapters possesses characteristics that turn the traditional account on its head.

In the nineteenth century, free contract yielded "unfree" labor at least as often as it yielded "free" labor. It could do so because in important respects free contract is an empty idea. A regime of free contract only receives its content from a detailed set of contract rules, and these rules cannot be deduced from any abstract idea of contract. In most cases, the state develops contract rules as courts, legislatures, and other governmental bodies go about answering a series of difficult but unavoidable "policy" questions: What kinds of contracts will we enforce? What kinds of contracts will we prohibit or refuse to enforce? How will duress or fraud be defined in determining whether to enforce a contract, or to prohibit a certain species of contract? What formalities will be required to bind a party? What remedies will we make available to the parties for contract breach? What remedies for contract breach will we allow the parties to establish for themselves? A range of quite different regimes of free contract can be constructed, depending on how the political entity answers these questions.[1] There can be no "natural" regime of contract, because there are no "natural" answers to these difficult questions. All regimes of contract are regulatory regimes involving conscious policy choices. In retelling the story of English wage labor, this book ends in the traditional place with a regime of free contract, but it is a regime of free contract that endorses

---

[1] Among modern theorists of contract, this is a completely conventional view. Even in the nineteenth century, theorists such as John Stuart Mill offered a similar view. John Stuart Mill, *Collected Works*, vol. III, *Principles of Political Economy with Some of Their Applications to Social Philosophy* (Toronto, 1965), Book V, chap. I, § 2.

policies and possesses a legal content associated today with "unfree" rather than "free" labor.

The systematic regulation of hired labor in England began with the Statute of Laborers in the middle of the fourteenth century. There is little mystery about why the statute was enacted when it was.[2] The Black Death reduced the laboring population of England between one-third and two-thirds. Those who survived took advantage of the labor shortages to demand higher wages and better working conditions.

The response of king and Parliament was to enact the Statute of Laborers.[3] It imposed a comprehensive, nationwide system of regulation on the hired labor market, comprising at least five interrelated parts. First was compulsory labor. The laboring poor were legally obligated to work if they were not artisans and did not hold enough land to occupy their time fully. Any employer who needed a laborer could require someone who was not otherwise occupied to enter his service, under threat of criminal compulsion. Second, the laboring poor had to hire themselves by the year (in agriculture) and not for shorter periods. Third, they had to fulfill these engagements under threat of criminal punishment. Fourth, if someone else hired them during their term, that person was also subject to criminal punishment. Finally, their wages were to be set by the state. This sweeping system of labor regulation was revitalized in the sixteenth century with the passage of the Statute of Artificers.[4]

Over the following two centuries, however, this broad system of regulation gradually fell into disuse. By the last quarter of the eighteenth century, wages were no longer being set, except on rare occasions.[5] Compulsory labor, except for paupers, had disappeared,[6] and enticement had become only a civil matter giving rise to money damages.

---

[2] It is not altogether clear why this law was directed toward hired labor, and no similar statutory effort was made to reinforce villeinage.

[3] What is referred to as the Statute of Laborers consisted of an ordinance enacted in 1349, 23 Ed. III, and a statute enacted two years later, 25 Ed. III, stat. 2.

[4] Statute of Artificers, 5 Eliz., c. 4 (1562–1563).

[5] Adam Smith, *An Inquiry into the Nature and Causes of the Wealth of Nations,* ed. Edwin Cannan (Chicago, Ill., 1976), I:158; William Holdsworth, *A History of English Law* (London, 1965), XI:471–72; see also Sidney Webb and Beatrice Webb, *The History of Trade Unionism* (London, 1920), 49–60.

[6] Daphne Simon, "Master and Servant," in *Democracy and the Labour Movement: Essays in Honour of Dona Torr,* ed. John Saville (London, 1954), 198. Compulsory labor does seem to have survived well into the eighteenth century, however: "Indictments at Quarter Sessions to force unmarried people into service seem to have become much less common after about 1750. In Essex, for example, after thirty-two such cases between 1748 and 1753, there were then three cases between 1754 and 1757, and none subsequently." K. D. M. Snell, *Annals of the Labouring Poor: Social Change and Agrarian England, 1660–1900* (Cambridge, 1987), 100 n. 73. For examples of compulsory service in the late seventeenth and

"Unfree" Wage Labor in Nineteenth-Century England   41

By the early years of the nineteenth century, a significant portion of the governing classes had been converted to laissez-faire ideas, in many cases no doubt believing that such ideas would also advance their economic interests.[7] In 1811, a Select Committee of Parliament declared that

> no interference of the legislature with the freedom of trade, or with the perfect liberty of every individual to dispose of his time and of his labour in the way and on the terms which he may judge most conducive to his own interest, can take place without violating general principles of the first importance to the prosperity and happiness of the community.[8]

Over the next few years, the provisions of the sixteenth-century Tudor legislation began to be repealed. In 1813, the wage setting provisions of the 1563 statute were removed from the statute books,[9] followed by the apprenticeship clauses in 1814.[10] With the repeal of these provisions of the Tudor legislation, state regulation of the labor market is thought to have been largely eliminated, leaving the terms of labor to be set primarily through bargaining between employers and workers under the common law of contract, which included a strict rule against granting orders for the specific performance of contracts of personal service. In most cases, only money damages could be recovered from breaching parties.[11]

One feature of the earlier system of labor regulation, however, remained in place: criminal sanctions for contract breaches. A number of historians have written about criminal sanctions, but they have mainly depicted them as trivial or anomalous in an advanced market society with a large population of propertyless workers.[12] All accounts trace criminal sanctions back to the medieval statutes of laborers and to the later Statute

---

early eighteenth centuries, see Anthony Fletcher, *Reform in the Provinces: The Government of Stuart England* (New Haven, Conn., 1986), 223–26; and Ann Kussmaul, *Servants in Husbandry in Early Modern England* (Cambridge, 1981), 166.

7   Webb and Webb, *History of Trade Unionism*, 59–63.

8   Quoted in ibid., 60.

9   53 Geo. III, c. 40 (1813).

10   54 Geo. III, c. 96 (1814).

11   Courts of Equity, however, did sometimes grant negative injunctions. See Lea S. VanderVelde, "The Gendered Origins of the *Lumley* Doctrine: Binding Men's Consciences and Women's Fidelity," *Yale Law Journal* 101 (1992).

12   Recently, a number of historians have begun to reject these views. Among them, Douglas Hay has argued that criminal sanctions were quite important in English labor markets in the nineteenth century. Douglas Hay, "Penal Sanctions, Masters, and Servants" (Unpublished manuscript, 1990), and "Masters, Servants, Justices and Judges" (Unpublished manuscript, 1988), 24. See also D. C. Woods, "The Operation of the Master and Servants Act in the Black Country, 1858–1875," *Midland History* 7 (1982): 109–13; and Paul Craven, "The Law of Master and Servant in Mid-Nineteenth-Century Ontario," in *Essays in the History of Canadian Law*, ed. David Flaherty (Toronto, 1981), I:175–211,

of Artificers, but until recently these sanctions were seen as part of a world that had passed away by the nineteenth century. Of course change was supposed not to have come all at once, and so the provisions of the Tudor legislation were repealed only gradually, piecemeal, over the course of the nineteenth century. In 1875, however, the inevitable occurred: The final clauses of the functionally and ideologically archaic Tudor system were finally taken off the statute books.[13]

This account of the rise and fall of criminal sanctions for labor contract breaches, however, does not fit the evidence well. Even as a number of the provisions of the Tudor legislation were falling into disuse over the eighteenth century, others were being revitalized. Between 1720 and 1843 Parliament passed more than half a dozen new statutes aimed at punishing criminally the breach of labor contracts. The first of these covered a few specific trades, but later statutes were more general.[14] At the time the first of these new statutes appeared (1720), nearly a century and a half had elapsed since Parliament had last passed such legislation. These eighteenth- and nineteenth-century statutes represented a genuinely new departure.[15] They imposed criminal sanctions for contract breach not, in the main, as part of a comprehensive system of regulation, as earlier statutes

especially 204; and Adrian Merritt, "The Historical Role of Law in the Regulation of Employment – Abstentionist or Interventionist?" in *Australian Journal of Law & Society* 1 (1982).

[13] Daphne Simon is the main modern exponent of this position (Simon, "Master and Servant," 197–200), but David Galenson has recently offered a similar view; see "The Rise of Free Labor: Economic Change and the Enforcement of Service Contracts in England, 1351–1875," in *Capitalism in Context: Essays on Economic Development and Cultural Change in Honor of R. M. Hartwell*, ed. John A. James and Mark Thomas (Chicago, Ill., 1994), 114–37.

[14] 7 Geo I, stat. I, c. 13 (1720) (journeymen tailors); 9 Geo. I, c. 27 (1722) (journeymen shoemakers); 12 Geo. I, c. 34 (1725) (woolcombers and weavers); 13 Geo. II, c. 8 (1740) (journeymen and other persons in the leather trades); 20 Geo. II, c. 19 (1747) (wide range of workers: artificers, handicraftsmen, miners, colliers, keelmen, pitmen, glassmen, potters, and other labourers); 22 Geo. II, c. 27 (1749) (variety of trades); 6 Geo. III, c. 25 (1766) (essentially same workers as covered in 1747 statute); 4 Geo. IV, c. 34 (1823) (wide range of workers). For a complete list of these statutes see Webb and Webb, *History of Trade Unionism*, 250–51 n. 2. See also John Orth, *Combination and Conspiracy: A Legal History of Trade Unionism, 1721–1906* (Oxford, 1991), 108–9.

[15] I should add here that there was another area in which a similar countertrend can be observed. Between 1720 and 1824, more than half a dozen anti-combination statutes were passed by Parliament. See Sir James Fitzjames Stephen, *A History of the Criminal Law of England* (London, 1883), III:206–7. Anti-combination measures do not necessarily impose substantive terms on the parties. They establish ground rules for bargaining, defining acts that are permissible and impermissible in trying to bring another party to terms. The Webbs, however, argued that the eighteenth-century anti-combination statutes were enacted not to regulate bargaining tactics in the market but primarily to support the wage setting and other traditional regulatory functions of the state (Webb and Webb, *History of Trade Unionism*, 65). Orth makes a similar argument in *Combination and Conspiracy* (59–60). Only in the Anti-combination acts of 1799–1800, according to this view, did Parliament

had, but as stand-alone remedies for breach of contract. With one exception early in the eighteenth century, Parliament made no attempt to re-enact the compulsory labor provisions of the earlier statutes,[16] the requirements that hirings be for a specific term, or, with only a relatively few exceptions in specific trades, the wage setting provisions of earlier statutes.[17] Market activity expanded rapidly in eighteenth-century England in both the commercial and industrial sectors of the economy. The first of the new eighteenth-century statutes regulated contracts not in agriculture, as the old statutes primarily had, but in the rapidly growing manufacturing sector: tailors (1720), shoemakers (1722), woolen trades (1725), and leather trades (1740).[18] Later, more general statutes were passed that covered a wide range of manual wage workers.[19] These statutes were enacted in direct response to the heightened demand for labor created by expanding markets. In thriving sectors of the economy, employers felt that it was absolutely essential that they be able to hold workers to their agreements.[20]

relinquish these traditional regulatory ambitions and transform anti-combination legislation into regulation of bargaining tactics in the market. However, at another point in their book the Webbs had noted that by the end of the eighteenth century, "[s]o completely had these [wage setting] statutes fallen into disuse that their very existence was in many instances unknown to the artisans" (57). They also wrote that with the 1757 repeal of the previous year's wage setting act for the woolen cloth weavers, "Parliament was now heading straight for *laisser-faire.* . . . [The 1757 act] marks the passage from the old ideas to the new" (51). Indeed, of all the eighteenth-century Anti-combination acts, only those regulating tailors and weavers included both anti-combination and wage setting clauses in the same act. Anti-combination law was transformed over the course of the eighteenth century into a rule about bargaining tactics in a free market, a rule that was far from being an archaic relic in the nineteenth century.

The earlier Anti-combination acts were repealed in 1824 to 1825, but union activity continued to be subject to the common law of criminal conspiracy and to the restrictions contained in the 1825 act as interpreted by the common law courts. Webb and Webb, *History of Trade Unionism,* 261–95; and Orth, *Combination and Conspiracy.*

[16] For the exception, see 7 Geo. I, c. 13 (1720). It was the first of these eighteenth-century statutes and covered only tailors in and around the cities of London and Westminster.

[17] 7 Geo. I, c. 13 (1720) amended by 8 Geo. III, c. 17 (1768) (wage rates for tailors); 29 Geo. II, c. 33 (1756) (wage rates for woolen cloth weavers) under pressure from the weavers; repealed the next year, 30 Geo. II, c. 12 (1757) under pressure from the clothiers; 10 Geo. III, c. 53 (1770) (wage rates for London coal heavers on the Thames); 13 Geo. III, c. 68 (1773) (wage rates for London and Westminster silk weavers) under pressure from the weavers; extended to weavers of silk mixed with other materials; 32 Geo. III, c. 44 (1792).

[18] 7 Geo. I, c. 13 (1720); 9 Geo. I, c. 27 (1722); 12 Geo. I, c. 34 (1725); 13 Geo. II, c. 8 (1740).

[19] 20 Geo. II, c. 19 (1747); 6 Geo. III, c. 25 (1766); 4 Geo. IV, c. 34 (1823).

[20] See Daniel Defoe, *The Great Law of Subordination Consider'd: Or, the Insolence and Unsufferable Behavior of Servants in England Duly Enquir'd Into* (London, 1723), ii, 92–103: "[T]he Husbandmen are ruin'd, the Farmers disabled, Manufacturers and Artificers plung'd, to the Destruction of Trade, and Stagnation of their Business; and . . . no Men who, in the

The later statutes actually began to punish contract breaches more severely than earlier statutes had. The sixteenth-century Statute of Artificers had condemned craftsmen and laborers to a maximum of one month's confinement for failing to complete their work. A majority of the statutes enacted during the early eighteenth century mandated the same maximum one-month term of confinement for contract breaches.[21] However, in 1766 the maximum punishment was increased to three months for workers covered by that statute, and the same maximum was carried for-

Course of Business, employ Numbers of the Poor, can depend upon any Contracts they make, or perform any thing they undertake, having no Law, no Power to enforce their Agreement, or to oblige the Poor to perform honestly what they are hir'd to do, tho' ever so justly paid for doing it" (ii). Based on Defoe's pamphlet, Christopher Tomlins argues that until this eighteenth-century legislation was passed, employers actually had no legal recourse (aside from a common law action for damages) against skilled piece workers who breached their agreements. See Christopher Tomlins, "Law and Authority as Subjects in Labor History," *ABF Working Paper #9312*, 7–11. But this position ignores the piece work clause of the Statute of Artificers, which had been enacted in the sixteenth century. Defoe may well have been exaggerating when he talked about the absence of legal remedies in the interests of carrying his argument that new contract laws were necessary. Later in his pamphlet, for example, he says that husbandmen have no legal remedy against departing servants in husbandry who have agreed to work for a certain time (see 300–1). I have to doubt the accuracy of this statement given that servants in husbandry were regularly proceeded against under the provisions of the Tudor Statute of Artificers, although it is possible that the Statute of Artificers was interpreted not to extend to servants hired for less than a year. Hirings in husbandry for less than a year became more common in the eighteenth century. How often the piece work clause of the Statute of Artificers was used before 1720 is more difficult to say. Even if it was not widely used before 1720, over the next century, it, along with the newly enacted contract breach statutes, would increasingly come to be relied on by employers. By 1823, repeal of the piece work clause of the Tudor statute was singled out in Peter Moore's 1823 bill to reform master and servant law as an especially oppressive aspect of that law. The piece work clause "has been much abused. . . . Very few prosecutions have been made to effect under the Combination Acts, but hundreds have been made under this law, and the labourer or workman can never be free, unless this law is modified." George White and Gravener Henson, *A Few Remarks on the State of the Laws, at Present in Existence, for Regulating Masters and Work-People, Intended as a Guide for the Consideration of the House, in Their Discussions on the Bill for Repealing Several Acts Relating to Combinations of Workingmen* (1823), 51. See also Simon, "Master and Servant," 165 n. 3 (the Statute of Artificers was still the basis of some prosecutions in the nineteenth century). Nevertheless, it seems clear that the status of piece work under the master and servant statutes represented contested terrain over a long period of time, and the question of the status of piece work revived again in the nineteenth century; see Chapter 4.

[21] Two exceptions seem to have been a 1725 statute, 12 Geo. I, c. 34 (1725) (woolen manufactures), which prescribed a maximum three-month prison sentence, and a 1720 statute, 7 Geo. I, stat. I, c. 13 (journeymen tailors) (maximum two-month sentence). Although the 1747 statute, 20 Geo. II, c.19, prescribed a maximum one-month term, it required that workers sent to the house of correction also be whipped. Three-month maximum terms only became the norm in later statutes.

ward into the 1823 statute. If we think of historical change not in terms of one stage of social/economic organization supplanting another, but rather in terms of societies making their futures *ad hoc,* discarding certain past practices, adapting others to new circumstances, and introducing entirely new ones, we will have a better understanding of the fate of the different provisions of the Tudor legislation. Penal sanctions for contract breaches, a centuries-old practice, was revived and redefined. Over the course of the eighteenth and early nineteenth centuries the master and servant relationship was progressively stripped of its mandatory legal incidents. Increasingly, it became a relationship whose terms were established by the parties. Penal sanctions were transformed from a mode of publicly regulating conduct in and exit from a legal status voluntarily entered (in the same way that divorce publicly regulates exit from another legal status also entered voluntarily) into a means primarily to enforce agreements, as status voluntarily entered evolved into contract. Penal sanctions, however, never completely lost their public character.

Criminal sanctions for contract breaches were revived by Parliament in the eighteenth and nineteenth centuries because they served the economic objectives of many employers in the contemporary English labor market *and* because they promoted the project of basing labor markets on contracts. The provisions of the Tudor legislation that fell into disuse and were repealed were inconsistent with this new emphasis on voluntary agreements, imposing as they did substantive terms on employers and workers. They were also the provisions to which workers were appealing in an effort to keep up their living standards.[22] The language of the 1766 statute makes clear that by the time it was enacted,[23] Parliament primarily viewed criminal sanctions as stand-alone remedies to enforce labor agreements.[24]

Free-market rhetoric often creates the impression that law can only interfere with the otherwise natural functioning of free markets; lawyers and institutional economists know better. All large-scale markets are legally regulated, if only by rules defining contract and property rights. In a sense, markets are "constituted" by rules of property and contract as much as they are "regulated" by them. It is difficult to imagine extensive,

---

[22] In a turnaround from earlier centuries, during the eighteenth century working people primarily pressed for wage setting. Employers fought tenaciously against attempts to enact new wage setting legislation or to base wage setting on the old statutes. Laboring people also fought a losing battle to retain the apprenticeship provisions of the old Tudor legislation. On the reversal of views about wage setting, see White and Henson, *A Few Remarks on the State of the Laws,* 54–56; see in general Webb and Webb, *History of Trade Unionism,* 49–62.

[23] 6 Geo. III, c. 25 (1766).

[24] Orth, *Combination and Conspiracy,* 109.

complex markets at all without state enforcement of contracts.[25] As one historian has observed,

> it was not until the eighteenth century, in Western Europe, England, and North America, that societies first appeared whose economic systems depended on the expectation that most people, most of the time, were sufficiently conscience ridden (and certain of retribution) that they could be trusted to keep their promises. . . . Only to the extent that [the] norm [of promise keeping] prevails can economic affairs be based on nothing more authoritative than the obligations arising out of promises.
>
> Both the growing force of the norm of promise keeping and its synchronization with the spread of market relations are clearly inscribed in the history of the law of contract. . . . For the first time the law strained to make promisors generally liable for whatever expectations their promises created. Never before had promises counted for so much in human affairs, and never before had the penalties for being short-willed and unreliable been so severe.[26]

The proliferation of new contract breach statutes in the eighteenth century must be seen as part of the process of freer market creation in England. Freer labor markets, it was widely believed, would not function properly unless workers could be held to their promises. It was an article

---

[25]   Enforcement poses no problem when it is in the interests of the other party to live up to agreements. But without institutional constraints, self-interested behavior will foreclose complex exchange, because of the uncertainty that the other party will find it in his or her interest to live up to the agreement. . . . Throughout history . . . this [risk of defection] has largely foreclosed complex exchange. . . . [State enforcement of contracts] has been the critical underpinning of successful modern economies involved in the complex contracting necessary for modern economic growth. . . . [N]either self-enforcement by parties nor trust can be completely successful. . . . [T]he returns on opportunism, cheating, and shirking rise in complex societies. A coercive third party is essential.

Douglass C. North, *Institutions, Institutional Change and Economic Performance* (Cambridge, 1990), 33–35. Cf. Avner Greif, "On the Social Foundations and Historical Development of Institutions That Facilitate Impersonal Exchange: From the Community Responsibility System to Individual Legal Responsibility in Pre-modern Europe," *Stanford University Department of Economics Working Papers* (1997) ("whether or not a legal system is required to support impersonal exchange depends upon a society's social structure, its intra-community contract institutions, and, in particular, the extent to which its social structure is common knowledge").

[26]   Thomas L. Haskell, "Capitalism and the Humanitarian Sensibility, Part 2," *The American Historical Review* 90 (1985): 553–55. Haskell may be exaggerating a bit here, but the increase in the maximum penalty for contract breach in the case of artisans and laborers is a good example of his point.

of faith among many employers that propertyless workers could not be held to their promises through civil suits for money damages:

[I]n the absence of any other remedy, [a worker] might set his employer at defiance. Has not the master a just right to say, "Satisfy me either in damages, or by performance of your engagement. The former you cannot do, therefore the latter you must do, even on the pain of imprisonment for refusal"?[27]

Criminal penalties for breaches of labor agreements were no different in principle than common law contract remedies. Both were state-made rules to enforce agreements, making extensive, complex markets possible. As the earlier system of comprehensive, substantive regulation of labor fell into disuse and was dismantled, many of those who governed England increasingly sought to place market relations on a new footing of private property and free contract. Penal sanctions were revived as an integral part of this market revolution, providing a legal remedy for breach of promise where other remedies were not considered to be effective.

Penal sanctions for contract breach were abolished in 1875, not because they had become an archaic relic, the result preordained, sooner or later, by the triumph of free markets, but because organized labor finally prevailed in a campaign to have them repealed. Had labor not waged that battle or not been successful, penal sanctions might have remained in place indefinitely, an unexceptional feature of free contract in English labor markets.

WHAT ENGLISH LAW WAS

Under the 1823 Master and Servant Act, English employers could have their workmen sent to the house of correction and held at hard labor for up to three months for breaches of their labor agreements.[28] Actions that exposed a worker to criminal sanctions included not only quitting before

---

[27] James Edward Davis, *The Master and Servant Act, 1867* (London, 1868), 7. See also William Holdsworth, *A History of English Law* (London, 1965), XV:20: "A civil remedy against a master will usually be sufficient because a master is usually solvent: it will usually not be sufficient against a servant because he is often not solvent; and it is most undesirable that a poor man, because he is poor, should be allowed to break his contract with impunity."

[28] 4 Geo. IV, c. 34, s. III (1823). Both 6 Geo. III, c. 25, s. IV (1766) and the Statute of Artificers (1563) were apparently still also the basis of some prosecutions in the nineteenth century. Simon, "Master and Servant," 165 n. 3. The Court of Queen's Bench interpreted this legislation to mean that workers could be imprisoned for up to three months for each breach of an agreement.

one had served out one's term or one's notice but also temporarily absenting oneself from work for a day or an afternoon or merely being neglectful or disobedient at work.[29] Other statutes subjected cottage workers to fines or imprisonment for failing to finish work timely.[30] The 1823 act contained broad language that could be read to cover the overwhelming majority of manual wage workers.[31] However, as I discuss in Chapter 4, the scope of the act became the subject of an extended struggle between employers and workers. Each party attempted to persuade the common law courts to adopt narrower or broader interpretations of its coverage and to impose those interpretations on justices of the peace.

More than three-quarters of a century after the beginning of what is conventionally termed the Industrial Revolution, English employers had lost none of their enthusiasm for criminal sanctions as a means for enforcing labor agreements. Quite simply this was because criminal sanctions continued to be of great economic use to them in nineteenth-century labor markets. First, and perhaps foremost, employers used criminal sanctions to compel workers to serve out their contract terms. This statement requires some explanation because before 1867 the justices of the peace, who administered the labor legislation, possessed only the power to pun-

---

[29] 4 Geo. IV, c. 34, s. III (1823).

[30] See 17 Geo. III, c. 56 (1777), and 6 & 7 Vict., c. 40 (1843).

[31] 4 Geo. IV, c. 34, s. III (1823) covered the following kinds of workers: "*any Servant in Husbandry or any Artificer,* Calico Printer, *Handicraftsman,* Miner, Collier, Keelman, Pitman, Glassman, Potter, *Labourer, or other Person* [who] shall contract with any Person or Persons whomsoever, to serve him, her, or them *for any Time or Times whatsoever, or in any other manner*" (emphasis added). Oral agreements were enough to bind a worker once he or she had begun work. The precise coverage of this act was unclear. On the one hand, it listed workers in a number of specific trades. On the other, it also included "any Artificer [or] Handicraftsman [or] Labourer . . . or other Person," apparently covering both skilled and unskilled manual workers generally. Numerous cases were successfully brought against skilled workers who were not members of one of the listed trades, but, as I discuss in Chapter 4, there were also decisions that placed certain workers beyond the reach of the act. Everyone agreed that domestic servants were not covered by the act. See the opinion of Lord Ellenborough in *Lowther v. Radnor,* 8 East 113, 103 Eng. Rep. 287 (1806), and the failed attempt in Parliament in 1801 to add domestic servants to the list of those covered by the Master and Servant acts, *Parl. Papers* (1801), I:177, and I:389. In 1866 George Newton, a potter, testified to his understanding of the scope of the 1823 act in the "Report from the Select Committee on Master and Servant; Together with the Proceedings of the Committee, and Minutes of Evidence" [hereinafter "Select Committee on Master and Servant"], *Parl. Papers* (1865), VIII:1, and (1866), XIII:1; testimony from (1866), XIII:Q. "36. The Act applies practically, does it not, to all trades? – Yes, there are a number of trades specified in the Act, but there is a very inclusive term, 'handicraftsmen,' 'or other person,' who shall enter into any contract to serve. 37. It likewise specifies agricultural labourers? – They are not exempted. 38. The only exemptions are domestic servants? – Yes."

ish contract breaches with a term of confinement or other sanctions and not the power to order the performance of contracts.[32]

The 1823 statute, and its predecessors, might have been read simply as criminal legislation designed to "punish" wrongs, breaches of labor agreements, but not to "compel" performance. "Punishment" would also have deterred future breaches, of course. Even so, the deterrence of the criminal law is something quite different than a court order to perform a contract. Take the case of a worker who quit before his agreed-on term of service was complete. A decree of specific performance would have ordered that person to do what he had promised to do, return to work to complete his term. If he did, he would not be subject to further imprisonment. If he refused, he could be imprisoned indefinitely until he changed his mind and returned to work, at which time he would be released. The compulsion to perform would have been achieved through the threat or actuality of indefinite confinement, but the goal would have been to secure performance, not to punish a wrong. Once performance was secured the threat of confinement would have been lifted.

Narrowly viewed, criminal punishment worked differently. First, once a person committed a breach, such as quitting before the end of his or her term, justices of the peace were only authorized to punish that person with confinement, regardless of whether he or she now agreed to return to work. Second, a justice was only authorized to confine a breaching worker for up to three months, not, as in the case of a finding of contempt following an order of performance, for an indefinite period.

From the point of view of employers, this interpretation of the legislation would have had two serious drawbacks. First, quite often employers did not want a valuable worker imprisoned; they wanted that worker returned to the job. They wanted him or her to be held to his or her agreement, not punished.[33] Second, the threat of a short prison term was not likely to be as effective as the threat of indefinite incarceration in pressuring workers to perform their agreements. Fortunately for employers, practically no one in authority, neither legal commentators, justices of the peace, nor judges of the common law courts, read the legislation as simple criminal legislation designed solely to punish wrongs.

---

[32] Justices were also authorized to abate wages or to dissolve the contract. 4 Geo. IV., c. 34, s. III (1823). The 1867 revision of the law did give justices of the peace the authority to order performance, 30 & 31 Vict., c. 141 s. 9 (1867). By the nineteenth century English equity courts had adopted a rule against ordering the specific performance of personal services contracts in actions for contract breach. See M. R. Freedland, *The Contract of Employment* (Oxford, 1976), 273–74. I discuss the question of the specific performance of contracts for personal services in a later section of this chapter.

[33] Woods, "Operation of the Master and Servants Act in the Black Country," 106.

Legal commentators were quite clear that the purpose of the legislation was not only to punish wrongs, but also to compel performance. One wrote that

> [i]n the first place, . . . [imprisonment is warranted] when a workman wilfully leaves his work unfinished[, because] there is something of a public wrong, considering how many persons, often fellow-workmen in the same class of life, suffer from the sudden neglect of work. In the second place, imprisonment may be viewed as a mode of compelling the performance of contracts. The law of England in a variety of cases allows imprisonment as the mode of compelling the performance of contracts.[34]

Judging by their conduct, many justices of the peace would have heartily agreed with this reading of the legislation. Justices commonly pressured workers into returning to their jobs rather than sending them off to the house of correction. A typical case would begin with an employer filing a complaint against a worker. The worker would be arrested (after the passage of Jervis's Act in 1848, summoned in many cases)[35] and brought before a justice of the peace. There, a settlement would be arranged. The justice would threaten the worker with penal confinement if he refused to return to his employer, and the worker would usually agree to go back. The case would then be dismissed.[36] William Roberts, a lawyer for the trade unions, described this process in testimony before the Select Committee on Master and Servant in 1866. Arrested workers were brought before a local magistrate:

> The law is not always applied as a means of punishing. Frequently the course is pursued which was pursued in this case, which was this; the master said, "I can send you to prison for three months with hard labour, will you go back to your work?" So it is, as it were, that exemption from punishment is sold to the men. These men agreed to go back to their work.[37]

---

[34] Davis, *Master and Servant Act, 1867,* 6. See also the opinion of Mr. Baron Watson in *In re Baker,* 2 H. & N. 219 (Exch., 1857), 235: "The master, for the purpose of compelling the workman to perform his contract, obtains the adjudication of a magistrate that he shall be sent to prison."

[35] 11 & 12 Vict., c. 43, s. 1 (1848) (the justice of the peace was authorized, in his discretion, to initiate proceedings by summoning a worker, rather than automatically issuing an arrest warrant).

[36] One student of the subject has concluded "that employers used the courts as a warning and as a means of getting men back to work. [Cases] would often be dismissed with the employer's consent, if the worker agreed to return and accept the conditions of his contract." Woods, "Operation of the Master and Servants Act in the Black Country," 101.

[37] Testimony of W. P. Roberts (lawyer for working men) before the "Select Committee on Master and Servant" (1866), XIII:Q. 1665. See also testimony of T. E. Forster, Esq.

Indeed, as the law was applied, employers enjoyed the best of both worlds. They were given the benefits of specific performance but also retained the advantages of the criminal law. Sometimes, an employer simply didn't want an obstinate worker back. He wanted to punish and make an example of him. In these cases, employers enjoyed advantages they would not have enjoyed under a regime of specific performance. Another witness before the Select Committee in 1866 testified that in one case he knew of,

> [t]he employer . . . refused to take the man back, and he demanded that the man should be punished. The justice . . . urged that it would not be fair to send so respectable a journeyman to prison, and was very indignant at the matter being insisted upon, but [the employer] said that he had a painful duty to discharge, under the circumstances, and insisted that the man should be sent to prison, and the man was accordingly sent to prison for seven days [at hard labour].[38]

But I have also found one case in which an apparently overly zealous local magistrate decided to send a workman to prison even though his employer had only asked for a specific performance of the agreement.[39]

For employers, the second serious drawback of criminal punishment might have been that the threat of a three-month prison term was much less effective in pressuring workers than the threat of indefinite incarceration for refusing to follow an order of performance. The common law

(President of the North of England Institute of Mining Engineers and manager of several collieries), Q. 1534: "Do the cases generally end in imprisonment, or in the men returning to their contracts without suffering the penalty? – Generally speaking, the men return to their contracts." For similar examples, see Simon, "Master and Servant," 172; and Woods, "Operation of the Master and Servants Act in the Black Country," 101. For eighteenth-century examples, see Robert Steinfeld, *The Invention of Free Labor: The Employment Relation in English and American Law and Culture* (Chapel Hill, N.C., 1991), 114–15.

[38] Testimony of George Newton before the "Select Committee on Master and Servant" (1866), XIII:Qs. 90–91; see also Simon, "Master and Servant," 168 n. 1.

[39] This case arose after the 1867 reform act had given magistrates authority, for the first time, to order the performance of agreements. See the case of *Bracewell and Lowe* (1871), reported in the "First Report of the Commissioners Appointed to Inquire into the Working of the Master and Servant Act, 1867, and the Criminal Law Amendment Act . . . ," *Parl. Papers* (1874), XXIV (Notes of Cases): 118. "William Lowe . . . factory operative, hereafter called the said employed, within the space of three calendar months last past . . . being then and there the servant of William Bracewell, . . . cotton spinner, hereafter called the said employer, in his trade or business of a cotton spinner under a certain contract of service for a period now unexpired, did neglect, and has ever since neglected, to fulfil the said contract, and has absented himself from the service of the said employer without just cause or lawful excuse . . . wherefore the said employer by his said agent further says, that the remedy which he claims for the said breach and nonperformance of the said contract is that the said employed shall fulfil the said contract." The defendant was convicted and sentenced to one calendar month with hard labor. The information was filed on September 30, 1871.

judges supplied an interpretation of the legislation that remedied this potential problem. They were of the opinion that punishment for a breach did not discharge the underlying contract. The contract subsisted. Hence, a worker who served a prison term for contract breach found on his release that he must still perform the agreement should the employer insist. If the worker refused again, this would constitute a new breach of the contract, exposing that worker to the possibility of a new three-month prison term.[40] In theory, a worker could be committed and recommitted indefinitely.[41] This was precisely the threat that defendants faced under orders of specific performance. In a sense, English wage labor operated under a permanent, standing order of specific performance.

English judges were quite self-conscious about the need for such an interpretation. They feared that if workers were not subject to reimprisonment, they might choose a short prison term over performance. A lawyer in one well-known case argued that

> [t]he object of 4 Geo. 4, c. 34, was to afford protection to masters, but it would be of little avail unless they could compel their workmen to perform their contracts. Suppose a workman enters into a contract to serve for two or three years, on the faith of which his master enters into large engagements, and after a few weeks' service the price of labour rises, the servant might be willing to submit to a conviction in order to get rid of his contract.[42]

---

[40] Lord Ellenborough's opinion in *The King v. The Inhabitants of Barton-Upon-Irwell*, 2 M. & S. 329, decided in 1814, seems to have been the source of this rule. Thereafter, it was strictly adhered to by the Court of Queen's Bench throughout the period being considered in this book. See *Ex parte Baker*, 7 El. & Bl. 697 (1857); *Unwin v. Clarke*, 1 L.R. 417 (1866) (Justice Shee doubting the correctness of the rule but abiding by the earlier decisions of the court); *Cutler v. Turner*, 9 L.R. 502 (1874) (imprisonment for three months for failure to comply with an order of performance under the 1867 act does not discharge the contract and does not exhaust the justices' power to imprison under another section of the act). In 1857, Pollock, C. B., dissenting in *In re Baker*, 2 H. & N. 219, 12 Eng. Rep. 92 (1857), in the Court of Exchequer, argued that the 1823 statute "did not intend that a workman should be imprisoned more than once for not fulfilling his contract" (104). A majority of the court, however, endorsed the established rule that a single conviction did not dissolve the underlying contract; see the opinions of Barons Bramwell and Watson. Four years later, a divided Court of Exchequer did adopt Pollock's view; see *Youle v. Mappin*, 30 L.J. (n.s.) (mag. cases) 234 (1861) (Baron Martin agreeing with Pollock, but Baron Bramwell dissenting). When the issue came before the Court of Queen's Bench again in 1866 in *Unwin v. Clarke*, 1 L.R. 417 (1866), the court rejected the Exchequer rule of *Youle v. Mappin* and once again held that a single conviction did not dissolve the underlying contract.

[41] See *Ashmore v. Horton*, 29 L.J. (n.s.) (mag. cases) 13 (1860) (comments of Chief Justice Cockburn, 15, and Justice Wightman, 16).

[42] *In re Baker*, 2 H. & N. 219, 157 Eng. Rep. 92 (Exch., 1857), 96.

In a case decided in 1866, a workman bound by a multiyear contract "declared that he would not return to his work, but would go to prison, and break his agreement."[43] The Court of Queen's Bench ruled that he could be reimprisoned until he returned to work. Justice Blackburn observed that

> it would be hard upon the master when he engages a servant for three years if the servant could, by being once punished for his breach of contract, get rid of it, and so by his wrongful act the master should lose his service for the rest of the time.[44]

Although contract enforcement took the form of penal sanctions, in practice employers not only enjoyed the practical equivalent of specific performance, but at their option also enjoyed the advantages of the criminal law.

THE RULE AGAINST
SPECIFIC PERFORMANCE
OF PERSONAL SERVICES CONTRACTS

At this point it is necessary to digress to answer a question that will immediately occur to American lawyers and legal academics: How can we possibly reconcile your account with the longstanding rule, adopted by English courts, that personal services contracts were not enforceable through orders of performance? This question arises because for generations American lawyers have been taught that English and American courts have always refused to order the performance of personal services contracts. At the same time, they have been taught literally nothing about the existence of criminal sanctions for labor contract breaches. As a result, the rule against specific performance has come to play a pivotal role in the story of the English legal system's supposed longstanding devotion to free labor.

When we examine the rationale for the rule, however, and place it in the context of the wider law of labor relations in nineteenth-century England, it loses practically all of its larger political significance. A handful of decisions issued by English equity courts beginning in 1819 established the modern rule, and none of these cases involved an ordinary manual wage worker. One involved a court reporter who had contracted to publish volumes of his case reports, another involved a map maker, a third

---

[43] *Unwin v. Clarke*, 1 L.R. 417 (1866), 418.

[44] Ibid., 423; see also *Cutler v. Turner*, 9 L.R. 502 (1874), 503.

involved an actor.[45] There would have been no need to go through the procedurally complex and expensive business of seeking an injunction from a court of equity in the case of an ordinary wage worker because an inexpensive and simple summary criminal process was available. Although the question was raised, it was decided in 1827 that the master and servant statutes did not extend to workers such as actors, court reporters, or map makers, who were higher status workers in trades not explicitly mentioned in the statutes.[46] If the monetary stakes were high enough, however, a contracting party might be tempted to try to obtain an

[45] *Clarke v. Price*, 2 Wils. Ch. 163, 37 Eng. Rep. 270 (1819) (court reporter); *Baldwin v. Society for Diffusion of Useful Knowledge*, 9 Simons 393, 59 Eng. Rep. 409 (1838) (map maker). In *Kemble v. Kean*, 6 Simons 333, 58 Eng. Rep. 619 (1829) (actor) the primary issue the vice-chancellor faced was whether a negative injunction could be granted, but his decision was based in large part on the rule that equity courts did not grant direct orders of performance.

[46] In *Branwell v. Penneck*, 7 B. & C. 536, 108 Eng. Rep. 823 (1827), a person employed by a lawyer to keep possession of certain goods seized under a *fieri facias* issued by the lawyer for a client sought the assistance of a justice of the peace in recovering wages from the lawyer. He argued that he was covered by the language "and other Labourers" included in an eighteenth-century master and servant statute (20 Geo. II, c. 19), which gave workers a summary process for collecting wages. The justice of the peace took jurisdiction of the case, but the Court of King's Bench ruled that the language of the statute did not cover such a worker. Justice Holroyd wrote that "if his construction of the statute 20 G. 2, c. 19 were correct, I know not how we could say that its provisions do not extend to bankers' or merchants' clerks, and other persons of that description" (825). In a later case, however, the courts did interpret the language of the 1823 statute to cover a higher status worker in a trade explicitly mentioned by the statute. In *Ex parte Eli Ormerod*, 13 L.J. (n.s.) (mag. cases) 73 (1844), a designer "who invents and draws patterns later engraved on rollers to be used in calico printing" was held to be covered by the statute. His lawyer had argued that he was "an artist" "of a higher grade," "not at all of the humble character of the persons enumerated," and "not engaged in the manual occupation of any trade" (73). Unfortunately, calico printer was one of the trades listed in the statute, and Justice Williams rejected this argument, writing that "I cannot conceive that the term 'artificer,' used in the statute, is confined to those instances only in which great manual labour is required. . . . The person in question plays a very important part in the particular branch of the manufacture of cotton, in which he is engaged. . . . I am not prepared to say, that the occupation of the party here was so different from the employment of the persons specified, as not to bring him within the words 'or other person,' mentioned in the act" (74). But in *Davies v. Baron Berwick* the court rejected the contention that a "person engaged by the owner of a farm, to keep the general accounts belonging to such farm, to weigh out the food for the cattle, to set the men to work, to lend a hand to anything if wanted, and in all things to carry out the orders given to him" fell under the rule of *Ex parte Ormerod*, and should be considered a "servant in husbandry" covered by the 1823 act. Justice Crompton wrote, "The provision in the act of parliament applies to persons who are engaged to do some manual work as in the case of calico-printers. . . . [T]he appellant . . . seems to have been rather in the position of a steward or bailiff. . . . The principal thing which he had to do was to keep the general accounts." 30 L.J. (n.s.) (mag. cases) 84 (1861) 84–86. On the interpretive struggles over the coverage of the master and servant statutes, see Chapter 4.

injunction. *Morris v. Colman*, decided by chancery in 1812, may have given potential plaintiffs reason to hope that equity courts would be inclined to order performance in some cases.[47] However, it is important to emphasize that English equity courts only saw cases that involved higher status purveyors of services.

After *Morris v. Colman*, chancery judges began to refuse to order the performance of such contracts. The rationale for this rule was that if defendants resisted such an order it would be futile to try to compel performance where the quality of the performance counted for everything. Where defendants performed, it would be unduly burdensome for the court to evaluate the performance to determine whether it complied substantially with the order.[48] A similar concern was not shown in the case of agreements to perform ordinary manual wage work, it may be supposed, be-

---

[47] 18 Ves. Jun. 436, 34 Eng. Rep. 382 (1812).

[48] Freedland, *Contract of Employment*, 273–74, citing *Clarke v. Price*, 2 Wils. Ch. 163, 37 Eng. Rep. 270 (1819), and later cases. In *Kemble v. Kean*, 6 Simons 333, 58 Eng. Rep. 619 (1829), the vice-chancellor noted,

> [i]n the first place independently of the *difficulty of compelling a man to act,* there is no time stated; and it is not stated in what characters he shall act; and the thing is, altogether, so loose that it is perfectly impossible for the Court to determine upon what scheme of things Mr. Kean shall perform his agreement. There can be no prospective declaration or direction of the Court as to the performance of the agreement; and, [apparently now returning to his first point] *supposing Mr. Kean should resist, how is such an agreement to be performed by the Court?* . . . [C]an it be said that a man can be *compelled* to perform an agreement *to act at a theatre by this Court sending him to the Fleet for refusing to act at all?* (emphasis added),

implying that it would be fruitless to try to get a satisfactory performance out of an actor by imprisoning him, but not mentioning any concern that Kean's personal liberties would have been violated by such an attempt (620–21). Equity courts refused equitable relief not only on the grounds that contracts were indefinite and that enforcing their performance would be enormously difficult, but also on the grounds that the plaintiff had driven a "hard bargain" that equity should not enforce. Chancery judges expressed great concern for the economically weaker party in the relatively few and higher status cases they saw: "Equity will not give any assistance to a party seeking to enforce a hard bargain." *Kimberly v. Jennings*, 6 Sim. 340, 58 Eng. Rep. 621 (1836), 621. Where *employees* sued to enforce an agreement *against employers,* equity courts often refused equitable relief on the ground that it would be unconscionable to compel one person to employ another against his will. See *Pickering v. The Bishop of Ely*, 2 Y. & C.C.C. 249, 63 Eng. Rep. 109 (1843), and *Johnson v. The Shrewsbury and Birmingham Railway Company*, 3 De G.M. & G. 914, 43 Eng. Rep. 358 (1853). On *employee* suits for equitable relief, see Freedland, *Contract of Employment*, 274–76. See also the discussion of specific performance in Galenson, "Rise of Free Labor," 120–22.

New York's Chancellor Walworth, writing in 1833, captured perfectly (although with tongue in cheek) the nature of the equity court's concern with issuing an order of specific performance in the case of an opera singer who was accused of preparing to breach his contract: "Upon the merits of the case, I suppose it must be conceded that the complainant is entitled to a specific performance of this contract; as the law appears to have been

cause such agreements were thought to involve common workers lacking exceptional skills.[49] Until the 1890s, it must be stressed, no English equity opinion mentioned that the rule was based on a concern for the defendant's personal liberty.[50] Indeed, we have seen that the multiple imprison-

---

long since settled that a bird that can sing and will not sing must be made to sing. . . . Although the authority before cited shows the law to be in favor of the complainant, so far at least as to entitle him to a decree for the singing, I am not aware that any officer of this court has that perfect knowledge of the Italian language, or possesses that exquisite sensibility in the auricular nerve which is necessary to understand, and to enjoy with a proper zest, the peculiar beauties of the Italian opera. . . . There might be some difficulty, therefore, even if the defendant was compelled to sing under the direction and in the presence of a master in chancery, in ascertaining whether he performed his engagement according to its spirit and intent. It would also be very difficult for the master to determine what effect coercion might produce upon the defendant's singing, especially in the livelier airs; although the fear of imprisonment would unquestionably deepen his seriousness in the graver parts of the drama." *De Rivafinoli v. Corsetti*, 4 Paige (N.Y. Chancery) 264 (1833), 270.

[49] In 1900, this was precisely the interpretation placed on these cases by the American jurist Christopher Tiedeman:

It is not true that courts of equity have in the past refused to enforce specifically contracts for personal services, where the character of the services did not require the exercise of any unusual skill. The rule of equity has been that a mandatory injunction will issue for the specific performance of a contract of personal services, where the services were of such a nature that the court could secure their specific performance. But where peculiar skill is required in the performance of the services, the courts of equity have refused to issue an injunction, for the reason that they cannot by any process of the court compel the exercise of the necessary skill [cites to *Kemble v. Kean; Kimberley v. Jennings;* and others].

A Treatise on State and Federal Control of Persons and Property in the United States (St. Louis, 1900), I:342 n.1.

[50] In *Contract of Employment*, M. R. Freedland writes:

The cases in which it was established that specific performance would not be ordered of an obligation to perform personal services proceed on the ground that equity will not make an order whose performance it cannot effectively supervise or whose performance would require constant supervision. . . . It was not until a rather later date that the refusal to make an order which would directly or indirectly compel persons to perform personal services was stated in terms of a humanitarian objection to involuntary servitude.

It is not surprising that the humanitarian objection to orders to work was not strongly felt at an earlier date, for the law was not lacking in processes whereby pressure was put upon employees or upon other employers tending to ensure that obligations to render personal services were performed. . . . There was in force until 1867 a series of Master and Servant Acts which enabled manual employees to be imprisoned for absence in breach of their contracts of employment. The Master and Servant Act 1867 provided for the making of orders of specific performance against employees (273–74).

From 1821 on, courts in some states in the United States did place the refusal to grant specific performance on the ground that it would result in involuntary servitude. But other states explicitly rejected this view; see Chapter 8.

ment interpretation placed on master and servant legislation by judges of the common law courts showed little regard for the personal liberties of ordinary English workers. It was not until fifteen years after criminal sanctions for contract breach had been repealed by Parliament that judges and commentators began to reinterpret the rationale for the rule against specific performance and to say that one of its purposes was to prevent contractual slavery.[51]

The rule that common law courts awarded damages (and at times negative injunctions) but never specific performance in the case of personal services contracts has been made to bear a political significance that it simply did not possess during most of the nineteenth century. More important was that criminal punishment was widely available for breaches of ordinary contracts of service until 1875. In 1867, moreover, justices of the peace were also given the authority to order manual wage workers specifically to perform their labor agreements. We have had a basically distorted view of the rule against the specific performance of personal services contracts. A proper understanding of the use of criminal sanctions to enforce labor agreements makes necessary a complete reassessment of the historical significance of the rule against specific performance of contracts for personal services.

ECONOMIC BENEFITS FOR EMPLOYERS OF USING PENAL SANCTIONS

Why would an English employer have needed to hold a worker to a contract in 1860? For that matter, why would an English employer have wanted a worker to sign a term contract at all? By that time, wasn't wage work employment at will? Couldn't employers simply rely on an enormous pool of propertyless wage workers to meet their labor needs at subsistence wages on a moment's notice? The answer to the last question seems to have been, not always. A country with a dynamic economy like England's in the nineteenth century does not have a single labor market;

---

[51] Ibid. In the 1890 case of *De Francesco v. Barnum*, 45 Ch. D. 430, 438, Fry, L.J., declared that

> For my own part, I should be very unwilling to extend decisions the effect of which is to compel persons who are not desirous of maintaining continuous personal relations with one another to continue those personal relations. . . . I think the Courts are bound to be jealous, lest they should turn contracts of service into contracts of slavery.

By 1909, Maitland had laid down the rule in his lectures on Equity that "[a]n agreement to serve can not be specifically enforced, otherwise men might in effect sell themselves into slavery." Frederic William Maitland, *Equity, Also the Forms of Action at Common Law* (Cambridge, 1916), 240.

it has multiple labor markets.[52] And labor may be in quasi-permanent short supply in some of these, even as it is abundant in others. During upturns in the trade cycle, moreover, labor generally may be hard to come by.

English manufacturers often saw fit, even during the last half of the nineteenth century, to sign skilled workers to one-year, two-year, or even longer contracts. Contracts of this kind accomplished several purposes. First, they guaranteed a manufacturer access to the skilled labor he needed. If shortages developed, he would neither have to do without nor attempt to bid workers away from other firms by offering large wage premiums. Second, they guaranteed that the manufacturer would have the skilled labor he needed at a price he had locked in for the term. When trade was on the upswing and the demand for labor was increasing, these were especially valuable benefits. However, they ultimately depended on the ability to enforce the contract. One study of prosecutions in the Black Country revealed that

> [t]here is . . . a correlation between the working of the trade cycle and the number of prosecutions in these Black Country towns. The economic slumps of 1861–2 and 1866–9 are reflected in the fall of the numbers prosecuted. The upturn in the economy after 1870 resulted in a great increase in the numbers being prosecuted. This would suggest that a worker would be less likely to challenge his employer in a period of slump and unemployment and cases of leaving work without notice and neglect of work would be much less frequent. However, in a period of trade boom and prosperity, the worker could use his economic power to better effect. Skilled workers especially wanted the right to sell their labour to the most generous employer and therefore were tempted to break their contracts. . . . When labour was scarce, employers were doubly determined to enforce contracts, and with a sympathetic magistracy behind them many more cases were brought to court.[53]

This study showed that in one Black Country town where prosecutions were common in the period from 1858 to 1875, 21 percent of these prosecutions were for quitting without giving proper notice.

[52] On the "multiplicity of [English] labour markets" in this period, see Sidney Pollard, "Labour in Great Britain," in Peter Mathias and M. M. Postan, ed., *The Cambridge Economic History of Europe* (Cambridge, 1978), VII, Part I:103.

[53] Woods, "Operation of the Master and Servants Act in the Black Country," 98, Table 1, and Fig. 1; see also Simon, "Master and Servant," 186 n. 2. For a similar analysis finding a secular upward trend in prosecutions under the Master and Servant acts over the course of the eighteenth and nineteenth centuries as economic activity increased, see Hay, "Penal Sanctions, Masters and Servants," 10–13.

Employers commonly used criminal sanctions to hold skilled workers to long contracts. In 1856, for example, William Baker, a potter, signed a one-year contract to work for the Hawleys, earthenware and china manufacturers. The contract was to run from November 11, 1856, to November 11, 1857, but in February 1857, halfway through the term, Baker gave a month's notice that he was leaving. On March 10 he left his employer and on March 11 began work for William Barlow, another manufacturer of china and earthenware. The Hawleys prosecuted Baker and he was convicted of breaching his contract. He was sentenced to one calendar month at hard labor in the house of correction. When he was released on April 17, he thought he had put his relationship with the Hawleys behind him and returned to work for Barlow. But the Hawleys were not prepared to let Baker go. He had made an agreement to work for them for a year and they were going to hold him to it. On April 29, they asked him to return to work under his original contract, and he refused. On May 13, they brought him before a justice of the peace again, where he was again convicted of breaching his contract and again sentenced to a month at hard labor in the house of correction.[54] Quite probably, Baker left his original employer because Barlow was offering higher wages.[55]

Baker's experience was apparently not unusual in the pottery trades. In 1866, William Evans, editor of the *Potteries Examiner* and a former potter himself, testified before the Select Committee on Master and Servant that within the previous two years "the present prosperous state of trade" had led employers to try to impose annual contracts.[56] The years 1864 and 1865 saw extremely low unemployment.[57] Evans observed that "seeing that trade is now in a prosperous state, that long period of agreement takes from the workman the power of raising the price of his labour."[58]

---

[54] This account was developed by combining facts presented in two different adjudications of the case, *Ex parte Baker*, 7 El. & Bl. 697, 119 Eng. Rep. 1404 (Queen's Bench, 1857), and *In re Baker*, 2 H. & N. 219, 157 Eng. Rep. 92 (Exch., 1857), 96. The Court of Exchequer overturned Baker's second conviction on the ground that the justice of the peace had not abated wages.

[55] The lawyer who argued on behalf of the Hawleys certainly implied that this was the case. *In re Baker*, 2 H. & N. 219, 157 Eng. Rep. 92 (Exch., 1857), 96. The year 1857 was a peak year in the trade cycle; see W. W. Rostow, *British Economy of the Nineteenth Century* (Oxford, 1948), 33, Table II.

[56] According to Evans's testimony, employers were colluding to present workers with a standard contract form that called for a one-year term to begin on November 11 of one year and end on November 10 of the next. Evans referred to this form contract as "the Chamber of Commerce Agreement." In certain cases the workmen apparently resisted the form contract by stipulating at the bottom that they were entitled to terminate the agreement by giving a month's notice. Testimony of William Evans before the "Select Committee on Master and Servant" (1866), XIII:Qs. 1375–77, 1404–10.

[57] See Table 2.1 and Figure 2.1.

[58] Testimony of William Evans, Q. 1410.

The same situation existed in other trades. During the 1864 to 1866 upturn in the trade cycle, a worker named Clarke signed a two-year contract to work for a cutlery manufacturer. He agreed to work for the firm exclusively under a schedule of prices set forth in the contract. The contract was dated June 1, 1865. In November of that year, Clarke absented himself from his work and refused to perform his agreement. The manufacturer, Unwin, prosecuted him for breach of contract. In his answer, Clarke stated "that he had applied to [his employer] to make an advance in his wages in the same manner that the large majority of the cutlery manufacturers in Sheffield had recently done to their hired workmen, which the appellants had refused to do, and in consequence thereof he had felt himself justified in refusing to work for them at the low rate of wages."[59] The justices told Clarke that the agreement was fixed and certain and could not be altered except by mutual consent and that his employers were unwilling to raise the prices for his work. They said that "he would have to be committed to prison unless he promised to return to work and perform his agreement."[60] Clarke replied that he would sooner go to prison than return to work at the old prices. The justices obliged; Clarke was sentenced to twenty-one days at hard labor. When he was released, he went to his employer to retrieve his tools. There he was told that he must still return to work to complete his contractual term. He again refused and was again prosecuted. The Court of Queen's Bench ruled that he could be imprisoned a second time.[61] Rather than go to the house of correction again, Clarke decided to return to work under the terms of the original agreement.[62]

Workers like Clarke who signed long contracts were referred to as "hired" men. Apparently they were common not only in the pottery trades but in cutlery as well. William Dronfield, secretary to the organized trades of Sheffield, testified before the Select Committee on Master and Servant in 1866 that "we have had a number of cases in the cutlery trade, where men have been hired. That I believe to be a demoralising system to both employers and employed."[63] He proceeded to describe a system in which employers offered a lump sum advance to induce workers to sign a long contract:

> An employer of labour is busy, he offers the inducement of a 5£ or a 10£ note to a man to get him to work for him, but often when this

---

[59] *Unwin v. Clarke*, 1 L.R. 417 (1866), 418. Unemployment in 1865 has been estimated to have been extremely low, between 1.8 and 2.1 percent; see Table 2.1.

[60] Ibid.

[61] Ibid., 418–19.

[62] Testimony of William Dronfield before the "Select Committee on Master and Servant" (1866), XIII:Q. 864.

[63] Ibid.

money is obtained, . . . the man . . . begins to think that he has made
a mistake in getting hired; the consequence is, that he does not work
willingly for his employer. He is bound for a time, and he should fulfil his contract according to his agreement; but these cases give rise
to a great number of hearings before the magistrates.[64]

In the hiring system, these advances were loans that were to be paid off
by deductions from a worker's wages. Leaving an employer while under
contract *and* while in debt to him was a serious offence.[65] One might almost characterize this version of the hiring system as a form of peonage
or domestic contract labor.

Valuable workers were also signed to long contracts in other trades. In
1871, during another upturn in the trade cycle, when unemployment was
extremely low, William Cutler, a fire-iron forger, signed a contract to work
for a fender and fire-iron manufacturer for a term of five years. Two years
into the contract, he announced to his employer that "the prices of work
done by me in your employment will be increased by 20 per cent (the
same as given in Birmingham), and in case of non-compliance with the
same, [I] shall feel compelled to suspend myself from your service . . . until the same is conceded."[66] When Cutler stopped working the manufacturers summoned him to appear before a magistrate. The magistrate assessed damages against Cutler for absenting himself from his service and
assumed that he would return to fulfill the remainder of his contract term.
The damages were paid, but Cutler did not return to work and his employers did not give up. They were determined that he should work out
his term at the stipulated prices. Cutler was again summoned before a
magistrate, and this time it was ordered that he

> shall fulfil the contract forthwith, and that he shall forthwith find
> good and sufficient security by recognizance, himself in the sum of
> 50£, and two sureties in the sum of 25£ for the due fulfilment of the
> contract, and that he shall pay to his employers 15s. 6d. costs, and in
> default of finding such good and sufficient security, that the em-
> ployed be committed to the house of correction at Wakefield there to
> be confined and kept until he should find security, but so, neverthe-
> less, that the term of imprisonment do not exceed in the whole three
> calendar months.[67]

The 1867 reform of the master and servant law had given justices of the
peace power to order workers to perform their contracts and to find good

[64] Ibid.

[65] Woods, "Operation of the Master and Servants Act in the Black Country," 103–4.

[66] *Cutler v. Turner*, 9 L.R. 502 (1874), 503. Unemployment in 1873, according to the best estimates we have, was below 1.25 percent; see Table 2.1.

[67] Ibid., 504–5.

and sufficient security for performance.[68] For failure to comply with such orders, workers could be imprisoned for up to three months.[69] When Cutler did not comply with this order he was sentenced to a three-month term. On his release, he continued to absent himself from work. His employers were still not prepared to set him free. They summoned him yet again to appear before a magistrate, where they asked that he be ordered to perform the contract. The magistrate on this occasion, however, decided to assess damages against Cutler, ordering him to pay his employers the substantial sum of £11 14s.[70]

During upswings in the trade cycle, pressure was placed on wages by the frequent bidding wars for skilled labor that broke out between employers. Long contracts put a stop to this sort of problem, if they could be enforced. In his 1866 testimony, William Dronfield was asked: "Does it occur often that one master bribes another man's servant to leave"? He replied: "Frequently; and I have heard a manufacturer in the same trade say that another manufacturer ought to be horsewhipped for offering the inducement, because he has taken some of his men, offering a greater premium than he would." The answer to the follow-up question revealed that employers were quite determined not to let this happen; when asked: "Do you know of many cases in which men who have left their employ under such circumstances have been punished?" Dronfield answered: "I know of a number of such cases where men have left, but they have always been punished; the law has always been carried out against them."[71]

In summary, one way in which employers used criminal sanctions for contract breach in the 1850s, 1860s, and 1870s was to compel workers to remain in term laboring relationships with them. Once a worker had signed an agreement, he or she was not free to leave the relationship at will. Compelling performance accomplished a number of objectives. It helped guarantee that an employer would have access to the skilled labor needed during periods of high labor demand and helped him to control the cost of that labor by preventing workers from withholding it or shopping it around for the best price. It is, of course, difficult to say how effective this system was in controlling wages during upswings in the business cycle. However, one analyst has concluded that, in a later period, during World War I, under admittedly different circumstances, once restrictions on leaving one's employer were eliminated from the government's wartime program of wage control, "there is no doubt that . . . the difficulties of the employer in handling his men were increased, and that the wages

[68] 30 & 31 Vict., c. 141, s. 9 (1867).

[69] Ibid.

[70] *Cutler v. Turner*, 9 L.R. 502 (1874), 502–5.

[71] Testimony of William Dronfield, Q. 865.

situation rapidly reached a point when it is almost true to say that control was non-existent."[72]

It is equally difficult to say how common these kinds of term contracts were in the 1860s. However, the hiring system was well established in the cutlery trade and in some other small trades in the Black Country.[73] In the pottery trade, employers were still trying to impose annual contracts during upturns in the trade cycle.[74] At least some iron manufacturers were signing valuable men to long contracts.[75] Annual contracts were common among tinplate manufacturers in Wolverhampton[76] and were the norm in the Durham coal fields.[77] They were also widespread in agriculture.[78] As late as 1866, certain bleach works were also hiring men under one-, two-, or three-year contracts.[79]

Although long contracts continued to play a role in controlling skilled labor costs, in general, from the beginning of the nineteenth century there seems to have been a trend toward shorter agreements in most trades. By 1860,

> [m]ost industrial workers . . . had . . . established a practice of engagement by the week, fortnight or month. Some indeed, had embraced the extreme system of the so-called "minute contract," under which . . . it was understood that the employer was free to dismiss a workman (and the workman to leave) "at a minute's notice" – in practice usually at the end of the day.[80]

---

[72] Humbert Wolfe, *Labour Supply and Regulation* (Oxford, 1923), 230. Wolfe argues that "leaving certificates" were crucial to the success of the entire program of labor cost regulation.

[73] Woods, "Operation of the Master and Servants Act in the Black Country," 103. See also Testimony of William Dronfield, Qs. 785, 864.

[74] See testimony of William Evans, Qs. 1375–82, 1404–10.

[75] See *Cutler v. Turner*, 9 L.R. 502 (1874).

[76] Testimony of Thomas Winters before the "Select Committee on Master and Servant" (1866), XIII:Q. 1178 (annual contracts, workmen required to give six months' notice).

[77] Richard Fynes, *The Miners of Northumberland and Durham: A History of Their Social and Political Progress* (1873; reprint Sunderland, England, 1923), 206–57; Simon, "Master and Servant," 172, 193.

[78] Simon, "Master and Servant," 190–91.

[79] "Select Committee on Master and Servant" (1866), XIII:Q. 2498.

[80] Simon, "Master and Servant," 191; see also, Woods, "Operation of the Master and Servants Act in the Black Country," 102–3. Whether "minute contracts" were actually day contracts or employment at will is not completely clear. It is also not clear whether the distinction held any practical significance. See on the one hand Testimony of William Burns, Esq. (Secretary and Law Agent to the Association of Mine Owners of Scotland) before the "Select Committee on Master and Servant" (1866), XIII:Q.

Where "minute contracts" had been adopted, prosecutions under the Master and Servant acts came to a halt.[81] "Minute contracts" were popular in the Scottish coal fields and in a number of trades in and around Glasgow,[82] but many Scottish and almost all English trades worked under weekly, fortnightly, or monthly contracts, and the power to compel the performance of such "short" contracts was equally important to employers.[83]

> 2326. Are those contracts for a whole day? – Yes, I understand so; nobody, so far as I can learn, would think of employing a man by the hour, on the supposition that he was at liberty to leave his work when he pleased. 2327. So that the term "minute contract," as used before this Committee, is a misnomer? – It is a misnomer, and therefore, suppose all contracts were reduced to a day, and the Act 4 Geo. 4 remained in operation, it would still affect those contracts. If a man agrees to work with me to-morrow, he may put me to very great loss and inconvenience if he does not come; he is then failing to fulfil the contract he has made with me. Again, if he does come, but misconducts himself in the execution of his work during that day, the terms of the Act being 'misconduct or misdemeanour in the execution of his contract,' he is still liable to the statute.

On the other hand see Testimony of William Mathews, Esq. (owner of iron and coal works in England, a justice of the peace, and President of the Mining Association of Great Britain), before the "Select Committee on Master and Servant" (1866), XIII:Q. "2514. We have had it in evidence before us, that in Scotland minute or day contracts prevail very much? – So I have understood; I cannot offer the Committee any evidence upon that point, because, as far as I am aware, there are no such contracts in England; a day contract means no contract at all, in fact."

81   Simon, "Master and Servant," 191; Testimony of J. W. Ormiston before the "Select Committee on Master and Servant" (1866), XIII:Q. 2048 (it is a system of no warnings); and Testimony of J. Dickinson, before the "Select Committee on Master and Servant" (1866), XIII:Q. 2127 (where minute contracts are adopted, the law of master and servant is practically speaking a dead letter).

82   "Select Committee on Master and Servant" (1866), XIII:Qs. 383–86, 497, 703–4; see also Simon, "Master and Servant," 191.

83   When I use the phrase "weekly, fortnightly, or monthly contracts," it should be understood that I am using these words loosely to encompass two legally different kinds of contract. Weekly, fortnightly, or monthly contracts were sometimes periodic contracts that were contracts for a short term which automatically renewed themselves unless one party gave a period's notice of termination. A contract from month to month accordingly would be a contract for one month that would automatically renew itself for another month, and so on indefinitely unless a party gave a month's notice that he or she was terminating the relationship at the end of the next period. However, weekly, fortnightly, or monthly contracts were also commonly contracts of indefinite duration that were determinable upon a week's, a fortnight's, or a month's notice. There are examples of both kinds of contracts in the cases; see, for example, *In the Matter of George Bailey, In the Matter of John Collier*, 3 El. & Bl. 607, 118 Eng. Rep. 1269 (1854) (service for the term of one month, and so on from month to month, determinable on one month's notice); *Whittle v. Frankland*, 31 L.J. (n.s.) (mag. cases) 81 (1862) (service to employer until either party gives one month's notice to terminate). I lump the two forms together here because for most purposes under the Master and Servant acts it made no difference which kind of contract

Workers under these kinds of contracts were not entitled to leave their employment without first giving either a week's, or a fortnight's, or a month's notice, depending on the agreement. Key workers in integrated industrial processes were not free simply to walk out, possibly shutting down an entire operation.[84] The requirement of advanced notice gave employers time to replace departing workers in an orderly fashion and to avoid sudden stoppages brought on by the departure of essential workers. It is also gave them the power to break strikes and undermine unions. No strike could take place without the required notice. Strikers who failed to give notice were commonly prosecuted for breaching their contracts and imprisoned.[85] In 1859, a strike was called among coal miners at Seaton Delaval without the required one month's notice first being given:

> On the second day after the stoppage the village was startled by the evil news that nine workmen had been arrested by policemen during the night or in the early morning, while they were yet in bed, and hurried off . . . to be tried before the local magistrate for breach of contract. . . . After a hasty examination – it would be a mockery to call it a judicial trial – eight of them were sentenced to two months' imprisonment in the county gaol. . . . Nearly all the men who were sent to gaol had opposed the strike. . . . When the manager was told that he had selected the most respectable and the most reasonable of his workmen for punishment – the very men who had most resolutely opposed the strike – his reply was that he was well aware of that, but they were the men who would most acutely feel the degradation of prison life, and they should have done more than give good advice; they should have gone to work.[86]

Some persons sympathetic to labor believed that criminal sanctions for breach of contract were more important than the anti-combination laws in weakening the position of working people.[87] Several modern historians

---

a worker was serving under. In either case workers could be prosecuted for departure if they failed to give the required notice and could be prosecuted for breaches of conduct while they served. The one difference the distinction may have made was that in contracts of indefinite duration determinable after a certain amount of notice, that notice could be given at any time. In periodic contracts one could only give notice aimed at terminating the relationship at the conclusion of the next full period. However, I have found no cases in which this difference became an issue.

[84] Simon, "Master and Servant," 193 n. 3; Woods, "Operation of the Master and Servants Act in the Black Country," 105.

[85] Simon, "Master and Servant," 171–72, 195; Woods, "Operation of the Master and Servants Act in the Black Country," 111.

[86] Thomas Burt, *An Autobiography* (London, 1924), 130–32.

[87] Webb and Webb, *History of Trade Unionism*, 250 n. 2. In 1824 to 1825 all earlier Anti-combination acts were repealed. The 1825 act that replaced the earlier acts legalized unions for certain purposes but prohibited violence, threats, and intimidation.

concur, arguing that the Master and Servant acts were so effective that the Anti-combination acts were unnecessary.[88]

Where short contracts[89] were in effect employers also used criminal sanctions to force workers to comply with performance and behavior standards. A worker was subject to criminal punishment for neglect or disobedience as well as for quitting; these were also regarded as breaches of the labor contract. An employer could adopt any number of strategies to induce workers to improve their performance. He could establish a system of incentives: wage premiums, employment during trade slowdowns, promotion up the job ladder. He could adopt a system of punishments: fines, threats of dismissal (the latter, however, are less effective just when employers need their workers most, when unemployment is low). The power to send a worker to prison for breaches of conduct at work was a formidable addition to any employer's arsenal of measures for eliciting greater effort and more consistency from his workers. It was particularly effective where labor markets were tight and threats of dismissal largely ineffective, but it was useful even where demand for labor was slack. In situations in which positive inducements work, why not use them? In situations in which negative inducements – fines, threats of dismissal where these would be effective, threats of prosecution where these would be effective – work, why not use them? The more disciplinary options an employer had available, the better off he was. English employers found criminal sanctions for contract breach quite useful in regulating their workers.

A study of the Black Country found that 38 percent of prosecutions in a small town there were for "neglect of work" or "unlawful absence from work" rather than for quitting without proper notice.[90] Unlawful absence and neglect involved missing work for a day or several days, being late for work, or leaving early:

> "Neglecting work for drink" was quite a common charge which before 1867 could result in imprisonment. John Goodman, a Wolverhampton japanner who worked at the Old Hall for twenty-eight years, occasionally missed time because of "intemperate ways." His employer brought him to court for this offence in March 1862 and he received fourteen days in prison.[91]

---

[88] G. J. Barnsby, *Social Conditions in the Black Country* (Wolverhampton, England, 1980), 46; and Douglas Hay and Paul Craven, "Master and Servant in England and the Empire: A Comparative Study," *Labour/Le Travail* 31 (Spring 1993): 176.

[89] See note 83.

[90] Woods, "Operation of the Master and Servants Act in the Black Country," 102.

[91] Ibid., 104.

Henry Massey, a Dudley fender maker, received a fourteen-day sentence because he had missed a day's work.[92] Alfred Farnsworth, a shingler, left work early because "he was very stiff and sore and could not cut through anymore." His departure left other men unable to continue work. He was prosecuted and sent to the house of correction for fourteen days.[93] Employers used criminal sanctions in the Black Country to combat the custom of St. Monday.[94] Sloppiness or loafing at work could also lead to a term at hard labor in the house of correction:

> George Heywood of West Bromwich was a bundler at the furnace of an iron works with both puddlers and millmen dependent upon him. Because he left his labour for a few hours, "the work was very much in arrears and other men were idle." He was given the option of paying £5 damages or having two months in prison and remarked that "he would have to have the two months."[95]

A puddler working the night shift at an iron works in Walsall left some iron in the furnace, where it spoiled, causing considerable damage to his employer. He was given a twenty-one day sentence.[96]

Criminal sanctions were also used against outworkers to enforce performance standards. Under an eighteenth-century statute, outworkers in a number of trades, including the leather trade, had eight days, after notice, to return the work they had taken in.[97] George Odger, Secretary to the London Trades, who was himself a shoemaker, testified before the Select Committee in 1866 that this legislation was often used to "drive workmen."

> Any decent man . . . when he has had work out by him eight days is apt to be terrified with the thought that his employer would feel disposed to have him before a magistrate for this breach of contract. . . . I have heard the threat made; I think it would be about two months ago. . . . I went over the time, the first time I ever did in my life; [my employer] called at my house when I was out and threatened that if he had not the work in a given time he would proceed against me in the ordinary way for breach of contract. I went home and then went to the workshop and worked nearly all night to get the work to him the next day, which embarrassed me a good deal because I had been

---

[92] Ibid.

[93] Ibid.

[94] Ibid., 105.

[95] Ibid.

[96] Ibid.

[97] 17 Geo. III, c. 56 (1777).

at work all the day before. I do not know whether he would have carried out his threat or not, but I was within his clutches if I did not make the boots.[98]

Contrary to conventional wisdom, legal coercion of waged labor in the form of penal sanctions for contract breaches persisted well into the nineteenth century in the mature markets of the English metropolitan core for the simple reason that it served the economic interests of employers. Penal sanctions may be said to have helped employers lower both "turnover" and "agency" costs. "Turnover" costs are costs an employer is forced to bear as the result of a worker leaving his or her job. There are several different kinds of "turnover" costs:

> costs of searching for [and acquiring] a new worker, going without labor in the meantime, and providing a new hire with firm specific skills.[99] . . . Firm-specific human capital, for example, is an asset that loses value when an employment relation is broken off. But replacing firm-specific human capital is not the only cost to a firm when a worker quits. It can be costly to find potential replacement workers and collect information about them. Most important, perhaps, is the cost of going without labor while searching for a replacement worker. One study found that the "implicit cost of lost output resulting from the lag between the separation and subsequent replacement of a worker," was the biggest single cost of replacing unskilled workers.[100]

When labor markets were tight, employers quite likely faced higher "turnover" costs. More workers were likely to leave, and the turnover cost per worker was probably higher as it became more expensive to find and acquire replacement workers. Moreover, the amount of lost output per departing worker may also have gone up during periods of peak demand. Long contracts enforceable through penal sanctions may well have helped to reduce these kinds of costs. Even short contracts of a fortnight or a month that required advanced notice before departure may have helped to slow turnover and reduce the cost of lost output. These kinds of contracts made it more difficult for workers to leave immediately just when another employer wanted them and gave employers the time to locate replacement workers. Even when labor markets were not tight, however, "turnover" was not costless, and short contracts may have helped to re-

---

[98] Testimony of George Odger before the "Select Committee on Master and Servant" (1866), XIII:Q. 1813.

[99] Christopher Hanes, "Turnover Cost and the Distribution of Slave Labor in Anglo-America," *The Journal of Economic History* 56 (June 1996): 311.

[100] Ibid.

duce these costs by making the replacement process more orderly. It is not even necessary to mention the cost reductions that were obtainable if prosecutions could keep labor from organizing effectively.

Agency costs also may well have been reduced through the use of penal sanctions. There are two main components of agency costs, monitoring or supervision costs designed to enforce effort and ensure quality and the residual costs of reduced output and quality that cannot be eliminated by any economical amount of supervision. "Agency" costs and "turnover" costs, moreover, are intricately interrelated. "Turnover costs not only make it difficult for an employer to replace an incumbent worker. They also increase the cost of extracting effort on the job, because the employer cannot (cheaply) enforce the terms of employment in the simplest way – by firing a worker observed to slack off."[101] It seems intuitively plausible that subjecting workers to the possibility of confinement at hard labor for shirking or negligence at work enforceable through a quick and inexpensive legal process would raise shirking costs for workers, at little additional cost to employers. Penal sanctions may very well have served to reduce "agency" costs for employers, particularly in tight labor markets.

Consequently, penal sanctions may have served as a partial or complete substitute for efficiency wages in nineteenth-century England, making it feasible for some employers to pursue and maintain a low wages policy.[102] Efficiency wage theory holds that employers can profit in certain circumstances by raising wages above the market rate. An extra dollar spent on wages, the theory proposes, may return more than a dollar to employers

[101] Ibid. Hanes argues that "turnover" costs are higher and hence more significant in "thin" labor markets (remote rural settings, for example) than they are in the kind of "thick" market that characterizes mature urban labor settings. He also argues that "turnover" costs are higher and hence more significant in the case of certain kinds of workers, such as servants who will live in the home, than in the case of many other kinds of workers. Because of these higher turnover costs in particular sectors of the labor market, he argues, the labor used in those sectors tended to be bound labor, whereas other labor was free labor. But Hanes empirically verifies his hypothesis using examples drawn only from the United States. He does not take into account that wage labor as a whole in nineteenth-century England was often bound labor. It may be true, as he argues, that turnover costs are higher in certain sectors, but turnover is not costless even in "thick" markets, especially during periods of intense demand for labor. Binding labor may be a good way of reducing "turnover" costs even in "thick markets," so long as the political authorities are willing to make that expedient available.

[102] It was still common in the nineteenth century for employers to argue that low wages were the only way to ensure that labor would be available and productive. See, for example, Peter Mathias, *The Transformation of England; Essays in the Economic and Social History of England in the Eighteenth Century* (New York, 1979), 148–65; and Stanley L. Engerman, "The Land and Labour Problem at the Time of the Legal Emancipation of British West Indian Slaves," in *West Indies Accounts: Essays on the History of the British Caribbean and the Atlantic Economy in Honour of Richard Sheridan,* ed. Roderick McDonald (Barbados, 1996).

in reduced worker shirking and in reduced turnover costs.[103] Employers would benefit therefore by paying above-market wages just to the point where an extra dollar of wages elicits just an extra dollar of savings in reduced agency and turnover costs. This level of wages represents an efficient wage. There are various theories explaining why efficiency wages may work. One theory holds that as more and more employers pay higher than market wages, involuntary unemployment results because labor markets cannot clear. It is this unemployment that leads to reduced worker shirking because it makes shirking more costly to workers. The cost of shirking to a worker will be the cost of dismissal (much higher when unemployment is high) discounted by the probability of getting caught.[104] Other theories hold that efficiency wages work because workers are made to feel that they have been given a fair deal and will reciprocate with a fair effort.[105] Efficiency wages are a particularly appealing strategy where increased supervision is not possible or is too costly.

There is some evidence from the nineteenth century that certain employers may have used penal sanctions as an alternative to paying efficiency wages as they pursued a low wages policy. Michael Huberman has studied the textile industry in Lancashire in the nineteenth century. He finds that as the size of certain cotton mills increased, supervision of the operatives did not increase with it.[106] Nineteenth-century management in many cases apparently did not try to reorganize work or add supervisors to oversee the larger number of workers collected together, and as a result larger firms began to face an "effort" problem.[107] In the end, according to Huberman, large textile firms in certain urban areas in Lancashire adopted a "fair wages" policy to try to deal with the "effort" problem among their factory operatives. But in one town in the county, Preston, the large textile firms pursued a different strategy. "Horrockses [a leading Preston firm and one of the largest in the world in the early nineteenth

---

[103] There are several versions of efficiency wage theory. Some hold that efficient wages will reduce turnover costs, others that efficient wages will reduce agency costs. In addition, several different mechanisms are invoked to explain why efficiency wages produce these results. For an excellent summary of the various efficient wages theories, see Andrew Weiss, *Efficiency Wages: Models of Unemployment, Layoffs, and Wage Dispersion* (Princeton, N.J., 1990).

[104] Carl Shapiro and Joseph E. Stiglitz, "Equilibrium Unemployment as a Worker Discipline Device," in *Efficiency Wage Models of the Labor Market*, ed. George A. Akerloff and Janet L. Yellen (Cambridge, 1986).

[105] George A. Akerlof and Janet L. Yellen, "Fair Wage-Effort Hypothesis and Unemployment," *Quarterly Journal of Economics* 105 (May 1990).

[106] Michael Huberman, *Escape from the Market: Negotiating Work in Lancashire* (Cambridge, 1996), 49–60.

[107] On the autonomy of American craft workers, see David Montgomery, *Workers' Control in America: Studies in the History of Work, Technology, and Labor Struggles* (Cambridge, 1979).

century] was well known for its harsh regime and it did not rely exclusively on the specter of high turnover to elicit effort. . . . [I]t regularly prosecuted operatives for quitting work without notice, for absenteeism, and for other acts of indiscipline."[108] These large Preston mills paid low wages and dealt with the "effort" problem in part by levying fines and prosecuting workers under the Master and Servant acts. This strategy was successful until at least the last quarter of the nineteenth century.[109]

Nineteenth-century management in other industries as well apparently did not place a great deal of emphasis on organizing work so as to permit effective supervision at the point of production. This was true, for example, of coal mining in the northeast.[110] In the absence of effective strategies for supervision in these industries, many employers may well have chosen to use penal sanctions to make shirking more costly to workers to elicit higher levels of effort as an alternative to paying higher wages.

Where unemployment rates were low, as they were during many years after the middle of the nineteenth century,[111] even firms that had developed effective supervision would have found it difficult to elicit effort through the threat of dismissal. Turnover costs also would have been higher under such conditions. One response to both problems might have been to pay efficiency wages, but an alternative response English employers had available while penal sanctions remained in effect was to prosecute and threaten to prosecute workers for quitting without notice and for negligence or disobedience on the job. The latter seems to have represented a viable strategy for controlling agency and turnover costs under the conditions that prevailed in nineteenth-century England.

Modern economic historians like to say that employers face a choice in the kind of labor force they can recruit. They can either choose to pay high wages and attract high-quality labor whose turnover is low, or they can choose to pay low wages and attract a low-quality work force that turns over often.[112] Wage labor markets under penal sanctions may have given employers yet a third option. Employers may have been able to adopt a wages/labor package that would not otherwise be possible, a low-wage, lower turnover, higher effort package made possible by kinds of threats that can no longer be used against wage workers.

The conventional view of wage labor requires revision. The dull compulsion of economic relations may have worked well enough for employ-

---

[108] Huberman, *Escape from the Market*, 53.

[109] Ibid., 53–54, 123.

[110] James A. Jaffe, *The Struggle for Market Power: Industrial Relations in the British Coal Industry, 1800–1840* (Cambridge, 1991), 65, 99–101, 149–50.

[111] See Table 2.1.

[112] See, for example, Gavin Wright, "Labor History and Labor Economics," in *The Future of Economic History,* ed. Alexander J. Field (Boston, Mass., 1987), 334.

ers under many circumstances, but it should now be clear that there were real economic advantages to be gained in many cases by using penal sanctions in waged labor markets. Just as it was possible to make slaves work harder and to stay put through physical compulsion, many employers seem to have believed that they could also elicit greater effort and reduce worker mobility in wage labor markets by utilizing a form of legal compulsion, albeit a much milder form. At the very least, where the state had made these kinds of remedies available to employers, they did not shy away from using them.

LAW IN THE BOOKS VERSUS LAW IN ACTION

Well into the second half of the nineteenth century, English wage workers were being imprisoned for breaching their labor agreements. Were these relatively rare events, or were they common? The anxiety that drives this question is one that is widely shared by historians: Laws are sometimes placed on the statute books but quickly become dead letters. Such laws may have little impact on the real lives of most people. Consequently, historians usually want to know whether a law has been "enforced." To find out, they examine police and court records, count the number of prosecutions, and identify the locales where prosecutions did and did not take place.

Before providing the statistics that are available for England, I must express some skepticism about this form of empiricism. What historians really want to know when they examine enforcement statistics is to what extent the legal rules affected the behavior of ordinary people. Court records cannot really answer this question. They *can* tell us how much formal enforcement there was, how many peoples' lives were directly touched by the legislation. But they *cannot* tell us how many people followed or broke the rules. There is no reason to suppose that levels of enforcement bear a universally fixed ratio to conformity levels. There may be little enforcement and widespread disobedience, little enforcement and lots of compliance, a lot of enforcement and little disobedience, or a lot of enforcement and a lot of disobedience.

Suppose a legislature passed a statute prohibiting murder. When we consult the court records, we find no prosecutions for murder. On the basis of this evidence we may draw two opposite inferences. On the one hand, the formally promulgated statute was never enforced, and murder was common; on the other hand, people obeyed the rule because they feared the police, because they believed it was a just rule, or for other reasons.[113] In terms of what we most want to know, whether the rule was fol-

---

[113] I draw this example from Duncan Kennedy, "The Stakes of Law, or Hale and Foucault!" *Legal Studies Forum* 15 (1991): 347.

lowed, those are two very different conclusions. The information we get by counting prosecutions is an inadequate substitute for the information we most want. Unfortunately, when it comes to the past there may simply be no good way to obtain this kind of information. Consequently, we must be humble in our claims about how much we can learn by counting prosecutions. Consider the situation of English wage workers in the second half of the nineteenth century.

For centuries, prosecutions for contract breach had normally been handled by a single justice of the peace. Often the proceedings were conducted in the justice's home. The process was a summary one, and comprehensive records are not available for periods before the mid-1850s. In earlier periods, justices seem to have been quite lax about reporting proceedings at all.[114] Hence, the reports of prosecutions in earlier centuries are scattered and fragmentary. Nevertheless, a few historians have been able to venture guesses about the incidence of prosecutions over time, based on evidence from local records.

One historian, Douglas Hay, has very tentatively concluded that as market activity intensified over the course of the eighteenth and nineteenth centuries, prosecutions increased. Hay speculates that the law was used less frequently in the eighteenth century than in the early years of the nineteenth century and less frequently in the early years of the nineteenth century than in the middle years of the nineteenth century.[115] Hay's guess, in other words, is that as the demand for labor picked up as a result of a secular expansion in market activity, employers resorted to criminal prosecution more and more frequently to coerce their workers into complying with their agreements. In earlier centuries, employers may have had less need to prosecute workers. This is hardly the picture we have been led to expect. As "free" markets and industrial capitalism developed in England, freer labor was not apparently the result. On the contrary, employers seem to have resorted more and more frequently to criminal coercion of their workers.

In the 1860s, criminal prosecutions were common in coal mining, in iron manufacturing and the building and printing trades and among glass, pottery, and cutlery workers, transport workers, engineers, tool makers, coach builders, boiler makers, and common laborers.[116] One study of prosecutions in the Black Country has concluded that

all types of employers regarded the Master and Servants Acts as a useful and a convenient weapon with which to subordinate labour.

---

[114] Hay, "Masters, Servants, Justices and Judges," 5–6.

[115] Ibid., 8.

[116] Simon, "Master and Servant," 192–95; Woods, "Operation of the Master and Servants Act in the Black Country," 109–11 (based on a relatively small sample from Walsall).

... The small masters. . . would have tended to use the Acts as an essential legal prop to their economic position. . . . However, . . . large scale employers in the iron and coal trades also used the Acts to enforce industrial discipline and to ensure regular working which was so important to them.[117]

Beginning with 1857, there are comprehensive statistics by county and police district of "Offences Relating to Masters, Servants and Apprentices" for England and Wales.[118] What they show is that between 1857 and 1875 about 10,000 people each year were proceeded against for mas-

[117] Woods, "Operation of the Master and Servants Act in the Black Country," 109–10. Daphne Simon argued that the cotton mills made "virtually no use of [the master and servant] laws." "Master and Servant," 190. But see H. I. Dutton and J. E. King, "The Limits of Paternalism: The Cotton Tyrants of North Lancashire, 1836–1854," *Social History* 7 (January 1982): 66: "Daphne Simon argues that prosecutions were essentially a weapon for small, backward employers, and were rarely used by larger, more progressive concerns in industries such as cotton. Whatever the merits of this assessment for the early 1870s, it is very wide of the mark for the period 1836–54. In Preston and Blackburn during those years the prosecution of operatives for leaving work without notice was an almost weekly occurrence, providing yet another indication of the absence of 'kind sentiments of mutual regard' between cotton lords and their hands." For an example of a cotton spinner being proceeded against under the 1867 Master and Servant Act, see the case of *Bracewell and Lowe* (1871) reported in the "First Report of the Commissioners Appointed to Inquire into the Working of the Master and Servant Act, 1867," XXIV (Notes of Cases): 118. Simon also argued that overwhelmingly it was small employers who used the Master and Servant acts (190). Both Woods and Dutton and King disagree with her assessment, but it finds some support in the Testimony of William Evans, Qs. 1379–81. However, when asked "how many men do these [small] employers generally employ?" Evans replied "I should say from 50 to 200 men" (Q. 1408). Factory operatives in cotton mills were frequently prosecuted for "leaving work without notice" in Preston, Lancashire, and surrounding towns during 1865 and 1866. See, for example, *Supplement to the Preston Herald for the Week Ending September, 9, 1865,* 2 (Margaret Smith prosecuted for leaving the mill of Messrs. George Smith and Son); *Preston Herald, September 16, 1865,* 6 (Michael Dunlavey and John Caton summoned by Messrs. T. and J. Aitken, cotton spinners, for leaving their employ without giving the required notice); *Supplement to the Preston Herald for the Week Ending September 23, 1865,* 3 (Margaret Hodgson charged with leaving the employ of Mr. Goodair, Springfield Mill, without serving the usual notice); *Preston Herald, Saturday, October 7, 1865,* 6 (Bridget Emerson charged with leaving the mill of Mr. Furness, cotton spinner, without serving the usual notice); *Preston Herald, Saturday, October 21, 1865,* 5 (James Stephenson summoned by card master Robert Johnson for leaving the employ of Messrs. Horrockses, Miller, and Co. without serving the usual notice).

[118] See *Judicial Statistics, England and Wales, 1857–1875*, 19 vols. (London, 1858–1876); see also Simon, "Master and Servant," 186 n. 2: Complete statistics begin in 1857 except for "one isolated return of imprisonments of servants for breach of contract for 1854 and 1855." Beginning with the 1858 volume, Table 7 in *Judicial Statistics* gives the numbers of persons prosecuted in each police district.

ter and servant offences.[119] There were at least a few prosecutions in the overwhelming majority of police districts throughout the country. In certain counties, like Lancashire, Staffordshire, and Yorkshire, there were large numbers of prosecutions.[120] In 1860, to take one example, 11,938 people were prosecuted.[121] Of these, 7,059 were convicted; the remainder were discharged. A percentage of these were discharged because they had agreed to return to work. Of the 7,000-odd convicted, 1,699 served a sentence in the house of correction, 1,971 were fined, 3,380 received other punishments (wages abated and costs assessed, in all likelihood),[122] and one person was ordered whipped.[123] Of those sentenced to the house of correction, the overwhelming majority received terms of one month or less. The total number of prosecutions in England and Wales under the Master and Servant acts each year from 1857 to 1875, together with estimated unemployment rates in those years, is shown in Table 2.1.

Figure 2.1 depicts the relationships presented in Table 2.1. Prosecutions (upper line) are in thousands.[124] Estimated unemployment rates (lower lines) are derived from Pigou and Beveridge.[125] In general, as unemployment rates fell, the annual number of prosecutions rose, and as unemployment rates rose, the annual number of prosecutions fell. The strong negative correlation between unemployment rates and prosecutions can be represented statistically, −0.7693 in the case of Beveridge's

[119] Workers brought a certain percentage of cases against their employers for back wages or wrongful dismissal. In one small sample from Walsall, these amounted to 13.4 percent of the total. Woods, "Operation of the Master and Servants Act in the Black Country," 102. It is unclear whether the figures contained in *Judicial Statistics* include worker cases brought against employers, but they probably did not. The *Judicial Statistics* reported *criminal offences* disposed of by summary process and probably did not include worker-initiated actions.

[120] See *Judicial Statistics, England and Wales, 1857–1875*.

[121] *Judicial Statistics, England and Wales, 1860* (London, 1861), Table 8.

[122] A note in the 1872 volume of the *Judicial Statistics* provides a brief, unsatisfactory explanation of the "other punishments" category of Table 8. It says that "[t]he majority of the cases enumerated under the heading 'Other Punishments,' are those in which offenders were ordered to pay costs."

[123] In 1857, eleven people were ordered whipped, two each in 1858 and 1859, and one in 1860. Thereafter, no whippings were ordered until 1866, when one person again was ordered to receive this punishment. This appears to be the last such order for a master and servant offence. *Judicial Statistics*, Table 6 (1857); Table 8 in all other years.

[124] Annual number of prosecutions derived from *Judicial Statistics, England and Wales,* Table 8, except for the year 1857, when the comparable statistics appear in Table 6.

[125] Estimated unemployment rates are derived from A. C. Pigou, *Industrial Fluctuations,* 2d ed. (London, 1929), Appendix, Table 1, and from William Beveridge, *Full Employment in a Free Society,* 2d ed. (London, 1960), Appendix A ("Trade Union Unemployment Rate").

Table 2.1. *Unemployment Rates and Annual Prosecutions*

		Estimated Percent Unemployment	
Year[126]	Total Prosecutions[127]	Beveridge[128]	Pigou[129]
1857*	9,687	4.20	6.0
1858	8,301	7.35	11.9
1859	9,891	2.65	3.8
1860*	11,938	1.85	1.9
1861	10,393	3.70	5.2
1862	7,637	6.05	8.4
1863	8,504	4.70	6.0
1864	10,246	1.95	2.7
1865	10,412	1.80	2.1
1866*	12,345	2.65	3.3
1867	9,953	6.30	7.4
1868	8,204	6.75	7.9
1869	7,385	5.95	6.7
1870	8,670	3.75	3.9
1871	10,810	1.65	1.6
1872	17,082	.95	.9
1873*	16,230	1.15	1.2
1874	13,544	1.60	1.7
1875	14,353	2.20	2.4

*Indicates a peak in the trade cycle.

data and −0.7392 in the case of Pigou's, where 0 indicates no correlation and −1 indicates perfect negative correlation.

One potential problem with these results is that increases or decreases in the number of prosecutions from year to year may merely have reflected changes in the size of the work force itself.[130] It is possible, in other

[126] An asterisk beside the year indicates a peak in the trade cycle; see Rostow, *British Economy of the Nineteenth Century*, 33, Table II.

[127] Annual number of prosecutions derived from *Judicial Statistics, England and Wales*, Table 8, except for the year 1857, when the comparable statistics appear in Table 6.

[128] Estimated unemployment rates derived from William Beveridge, *Full Employment in a Free Society*, 2d ed. (London, 1960), Appendix A ("Trade Union Unemployment Rate").

[129] Estimated unemployment rates derived from A. C. Pigou, *Industrial Fluctuations*, 2d ed. (London, 1929), Appendix, Table 1.

[130] I am grateful to Professor Gillian Hamilton of the University of Toronto for helping me work through these statistics. Remaining errors are mine alone.

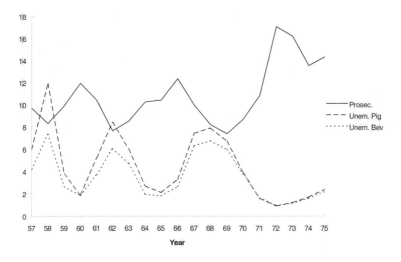

Figure 2.1. Annual Prosecutions Plotted against Unemployment Rates

words, that as unemployment fell and more workers were employed, more were prosecuted simply because there were more of them but the percentage of the workforce prosecuted did not change. If that were the case then employers would not really have been acting differently in tight as opposed to slack labor markets. If employment had increased by 2 percent from one year to the next, for example, and prosecutions had also increased by 2 percent, the number of prosecutions would have increased, but the same percentage of the workforce would have been prosecuted in the tighter labor market as in the slacker market. Did this happen?

Columns 2 and 3 in Table 2.2 demonstrate that the relationship between tight labor markets and increased prosecutions was real even when we discount for changes in the size of the workforce employed. In every set of years but three, when employment increased by a certain percentage, prosecutions increased by a much higher percentage, indicating that a larger percentage of the larger workforce was being prosecuted. In addition, the opposite applied as the workforce shrank. As unemployment rose and total employment fell, annual prosecutions fell at a much higher rate than employment did, indicating that a smaller percentage of the smaller workforce was being prosecuted. The only three exceptions were 1865–1866, 1868–1869, and 1874–1875, and all of these occurred at the end of a series of years in which employment had been fairly steady either at a relatively high or low level. It seems that at that point the level of employment became more important than the direction of the change. Where employment had been very high for a number of years a small de-

Table 2.2. *Employed Labor Force and Annual Prosecutions*

Years	Percent Increase or Decrease in Prosecutions	Percent Increase or Decrease in Employment
1857–1858	−14.30	−3.15
1858–1859	+19.15	+4.70
1859–1860	+20.69	+0.80
1860–1861	−12.94	−1.85
1861–1862	−26.51	−2.35
1862–1863	+11.35	+1.35
1863–1864	+20.48	+2.75
1864–1865	+1.62	+0.15
1865–1866	*+18.56*	−0.85
1866–1867	−19.37	−3.65
1867–1868	−17.57	−0.45
1868–1869	*−9.98*	+0.80
1869–1870	+17.40	+2.20
1870–1871	+24.68	+2.10
1871–1872	+58.02	+0.70
1872–1873	−4.98	−0.20
1873–1874	−16.54	−0.45
1874–1875	*+5.97*	−0.60

Note: Numbers in italics are those which do not conform to the general pattern described in the text.

crease in employment did not immediately reverse the trend toward greater numbers of prosecutions (1865–1866, 1874–1875). Similarly, where employment had been very low for a number of years a small increase in employment did not immediately reverse the trend toward fewer prosecutions (1868–1869). Table 2.2 shows these relationships year by year.[131]

Prosecutions by English county in 1860 are depicted in Figures 2.2 and 2.3.[132] They indicate that prosecutions were more common in the northern midlands and in certain of the northern counties than in the southeast. In general the counties with higher prosecution rates were those where manufacturing played a significant role in the local economy.

[131] The figures in Table 2.2 were calculated using the data presented in Table 2.1. Only Beveridge's employment estimates were used.

[132] Population and prosecution data in Figures 2.2 and 2.3 are taken from *Judicial Statistics, England and Wales, 1860.* Only English counties are included.

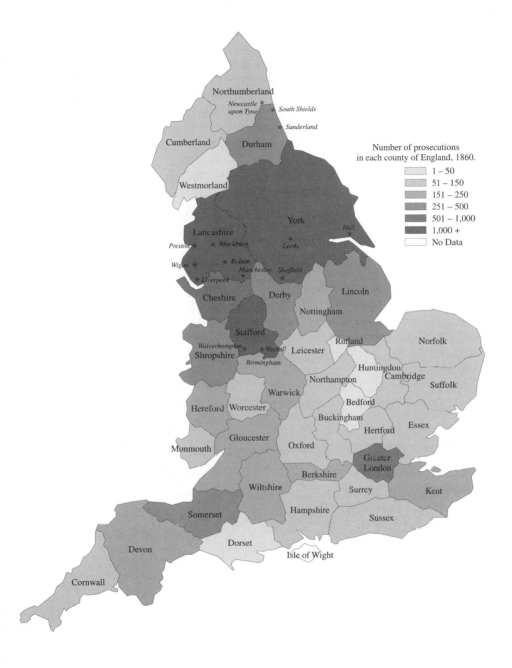

Figure 2.2   Number of Prosecutions in Each County of England, 1860

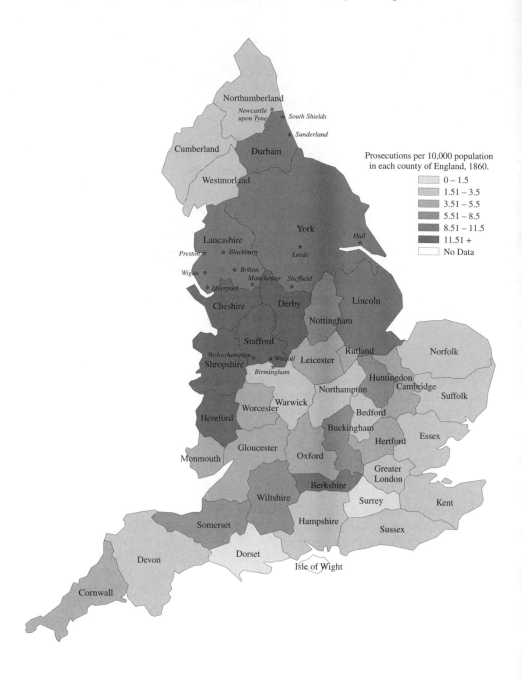

Figure 2.3. Prosecutions Per 10,000 Population in Each County
of England, 1860

What do these statistics tell us about the effect of master and servant legislation on the behavior of working people and their employers? A considerable number of working people each year between 1857 and 1875, on average about 10,000 in England and Wales, were dragged into the criminal justice system. There they faced the possibility that they would be confined for up to three months in the house of correction and held at hard labor. They found themselves in this position because their employers believed that they had violated their labor agreements in some way. These 10,000 or so served as an example and warning to the rest. The statistics also tell us that there was a strong correlation between the trade cycle and the annual number of workers prosecuted. When unemployment rates were low employers resorted to the disciplinary device of prosecutions more frequently. But even when unemployment was high, employers continued to find prosecutions useful, perhaps because even under those conditions prosecutions helped to control turnover and agency costs. In no year for which we have statistics were there fewer than 7,300 prosecutions. However, when the economy boomed in the early 1870s and labor became militant, the number of prosecutions more than doubled despite the fact that the 1867 reform act had reduced the number of prison sentences.[133] Employers may well have found the new power of the justices of the peace to order performance of contracts as useful as the old power to order a prison sentence directly on conviction.[134] In the very

[133] After the Master and Servant Reform Act was passed in 1867, the number of prison sentences fell substantially despite the fact that the annual number of prosecutions increased. Nevertheless, workers continued to be imprisoned under the new act. The new legislation made imprisonment available as an *initial* punishment only in cases of "aggravated breaches of contract, causing injury to persons or property." But often "aggravated breach" was interpreted broadly. Almost any breach would have caused some "injury to property."

Moreover, under the 1867 reform legislation, justices of the peace were given the power, for the first time, to order performance of the contract and to compel workers to find security for performance. For failure to comply with such orders, workers could still be committed to the house of correction for up to three months. Workers also continued to be subject to imprisonment in contract breach cases if they failed to pay any fine assessed by a magistrate. In 1854, 2,529 persons were committed for breach of contract in England and Wales, and 1,650 people were committed in the following year, 1855. See *Parl. Papers* (1856), L, 633, 637. Thereafter, "[p]rison sentences [each year during the period 1857–1867, before the reform legislation was enacted] averaged 1,240 of a month or less and 250 of more than a month; in [the period 1868–1871, after the reform legislation took effect], 380 and 125." Simon, "Master and Servant," 186 n. 2. But in 1872 and 1873 the annual number of prison sentences rose again, 553 of a month or less and 188 of more than a month in 1872; and 544 of a month or less and 200 of more than a month in 1873. *Judicial Statistics, England and Wales,* Table 8.

[134] For examples of magistrate orders to perform contracts, see "First Report of the Commissioners Appointed to Inquire into the Working of the Master and Servant Act, 1867," XXIV (Notes of Cases): *(Jones and Probert)*, 27; *(Parham v. Matthews)*, 29; *(Parham*

year criminal sanctions were abolished, 1875, prosecutions were just slightly below the record rates of 1872 and 1873.

What the statistics cannot tell us is, on the one hand, how much compliance with the law there generally was for one reason or another, and on the other, how much noncompliance there was. For each actual prosecution, how many times did an employer threaten a worker with prosecution should he quit or refuse to comply with orders and a worker stayed or complied to avoid confinement at hard labor? Were there only 5, or were there 50, 100, 200, 500, 1,000 such encounters for each prosecution? For every hostile encounter, how many more times did a worker simply decide to remain with an employer or to perform a task rather than risk the possibility of criminal prosecution? Were there only 5, or were there 50, 100, 500, 1,000 such silent decisions for each threat actually made?[135] On the other hand, how many times did a worker leave and an employer simply decide not to pursue the matter? Were there 5 unprosecuted breaches for each breach proceeded against, or were there 10, 100, 500?[136] These are the limits of what the criminal statistics can tell us about the effect of this legislation on the behavior of employers and workers. What seems likely is that this legislation played a significant role in the lives of working people, giving employers a powerful tool to enforce labor agreements in their ongoing struggles to keep wages down and productivity up.

CONTRACT LABOR AND WAGE LABOR

How well does what we have learned about American contract labor and English wage labor in the nineteenth century accord with the conventional wisdom about free and unfree labor? Poorly, I think. In the most advanced liberal market society of the nineteenth century, wage labor was, by modern standards, unfree labor. Free markets and free labor did

v. Wells), 30; (Colgan v. Doogan), 30; (Irvine v. McDonagh), 32; (Gluson v. Hogan), 35; (Walker v. Golden), 36; (Stephenson v. Maclaughlin), 44; (Lee v. Watson), 60; (Harrison v. Nash), 60; (Ranby v. Brown), 62; (Ranby v. Barrowcliffe), 62; (Eaton v. Green and Smith), 81; (Watts and Walker), 105; (Webb v. Watts), 114.

[135] "In your own experience have you very often been obliged to have recourse to the law? – No, not often, and to show how few cases there are, I have some statistics from our own district. *The moral effect of having the power is often sufficient*" (emphasis added). Testimony of J. Lancaster, Esq. (justice of the peace, Vice President of the Mining Association of Great Britain, and Chairman of the Wigan Coal and Iron Company) before the "Select Committee on Master and Servant" (1866), XIII:Q. 1441.

[136] "You say [prosecutions] occur in some works and not in others; is that owing to the nature of the works, or to the disposition of the employer? – The disposition of the employer; the processes of manufacture are precisely the same." Testimony of George Newton (a potter), ibid., Q. 34. "You say that the men had been previously in the habit of leaving without warning; had many men in consequence of so leaving been prosecuted under the Acts we are considering? – As far as I can recollect, I do not think, in all my experience as a manager, that I ever prosecuted a single man for leaving without warning."

not invariably occur together as fixed components of laissez-faire industrial capitalism. If conditions of labor scarcity could lead to the use of unfree labor, as they did in the colonial periphery, so apparently could conditions of general labor abundance, as they did in England. At the same
time, the American experience shows that conditions of relative labor
abundance could also lead to the use of free labor, as they did in the
northern United States. However, even conditions of labor scarcity could
lead to the use of free labor, as they did in the case of the free contract labor used in the United States after the 1830s. The conventional way of
looking at the history of labor turns out to be deeply flawed. The wage labor offered in free markets was not always free labor because sometimes
nonpecuniary pressures were used to compel work. Whether labor was
compelled through nonpecuniary pressures seems to have depended on
whether the state was willing to authorize imprisonment for breaches of
labor agreements. Furthermore, this decision does not seem to have depended on whether labor was abundant or scarce. However abundant labor may generally have been, conditions arose in advanced market
economies that made the enforcement of labor contracts through the
threat of physical confinement economically beneficial for employers. On
the other hand, however scarce labor may have been, a state might still
balk at authorizing the use of certain kinds of pressures to compel labor.
As a general matter it seems pretty clear that employers of both waged
and contract labor would ordinarily have wanted to possess the legal
power to use nonpecuniary pressure to enforce labor contracts. Only
where states failed to cooperate with these ambitions would we expect
employers not to possess this kind of power.

Even revised in this way the story fails to go far enough, because up to
this point we have accepted the conventional classification of labor into

Q. 2053. Practically, in your experience, as regards these Acts, they have been a dead letter? – Yes, since I became the manager of the Shotts Iron Works. At the time I was sub-
manager of the Glengarnock Works of Messrs. Merry & Cunningham, there were some
cases of prosecutions; but half-a-dozen cases altogether are all I can recollect." Testimony
of Mr. J. W. Ormiston (manager of the Shotts Iron Company in Scotland), ibid.,
Q. 2052–53. "[B]ut do many cases occur of men leaving their work, and breaking their
contract, who are not prosecuted? – Yes, if a man is a useless and poor workman, and is
not employed in any responsible position as an engineman, or in any post of that sort, we
should scarcely follow him." Testimony of J. Lancaster, Esq., ibid., Q. 1486.

It may be, of course, that some employers competed for labor by tacitly offering the
nonpecuniary inducement of freedom from prosecution under the Master and Servant
acts. Even during periods of low unemployment, however, this competitive strategy, if
pursued by some employers, did *not* lead to a general unraveling of the strategy of using
the Master and Servant acts to keep labor costs in check. On the contrary, during periods
of low unemployment, the percentage of the labor force prosecuted tended to rise. It may
be that the labor cost advantages that could be derived from using the Master and Servant acts in many cases outweighed the benefits that could be derived from this form of
nonpecuniary competition for labor.

free and unfree depending on whether penal sanctions were used. Dividing labor into these two categories obscures important truths about the complexities of compulsion in labor relations. To say that American contract labor and American wage labor were free labor is only to say that American employers could not legally avail themselves of physical violence or the threat of imprisonment to enforce labor contracts. It is to say nothing about the other remedies for labor contract breaches that they might have enjoyed, because other remedies are not viewed as "legally" coercing labor.

Yet we have seen that American importers of contract labor were able to pressure workers into performing their contracts by using a variety of remedies other than the threat of imprisonment. These more or less effective pecuniary alternatives to penal sanctions made it possible for some American employers to use contracts and contract enforcement to deal with their labor supply problems by importing foreign workers. These other "legal" means of pressuring the performance of labor become invisible when labor is simply divided into free and voluntary or unfree and coerced. The conventional classification creates the impression that contract labor without penal sanctions is not possible. It also creates the impression that in the absence of penal sanctions wage labor must necessarily be the legally unencumbered labor we imagine free wage labor always to have been.

In the remainder of this book I turn away from the depiction of labor relations in terms of free and unfree to investigate the particular legal rules that authorized, permitted, or prohibited the use of different kinds of nonpecuniary and pecuniary pressures in the wage labor of England, the United States, and, more briefly, some other countries. In this way we can begin to understand that, depending on these particular rules, employers were able to bring to bear against wage workers in different places a range of greater or lesser pressures, and that these should be understood as falling along a continuum rather than in terms of a binary opposition.

3

Explaining the Legal Content of English Wage Labor

CONFLICT, INTERESTS, IDEAS, AND NORMS

To the extent that an explanation has been offered by some labor historians for the rule that authorized criminal sanctions to enforce labor agreements, it is that criminal sanctions served the interests of English employers. During the eighteenth century, at a time when the English economy grew rapidly, the demand for labor intensified and Parliament enacted a series of statutes making penal sanctions available to employers for breaches of labor contracts. The problem of labor scarcity was not limited to the colonial periphery but posed difficulties for employers even in the midst of the general labor abundance of a developed market economy. Does the governing elite's response to scarce labor then account for the existence of penal sanctions in England?

Labor scarcity cannot be the entire explanation because it does not seem to have been either a necessary or a sufficient condition for the existence of penal sanctions. Penal sanctions were employed in England for centuries during long periods in which labor was in quasi-permanent surplus. In the nineteenth century employers continued to use penal sanctions with reduced frequency even at times when labor was not in great demand, during troughs in the trade cycle. They did so because there were economic advantages to be derived from using sanctions even under those circumstances.

If labor scarcity was not a necessary condition for the existence of a rule of penal sanctions, it was also not a sufficient condition. Labor markets might be tight, but any particular state might be unwilling to accommodate employers. The government of the United States, for example, failed to authorize stringent remedies to enforce contract labor agreements during the Civil War. Even if we add the problems of turnover and agency costs to the general problem of labor scarcity, these factors still do not explain why a state accommodated employers in certain cases but not in others. We face an additional explanatory problem, however. These kinds of labor problems can be dealt with in a variety of ways. Why were penal sanctions chosen rather than other possible measures?[1]

English employers and governing elites did not address their labor problems in a social vacuum, in a contextless, neoclassical economic universe. They grappled with these problems in a nation that had a particular history with a particular set of social institutions, norms, and legal rules. Without taking these into account it is not possible to explain why the responses to these problems took precisely the form they did. Why were English employers not authorized to enslave wage workers, for example? During the seventeenth century the Scottish Parliament passed legislation to make coal miners the serfs of mine owners.[2] During the nineteenth century, large numbers of Russian factory workers were serfs.[3] Why were English employers not permitted to whip their wage workers or have them imprisoned for a year at hard labor? Why could they not directly coerce them to enter the wage labor relationship in the first place? At an earlier point in English history, after all, employers could legally "require" certain wage workers to enter their service if they were not otherwise occupied. Why could they not do so in the nineteenth century? If "economic" coercion was not sufficient in the nineteenth century to keep workers disciplined and at their jobs during their terms of employment, why was it sufficient to compel them to enter wage work in the first place? It is always possible, of course, to generate untestable functionalist explanations (such as that the practice satisfied the needs of free markets for labor mobility) to try to account for these anomalies.[4] But ultimately, simple functionalism must fail because it explains social practices without taking into account the numerous possible solutions for a problem and the fact that a particular solution has only been arrived at through a path-dependent but partly contingent process of historical and social evolution.

To arrive at a satisfactory explanation for the existence of penal sanctions in nineteenth-century England, it is necessary to add historical, social, political, and legal dimensions to the undoubtedly crucial economic one. In the process, the nature of the explanation itself will change. It will

---

[1] Present-day American employers, for example, who cannot avail themselves of penal sanctions, have responded to similar problems through a number of different explicit and implicit contractual practices. For an overview of the literature discussing these contractual strategies, see Mark Kelman, "Progressive Vacuums," *Stanford Law Review* 48 (April 1996): 978 ns. 8, 9, and 986 n. 21.

[2] Christopher A. Whatley, "'The Fettering Bonds of Brotherhood': Combination and Labour Relations in the Scottish Coal-Mining Industry," *Social History* 12 (May 1987): 139.

[3] Reginald Zelnik, "The Peasant and the Factory," in *The Peasant in Nineteenth Century Russia,* ed. Wayne S. Vucinich (Stanford, Calif., 1968), 158–90.

[4] Jon Elster, *The Cement of Society: A Study of Social Order* (Cambridge, 1989), 147–48 (criticizing such efforts).

employ a causal narrative rather than invoke a general law.[5] The narrative presented in this and the following chapters is structured using a multistep framework. The first step describes how certain groups came to define their interests with respect to a legal rule. The second explains why groups failed or succeeded in having the state adopt the rule. The third step describes the interpretive struggles that took place over the proclaimed rule, struggles that may have restricted or expanded its scope. The fourth step describes the economic struggles that took place under the rule as interpreted. The final step explains how a long-established rule came to be challenged and ultimately changed.

By accepting the idea that penal sanctions served the material interests of employers of waged labor, we have called into question a fundamental tenet of the narrative of free labor. If nonpecuniary coercion of waged labor helped employers reduce turnover and agency costs, we should not be surprised to find wage labor widely subject to such pressures. To the extent that employers viewed nonpecuniary sanctions as promoting their interests, we should expect to find free wage labor in the modern sense only where states failed or refused to authorize the use of these kinds of pressures. In that case, the problem becomes to explain how free labor came into existence in the first place; why states prohibited the use of these kinds of pressures. The answer, contrary to the prevailing wisdom, has to be sought in something other than the interests of employing elites.

THE PROCESS OF DEFINING
GROUP INTERESTS

It is not altogether obvious why a group's definition of its interests has to be explained. After all, aren't interests transparent? The answer seems to be, not entirely. What James March has written about rational choice applies equally to what we commonly call group interest formation: "Rational choice involves two guesses, a guess about uncertain future consequences and a guess about uncertain future preferences."[6] In light of these uncertainties about any course of action, ideas, it seems, often turn out to be the final arbiters of group interests.[7] Take for example the case of wage

---

[5] On this form of explanation, see Don Herzog, *Happy Slaves: A Critique of Consent Theory* (Chicago, Ill., 1989), 19–20 ("No one thinks that the centrality of narration in ecology and evolutionary biology somehow impeaches their scientific credentials"). See also William H. Sewell, Jr., "Three Temporalities: Toward an Eventful Sociology," in *The Historic Turn in the Human Sciences*, ed. Terence J. McDonald (Ann Arbor, Mich., 1996), 245–80.

[6] James G. March, "Bounded Rationality, Ambiguity, and the Engineering of Choice," in *Rational Choice*, ed. Jon Elster (New York, 1986), 142.

[7] Herzog, *Happy Slaves*, 18. ("Realists counsel us to strip away ideas and focus on interests. But what are interests apart from ideas? Whatever interests I have depend partly on my

setting. For centuries, English elites had supported wage setting as a way to control wages in times of labor scarcity. Why did they change their minds over the course of the eighteenth century, pushing through the repeal of wage setting legislation over the strong objection of working people and some members of the governing elite as well? The answer has to do with the fact that wage setting always had two sides. During times in which labor was in great demand, wage setting helped to reduce the upward pressure on wages, promoting the interests of employers. However, at times in which the demand for labor was weak, wage setting tended to keep wages from falling below subsistence levels, arguably working against the interests of employers.

Given the double-sidedness of wage setting, is it possible to decide definitively whose long-term interests it served? Since repeal of wage setting legislation would mark a basic change in ground rules, one that would be viewed as permanent, it is precisely long-term interests that had to be assessed. Obviously, the answer depended in part on how wage setting was administered and what economic conditions prevailed. Employing elites had long controlled the state wage setting apparatus. Couldn't they ensure that wage setting was administered in their interests? For centuries, this had been a complaint of working people. However, different groups among employing elites defined their interests differently. In crude terms, some members of the gentry, who had traditionally controlled the wage setting machinery in the country, believed that their long-term interests were served by providing a basic wage to the laboring poor in bad times and by restraining wage increases in good times. Their interests were defined by a set of ideas about the way society should be organized and the political role they should play in that organization. The political identity and economic interests of many members of the commercial and industrial elite were constituted by a different set of ideas by this time, laissez-faire ideas. Just as the ideas of the gentry served to tell them what their interests were in the face of the double-sidedness of wage setting, laissez-faire ideas served to tell members of the commercial and industrial elite what their interests were in the face of the indeterminate long-run consequences of the same practice.

It is true that if employers had enjoyed a permanent oversupply of labor it might have been unambiguously in their interests to have gotten rid of wage setting. However, economic conditions are rarely permanent in a dynamic market economy like England's in the nineteenth century, and it was inevitable that labor would come into short supply from time to time,

self-image, my identity, my plans and projects; all those in turn are constituted partly by my ideas. . . . Realism then fails: it misses how systematically our concepts for understanding social life are informed by ideas. To occupy a social role, for instance, is to have a set of obligations dependent on our shared understanding of the role.")

and semipermanently in certain labor markets.[8] At those times and in those markets, the repeal of wage setting legislation worked against the interests of employers. Whether the long-term interests of employers as a class were served by the repeal of wage setting, therefore, depended on how many workers and employers were situated in markets where labor was in quasi-permanent short supply, how many in markets where labor was in quasi-permanent surplus, and how long these conditions could be expected to prevail. Needless to say, this would not have been easy to figure out. It is possible, however, to provide some sense of just how variable the state of the labor market was in England during the nineteenth century by looking at the trade cycle. Labor scarcity probably became a problem for certain groups of employers every time there was a sharp upturn in trade.[9] Over the first three quarters of the nineteenth century, the economy rapidly moved between peaks and troughs every few years. 1797, for example, was a trough year followed by a peak year in 1800 and then another trough year in 1801 followed by a peak in 1802. Between 1855 and 1873 trade moved between peaks and troughs four times. There was a trough in 1855 followed by a peak in 1857, another trough in 1858 followed by a peak in 1860, and then the trade cycle repeated itself. Another trough occurred in 1862 followed by a peak in 1866, then a trough in 1868 and a peak in 1873.[10]

In the face of the nearly impossible-to-calculate long-term aggregate costs and benefits of wage setting, it was laissez-faire ideas that provided a clear answer to the question of where employers' enduring interests lay. Similarly, the opposition to repeal of wage setting by working people was ground in ideological commitments and temporary conditions as much as in a fine calculation of long-term costs and benefits to wage workers as a whole.[11]

---

[8] On the multiplicity of nineteenth-century English labor markets and the quite different states of supply and demand in these markets, see Sidney Pollard, "Labour in Great Britain," in Peter Mathias and M. M. Postan, ed., *The Cambridge Economic History of Europe* (Cambridge, 1978), VII, Part I: 97–179.

[9] For estimated unemployment rates between 1857 and 1875, see Table 2.1 in Chapter 2.

[10] See W. W. Rostow, *British Economy of the Nineteenth Century* (Oxford, 1948), 33, Table II. It has been estimated according to a number of measures of wages that the duration of expansions in the first half of the nineteenth century was roughly equal to the duration of contractions. In other words, there were roughly as many years of upturn in trade cycle terms as years of downturn. See Arthur D. Gayer, W. W. Rostow, and Anna Jacobson Schwartz, *The Growth and Fluctuation of the British Economy, 1790–1850* (Oxford, 1953), II:939–40, Table 94a.

[11] The eighteenth century marked a reversal of opinion among working people on the subject of wage setting, precipitated by the agitation of workers in a few adversely affected trades:

What I have been arguing is that rules normally cut in more than one direction. In contests over rules a group's judgment that a rule will promote its long-run interests is almost never based on a genuine empirical weighing of the benefits and costs of the rule to the group as a whole. Such a calculation would necessarily involve a summing up of all the costs and benefits to different individuals in the group, some of whom might be small or large net losers under the rule, whereas others might be small or large net gainers under the rule. Such judgments are generally arrived at through an ideological decision about the best course for the group to pursue. In a sense, ideological commitments are as much *responsible for* creating group identity *and* group interests out of the often diverse and conflicting interests of group members as they are *reflective of* such interests.

CRIMINAL SANCTIONS

The adoption of criminal sanctions represents another example of a course of action in which ideas played an important role in the formation of group interests. Criminal sanctions for labor contract breaches had a number of clear benefits for employers that we have already talked about, but the rule also had its drawbacks. In tight labor markets employers who needed workers and were willing to pay for them could not always secure them because the law stood in their way.[12] According to testimony before

> The year 1773 produced a new era, and marks the strange vicissitudes of human events. The laws which had been heretofore so obnoxious to the workmen and artificers, were now in the most clamorous manner demanded by them. The silk weavers in Spitalfields, disgusted at the avaricious conduct of their masters, determined to throw themselves into the hands of the magistrates to fix the rate of their wages. . . . From 1349 till the era of Cromwell, 1649, the artificers and labourers had run the risk of being branded with red hot irons and treated as felons rather than submit to the rates fixed by magistrates, and then in little more than a century they become outrageous for the magistrates to have the power sooner than their masters.
>
> George White and Gravener Henson, *A Few Remarks on the State of the Laws, at Present in Existence, for Regulating Masters and Work-People, Intended as a Guide for the Consideration of the House, in Their Discussions on the Bill for Repealing Several Acts Relating to Combinations of Working-men* (London, 1823), 54–55.

This reversal of opinion too seems to have been dictated as much by a combination of traditional ideas, and economic conditions in certain labor markets, as by a fine calculation of long-term costs and benefits to working people as a whole. During earlier centuries many working people believed that wage setting operated against their interests.

[12] Writing of the employer role in the campaign to abolish serfdom among Scottish miners in the eighteenth century, Christopher Whatley describes one mine owner whose motives were to gain access to labor: "Having acquired a colliery in 1764, and with plans to sell coal in the large lucrative Edinburgh market as well as to inland towns to the south, but having only a handful of bound colliers, [James] Dewar's interest in reform can clearly be understood. As one of his opponents later asked, 'What significance was it . . . to stock his coal-works with colliers liable to be reclaimed as the law then stood?' There

the Select Committee on Master and Servant in 1866, workers engaged by one employer who were enticed away by another employer were invariably punished. The law was always used against them, depriving the second employer of their services.[13] Employers frequently used criminal sanctions to break strikes. On the other hand, criminal sanctions could also work against employer interests during strikes. Consider the following description from 1868:

> The other day two workmen left their employment in Kingston, attracted by the high wages offered at the gas works during the strike, and engaged themselves for the vacant places. Men, as we know, who had struck, were being sentenced every day to prison under the [Master and Servant act]. Yet those men who had come up from Kingston to take the places of the men on strike and do their work were sent to prison by the same rule.[14]

The gas works apparently had more difficulty replacing strikers because criminal sanctions were used to hold replacement workers to *their* agreements. In such situations, one result of the rule would have been to make strikes more effective.

To take full advantage of the rule, moreover, employers had to commit themselves to long contracts. To induce workers to sign such contracts employers often had to agree to supply work or wages during the contract term.[15] These commitments represented gambles that the demand for their goods would remain steady. If demand fell during the contract term,

---

are clearly grounds for suggesting that the liberty which he sought was *his own*, to expand his labour force by vigorously recruiting from neighbouring collieries free from the fear that their owners could recall their bound labour." "'The Fettering Bonds of Brotherhood,'" 146–47.

[13] Testimony of William Dronfield before the "Select Committee on Master and Servant" (1866), XIII:Q 866.

[14] Frederic Harrison, "Tracts for Trade Unionists – No. I, Imprisonment for Breach of Contract, or The Master & Servant Act," in *1868, Year of the Unions: A Documentary History,* ed. Edmund Frow and Michael Katanka (New York, 1968), 145.

[15] But see Chapter 4 for a discussion of the common law rule that allowed masters to bind piece workers for a term, impliedly binding themselves only to find reasonable work during the course of the term. In practice, in long contracts employers made more or less extensive promises about what their obligations would be during the contract term. In the case of contracts for a term that paid fixed wages periodically, the employer was obligated to pay those wages during the entire term even if demand for goods fell off, unless the contract provided that it could be sooner terminated by giving notice. In cases of contracts for a term based on piece work actually done, employers did in many cases obligate themselves to provide some earnings security for workers during the term. Some collieries at some points offered annual contracts that provided earnings protection when the pit was closed because of accidents, others provided wider protection against

workers might be able to seek wages while they were laid off.[16] How often employer gambles turned out badly is anybody's guess. It is also true, of course, that many employers sought to bind workers for a term without explicitly binding themselves to provide work during the term. In doing so, however, they ran a risk that the courts or the magistracy would find the contract unenforceable on the ground that it lacked mutuality, undermining the rationale for undertaking the contract in the first place.[17] By the 1850s, the common law courts were imposing a limited obligation on employers to find reasonable work during the term even where they had not explicitly undertaken such an obligation.[18]

The need to commit to long contracts to gain the full benefit of the rule must be counted one of the costs to employers of the rule's operation. Even a commitment to shorter contracts of a fortnight or a month meant that there might be some delay in laying workers off, given that they could not be dismissed without a period's notice. If they were let go, an

---

slack trade, and still others bound workers for a term but gave no guarantees. Long contracts in other trades could provide more or less wage protection during the contract term. For examples, see contracts referred to in cases discussed in Chapter 4. In many instances, employers explicitly promised to provide reasonable work during the term or wages in lieu of work but sometimes also reneged on these promises. See Testimony of William Evans before the "Select Committee on Master and Servant" (1866), XIII:Q. 1359.

[16] See *Beeston v. Collyer*, 4 Bing. 309, 130 Eng. Rep. 786 (1827); *Fawcett v. Cash*, 5 B. & AD. 904, 110 Eng. Rep. 1026 (1834); *Williams v. Byrn*, 6 L.J. (n.s.) (King's Bench) 239 (1837); *Aspdin v. Austin*, 5 Q.B. 671, 114 Eng. Rep. 1402 (1844). These were all cases in which fixed wages were to be paid periodically during the term. When the wages to be paid during the contract term were based on work by the piece actually done, whether a worker could recover depended on whether the employer had promised to provide reasonable work during the contract term. See *Williamson v. Taylor and Others*, 5 Q.B. 175, 114 Eng. Rep. 1214 (1843) (miner cannot recover because the contract did not expressly obligate the employer to provide reasonable work during the term). This rule was modified in the 1850s. For a contract where the employer did promise to provide reasonable work or wages in lieu of work during the entire term, see *Hartley v. Cummings*, 17 L.J. (n.s.) (C.P.) 84 (1847); for a separate report of the same case, see 5 C.B. 247, 136 Eng. Rep. 871 (1847).

[17] In an action for harboring a plaintiff's servant who had undertaken to serve for a year, Lord Denman upheld the verdict in favor of the defendant on the ground that there was no contract of service: "[T]he master not undertaking to employ [the servant], or to find him work . . . there is no consideration for the workman's hiring himself to the plaintiff exclusively." *Sykes v. Dixon*, 8 L.J. (n.s.) (common law) (1839), 102, 103–4. For a case in which magistrates refused to enforce a contract because it lacked mutuality, see *The Queen v. Welch and Another*, 22 L.J. (n.s.) (mag. cases) (1853), 145.

[18] These mutuality cases are discussed in greater detail in Chapter 4.

employer was open to a claim for wages or to damages for wrongful dismissal.[19]

Did the benefits of the rule outweigh the costs? Were some members of the group hurt by the rule while others were helped by it? If so, how were intragroup interest conflicts resolved? To my knowledge, no contemporary ever attempted to calculate overall costs and benefits to employers or differential impacts on different employers. How then did employers determine that this rule served their interests on balance as a group? The answer may be found in widely shared ideas about contracts of service and in widely shared employer self-conceptions. This is not to say that this judgment was not also solidly based on the significant economic benefits employers derived from the rule.

By the nineteenth century, there was wide agreement in certain segments of the English elite that the old system of comprehensive labor regulation violated "general principles of the first importance to the prosperity and happiness of the community."[20] These principles required that every individual must enjoy "perfect liberty . . . to dispose of his time and of his labour in the way and on the terms which he may judge most conducive to his own interest."[21] From the late eighteenth century on certain members of the English governing elite had worked to realize a vision of labor markets regulated by contract, which they undoubtedly also believed would promote their interests. However, the principle of free contract placed limits on the coercive measures they could justify in dealing with the problem of labor scarcity. Such measures had to be consistent with the general norm of perfect liberty to make labor agreements, and that norm was interpreted to mean that one person could not force another into entering a contract by using threats of physical violence or imprisonment.[22] Other aspects of the contract ideology of the time, however, pointed toward legitimate steps that might and should be taken. If labor markets were to function properly under the new system of contract, it

---

[19]   Admittedly, workers often did not prevail in such actions, but the threat of an action must have had a nuisance value for workers. On worker difficulties in maintaining these actions, see Daphne Simon, "Master and Servant," in *Democracy and the Labour Movement: Essays in Honour of Dona Torr*, ed. John Saville (London, 1954), 160–65; and D. C. Woods, "The Operation of the Master and Servants Act in the Black Country, 1858–1875," *Midland History* 7 (1982): 108–9.

[20]   "Report of Select Committee of Parliament" (1811), quoted in Sidney Webb and Beatrice Webb, *The History of Trade Unionism* (London, 1920), 60.

[21]   Ibid.

[22]   A. W. B. Simpson, *A History of the Common Law of Contract: The Rise of the Action of Assumpsit* (Oxford, 1975), 50, 99.

was thought to be crucial that employers be able to enforce the agreements of their workers. Moreover, it was right and proper that people should be held to their promises. In *Lumley v. Wagner*, the Lord Chancellor noted:

> Wherever this Court has not proper jurisdiction to enforce specific performance, it operates to bind men's consciences as far as they can be bound, to a true and literal performance of their agreements; and it will not suffer them to depart from their contracts at their pleasure, leaving the party with whom they have contracted to the mere chance of any damages which a jury may give.[23]

In the case of propertyless wage workers, it was widely believed that a system of enforceable contract could not be based on money damages. As one lawyer argued, "an Action is in effect, no remedy against person's in the appellant's rank of life, and the [Master and Servant] act has substituted an effectual remedy in lieu of an action."[24] People, especially people of low status, had an obligation to fulfill their contracts. They should not be permitted to walk away from these obligations at their pleasure, nor should they be allowed to defy their employers with impunity. Only penal sanctions could assure this result, and there was nothing particularly objectionable about using these kinds of sanctions to enforce agreements, given that they had been entered into voluntarily. In effect, strict enforcement of a contract was merely "giving effect to [the contracting party's] own expressed desire."[25]

Equally important, the interests of enticers of labor carried little legitimacy among employers even though many employers engaged in the practice. One manufacturer thought "that another manufacturer ought to be horsewhipped for offering inducement[s to his workers]."[26] Upright employers tended to imagine themselves in the position of those who had workers, rather than in the position of those who needed them. It would have been entirely possible for employers to have cultivated a self-image in which those who could afford to pay workers a premium would be thought to have won out fair and square in the competition of life in the market, but that was not the case in mid-nineteenth-century England.

It was these views – that labor markets should be based on voluntary agreements, agreements must be enforceable, agreements could not be enforced by suing for money damages, penal sanctions to enforce voluntary

---

[23] *Lumley v. Wagner*, 1 De G. M. & G. 618, 42 Eng. Rep. 687 (1852), 693.

[24] *Ashmore v. Horton and Another*, 29 L.J. (n.s.) (mag. cases) (1860) 13, 15; see also James Edward Davis, *The Master and Servant Act, 1867* (London, 1868), 7.

[25] John Stuart Mill, *Collected Works*, vol. III, *Principles of Political Economy with Some of Their Applications to Social Philosophy* (Toronto, 1965), Book V, Chapter I, § 2.

[26] Testimony of William Dronfield, Q. 865.

agreements were not particularly objectionable, those who lacked labor had no valid claim on the labor controlled by others – that filtered and channeled the response of English elites to the real problems of tight labor markets, turnover costs, and labor discipline. These views also led them to promote penal sanctions as a way of advancing their interests, in the context of the wider utopian project of remaking market relations so that they would henceforth be based on private property and free contract.

MAKING THE RULES

Once group interests had been formulated, didn't the ruling elites of nineteenth-century England have the power simply to put in place the rules they wanted? The answer seems to have been, not always. It is true that the mercantile and industrial classes succeeded in having wage setting repealed early in the century over the strong opposition of working people, and in 1823 Parliament did pass a new Master and Servant Act that reinvigorated criminal penalties for contract breaches. However, only a year later, in 1824, employers suffered a serious reverse when Parliament repealed all earlier Anti-combination acts.[27] The very next year the 1824 act was itself repealed and an Anti-combination act less favorable to labor was put in its place.[28] But the 1825 act also repealed all earlier anti-combination legislation and formally recognized the right of unions to exist for the purpose of bargaining over wages and hours. Although the 1825 act and the law of conspiracy continued to limit the kinds of activities unions were able to engage in,[29] the recognition of their basic legal right to exist represented a crucial improvement in the position of wage workers.

Why had workers lost out so badly in 1823 when criminal sanctions for contract breach were reaffirmed, but only two years later participated in a successful campaign to have the old anti-combination laws repealed? The 1824 Anti-combination Act was passed mainly as a result of the efforts of two men, Francis Place and Joseph Hume, who maneuvered the act through Parliament. They were motivated primarily by a commitment to a particular vision of laissez faire, a vision they believed would help to restore harmony to labor relations.[30] In their highly contested interpreta-

---

[27] 5 Geo. IV, c. 95 (1824). See Webb and Webb, *History of Trade Unionism*, 64–112, and John Orth, *Combination and Conspiracy: A Legal History of Trade Unionism, 1721–1906* (Oxford, 1991), 68–95.

[28] 6 Geo. IV, c. 129 (1825).

[29] Webb and Webb, *History of Trade Unionism*, 107, 261–95; and Orth, *Combination and Conspiracy*, 68–95.

[30] The abstract concept *laissez-faire* does not yield a clear answer to the question of whether labor should be permitted to form combinations. Freedom in the market can mean either that workers should be free to combine or not. Another contemporary version of freedom in the market held that *laissez-faire* meant that only *individuals* should be free to

tion, the principle of laissez-faire implied that workers should be free to bargain however they saw fit, by combining if they liked. Not surprisingly, a number of employer groups reacted strongly to the passage of the 1824 act, mounting a parliamentary campaign to have the new act repealed. For a while it looked as though the old Anti-combination acts might be reinstated:[31]

> When it seemed likely that they would be reinstated, in 1825, even the Government was shaken by the storm of protests, petitions, meetings, and deputations from every trade. "Vigilant and intelligent men" came down to watch the parliamentary proceedings, from Lancashire, Glasgow, Yorkshire, Tyneside. Any attempt to re-enact the Combination Acts, John Doherty, the leader of the Lancashire cotton-spinners, wrote to Place, would result in a widespread revolutionary movement.[32]

The 1825 legislation that emerged from Parliament preserved the core gains of the 1824 act. By contrast, criminal sanctions for contract breaches were given new life in 1823 with the passage of a new Master and Servant Act.

In 1823, Peter Moore, the Radical MP for Coventry, introduced a bill that sought to repeal practically all previous Master and Servant acts. In a pamphlet produced to accompany the bill, Gravener Henson, a leader of the Nottingham framework knitters, and George White, a clerk of committees at the House of Commons, made clear that one of the central concerns of the Moore bill was to rid workers of the piece work clause of the old Tudor Statute of Artificers, which punished failure to finish work: "Very few prosecutions have been made to effect under the combination Acts, but hundreds have been made under this law, and the labourer or workman can never be free, unless this law is modified."[33] The piece work clause, they went on to say, was

bargain with one another, indeed, that labor combinations represented an interference with the freedom of individuals to bargain in the market. See John Nockleby, "Two Theories of Competition in the Early 19th Century Labor Cases," *The American Journal of Legal History* 38 (1994) for a discussion of these two interpretations of laissez-faire in the American context. For an account of the politics of Place and Hume, see Webb and Webb, *History of Trade Unionism*, 96–108; and E. P. Thompson, *The Making of the English Working Class* (New York, 1966), 516–21.

[31] For a fuller discussion of these developments, see Webb and Webb, *History of Trade Unionism*, 107, 261–95; and Orth, *Combination and Conspiracy*, 68–95.

[32] Thompson, *Making of the English Working Class*, 518.

[33] White and Henson, *A Few Remarks on the State of the Laws*, 51.

a branch of the system to compel a man to work for low wages. . . .
[A] number of servants, on account of change of trade, &c. wish to
leave their master, if he will not give them fair wages; he says, I cannot prevent you from leaving WHEN you have finished your work;
but if a man leaves before he has finished, a gaol is his doom; instead
of acting with one impulse, to compel him to give fair wages, some
must stay a month, some two months, and perhaps some leave and
are made what the master calls examples of, by being imprisoned.[34]

Remarkably, Moore's bill did not propose to repeal the criminal sanctions provisions of the Master and Servant acts, merely to amend them.
Under the bill's provisions, workers would continue to be subject to
prison terms for contract breaches, not only for quitting, but also for idle-
ness or negligence at work.[35] Moore's bill proposed three main modifications of existing law. First, *piece* workers could, by giving fourteen days'
written notice, free themselves of their obligations to finish the work they
had agreed to perform. However, this provision only applied to those who
were engaged to do piece or task work. It did not extend to anyone
who was hired for a term.[36] Under Moore's bill, all workers hired for any
term continued to be subject to penal sanctions for failing to fulfill their
engagements. Second, the bill reduced the maximum sentence for first of-
fenses to an unspecified number of days rather than three months.[37]
Third, it made appeals to Quarter Sessions available even in the case of
orders of commitment, although not where the penalty was less than fourteen days' imprisonment.[38] That was all. Apparently, in 1823, total repeal
of criminal sanctions was not an imaginable possibility even for those
closest to working people in the parliamentary community. The rule of
penal sanctions seems to have been treated as part of the unchangeable
background scenery of social and economic life even by working people
during this period. Individual workers might denounce the Master and
Servant acts as an invasion of the sacred liberties of the people, but a
world without those laws does not seem to have presented itself as a real-
istic option at the time.

---

[34] Ibid., 52.

[35] *Parl. Papers* (1823), II:261–311 ("A Bill for Repealing Several Acts Relating to Combinations of Workmen, and for More Effectually Protecting Trade, and for Settling Disputes
between Masters and Their Workpeople"), clause 13, 275.

[36] Ibid., 275–76. See also White and Henson, *A Few Remarks on the State of the Laws*, 116.

[37] "A Bill for Repealing Several Acts," *Parl. Papers* (1823), II: c. 13, 275.

[38] Ibid., 306–8; and White and Henson, *A Few Remarks on the State of the Laws*, 90–91. 6 Geo.
III, c. 25 (1766) allowed appeals to Quarter Sessions except for orders of commitment (s.
IV).

The Moore bill aimed to free piece workers who had not agreed to work for a term from open-ended obligations to finish work.[39] As for those who had agreed to work for a time certain,[40] they should continue to be bound to complete their terms or work out their notice. What the bill, and White and Henson, sought in the case of these contracts was not freedom from the traditional obligation to perform but enforcement of the reciprocal obligations of employers. No worker hired "by the day, week, month or year, or longer period, shall be liable to be discharged from such hiring without his, her, or their own consent, previous to the expiration of the term of such hiring."[41] White and Henson explained that

> [i]f a man is hired by a master for his own convenience, he ought to be bound to give the real wages agreed on, and ought also to be compelled to keep that servant the whole of the time for which the agreement was made, unless he can show sufficient cause to discharge him, before a Justice. . . . *The master and servant ought to be reciprocally bound by their engagements.*[42] (emphasis added)

They went on to add that it

> is nothing but just, that if a master requires a workman, for his interest, to give up his services to him for a certain time, though he may have many opportunities in the time to mend his situation, the master ought to keep such servant for the whole term, as it was to obtain permanent employment that he was induced to engage.[43]

---

[39] White and Henson, *A Few Remarks on the State of the Laws,* 51, 117. The piece work clause of the Statute of Artificers

> has been much abused, as in many businesses they never finish their work, as the nature of the employment is such, that they are compelled to begin one before they finish another . . . therefore, if any dispute ariseth . . . or men leave their work, having words, the master prosecutes them for leaving their work unfinished . . . the labourer or workman can never be free, unless this law is modified. . . . This [proposed] clause is to set the workman free from any tyrannical master, who may wish to detain him under the pretext of not finishing his work. There are a number of trades who are compelled, from the nature of their employment, to begin one article before they finish the other; and masters frequently, in some trades, deliver out as much work as will take a workman six months to finish. . . . Fourteen days is sufficient for a master to obtain another workman: he can stop the workman any day he pleases, and 14 days is sufficient notice in return.

[40] This would encompass contracts for a term, short periodic contracts, and contracts of indefinite duration determinable on a fixed period of notice.

[41] "A Bill for Repealing Several Acts," *Parl. Papers* (1823), II:274.

[42] White and Henson, *A Few Remarks on the State of the Laws,* 94.

[43] Ibid., 116.

Appeals to Quarter Sessions from orders of commitment were to be allowed in the proposed legislation, according to White and Henson, because a single justice of the peace simply could not be trusted to deal fairly with workers, although the bill continued to allow single justices to adjudicate cases initially.[44] In addition, the bill made justices who were also employers in a particular trade ineligible to adjudicate master and servant cases arising within the trade.[45] On the other hand, the bill prohibited the common law courts from removing "by Certiorari, or any writ or process whatsoever" any order, judgment, conviction, determination, or dismissal made under the proposed act.[46]

Nowhere in White and Hensons's pamphlet is there the slightest indication that they considered penal sanctions an abridgment of the liberties of Englishmen in and of themselves. In their view, what could turn a contract of hire into a contract of slavery was the length of the engagement:

> *One step more in this "economy," and slavery is at hand immediately.* If a man is to make any agreement, unprotected, which his master can impose upon him, he has only got to sell, or hire himself, for life, and then, by his own agreement, he may become the property of his master. Such has been the want of employment in England, of late years, that there have been a great number of persons who would have sold themselves for life, to have had victuals, lodging, and clothing.[47] (emphasis original)

---

[44] "As to misbehaviour, one Justice is to be the judge of what may be so called; a few angry words, singing, appearing dirty, smoking tobacco, workman not finishing his work to please his master, or not doing enough, – in short, every thing that the master chuses to style misbehaviour, has been construed into an offence before one Justice, who sends the unfortunate man to the gaol, or house of correction, without an appeal." Ibid., 91. "No man ought to be sent to gaol, without an appeal, by one Justice, unless he is a well known and *convicted* rogue and vagabond." Ibid., 94. The proposed legislation, however, continued to allow a single justice to adjudicate initially and prohibited appeals from commitments of less than fourteen days; see "A Bill for Repealing Several Acts," *Parl. Papers* (1823), II:275, 307–308.

[45] "A Bill for Repealing Several Acts," *Parl. Papers* (1823), II:304; see also White and Henson, *A Few Remarks on the State of the Laws,* 132.

[46] "A Bill for Repealing Several Acts," *Parl. Papers* (1823), II:307; see also White and Henson, *A Few Remarks on the State of the Laws,* 136–37. The 1747 act (20 Geo. II, c. 19) had similarly prohibited the issuance of writs of certiorari. However, the 1823 act (4 Geo. IV, c. 34), enacted some time after Moore's bill was set aside, did not explicitly prohibit writs of certiorari although it did make justices' orders final, giving no appeals to Quarter Sessions.

[47] White and Henson, *A Few Remarks on the State of the Laws,* 108–9.

Peter Moore's bill contained a provision limiting contracts of hire to no longer than five years (with certain exceptions).[48]

In the event, even these timid proposals alarmed many members of Parliament, and Moore agreed to allow discussion on his bill to be postponed until the next session.[49] That occasion never presented itself because later in the year Parliament passed the 1823 Master and Servant Act, reenacting the existing system of criminal penalties for contract breaches.

Whether statutory rules persist or are changed in a society like that of nineteenth-century England depends on many factors, including the state of political and economic organization of the contending parties, the scope of the suffrage, and more. One important factor is whether the moral and political principles asserted by one side or the other have come to be widely accepted. To return to an earlier example, if a practice like wage setting had been advocated strictly instrumentally to promote group interests, we would expect employing elites to press for wage setting at times when it was in their interests to do so (when wages were rising) but to move to get rid of it at other times. The fact that this did not happen indicates that part of what was involved in the movement to repeal wage setting legislation at the beginning of the nineteenth century was a genuine normative judgment based on laissez-faire ideas about the way society should properly be organized. Furthermore, even though it might have been possible for employers to have argued that one principle was appropriate under one set of circumstances and another under other circumstances, such a strategy would have undermined the normative power of all their arguments. Their arguments would then have all come to be viewed as transparently self-serving. It is true that groups often manipulate normative arguments to gain instrumental benefits, but if they prevail, they are often forced to live with the results, good and bad.[50] Normative arguments are among the most powerful political tools groups have available for maintaining or changing ground rules.

Although many employers believed that criminal sanctions served their interests, many also believed that the anti-combination laws served their interests as well. That one rule remained in place while the other was changed seems to have been the result, on the one hand, of the success a few well-placed Benthamite radicals had in gaining just wide enough acceptance of a particular interpretation of laissez-faire, with support at one crucial moment from the working classes, and on the other hand, of a failure of the few parliamentary supporters of labor to see that criminal sanc-

---

[48] "A Bill for Repealing Several Acts," *Parl. Papers* (1823), II:271–72.

[49] Orth, *Combination and Conspiracy*, 69, citing Graham Wallas, *The Life of Francis Place, 1771–1854,* 3d ed. (New York, 1919), 208.

[50] Elster, *Cement of Society*, 128.

tions could be similarly recast as a violation of other basic English political norms. Instead, the principle that people must fulfill their voluntary
contracts (compelled by penal sanctions if necessary) held the field uncon-
tested. Although the earlier Anti-combination acts were repealed in 1824
to 1825, employers continued to enjoy the benefits of criminal sanctions
for another fifty years. Such were the different fates of two rules that
many employers believed were equally important to the profitable conduct of their businesses.

It was not until 1863 that labor launched a campaign to reform the
master and servant law, and it was here that labor advocates began to argue that criminal sanctions violated the basic political norm of equal treatment under law. I pick up the story of this ultimately successful campaign
to change basic ground rules in Chapter 6. The next chapters, however,
turn to the legal and social conflicts that took place while the rule of criminal sanctions remained in effect, a taken-for-granted part of the landscape.
These struggles occurred on at least two levels: interpretive struggles over
the meaning of the rules and tactical struggles for economic advantage
under the rules. Although they did not directly challenge the rule of criminal sanctions, they had the unintended consequence of reshaping the terrain on which the rule rested. One unanticipated result was that over time
these battles began to cut the ground out from under the previously unquestioned rule of penal sanctions, making thinkable a campaign to try to
change the rule outright.

4

Struggles over the Rules

The Common Law Courts, Parliament, the People, and the Master and Servant Acts

English legal history is generally of two kinds, common law and statutory. The history of common law is usually devoted to following the development of legal doctrine in the decisions of the common law courts. Statutory history is generally quite different, devoted to parliamentary politics or to politics in the country, with the object of laying bare the circumstances that produced a particular piece of legislation. Often the legislation is described in detail, and its subsequent history (amendments, repeals, etc.) is retold. Rarely does one find a statutory history in which the common law courts play a significant role. Almost never does one find a statutory history in which parliament repeatedly reacts to modify judicial interpretations of a previously passed statute. One supposes that this convention of English legal history flows from the fact of parliamentary sovereignty, which makes the legislative body supreme and the courts subservient to it, at least insofar as legislation is concerned. In the case of the Master and Servant acts, this convention of legal history writing has obscured an important part of the story. For centuries, the common law courts played a significant role in the legal development of the Master and Servant acts, and in a number of instances Parliament took steps to try to reverse court decisions by passing additional legislation.

From the late seventeenth century on, we find a steady stream of cases devoted to the question of whether justices of the peace possessed jurisdiction under the Tudor Statute of Artificers to hear wage recovery complaints brought by workers against employers. Early on the courts decided that the wage recovery jurisdiction of justices of the peace was limited to servants in husbandry hired for a year and did not extend to domestic servants or laborers.[1] The courts adhered to this position even when confronted with the argument that the Statute of Artificers gave justices jurisdiction to establish the wages of all kinds of workers, not merely

---

[1] See *Mr. De Vall*, 2 Jones 47, 84 Eng. Rep. 1140 (28 Car. II); *Dominus Rex And Devall*, 3 Keb. 626, 84 Eng. Rep. 917 (28 Car. II); *The King v. Champion*, Carth. 156, 90 Eng. Rep. 695 (2 Wm. and Mary).

servants in husbandry, and to criminally enforce the agreements of a range of workers other than servants in husbandry.[2]

In 1747, Parliament moved to change this situation by giving justices of the peace jurisdiction to order the payment of wages in the case of "*Servants in Husbandry,* who shall be *hired for one Year, or longer, or . . . Artificers, Handicraftsmen, Miners, Colliers, Keelmen, Pitmen, Glassmen, Potters, and other Labourers employed for any certain time, or in any other Manner*" (emphasis added).[3] Apparently, the scope of the 1747 statute itself became a subject of controversy, because ten years later Parliament moved to amend the statute:

> And whereas Doubts have arisen whether the Words *any Labourers employed for any certain Time, or in any other Manner, extend to Servants in Husbandry hired for a less Time than one Year:* For obviating the said Doubts, Be it enacted by the Authority aforesaid, That the Said Act, and all and every Clause and Matter therein contained, shall . . . be deemed and construed to extend to *all Servants employed in Husbandry, though hired for a less Time than one Year.*[4] (emphasis added)

Given that the system of annual hirings had been breaking down during the eighteenth century – servants in husbandry were being hired for a variety of different times – this amendment seems to have addressed an important problem.[5]

The common law courts interpreted the language of the 1747 statute to mean that justices of the peace had been given jurisdiction over servants in husbandry but not over other types of servants.[6] In 1801, a bill was introduced in Parliament "For the better settling of Disputes between Masters and Workmen, and also between Masters and Mistresses of Families and *Menial and Domestic Servants*" (emphasis added).[7] The opening section of the bill complained that "whereas the Laws now in being have, *by Construction,* been confined to Servants in Husbandry only" (emphasis

---

[2] See *The Queen v. London,* 6 Mod. 204, 87 Eng. Rep. 958 (3 Queen Anne) (argument of Brotherick, 958).

[3] 20 Geo. II, c. 19 (1747).

[4] 31 Geo. II, c. 11, s III. (1757).

[5] On the decay of the system of annual hirings in the eighteenth century, see K. D. M. Snell, *Annals of the Labouring Poor: Social Change and Agrarian England, 1660–1900* (Cambridge, 1987), 73–74.

[6] See *The King v. Hulcott,* 6 T.R. 583, 101 Eng. Rep. 716 (1796), 718 (opinion of Lord Kenyon, Ch. J.), and *Lowther v. Radnor,* 8 East 113, 103 Eng. Rep. 287 (1806), 291 ("these words [in 20 Geo. II, c. 19] certainly restrain the operation of the remedy, as to servants, to those in husbandry only." Opinion of Lord Ellenborough, C. J.) Where the 1747 act referred to "servants" as opposed to "artificers" or "labourers" it only mentioned servants in husbandry explicitly.

[7] *Parl. Papers* (1801) I:177.

added),[8] it had become necessary for Parliament explicitly to extend the jurisdiction of justices of the peace to "Menial or Domestic Servants."[9] The bill was later amended, but never did receive final parliamentary approval.[10]

Between the 1820s and 1860s, three main issues under the Master and Servant acts were repeatedly brought before the common law courts. These issues marked out the boundaries of *legal* conflict over penal sanctions in this period. Interestingly, these were essentially the same boundaries within which *political* conflict over the Master and Servant acts was confined during this period. Just as outright repeal of penal sanctions for contract breach was not addressed in Peter Moore's failed 1823 effort to reform master and servant law, the legitimacy of penal sanctions for contract breach was not a subject of dispute in the litigation over these acts. The subjects of legal dispute were essentially the same as the subjects of political controversy. The first was the issue of the reciprocal obligations of masters and servants. White and Henson in their pamphlet in support of Peter Moore's bill argued that it was essential in all cases in which workers had been hired for a term that employer and worker should be "reciprocally bound by their engagements." Employers should be obligated to keep a worker for the whole term for which that person had signed, "as it was to obtain permanent employment that he was induced to engage" in the first place.[11]

"Mutuality" became an important issue because increasingly, it seemed, employers were trying to have it both ways. They were trying to secure for themselves the benefits of long contracts while at the same time eliminating certain of their potential costs. As White and Henson put it,

> it has been the practice for masters in manufactures, &c. to hire servants for a great length of time, who are compelled [by the Master and Servant acts] to serve, but the master frequently dischargeth them at a moment's notice, without assigning any cause. If a master hires a servant for a length of period, he prevents him from making any other advantageous bargain until that period is transpired; and he ought to be compelled to keep that servant, who hires for the sake of the employment: to discharge him without cause is to defraud him.[12]

[8] Ibid.

[9] Ibid., 178.

[10] Ibid., 389.

[11] George White and Gravener Henson, *A Few Remarks on the State of the Laws, at Present in Existence, for Regulating Masters and Work-People, Intended as a Guide for the Consideration of the House, in Their Discussions on the Bill for Repealing Several Acts Relating to Combinations of Working-men* (London, 1823), 116.

[12] Ibid., 49.

The issue came before the courts in a number of different contexts. Sometimes it arose in a case in which an *employer sought to enforce a contract* whose terms expressly bound the employee to serve for a term, but did not expressly bind the employer to find work or wages for the worker during the term. Sometimes it arose in a case in which a *worker sought wages* for time he or she was laid off during the contract term. Over the period being examined here the position of the common law courts on the issue of "mutuality" changed subtly, placing workers in a worse legal position.

The second issue was also one the Moore bill had addressed. That bill proposed to permit piece workers to terminate their contractual obligations by giving fourteen days' written notice. It seemed unfair to the bill's drafters that workers who had only undertaken to perform a task, indeed who might be taking work from more than one employer, should be bound in the same way as those who had bound themselves for a term. A similar issue came before the common law courts as a question of statutory interpretation. Did the language of the Master and Servant acts, particularly the 1823 act, encompass piece or task workers? Were they subject to the penal enforcement of their agreements under the acts? In the early years of this period, the common law courts seemed inclined to exclude certain piece workers from the act, but over time that position changed, and not in ways that were beneficial to such workers.

The final issue that occupied the courts was also addressed in Peter Moore's bill. The Moore bill proposed to allow appeals to Quarter Sessions from a single justice's commitment order because justices frequently dealt unfairly with the workers brought before them. Some of the common law judges also were concerned with the quality of the justice delivered by local magistrates. During one period the Queen's Bench regularly quashed convictions and commitments where justices were shown not to have observed certain procedural formalities. Certain members of the court felt inclined to take these steps because they viewed the summary criminal jurisdiction that magistrates exercised as an abridgment of the guarantees of the common law, including guarantees of trial by jury. During the 1840s, trade union lawyers enjoyed a fair amount of success in winning freedom for workers on this ground. However, here, too, in the 1850s the courts retreated from their earlier position and grew more reluctant to set aside orders of a justice on the ground that he had failed to observe procedural formalities.

TERM CONTRACTS
AND GUARANTEED EARNINGS

In the paradigmatic case of a contract of hiring for a term, employer and employee would be reciprocally bound, the one to serve, the other to pay fixed wages periodically during the term or a predetermined amount at the conclusion of the term. Accordingly, if an employer dismissed an employee without cause during the term, the employee could bring an action to recover damages for lost earnings covering the balance of the term, if there were no provision to determine the contract on shorter notice.[13] Problems arose, however, where a contract was in writing and the employee had bound himself to serve the employer exclusively for a term but had also agreed to be paid by the piece for work actually done, and the employer had not expressly undertaken to furnish the worker with a reasonable quantity of work during the entire term. In the 1820s and 1830s, the common law courts seem to have taken the position that such a contract was not valid and binding because it lacked consideration and could not be enforced by the employer either against the employee in assumpsit or against a third party in an action for harboring or enticement.[14]

For example, *Sykes v. Dixon,* decided in 1839, was an action for harboring and enticement brought by one employer against another. The subject of the action was the workman William Bradley of Sheffield. John Sykes manufactured powder flasks and other articles, and William Bradley had signed an agreement to work for him "and no other person whatsoever" for twelve months "and so on from twelve months end to twelve months" until Bradley gave Sykes twelve months' written notice.[15] But Sykes never signed the agreement, and he made no other written promises to Bradley. After giving defective notice to Sykes, Bradley went to work for Dixon, and Sykes sued Dixon for enticement and harboring. The Court of Queen's Bench held that the actions could not be maintained. Lord Denman, C. J., was of the opinion that no contract of service existed between Sykes and Bradley:

> The contract of hiring was put in evidence, and, upon examination, it appeared, that it was all on one side. . . . [W]e are of opinion, that there was not [a contract of service], the master not undertaking to employ him, or to find him work. The answer to this objection was, that a consideration for the promise would necessarily result, because the plaintiff must have paid Bradley for his labour. But so he must have done under any contract; the work must have been balanced by the wages; but there is no consideration for the workman's hiring himself to the plaintiff exclusively.[16]

This was good news so far as workers were concerned. Where an employer had signed a worker to a term but had failed to undertake to em-

---

[13] *Beeston v. Collyer,* 4 Bing. 309, 130 Eng. Rep. 786 (1827); *Fawcett v. Cash,* 5 B. & AD. 904, 110 Eng. Rep. 1026 (1834); *Williams v. Byrn,* 6 L.J. (n.s.) (King's Bench) 239 (1837).

[14] *Lees v. Whitcomb,* 5 Bing. 34, 130 Eng. Rep. 972 (1828); *Sykes v. Dixon,* 8 L.J. (n.s.) (Queen's Bench) 102 (1839); see also *Young v. Timmins,* 9 L.J. (Exch.) 68 (1831).

[15] *Sykes v. Dixon,* 8 L.J. (n.s.) (common law) 102 (1839).

[16] Ibid., 103–4.

ploy and find that person work during the term, the employer could not be certain that he would be able to enforce the agreement. In other words, employers could not have it both ways, at least so far as formal common law contract doctrine was concerned.[17] They could not both legally bind the worker to a term and simultaneously eliminate their exposure under the contract. If they chose to eliminate the risks of long contracts by not promising to furnish an adequate quantity of work during the contract term, they could not be certain that they would be able to secure the benefits of such contracts at common law. To be certain of obtaining the benefits of a long contract they had simultaneously to assume some of the risks of such a contract.

However, there was also a downside from the worker's perspective to the common law doctrine as it then stood. The lawyer for Sykes, in arguing for the validity of the contract, had declared: "The court will imply an engagement by the master to employ the workman in this case; and if so, the engagement to employ him and to pay him wages would be a sufficient consideration for his engagement to serve."[18] The court rejected this argument. The corollary of the principle that an employer could not enforce such a contract was that the courts would refuse to imply such a promise to employ and furnish work. If the courts had been willing to imply such a promise then the contract, being valid and binding because supported by consideration, would have been enforceable. Under the doctrine as it then stood, therefore, an employee working under such a contract would be in the position of having promised to work for an employer exclusively during a term. Yet if that employer failed to furnish a reasonable amount of work, a worker would not be able to maintain an action for lost wages for the times he was not provided with work and therefore not paid.

This very issue was presented in *Williamson v. Taylor* when a coal miner brought an action in assumpsit against the owners of a coal mine for not

17 It must be emphasized, of course, that we do not know how the justices of the peace as a group treated one-sided contracts in this period. White and Henson, writing in 1823, leave the impression that in many cases long-term contracts were criminally enforced against workers, whereas employers felt free to terminate service summarily. It is possible that the justices did enforce an obligation on employers to pay lost wages where they had dismissed or laid off workers paid by the piece without cause, but we can't be certain. The actions of the justices of the peace were subject to review by the superior common law courts; as a result the views of the courts did have some impact on the practices of the local magistracy, but it is unlikely that common law contract doctrine was coextensive with these practices. It also seems quite clear that employers did in fact in many cases have it both ways, criminally enforcing long agreements while at the same time disclaiming any responsibility for finding work during the term of the contract. The common law courts did later explicitly decide, however, that common law contract doctrine requiring mutual promises applied to the validity of contracts for which criminal enforcement was sought. If such contracts were not valid and binding at common law, they could not be criminally enforced.

18 *Sykes v. Dixon*, 8 L.J. (n.s.) (common law) 102 (1839), 103.

supplying him with work during a reasonable number of working days "to wit forty days between [April 6, 1843] and the commencement of this suit, the same being reasonable working days and times . . . whereby plaintiff hath lost and been deprived of wages to a large amount . . . which he otherwise would and ought to have earned."[19] The defendants answered that they had not expressly undertaken to supply the plaintiff with work during a reasonable number of working days. At the hearing before the Queen's Bench the plaintiff's lawyer argued that "[i]t is true that the agreement contains no express contract by the defendants to the effect stated in the declaration. But such a contract arises, by necessary implication" given that the plaintiff "is to continue servant to the defendants 'during all the times the pit shall be laid off work.'"[20] "The promise," the lawyer argued, "would be implied from the relation of the parties, and the necessity of the case; the plaintiff had lost the opportunity of working for others, and must therefore be employed by the defendants or not at all."[21]

The miner had hired himself to the defendants, owners of a colliery, "as their servant, for a certain term, to wit from 5th April 1843 until 5th April 1844, to work at and in the said colliery, . . . as a hewer, for wages to be paid to plaintiff by defendants once a fortnight . . . *according to the quantity of work to be done* by plaintiff, at and after certain rates and prices." (emphasis added).[22] Under the agreement, workmen "hired shall, during all the times the pit shall be laid off work, continue the servants of the said owners, subject to their orders and directions, and liable to be employed by them at such work as they shall see fit."[23]

In his opinion, Lord Denman summarily rejected the miner's argument, declaring that, "We can judge of the meaning and intent of this agreement only by its terms: and we find nothing in them to warrant the allegation of the promise alleged in the declaration."[24] He also left little doubt about what had moved him to refuse to imply such a promise in this case:

> [T]he question is whether, upon a true construction of the agreement, the defendants were bound to keep the pit at work so as to give the plaintiff an opportunity of working and earning wages. On perusal of that agreement, we do not find anything in the terms of it, to make it imperative on the defendants to keep the pit at work

[19] *Williamson v. Taylor*, 5 Q.B. 173, 114 Eng. Rep. 1214 (1843), 1215.

[20] Ibid., 1216.

[21] From the report of the same case in 13 L.J. (n.s.) (Queen's Bench) 81 (1843), 82.

[22] From the report of the case in 5 Q.B. 173, 114 Eng. Rep. 1214 (1843), 1215.

[23] Ibid., 1216.

[24] Ibid., 1217.

any given time, or to find the plaintiff in employment all the year round.[25]

The *Williamson* case was initially tried at the 1843 Northumberland summer assizes. It is clear that it represented one front in a much wider conflict between the coal miners and coal operators of the region, a conflict over whether the operators should guarantee some minimum number of work days each fortnight to men who were bound under annual contracts. The dispute over guaranteed work had arisen on and off in the northern coal fields since the early 1830s. In 1831 the miners of Durham and Northumberland had formed themselves into a union under Tommy Hepburn's leadership and struck the northern coal fields. One of their demands had been that miners should be guaranteed a certain number of days of work each fortnight under the annual bond, which, after all, obligated them to serve their employers for an entire year. Under the existing bond the coal operators could lay off miners without pay for up to three days. The operators had been abusing this clause, and the men demanded a change:

> If [the men] are kept off work for three days, they can demand pay for the days after that, unless sent to work. To counteract this, the owners employ them the fourth day, and by that means can *cannily* keep them off the three days after without any further expense. In consequence of such conduct as this, the poor pitmen are often only employed four or five days in the fortnight.[26]

The owners resisted the miners' demands and Hepburn's union collapsed. The 1832 annual bond "excluded the guaranteed minimum wage, and although it was reintroduced in 1838 re-emerged as a central issue in the dispute of 1844."[27] In 1842 and 1843 the miners of Durham and Northumberland began to organize themselves again after a period of inactivity. By 1843, "a general spirit of revolt" had developed in the coal fields in the region.[28] In late 1843, the coal operators at a colliery in Durham had sixty-eight men arrested for breach of contract when they refused to work under unsafe conditions. The miners hired W. P. Roberts to fight their case; after a long hearing before the justices of the peace they were convicted. Roberts sued out a writ of *habeas corpus* and won their re-

---

[25] From the report of the case in 13 L.J. (n.s.) (Queen's Bench) 81 (1843), 82.

[26] Quoted in James A. Jaffe, *The Struggle for Market Power: Industrial Relations in the British Coal Industry, 1800–1840* (Cambridge, 1991), 155.

[27] Roy Church, *The History of the British Coal Industry, 1830–1913: Victorian Pre-eminence* (Oxford, 1986), 260.

[28] Friedrich Engels, *The Condition of the Working Class in England* (Stanford, Calif., 1968), 287.

lease before the Court of Queen's Bench.[29] In late 1843 and early 1844, Roberts mounted a broad legal campaign on the miners' behalf:

> Whenever a miner was sentenced by a magistrate, Roberts secured a writ of *habeas corpus* from the Court of Queen's Bench, brought his clients before the Court in London and always secured their freedom. In the Queen's Bench on January 13th, 1844, Mr. Justice Williams set free three miners who had been sentenced by the Bilston (South Staffordshire) magistrates. . . . In a previous case Mr. Justice Patteson had freed six workers, so by this time the name of Roberts was beginning to alarm the magistrates in the coalmining districts. In Preston six of Roberts's clients were in prison. Early in February he went there to look into their case only to discover that the miners had already been let out of gaol *before* completing their sentences. In Manchester seven of Roberts's clients were in prison. He applied to Mr. Justice Wightman for a writ of *habeas corpus* and secured the unconditional release of all seven miners.[30]

Roberts later observed of his activity, "When I was acting for the Colliers' Union in the North we resisted every individual act of oppression, even in cases where we were sure of losing; and the result was that in a short time there was no oppression to resist."[31]

The *Williamson* suit, brought before the Queen's Bench in November 1843, marked an attempt by the miners to win their point about a guaranteed number of work days in a court of law. Its failure sent them back to collective action. The issue of reciprocal obligations under the annual bond was a chronic source of discontent. The coal miners of the north fervently believed that justice required that they be guaranteed a certain minimum amount of work or wages each fortnight during the term, in view of the fact that the pit bond required that they "shall, during all the times the pit shall be laid off work, continue the servants of the said owners, subject to their orders and directions, and liable to be employed by them at such work as they shall see fit."[32] When the annual pit bond was about to expire in March 1844, the miners had W. P. Roberts draw up a proposed new contract. Among other matters, it provided that "Owners . . . agree to find at least four days' work a week for miners whom they regularly employed. In default of four days' work in the week the miners

---

[29] See Richard Fynes, *The Miners of Northumberland and Durham: A History of Their Social and Political Progress* (1873; reprint Sunderland, England, 1923), 37–49.

[30] Engels, *Condition of the Working Class in England,* 288.

[31] Quoted in Sidney Webb and Beatrice Webb, *The History of Trade Unionism* (London, 1920), 184.

[32] From the report of the case in 5 Q.B. 173, 114 Eng. Rep. 1214 (1843), 1216.

should receive pay for four days' work."[33] In the event, the miners could neither litigate nor negotiate their way to a general system of guaranteed work or wages in the north in 1844.[34]

This is where matters stood in the early 1840s.[35] Workers might not be bound at common law by long piece work agreements if an employer failed to promise to find them work or pay them wages during the term, precisely because the courts refused to imply such a promise.[36]

Between 1846 and 1848, however, the legal ground began to shift, as a result, at least in part, of the increasing difficulty employers were having in enforcing long piece work contracts where they had not expressly promised to find work or wages during the term. In the 1850s, building on these decisions, the position of the courts changed even more.

In *Pilkington v. Scott*, decided in 1846, employer plaintiffs sought to enforce the contract of one of their workmen by bringing an action on the case against a second employer for wrongfully harboring their servant.[37] Joseph Leigh, a crown glass maker, had signed an exclusive seven-year contract with the plaintiffs. In the agreement, the plaintiffs had promised Leigh that "during any depression of trade, he should be paid a moiety of his wages; [but] that, if he should be sick or lame, the plaintiffs should be at liberty to employ any other person in his stead without paying him any wages."[38] The contract also stipulated, however, "that the plaintiffs should pay him *when and so long as he should continue to be employed . . . wages by the*

---

[33] Engels, *Condition of the Working Class in England*, 287–88.

[34] As Engels pointed out, different collieries adopted different practices, and in some the miners were guaranteed wages during the term, although this obligation was often circumvented in practice (286). In others, wages were guaranteed should the pit be closed as the result of an accident or broken machinery. Fynes, *Miners of Northumberland and Durham*, 293–94.

[35] Lord Denman again refused to imply a promise to employ in *Aspdin v. Austin*, 5 Q.B. 671, 114 Eng. Rep. 1402 (1844), and in *Dunn v. Sayles*, 5 Q.B. 685, 114 Eng. Rep. 1408 (1844), on similar grounds.

[36] The decision in *Williamson v. Taylor* may not have sustained symmetry in practice, as it did in legal doctrine; rather, it may well have had just the opposite effect. It may well have exacerbated the injustice of the situation by making it impossible for miners to sue for lost wages where no explicit undertaking to find work had been made in a pit bond, although not altering the common practice of criminally enforcing promises to serve for a year. The symmetry of the common law doctrine, however, was not completely irrelevant to the situation on the ground.

[37] *Pilkington v. Scott*, 15 M. & W. 657, 153 Eng. Rep. 1014 (1846).

[38] Ibid., 1014. The final clause of the cited section appears to be an attempt to contract out of an old obligation imposed on masters. An 1830 edition of Richard Burn's *The Justice of the Peace and Parish Officer* (London), V:115 still included the following quote from Dalton's *Country Justice*: "If a servant retained for a year, happen within the time of his service to fall sick, or to be hurt or disabled by the act of God, or in doing his master's business; yet the master must not therefore put such servant away, nor abate any part of his wages for such time."

piece (stating them), and £8 per annum in lieu of house-rent and firing"
(emphasis added), but that they could terminate his contract by giving
him "a month's wages or a month's notice."[39] When Leigh left to take
work elsewhere the plaintiffs brought this action for harboring against
Leigh's new employer.

The defendants argued that the agreement sued on was not binding because it lacked consideration:[40]

> [T]here is no contract or stipulation on the part of the masters to em-
> ploy the party at all. They only contract to pay him wages "when
> and so long as he shall continue to be employed." That is no contract
> to employ him [citing *Aspdin v. Austin* decided two years earlier].
> Then, if so, supposing, immediately after the signing of the contract,
> the plaintiffs refuse to give him employment, he nevertheless cannot
> for seven years work for any other person.[41]

Two years earlier, in *Aspdin v. Austin* and *Dunn v. Sayles*,[42] Lord Denman
had indeed decided that a promise to employ should not be implied by
the court where it had not been expressly made in a contract. That would
impose an obligation on an employer to continue to operate a business
when it was no longer economically feasible to do so. In those cases, however, the contracts had stated that the employee was to be paid a sum certain in annual wages. Although refusing to raise a promise to employ, the
court did say that the person hired could sue on the promise to pay these
wages so long as he held himself out as ready and willing to perform the
services.[43] In the contract in the *Pilkington* case, the only sum certain mentioned was the £8 per annum in lieu of house rent and firing. For the rest,
the wages were to be by the piece for work actually done. No sum certain
in wages had been promised, and if no undertaking to give work could be
implied then, except for the promise to pay £8 per annum, there might be
no consideration to support the contract, just as the lawyer for the defendants argued. On a strict reading of *Aspdin v. Austin* and *Dunn v. Sayles*,
therefore, this agreement might well not be valid and binding, and not,
therefore, enforceable.

There was a second basic problem with the contract. The workman
was bound for the entire term, but the plaintiff employers had reserved to
themselves the power to terminate the agreement on a month's notice. In

[39] *Pilkington v. Scott*, 15 M. & W. 657, 153 Eng. Rep. 1014 (1846), 1014.

[40] Ibid., 1015.

[41] Ibid.

[42] *Aspdin v. Austin*, 5 Q.B. 671, 114 Eng. Rep. 1402 (1844); *Dunn v. Sayles*, 5 Q.B. 685, 114
Eng. Rep. 1408 (1844).

[43] *Aspdin v. Austin*, 5 Q.B. 671, 114 Eng. Rep. 1402 (1844), 1408.

Young v. Timmins, decided in 1831, such a unilateral power to determine the contract was one of the grounds for holding the contract legally invalid.[44]

The decisions in *Williamson v. Taylor, Aspdin v. Austin,* and *Dunn v. Sayles* had all been rendered by the Court of Queen's Bench. The *Pilkington* case was heard by the Court of Exchequer. A distinct change in tone occurs in Mr. Baron Alderson's opinion. He observes that in *Hitchcock v. Coker,* decided several years earlier, it had been decided that courts would not inquire into the adequacy of consideration in contracts of this kind. They would merely ask whether consideration, in legal contemplation, was present. Mr. Baron Alderson took advantage of this doctrinal shift to reduce the extent of the obligations employers would henceforth have to undertake to make contracts binding. Then, turning his back on the earlier Queen's Bench decisions, he went on to read in a promise to employ where such a promise had not explicitly been made. In doing so, however, he had the promise to pay half (piece) wages during trade depressions and the £8 per annum to rest this reading on. "All [the contractual] provisions being taken together," he concluded, "it appears to me that the agreement points clearly to an undertaking on the part of the masters to employ the workman for the seven years, subject to the notice, and on the part of the workman to serve them for that period on the same terms. That is *a reasonable bargain,* having its foundation in a good consideration, namely, *the agreement to employ him,* and the amount or the adequacy of that consideration the Court will not inquire into" (emphasis added).[45]

In a perverse twist, Mr. Baron Rolfe declared that the unilateral right to terminate the agreement on a month's notice or a month's wages, which the plaintiffs had reserved for themselves, itself implied that they had undertaken to employ the workman for the term, "else why should they introduce a power enabling them to do that upon notice, which, ex hypothesi of the other side, they might do without any notice?"[46] The crucial factors that allowed the court to uphold the contract in this case, it appears, were the plaintiffs' promises to pay £8 per annum and half piece wages during trade depressions. However, those promises fell distinctly short, as the defendant's lawyer pointed out, of an explicit undertaking to provide a reasonable amount of work during the term. The court's willingness to "read in" a promise to employ in the absence of an explicit promise represents a significant shift in the direction of implying such promises in situations where an employer had promised less, making contracts binding, and therefore enforceable, where they previously might

---

[44] *Young v. Timmins,* 9 L.J. (Exch.) 68 (1831), 74 (opinion of Mr. Baron Vaughan: "This proviso is unjust").

[45] *Pilkington v. Scott,* 15 M. & W. 657, 153 Eng. Rep. 1014 (1846), 1015.

[46] Ibid., 1016.

not have been. Because the plaintiff employers had in fact explicitly undertaken some obligations, however illusory these might have been in light of the unilateral power to determine the contract on a month's notice, this was a good case to begin to change doctrine.

In 1847 a case with even better facts arose in the glass trade and led to a similar result in the Court of Common Pleas. Thomas Pike, a glass maker, signed an exclusive seven-year contract to work for James Hartley, a glass and alkali manufacturer. The contract stipulated that Hartley would pay Pike "*so long as he continues to be employed* . . . 24s. per week, for 1,200 tables; and, for all . . . tables over and above 1200, at and after the rate of 10s. per hundred" (emphasis added) up to a maximum of 2,400 tables.[47] In addition,

> the said J. Hartley agrees to find the said Thomas Pike some other description of work, provided the said James Hartley does not require 1,200 tables, so that the wages of the said Thomas Pike shall not be less than 24s. per week, except when a furnace shall be out, when he, the said Thomas Pike, engages to work for 21s. per week.[48]

Hartley reserved the right not to pay Pike's wages if Pike became sick, lame, or incapacitated and was not able to work. He also reserved the right not to pay wages if Pike "shall not, in [Hartley's or any of his partners'] opinions, have conducted himself properly, or as he ought to do, *or if the said James Hartley, or his partner or partners . . . shall discontinue the said trade or business during the said term of seven years*" (emphasis added).[49] Pike apparently left Hartley during the term of the contract to take work with another employer, and Hartley sued the second employer for enticement and harboring.

As in *Pilkington v. Scott,* the lawyer for the second employer argued in *Hartley v. Cummings* that the contract was not valid and binding because it lacked sufficient consideration. Citing *Aspdin v. Austin,* he argued that a promise to employ could not be implied: "[T]he agreement binds the servant to work for no one else during the seven years: but it does not bind the master to employ him during that period; he may suspend the works, and yet make no remuneration to the servant."[50] However, the defendant's lawyer now had the precedent in *Pilkington v. Scott* to contend with. He also had to deal with the explicit undertakings in the contract to guarantee Pike minimum wages of 24 shillings a week even if the plaintiffs did not require 1,200 tables and the promise to pay 21 shillings per week when the furnace was out.

---

[47] *Hartley v. Cummings,* 5 C.B. 247, 136 Eng. Rep. 871 (1847), 873.

[48] From the report of the same case in 17 L.J. (n.s.) (C.P.) 84 (1847), 86.

[49] Ibid.

[50] From the report of the same case in 5 C.B. 247, 136 Eng. Rep. 871 (1847), 875.

In the event, as in *Pilkington,* the court construed the agreement as containing a promise to employ. The plaintiff employers might not have been altogether happy with this construction because it placed burdens on them that they might not have meant to undertake. The court construed the contract in this way to find sufficient consideration to support its validity:

> It is not necessary to deny that this agreement might operate in restraint of trade to an extent that would vitiate it, if it gave the plaintiff a right to keep Pike unemployed during any part of the seven years. It is enough to say that this agreement gives him no such right. The master engages to employ the workman for the seven years at a given rate of wages, except in the events that are specially provided for, viz. incapacity or misconduct of the workman, or the master ceasing to carry on the trade.[51]

Cresswell, J., went on to add, "[t]he provision as to the discontinuance of the business means a substantial and bona fide ceasing to trade, and not a mere temporary suspension."[52]

In such an event Pike need not worry about breaching the contract by taking work elsewhere, for "[u]pon the business ceasing, it follows that the agreement falls to the ground on both sides."[53] To find contracts of service for a term valid and binding and therefore enforceable, the common law courts began to move away from the position that a promise to find work would not be "read in" to a contract of service. Needless to say, this change too could be a mixed blessing for both workers and employers. The contracts of workers would be more likely to be enforced, but employers would now have an implied obligation to find work for them during the term. The remaining question was how extensive this obligation might be. In *Hartley v. Cummings* the language of the contract was read to require the employer to find work or wages for the workman during the entire seven-year period, except if the business was permanently ended.[54] The employer apparently had no right to suspend business temporarily without continuing to pay the workman the guaranteed minimum earnings he had been promised.

Just as the common law courts were beginning to change course, the decisions in some of the earlier common law cases began to filter into the arguments made over the criminal enforceability of contracts of service. On November 11, 1845, Seth Turner signed an agreement with John Darlington in which he agreed "to serve, and hires himself to the said John

---

[51] Ibid., 876 (opinion of Maule, J.).

[52] Ibid., 877 (opinion of Cresswell, J.).

[53] Ibid., 876 (opinion of Maule, J.).

[54] And except for misbehavior on the part of the workman.

Darlington exclusively as his hired servant, in the capacity of a miner, for the term of eleven calendar months."[55] Turner was to work at piece rates. On his side Darlington agreed "to accept and employ the said Seth Turner as his servant in mining, at the wages and on the terms above mentioned, exept when and so often as he may be prevented by an unavoidable or accidental damage or obstruction to any engine, gearing, or machinery, or to the said mines or any of them, or to the workings thereof."[56] Apparently, a dispute about wages arose and several men walked off the job. Proceedings were brought before a justice of the peace and the men were committed to the house of correction "there to be held to hard labour for the term of three months" for absenting themselves from their service.[57] A writ of *habeas corpus* was sued out and the men were released on bail "to abide the judgment of the Court upon the validity of the warrants of commitment."[58] Two years after W. P. Roberts had traveled all over the coal fields in the North contesting the convictions of miners, one of the arguments Bodkin made on behalf of the miners in this case was that

> the contract was altogether invalid, being an absolute binding of the servant for eleven months, to the exclusion of his employment by any other person, for a remuneration depending upon the quantity of work done; and, at the same time, with no provision binding the master to provide him with work. This is, therefore, an oppressive and unreasonable agreement, void as being in restraint of trade.[59]

The Court of Queen's Bench ordered the prisoners discharged, finding the warrants of commitment bad on other grounds. But Lord Denman also considered the miners' argument about the employer's failure to make an explicit promise to find work. It may well have been the first time this argument had been presented to him in the criminal context, because he seemed somewhat at a loss how to react, although he was clearly predisposed to react negatively. He was reported to have said that, "I should be slow to say that any opinion of ours as to the validity of this contract, on the ground of public policy, would prevent either party to it from being

---

[55] *In the matter of Turner, Ollerton, and Others*, 15 L.J. (n.s.) (mag. cases) 140 (1846), 141. There was also a provision in the contract that obligated Turner to serve beyond the eleven months if he failed to work at least eleven days in every fortnight, "such further time as shall be wanting to complete the said period of eleven days' work in each and every fortnight of the said term."

[56] Ibid.

[57] Ibid., 142.

[58] Ibid., 140.

[59] Ibid., 143. Because these contracts bound workers to serve one person exclusively for a term, they were also sometimes attacked and defended under restraint of trade doctrine. The lawyers on the other side cited *Pilkington v. Scott* among other cases in arguing for the validity of the contract (144).

amenable to the summary jurisdiction provided for the breach of it, when they have both voluntarily entered into it."[60]

However, just two years later Lord Denman did exactly what he said he should be slow to do. In a case brought to the court on a *certiorari* he quashed a conviction of a servant for absenting himself from his master's employment on the ground that the contract was "wholly void."[61] There were special circumstances in this case – the workman was a minor – but the court applied common law principles to determine whether this one-sided contract signed by a minor was valid and binding. Having found it invalid, the conviction under the Master and Servant Act was overturned. Lord Denman declared:

> Among many objections one appears to me clearly fatal. He was an infant at the time of entering into the agreement which authorizes the master to stop his wages when the steam-engine is stopped working for any cause. An agreement to serve for wages may be for the infant's benefit; but an agreement which compels him to serve at all times during the term, but leaves the master free to stop his work and his wages whenever he chooses to do so, cannot be considered as beneficial to the servant. It is inequitable and wholly void.[62]

Apparently, not only had developments in the common law of contract begun to filter into the arguments made before the courts on the question of the criminal enforceability of contracts of service, they also had begun to affect the practice of some justices of the peace.

In December 1852, Robert Whittaker had signed an agreement with Griffiths, Browett, and Goodman to serve as a tin-plate worker "and not to work for or serve any one else without their leave . . . from the date hereof during and until the full term of twelve months."[63] After the twelve months had ended, either party could terminate the agreement on three months' notice. The employers had lent and advanced 3£ to Whittaker in consideration for his signing the agreement. The loan was to be repaid through deductions from his wages of 10 shillings per week. His employers had agreed "to pay unto the said R. Whittaker on the Saturday night in every week during the aforesaid term, usual holidays excepted, *all such wages as the articles made by the said R. Whittaker . . . shall amount to at their usual workmen's prices for similar articles*" (emphasis added).[64] A little more than a month later Whittaker "left, and had ever since absented himself."[65]

[60] Ibid., 144.
[61] *The Queen v. James Lord*, 17 L.J. (n.s.) (mag. cases) 181 (1848), 183.
[62] Ibid.
[63] *The Queen v. Welch and Another*, 22 L.J. (n.s.) (mag. cases) 145 (1853), 145.
[64] Ibid.
[65] Ibid.

One of the partners obtained a summons requiring Whittaker to appear before the justices of the peace to answer for his transgression. On January 22, 1853, both the partner and Whittaker did appear. The justices "having heard the matter and examined the witnesses, refused to make and did not make any adjudication on the hearing, and also refused to order R. Whittaker to return to the service, on the ground that the agreement was bad on the face of it, for want of mutuality."[66] The partners obtained an order to have the justices of the peace show cause why they should not hear, determine, and adjudicate the complaint. The lawyer for the justices argued before the Queen's Bench that the justices "thought that the contract could not be enforced on the ground that it did not bind the employers to find employment, and they were right."[67] Invoking several of the common law decisions we have just discussed, he argued that "[i]n *Williamson v. Taylor*, the party retained endeavoured to recover for non-employment, on an agreement like this, and failed."[68] In that case "a stipulation to pay wages in proportion to the work done, was held not to warrant a contract to provide work being implied. And to the same effect is *Sykes v. Dixon*, and *Lees v. Whitcomb*."[69]

Relying on *Pilkington v. Scott*, however, which had marked a departure from earlier cases, Lord Campbell was of the opinion that looking at the agreement as a whole "it is surely *a necessary implication* that the employers shall find reasonable work for the servant as well as pay him wages for the articles which he makes" (emphasis added).[70] What was the obligation cast on employers? "To find *reasonable employment according to the state of the trade*" (emphasis added).[71] Lord Campbell concluded:

> This being so, the contract is not a unilateral one, but one binding each party to the performance of some obligation, and therefore valid. This decision does not conflict with the authorities. . . . On the contrary, I think *Pilkington v. Scott* is in point to support it. Being then a valid contract within the [master and servant] statute, it ought to be enforced, and the Justices had jurisdiction to make the order.[72]

All the justices were of this opinion.

[66] Ibid., 146.

[67] Ibid.

[68] From the report of the same case in 2 El. & Bl. 357, 118 Eng. Rep. 800 (1853), 802.

[69] From the report of the same case in 22 L.J. (n.s.) (mag. cases) 145 (1853), 146.

[70] Ibid.

[71] From the report of the same case in 2 El. & Bl. 357, 118 Eng. Rep. 800 (1853), 802.

[72] From the report of the case in 22 L.J. (n.s.) (mag. cases) 145 (1853), 147.

The lesson was driven home the next year in *Ex parte Bailey, Ex parte Collier,*[73] when a decision by the justices to enforce the contracts of two coal miners under the Master and Servant acts was upheld by the Queen's Bench in the face of a similar challenge. George Bailey and John Collier served Messrs. Marshall & Co. as colliers under a month-to-month agreement that required a month's notice to terminate. Following a dispute over wages, a strike was called. Bailey and Collier were brought before a justice of the peace for absenting themselves from their service without a month's notice in the course of this strike. After hearing the matter, the justice committed the men to the house of correction "there to remain and be held to hard labour for the term of two calendar months."[74] A writ of *habeas corpus* was applied for, and in a preliminary hearing Mr. Justice Erle discharged the men on their own recognizance pending a decision of the Court of Queen's Bench. At the hearing before the full court affidavits were presented as to the terms of the agreement. In their affidavits the men claimed that they were

> not bound under the said contract to any hours of working; nor bound to cut any quantity of coal: that the employment in the said colliery depends on the demand for coal: that there is not always full employment: that deponent[s] [are] only paid by the ton of coal: that no allowance is made for loss of time when trade is slack or the works stopped by accident.[75]

There was a serious factual disagreement about the terms of the agreement. The employers apparently found it expedient to counter the assertion made by the men that under the contract the company owed no obligation to find them work or wages during the term. In an affidavit produced by an agent for the company, it was claimed that

> if trade was slack, or works stopped by accident, the [company] *would consider themselves,* by the said contract, compelled, either to provide the said George Bailey, and the other colliers employed at their said colliery, with work, or pay them reasonable wages.[76] (emphasis added)

---

[73] 23 L.J. (n.s.) (mag. cases) 161 (1854), reported separately in 3 El. & Bl. 607, 118 Eng. Rep. 1269 (1854).

[74] From the report of the case in 3 El. & Bl. 607, 118 Eng. Rep. 1269 (1854), 1271.

[75] Ibid., 1270.

[76] Ibid., 1270–71.

It appears that the employers were not the only ones who were uneasy about the state of their case. The committing justice also seems to have been concerned that should the contract be found invalid, he would be vulnerable to an action for false imprisonment.[77]

At the hearing before the full court, Smythies argued for the miners that in *Williamson v. Taylor* it was decided by the Queen's Bench that a pit bond that had not expressly committed the company to find work or wages imposed no such obligation on the employer. As a result, Smythies noted,

> there was no consideration for the contract. The employers were not bound to find work for the prisoner; *Williamson v. Taylor* (5 Q. B. 175). It would have been a very improvident bargain if they had contracted to do so; for their colliery might be stopped by flood, or some other accident over which they had not controul.[78]

If there was no consideration for the contract "no valid contract could be inferred by the Justice."[79] Huddleston, responding on behalf of the justice of the peace, "referred to that part of the affidavit of Hutchinson in which it was stated that the employers *considered themselves bound* either to provide the men with work or pay them wages" (emphasis added).[80] Mr. Justice Crompton added that "*Regina v. Welch* [decided the previous year] and *Pilkington v. Scott* . . . go far to shew that the employers were so bound."[81]

In deciding that the contract was valid and enforceable, Lord Campbell spelled out in a little more detail the implied obligations of employers to find work or wages in such situations:

> [T]he justice was fully warranted in inferring that this was a contract to serve for a month, and to be paid according to the work done. It has been said that there was no consideration for such a contract; but I, on this evidence think that there was an obligation on the part of the employers, not merely to pay for the work done, but also to

---

[77] "J. W. Huddleston, for the committing magistrate, objected to the use of the affidavits. He stated that there was reason to believe that, if the conviction were quashed, an action would be commenced against his client . . . but he offered to waive all technical points . . . if an undertaking to bring no action were given." Ibid., 1272. Actions for false imprisonment were sometimes brought against justices of the peace. If a justice was shown not to have had jurisdiction in a case, he might be held liable for damages; see, for example, *Lancaster v. Greaves*, 9 B. & C. 628, 109 Eng. Rep. 233 (1829); *Hardy v. Ryle, Esq.*, 9 B. & C. 603, 109 Eng. Rep. 224 (1829); and *Wiles v. Cooper, Esq., and Two Others*, 3 AD. & E. 524, 111 Eng. Rep. 513 (1835).

[78] *Ex parte Bailey, Ex parte Collier*, 3 El. & Bl. 607, 118 Eng. Rep. 1269 (1854), 1272.

[79] From the report of the same case in 23 L.J. (n.s.) (mag. cases) 161 (1854), 164.

[80] From the report of the same case in 3 El. & Bl. 607, 118 Eng. Rep. 1269 (1854), 1272.

[81] Ibid.

employ the men: not, I think, necessarily to find them work day by day; but an obligation to continue the relation of master and servant; so that, if the master *causelessly refused to give the servant work whilst the colliery was open* he would have broken his contract. That obligation on the part of the master would be ample consideration for the servant's promise.[82] (emphasis added)

Earlier in the argument Lord Campbell had opined that "[i]t may very well be that they did not contract to keep their colliery open, and *yet that if, the colliery being open, they excluded the prisoner they would have broken their contract*" (emphasis added).[83] In a different report of the case, his words are reported slightly differently: "It may be that [the company was] not bound to keep open their colliery: but could they have excluded these men and taken in others to work while their colliery was open?"[84]

Eight years later the position of the court remained the same. In *Whittle v. Frankland,* a coal miner who had left work after a dispute about wages without giving the required twenty-eight days' notice (under a contract of indefinite duration determinable on twenty-eight days' notice) was brought before the justices of the peace of Rotherham. It was argued on Whittle's behalf at petty sessions, "[t]hat the agreement did not bind the masters to find work or pay wages and was therefore bad for want of mutuality."[85] "The Justices, however, were of the opinion . . . that, *by reasonable implication,* the agreement bound the masters to find work and pay wages and was a valid agreement" (emphasis added).[86] They convicted Whittle of unlawfully absenting himself from his service and committed him to one month's imprisonment with hard labor.[87] However, because a full-blown case had been mounted against the validity of the contract at petty sessions and the justices may have feared an action for false imprisonment, they sought the opinion of the Court of Queen's Bench as to whether they were correct in their determination. In the course of the argument Mr. Justice Crompton declared that "There is no case, as far as I am aware, which seems to go so far as to decide that, under a contract like the present, *if the master had work he would not be bound to give it, to a reasonable extent under surrounding circumstances*" (emphasis added).[88] In his opinion in

---

[82] Ibid., 1273–74.

[83] Ibid., 1272.

[84] From the report of the same case in 23 L.J. (n.s.) (mag. cases) 161 (1854), 164.

[85] *Whittle v. Frankland,* 31 L.J. (n.s.) (mag. cases) 81 (1862), 83. Also reported in 2 B. & S. 49, 121 Eng. Rep. 992 (1862), 993.

[86] *Whittle v. Frankland,* 2 B. & S. 49, 121 Eng. Rep. 992 (1862), 993.

[87] From the report of the same case in 31 L.J. (n.s.) (mag. cases) 81 (1862), 82.

[88] Ibid., 84.

the case Mr. Chief Justice Cockburn concluded by saying: "There is no express agreement that they will find him work, but that arises by necessary implication."[89] The justices of the peace were correct, therefore, in finding that the agreement was valid and binding, and the conviction was affirmed.

Nineteen years earlier, in 1843, a Northumberland coal miner working under an annual pit bond had tried to recover damages based on lost earnings for nonemployment during the contract term. The court told him in no uncertain terms that where an employer had not explicitly promised to provide work or wages during the contract term, the courts would not raise such a promise. He had no legal recourse against his employer for the days he was not given work.

Based on common law doctrine as it then stood, however, this coal miner could at least hope that if his employer was not bound to find him work or wages during the entire term, he would not legally be bound to serve out his term. He could hope that the courts would not sustain the criminal enforcement of *his* obligations under the contract. However, by the time the courts got around to deciding the matter, their views on the implied obligations of employers had changed enough so that by the 1850s the coal miner found that such a contract *did* bind him under criminal law. Unfortunately their views had not changed so much that they would have reversed the earlier decision refusing him lost wages for nonemployment.

By the 1850s an employer's implied obligation was to provide work, but only if circumstances in the trade allowed him, in his judgment, to do so. A contract that did not expressly bind an employer to furnish a minimum amount of work or wages in lieu of work during the term nevertheless bound a worker to his service during the entire term. After twenty-odd years of litigation on the question of reciprocal obligations, by the early 1850s the outcome was doubly unfavorable to workers.[90] Employers, it appeared, could now legally have it both ways to a greater or lesser extent. The implied obligations imposed on employers under the new doctrine were limited, but they did nevertheless exist. An employer could not *legally* dismiss a worker without just cause during the contract term. He could not *legally* dismiss an otherwise diligent worker who was promoting union activity and also could not *legally* replace a worker with another worker who was prepared to take the job for less. It is not clear how the courts would have reacted to layoff schemes in which the plant or

---

[89] Ibid., 85.

[90] I am not suggesting here that workers had been pursuing a systematic litigation strategy like the one the NAACP pursued in the United States in the twentieth century. I am suggesting only that as reciprocal obligation issues arose, were litigated, and were disposed of, the outcomes were unfavorable to workers.

mine remained open, but some workers under contract were temporarily furloughed. Temporary or even longer suspensions of all work to reduce production in light of the circumstances of the trade, or reductions in everyone's hours of work (short time), a common practice, clearly did not render contracts unenforceable against workers. However, they also did not give workers any claim for lost wages so long as an employer had not explicitly promised to provide a guaranteed minimum amount of work or minimum wages in lieu of work.

It may have been true that as a practical matter working people were no worse off than they had been twenty years earlier despite these doctrinal changes. However, this does not quite capture the full significance of these legal developments. Although organized working people had not laid out and pursued a systematic litigation strategy over the years, it was no accident that the cases arose in the order they did. In the early years, between the 1820s and mid-1840s, working people were principally focused on trying to secure a guaranteed minimum amount of work and hence a guaranteed minimum level of earnings under long contracts, *given that* they were bound criminally to serve during the entire term. White and Henson seemed to express a widespread sentiment when they wrote in 1823 that "If a master hires a servant for a length of period, he prevents him from making any other advantageous bargain until that period is transpired; and he ought to be compelled to keep that servant, who hires for the sake of the employment."[91]

Lengthy contracts, per se, and the enforcement of such contracts under master and servant laws, do not appear to have been regarded by working people as the main problem during this period. Workers often viewed such contracts as beneficial. In certain cases they even struggled against their employers to maintain long contracts. What was a source of discontent for them at this time was that employers were circumventing their perceived responsibilities under these long contracts.[92] In the line of cases

---

[91] White and Henson, *A Few Remarks on the State of the Laws*, 49.

[92] There is now an extensive literature dealing with the subject of "implicit contracts" in labor relations. These contracts represent implicit bargains between workers and employers that in exchange for a worker's loyalty and best efforts an employer will guarantee the worker a steady income over the course of the trade cycle, with layoffs occurring only where absolutely necessary. We have been dealing with explicit rather than implicit contracts here, but workers appear to have believed that these explicit contracts contained an implicit guarantee. Even though an employer had not expressly promised to provide a minimum amount of work or wages in lieu of work during the contract term, workers seem to have believed that such an undertaking should have been implicit, given that they were explicitly bound for the term. In the end courts appear to have agreed, imposing on employers an implicit obligation to provide a reasonable amount of work given the circumstances of the trade. In a sense workers seem to have believed that employers were violating this implicit contract lodged within an explicit contract by employing them too little during the term. The courts did not really remedy this problem by imposing an

we have just reviewed the legal attempt to impose on the coal masters an implied legal obligation to provide work or wages came first. It was only after this legal battle had been lost that the enforcement of lengthy contracts against workers under the Master and Servant acts began to seem more problematical. If employers were not legally bound to provide some guaranteed minimum amount of work or wages in lieu of work during the term, why should workers be bound to their employers for the entire term? When the courts nevertheless found that they were, this result may well have been one of the factors that contributed to a basic redefinition of the terms of struggle. In the 1860s working people began to demand fundamental reform of the Master and Servant acts. What began as an effort to secure guaranteed minimum earnings under long contracts ended with the feeling that the law was basically inequitable. It bound workers criminally to their contracts for the entire term while employers were legally free to provide work or not provide work as they saw fit given the circumstances of the trade.

It seems unlikely that by themselves these narrow legal developments could have produced such a change in sentiment. However, in combination with a number of other small and large developments that had taken place over the period since the 1820s, they may have had enough cumulative weight to deflect the path of historical inertia. They may have begun to induce working people to reconsider the value of long piece work contracts when no promise to find work or wages had been made, perhaps reinforcing a trend toward shorter contract terms. They also may have begun to induce workers seriously to question the entire justification for being held criminally to their agreements in the first place. That justification had drawn whatever legitimacy it may have possessed in the minds of working people from the obligations that were supposed to bind employers and employees to one another reciprocally. The actions of the common law judges may have served to buttress an unfair system by giving it the imprimatur of law, but in the process may also have begun to undercut one of the main rationales for penal sanctions. This was especially dangerous by the 1850s because working people had begun to find their voices, were beginning to establish permanent trade unions, and were striking not only to improve their material conditions but also for a say in the terms of work.

anemic implicit duty that left employers free to do pretty much as they saw fit while workers continued to be strictly bound. We might in fact expect employers to defect from these implicit contracts more often under the circumstances because much of what they could hope to accomplish through implicit contracts, reductions in turnover and agency costs, could be accomplished instead through the strict enforcement of the explicit contract under the Master and Servant acts. On implicit contracts, see generally Morley Gunderson and W. Craig Riddell, *Labour Market Economics,* 3d ed. (Toronto, 1993), 289–97.

COVERAGE OF THE MASTER
AND SERVANT ACTS

Struggles over the interpretation of the master and servant rules in this period were not limited to the issue of the reciprocal obligations of employers and employees. A second major battle was fought in the courts over the precise coverage of the Master and Servant acts. Which kinds of workers fell under the acts and were therefore exposed to criminal liability for contract breaches, and which kinds fell outside the acts and could escape criminal liability? The most important aspect of this battle was the status of piece or task workers who had not been hired for any term. This was a significant issue, because an important segment of the skilled work force in this period was employed in the putting out system or inside a shop as task workers not engaged to serve for a term.[93]

Like the issue of reciprocal obligations, the issue of piece or task work was also a subject of political controversy. Peter Moore's failed 1823 effort to reform master and servant law included, as one of its most important proposals, that piece and task workers be freed from criminal liability for failing to finish their work on giving fourteen days' written notice of their desire to terminate their employment. The status of piece and task work was another one of the issues that defined the boundaries within which the struggles over the Master and Servant acts were taking place in the period between the 1820s and the 1850s. On this issue also workers eventually lost in the courts, one more factor leading them to move the struggle over the Master and Servant acts beyond the narrow channels to which it had been confined.

Most of the litigation over piece and task work arose under 4 Geo. IV, c. 34 (1823), the newest comprehensive Master and Servant Act. By its terms the statute covered the following categories of workers: "any Servant in Husbandry, or *any Artificer,* Calico Printer, *Handicraftsman,* Miner, Collier, Keelman, Pitman, Glassman, Potter, *Labourer, or other Person"* (emphasis added).[94] Two important questions were raised by the statute: Were the words of general description restricted only to persons employed in the specific trades listed, or were they meant to include all artificers, all laborers? and Whatever kinds of workers were covered, what did such workers have to do to bring themselves within the act? The statute provided that if any of the specified workers

> shall *contract* with any Person or Persons whomsoever, *to serve him,* her,
> or them *for any Time or Times whatsoever, or in any other manner,* and shall
> not enter into or commence his or her Service according to his or her

---

[93] F. M. L. Thompson, *The Rise of Respectable Society: A Social History of Victorian Britain, 1830–1900* (London, 1988), 31–40.

[94] 4 Geo. IV, c. 34, s. II. (1823).

Contract (such Contract being in Writing, and signed by the contracting Parties), or having entered into such Service shall absent
himself or herself from his or her Service *before the Term of his or her
Contract . . . shall be completed, or neglect to fulfill the same,* or be guilty of
any other Misconduct or Misdemeanor in the Execution thereof
[then such person may be committed by a magistrate to the house of
correction].[95] (emphasis added)

The wording of the 1823 act followed closely the wording in an earlier
statute, enacted in 1747 and amended in 1757.[96] The first important nineteenth-century case that tested the scope of the Master and Servant acts,
in fact, arose under the earlier act.

In 1806, G. Lowther brought an action in trespass against two justices
of the peace. It was alleged that they lacked jurisdiction to order him to
pay wages to one J. Sopp, who had been employed by him to dig and
stean (line with rocks) a well. Sopp had engaged another workman to help
him complete the project and was to pay this workman out of his wages.
When Lowther refused to pay Sopp following the justices' order,[97] they
followed up with a distress warrant, which was executed against his
goods. The trespass alleged in the suit was for this act, ordered by justices
who, it was argued, did not have jurisdiction over the matter.

Lord Ellenborough decided that the justices did have jurisdiction, and
in the course of his opinion made two important rulings. First, the term
"labourer" in the Master and Servant Act was not confined to laborers in
the specific trades mentioned in the act, but extended to all laborers.[98]
Moreover, the fact that Sopp had retained another workman to work under him did not negate his status as a laborer, for this was "a common
practice with labourers as well in husbandry as in other business."[99]

Second, the act covered "labourers employed for any certain time, *or in
any other manner.* The latter words are as general as may be; and we cannot
find any reason in law or policy to say that they do not comprehend the
case of Sopp" (emphasis added)[100] who "was employed to do the work
either by the day or the piece."[101]

---

[95] Ibid.

[96] 20 Geo. II, c. 19 (1747), amended by 31 Geo. II, c. 11 (1757). After the 1757 amendment,
the main differences between the 1823 act and the 1747 act were that the 1747 act did
not include calico printer and instead of the words, "labourer, or other person" contained the words "and other labourers." The 1747 act also required whipping on commitment to the house of correction, whereas the 1823 act did not authorize whipping.

[97] *Lowther v. Radnor*, 8 East 113, 103 Eng. Rep. 287 (1806) (order was affirmed on appeal to
Quarter Sessions), 288.

[98] Ibid., 291.

[99] Ibid., 290.

[100] Ibid., 291.

[101] Ibid., 290.

In the 1820s, however, a shift began to take place as the Court of King's Bench developed a more restrictive reading of the Master and Servant acts. The first important case to come before the courts in this period, however, did not require the judges directly to confront Lord Ellenborough's decision. *Branwell v. Penneck*, like *Lowther v. Radnor*, was an action for trespass brought by an aggrieved employer against a justice of the peace for wrongfully distraining his goods pursuant to an order to pay wages. In this case, however, the person who had originally complained to the justice for his wages was not a manual laborer. He had been engaged by Branwell, a lawyer, to keep possession of certain goods seized under a *fieri facias* issued by Branwell on behalf of one of his clients. When Branwell refused to pay him for his efforts, he sought the assistance of a justice of the peace.

All the justices of the Court of King's Bench thought that the local magistrate lacked jurisdiction in this case. The case had arisen under the 1747 statute,[102] and Mr. Justice Bayley was of the opinion that "the Legislature had principally in view outdoor work or country labour. . . . In the present case, there was no work or labour done."[103] Mr. Justice Holroyd thought that if the construction of the act contended for by the justice of the peace were adopted, "I know not how we could say that its provisions do not extend to bankers' or merchants' clerks, and other persons of that description."[104] Mr. Justice Littledale declared that, "The words other labourers . . . are only applicable to persons of the same description as those specially mentioned," by which he seems to have meant workers in the trades or those performing manual tasks.[105] The Master and Servant acts would apply to a range of workers who performed manual labor in the trades and in agriculture but not to a range of other workers like clerks or higher servants who did not fall under the categories laborer, artificer, or handicraftsman.

Two years later, the issue of piece and task work was presented squarely to the Court of King's Bench, and the justices began to trim back Lord Ellenborough's decision, adopting a more restrictive reading of the applicability of the Master and Servant acts to piece and task workers. In 1828 Lancaster brought an action against Greaves, a justice of the peace, for trespass and false imprisonment. Lancaster had been brought before the magistrate by one Ullock, with whom he had contracted in writing "to make and complete a new carriage road . . . for the sum of 27£, . . . the said road was to be completed . . . before the latter end of the month

---

[102] 20 Geo. II, c. 19 (1747).

[103] *Branwell v. Penneck*, 7 B. & C. 536, 108 Eng. Rep. 823 (1827), 824–25.

[104] Ibid., 825.

[105] Ibid., 825.

of November."[106] In one report of the case, it was said that the extent of the work would have required Lancaster to employ twenty laborers.[107] Lancaster performed part of the work but did not finish it; the magistrate convicted him of absenting himself from his service and committed him to jail for one month. Lancaster's suit for trespass and false imprisonment came before the Court of King's Bench in 1829, posing the question: Did the magistrate have jurisdiction over the case under the Master and Servant Act, 4 Geo. IV, c. 34, s. 3 (1823)?

Lord Tenterden was of the opinion that for a magistrate to have jurisdiction under the act, "it must appear that the *relation* of master and servant has been established. The information in the present case did not shew this, but that [Lancaster and Ullock] stood in the situation of two contracting parties for the making of a road" (emphasis added).[108]

Evidently, Lord Tenterden believed that contracts of service were a distinct species of contract. Contracts of service in his mind apparently still represented a means of entering a legal status, the master and servant "relation," which legally subordinated one party to the other party. Other species of contracts were apparently made and implemented between people who started out and remained juridical equals. Mr. Justice Littledale thought that this view of the Master and Servant Act could be supported by the language in the statute that spoke of "labourers or other persons having *contracted to serve*" (emphasis added).[109] But what precisely made a contract a contract to serve as opposed merely to a contract between two parties to perform some task that called for manual labor? Mr. Justice Parke observed that, "There may indeed be a service, not for any specific time or wages, but to be within the statute there must be a contract for service *to the party exclusively*. Here there was no such contract but a contract to make a certain road for a certain price" (emphasis added).[110]

Task work might be brought under the statute, in Mr. Justice Parke's view, if the task worker agreed to work exclusively for the employer during the time it took to complete the task. The distinction, it appears, between being inside and outside the master and servant relation turned on whether workers left themselves free to accept work from more than one employer. If they had not made an exclusive commitment they could not have placed their labor under any one person's control. One could not, apparently, serve more than one master at a time. In this view, alienating one's labor to another person exclusively implied that one had turned over control of one's energies and person to another person to some de-

---

[106] *Lancaster v. Greaves*, 9 B. & C. 628, 109 Eng. Rep. 233 (1829), 234.

[107] Report of the same case in 7 L.J. 116 (mag. cases) (1829), 116.

[108] Report of the same case in 9 B. & C. 628, 109 Eng. Rep. 233 (1829), 234.

[109] Ibid.

[110] Ibid., 234–35.

gree and that the enforcement of the agreement against one's person was little more than the logical corollary of this act of self-alienation.

In this case, the fact that the job required Lancaster to employ lots of other men may also have influenced the court's decision. It would imply that the contract did not bind his labor personally; he was merely obligated to produce a road, however he could manage to get that done. The justice, it was found, lacked jurisdiction under the 1823 Master and Servant Act.

Lancaster v. Greaves carved out a category of independent contractor that allowed a certain category of persons who contracted to make or do things, especially those who employed others in the process, to retain their bodily separateness, quite literally their personal independence. *Hardy v. Ryle,* decided by the King's Bench in the same year, carved out an even larger exemption, placing home piece workers beyond the reach of the 1823 Master and Servant Act. This decision posed a serious challenge to labor discipline in the putting out system as a whole.

Henry Hardy, a home silk weaver, had agreed with Thomas Hall on October 10, 1827, that he would weave into silk crape certain materials furnished to him by Thomas Hall. But on October 20, it was alleged, Henry Hardy "did neglect the said service before the whole of the said materials were so woven . . . and did leave the same in an unfinished state . . . the said Henry Hardy hath . . . neglected to fulfil the said contract."[111] Hardy was brought before a justice of the peace, convicted of the offence, and committed to the house of correction to "be held to hard labour for the space of one month."[112] When he was released, he brought an action for trespass and false imprisonment against Ryle, the justice of the peace who had convicted and committed him. The case was tried at the Cheshire Summer Great Sessions for 1828. Having been nonsuited there, Hardy's lawyer obtained a rule *nisi* to set the nonsuit aside or to enter a verdict for the plaintiff. The King's Bench scheduled the case to be heard beginning in April 1829. Someone in parliament must have been watching the progress of the case, because before the King's Bench got around to hearing the substantive jurisdictional claim, which it did ultimately hear on July 2, 1829, Parliament acted.

The 1823 Master and Servant Act, under which Hardy had been convicted, did not specifically list silk weavers. On June 19, 1829, just before Hardy received his hearing, 10 Geo. IV, c. 52 became law and remedied this omission by amending the 1823 act. It extended the 1823 act to all persons mentioned in an earlier statute, 17 Geo. III, c. 56 (1777), and that earlier statute did include "silk manufacturers." But if Parliament thought

---

[111] *Hardy v. Ryle,* 7 L.J. (mag. cases) 118 (1829), 118–19.
[112] Ibid., 119.

that it had foreclosed an adverse decision from the King's Bench by taking this step, it was sadly mistaken.

In issuing his opinion in the case, Mr. Justice Bayley began by saying that, "It is not necessary to decide whether the act 4 Geo. 4. c. 34 (the 1823 act) does apply to persons employed in the silk trade"[113] because there were other grounds for finding that the justice of the peace lacked jurisdiction. Justice Bayley continued,

> it is clear to me that the party, to come within [the 1823 act] must not only be a person within the descriptions enumerated, but must also have contracted to serve, or have entered the complainant's service. But there is a plain distinction between a contract to receive and to act as a servant, and a contract between individuals that, for a sum certain, specified work shall be done. A man might contract with many different persons to do work for all, and by so doing would not properly be brought within the meaning of this act, and could not be said to have contracted to serve each; for where a party is a servant, he is so exclusively to one master.[114]

Mr. Justice Parke, wanting to limit the potential scope of the decision, pointed out that a master and servant relation could be established on the basis of an agreement to do specified work for a sum certain, but it would have to be clear that the service was to be exclusive while the work was being done. "The service contemplated by the act," Mr. Justice Parke noted, "is a service for a definite time, *or till some particular thing is done*. . . . It does not appear that the party was in Hall's service for this particular purpose"(emphasis added).[115]

It is not clear what Parliament intended in passing the 1823 act, although its 1829 amendment of the act suggests that it wanted home silk weavers included. It is certainly the case, nevertheless, that the language of the statute was broad enough to support a reading that would have included piece workers: "contract . . . to serve . . . for any Time or Times whatsoever, *or in any other manner . . . neglect to fulfill same*" (emphasis added).[116] By projecting its version of the common law master and servant relationship onto the act, the court generated a restrictive interpretation of its coverage.[117]

---

[113] Ibid., 122.

[114] Ibid.

[115] Ibid., 123.

[116] 4 Geo. IV, c. 34 (1823).

[117] The precise boundaries of the common law master and servant relationship in the case of home workers was itself a subject on which judges could disagree. In *Hart v. Aldridge*, 1 Cowp. 54, 98 Eng. Rep. 964 (1774), a common law enticement action, Lord Mansfield and Mr. Justice Aston appeared to differ on the question. "I think," Lord Mansfield said

Whatever Parliament may or may not have intended in passing the 1823 act, there was no question that in other Master and Servant acts it had specifically subjected domestic piece workers to criminal liability for breaches of their agreements. The 1777 Master and Servant Act covered outworkers explicitly. It provided that "if any Person, being hired, retained, or employed, to prepare or work up any Materials . . . shall wilfully neglect or refuse the Performance thereof for eight Days successively" (after notice), he could be brought before two or more justices of the peace and if convicted committed to the house of correction to be kept at hard labor for up to three months.[118] Mr. Justice Littledale, recognizing that outworkers such as Hardy were covered by the 1777 act, observed that that act "does not apply [in this case], for the party was not punished for neglecting his work for eight days."[119]

It is difficult to say what the consequences of the decision in *Hardy v. Ryle* actually were. If employers and justices of the peace were sophisticated enough to frame prosecutions and convictions in the proper way, domestic piece workers in the specified trades would have continued to be subject to the discipline of the criminal law.[120] On the other hand, it is not clear that magistrates did interpret the decision this way. Some may have interpreted the decision to foreclose prosecutions of outworkers altogether. It is difficult to reach firm conclusions one way or the other. What does seem clear is that this decision and several later ones seem to have

on the one hand, "the point turns upon the jury finding that the persons enticed away were employed by the plaintiff as his journeymen. It might perhaps have been different if the men had taken work from every body and after the plaintiff had employed them the defendant had applied to them, and they had given the preference to him in point of time. For if a man lived in his own house and took in work for different people it would be a strong ground to say that he was not the journeymen of any particular master." On the other hand, Mr. Justice Aston thought that "even supposing, as my Lord has stated, that the servant did live in his own house, if he were employed to finish a certain number of shoes for a particular person by a fixed time, and a third person enticed him away, I think an action would lie. If not, it might be of very bad consequence in trade" (964–65).

[118] 17 Geo. III, c. 56, s. VIII (1777).

[119] From the report of *Hardy v. Ryle* in 9 B. & C. 603, 109 Eng. Rep. 224 (1829), 228. The 1777 act, however, only listed about a dozen specific trades although it included most of the major ones.

[120] We know from the testimony of George Odger in 1866 that shoemakers were being prosecuted under the 1777 act at that date; see Select Committee on Master and Servant, 1866, XIII:Q. 1813. In 1843 Parliament adopted a new home worker statute. It repealed the 1777 act as it applied to a number of trades, silk hosiery manufactures included, and softened the penalties for breach of contract in those trades, substituting an initial fine for immediate imprisonment. Imprisonment could follow, however, if the fine was not promptly paid; see 6 & 7 Vict., c. 40, s. VII. However, trades not named in the new act continued to be covered by the 1777 statute. Iron and leather manufacturers were among those who continued to be subject to the 1777 act.

had a symbolic impact beyond what we might have expected. Certain elements in the working classes apparently came to believe that as a result of these decisions piece workers were simply not covered by the Master and Servant acts.[121] This is discussed more fully below.

At the time, the stakes with respect to outwork were quite high. Up to 1850, 100,000 woolen handloom weavers and 50,000 cotton handloom weavers were employed, most of them outworkers.[122] "The silk industry grew rather rapidly from the 1830s, practically doubling its workforce between then and the early 1860s; at that time nearly two thirds, or about 100,000 people, were domestic outworkers, chiefly weavers."[123] F. M. L. Thompson has described the integral relationship between the growth of the factory and the growth of domestic outwork in England in this period:

> Industrialization, even considered in the restrictive and potentially misleading sense as something that happened simply to manufacturing industry rather than to all sectors of the economy, was far from being a one-way procession into the factory. Mechanization of one sector or process in an industry, and its move into the factory could well generate increased demand for hand work and outwork in other sectors. The classic example was in the cotton industry, where from the later eighteenth century the rise of spinning mills had led to an enormous expansion in the number of handloom weavers, most of them outworkers.[124]

Over the next decade, the King's Bench continued to maintain a restrictive view of the powers of the justices of the peace in resolving master and servant disputes. In 1835, in *Wiles v. Cooper*, local magistrates had ordered an employer imprisoned when he failed to pay the wages the justices had ordered paid to a carpenter who had done work for him. The magistrates had the employer imprisoned on the basis of powers given to them in an act of Parliament, 5 Geo. IV, c. 18, s. 25 (1824), entitled "An Act for the More Effectual Recovery of Penalties before the Justices and Magistrates on Conviction of Offenders."[125] After spending eight days in prison, Wiles paid the money that was due and was released. He promptly sued the justices for trespass and false imprisonment. As the case was presented to the King's Bench, there were two principal issues. First, did the 1823 act cover carpenters working under the terms on which this carpenter had been engaged? Second, did the recent act of Parliament empower justices

---

[121] See Hansard's *Parl. Debates*, 74, 517–31 (May 1, 1844).

[122] F. M. L. Thompson, *Rise of Respectable Society*, 31–33.

[123] Ibid., 34.

[124] Ibid., 31.

[125] *Wiles v. Cooper*, 3 AD. & E. 524, 111 Eng. Rep. 513 (1835), 513–14.

of the peace to imprison employers for failing to obey wage payment orders? The Court of King's Bench did not reach the substantive question of jurisdiction because it disposed of the case on the basis of the threshold issue. It ruled that the recent act of Parliament was "applicable to the case of penalties and forfeitures, and *not* to that of orders for the payment of wages" (emphasis added).[126] I include this decision because it played a role in a parliamentary bill that was introduced in 1844 in an effort to reverse this and several other crucial King's Bench decisions that were handed down beginning in 1827.

Over the course of the next few years the King's (beginning in 1837 Queen's) Bench continued to hand down similar decisions. In 1837, the court heard a case in which a domestic servant was bringing an action for false imprisonment against a local magistrate for having imprisoned her for breaching her contract.[127] The court reaffirmed several centuries of precedents by holding that the 1766 Master and Servant Act[128] did not cover domestic servants.[129] In his opinion, however, Lord Denman arguably moved to overturn Lord Ellenborough's earlier ruling that the words of general expression in the Master and Servant acts were not limited to the specific trades listed in the act: "We find ourselves compelled to say that the 'other persons' are not all persons whatever who enter into engagements to serve for stated periods, but persons of the same description as those enumerated; and that the generality of the words must have been so restricted."[130]

Some of what had been going on in the King's Bench must have filtered down to the justices of the peace. If nothing else, their vulnerability to actions for false imprisonment would probably have induced them to keep abreast of the proceedings in the King's Bench. For example, in 1838 a justice of the peace dismissed the complaint of an employer who had contracted with a person to build some houses for him. The magistrate's dismissal of the action probably reflected his understanding of recent developments.[131]

The narrowest reading of the 1747 and 1823 acts with respect to task work was still to come. In 1839, William Johnson was brought before Mr. Justice Williams pursuant to a writ of *habeas corpus* asking to be discharged from the house of correction at Brixton. Johnson had been committed to "the said house of correction, there to remain, and be *corrected* and held to

---

[126]　Ibid., 516 (opinion of Lord Denman).

[127]　*Kitchen v. Shaw*, 6 AD. & E. 729, 112 Eng. Rep. 280 (1837).

[128]　6 Geo. III, c. 25 (1766).

[129]　*Kitchen v. Shaw*, 6 AD. & E. 729, 112 Eng. Rep. 280 (1837), 281–82.

[130]　Ibid., 282 (opinion of Lord Denman).

[131]　*West v. Smallwood*, 7 L.J. (n.s.) (common law) 144 (1838).

hard labour for the space of six weeks" (emphasis added)[132] for leaving his work unfinished and for leaving his employer's service without permission. Johnson was a calico printer who worked on the premises of his employer. His employer supplied him with materials, and he was paid according to the work he turned out, not by the day or week, a common arrangement.[133] His case was different from Thomas Hardy's in that Johnson did not work at home and was probably only taking work from the person on whose premises he was employed, at least for the time he was working there. However, there was no explicit agreement that this was to be an exclusive contract with his employer, and Johnson had not explicitly been engaged for any term.

Under Mr. Justice Parke's view of the 1823 act, set out in his opinion in *Hardy v. Ryle* ("service till some particular thing is done"),[134] it seems likely that Johnson would have been subject to criminal liability. But Mr. Justice Williams did not read *Hardy v. Ryle* and *Lancaster v. Greaves* this way. Because there was no agreement that Johnson was to work exclusively for his employer, it "was nothing more or less than a contract to perform a particular work, wholly distinct from entering into a service in the familiar meaning of the term. It is clear, that this contract might have been performed, and yet the prisoner might notwithstanding his engagement . . . have entered into divers other contracts with, and been working for divers other persons at the same time."[135] Johnson was ordered discharged from

132 *Johnson v. Reid,* 7 L.J. (n.s.) (mag. cases) 25 (1840), 26 (false imprisonment action brought by Johnson against committing justice of the peace). Johnson's lawyer questioned the authority of the justice to order the whipping in an earlier *habeas* proceeding, but the court did not decide that issue; see *The Queen v. William Johnson,* 7 L.J. (n.s.) (mag. cases) 27 (1839), 28–29. The 1747 statute had authorized correction as part of the punishment following commitment to the house of correction for "any misdemeanor, miscarriage or ill-behaviour" by a worker for which his master had complained to the justice of the peace ("to punish the Offender by Commitment to the House of Correction, there to remain *and be corrected,* and held to hard Labour for a reasonable Time, not exceeding one Calendar Month" [emphasis added]) 20 Geo. II, c. 19 (1747). The 1823 statute did *not* contain this language, and Johnson's lawyers had argued that Johnson had been committed under the latter statute and could not therefore be punished with whipping. It was not unheard of during the first several decades of the nineteenth century for justices of the peace to order workers whipped on commitment to the house of correction under the 1747 statute; see *The King v. Hoseason,* 14 East 605, 104 Eng. Rep. 734 (1811), and Douglas Hay, "Patronage, Paternalism, and Welfare: Masters, Workers, and Magistrates in Eighteenth-Century England," *International Labor and Working Class History* 53 (Spring 1998): 39–43.

133 For these facts, see *Johnson v. Reid,* 7 L.J. (n.s.) (mag. cases) 25 (1840), 26.

134 *Hardy v. Ryle,* 7 L.J. (mag. cases) 118 (1829), 123 (opinion of Mr. Justice Parke).

135 *The Queen v. William Johnson,* 7 L.J. (n.s.) (mag. cases) 27 (1839), 29.

the house of correction[136] and promptly proceeded to sue the justice of the peace for false imprisonment.[137]

The Queen v. Johnson represents the high water mark of the court's restriction of the 1747 and 1823 acts in the case of piece workers. This decision arguably freed from liability under these acts any person who worked by the piece in any shop or factory but who had not expressly undertaken to work for his or her employer exclusively until certain tasks were completed, or for some period of time. Johnson's was a very common form of hiring in the trades, piece work for no stated term. Parliament had long imposed the obligation on piece workers under the Master and Servant acts to finish the work they had undertaken, regardless of whether a piece worker might also be in a position to accept work from other employers.

In 1843 Parliament reacted to the accumulated weight of these decisions. It enacted 6 & 7 Vict., c. 40, amending the 1777 act (17 Geo. III, c. 56), among others. The 1843 act, however, only covered piece workers in seven listed trades. The 1777 act continued to apply to a number of other trades.[138] With respect to the listed trades, the 1843 act was as explicit as Parliament could make it. The first part of section VII covered domestic outworkers in the same way the 1777 act had, requiring them, if requested, to work up and return materials within a prescribed period, in this case seven days.[139] The second part of section VII went further. It was directed at persons who

> shall contract or engage to *work . . . in any of the said Manufactures . . .* either by himself *or by* any Person or *Persons to be employed by or under him,* and whether such Contract or Engagement shall be to work or be employed for any *Person exclusively, or for all or Part of his Time, or for specific Work, or otherwise, and whether such Person is to be paid according to the Value or Amount of the Work done, the Time employed, or in any other Manner whatsoever, and shall neglect to fulfil such contract or Engagement, or absent himself from such Work or Employment* before such notice (if any) as shall have been agreed upon between the said Parties. . . . [such person shall be subject to a fine and in default of payment imprisonment].[140] (emphasis added)

---

[136] Ibid.

[137] *Johnson v. Reid,* 7 L.J. (n.s.) (mag. cases) 25 (1840).

[138] "Manufacture of Hats, and in the Woolen, Linen, Fustian, Cotton, Iron, Leather, Fur, Hemp, Flax, Mohair, and Silk Manufactures; [also] Journeymen Dyers" 17 Geo. III, c. 56 (1777). 6 & 7 Vict., c. 40 (1843) repealed the 1777 act as it applied to "Woolen, Worsted, Linen, Cotton, Flax, Mohair, and Silk Hosiery," leaving the hat, iron, leather, fur, and hemp trades and journeymen dyers to be regulated by the 1777 act.

[139] 6 & 7 Vict., c. 40 (1843).

[140] Ibid.

It appears that Parliament was trying to cover all the bases, bringing all workers employed on any terms in these trades within the scope of the act and implicitly overturning a series of King's Bench decisions, at least with respect to the specific trades. However, in 1844 an even more ambitious bill was introduced. It was designed to amend the comprehensive 1823 act, along with the main eighteenth-century Master and Servant acts. It was styled "A Bill For Enlarging the Powers of Justices in Determining Complaints between Masters, Servants and Artificers, and for the More Effectual Recovery of Wages before Justices."[141]

Cleverly, this bill was presented as an attempt to extend the wage recovery jurisdiction of justices of the peace, a pro-worker bill. Indeed, the bill would have extended the jurisdiction of justices in cases of wage recovery, but it would simultaneously have extended their jurisdiction in the case of worker contract breaches. After reciting the earlier acts, the bill presented a clause that made it easier for workers to recover wages from absentee employers. Then it continued:

> And whereas doubts have arisen whether the word "Labourers," expressed in the said several recited Acts [20 Geo. 2, c. 19 (1747), 31 Geo. 2, c.11 (1757), 6 Geo. 3. c. 25 (1766), 4 Geo. 4, c. 34 (1823)], and also whether the words "or other person," mentioned and expressed in the said two last mentioned Acts, extend or apply to any Labourers or other persons, except such as are employed in the various trades enumerated in the same several Acts, *or to any cases except where the relation of Master and Servant exists.* . . . For obviating such Doubts Be it Enacted and Declared [that the several recited acts] *and all and every the powers, authorities, clauses and matters therein contained,* so far as the same affect, concern or relate to Labourers, or other persons, *shall . . . extend, and be deemed and construed to extend,* and apply *to all Labourers and other persons, although not employed in any of the trades enumerated in the said several recited Acts, and although the relation of Master and Servant may not actually subsist between such Labourers, or other persons, and their Employers.*[142] (emphasis added)

This was a lawyer's bill. It would have quietly extended criminal liability under the 1823 and earlier acts to persons who had been exempted from liability by the decisions in *Hardy v. Ryle* and *The Queen v. Johnson*. It would also have enacted into law Parliament's own interpretation of the words of general expression contained in earlier acts, rendering irrelevant Lord Denman's gloss of those words in *Kitchen v. Shaw*. The bill, however, certainly did include benefits for working people. Besides making it easier to recover wages from absentee employers and extending wage recovery

---

[141] *Parl. Papers* (1844), III:223.

[142] Ibid., 225–26.

jurisdiction to the workers who would now also be subject to criminal liability, the bill also proposed to reverse the decision in *Wiles v. Cooper*. It would have given justices of the peace authority to use "An Act for the More Effectual Recovery of Penalties" in the case of orders for the recovery of wages.[143]

The bill was subtle enough so that it was greeted as "harmless,"[144] but the government was not satisfied. When the bill was sent to committee for amendment, the government took it over and rewrote it. The new text made explicit what had been veiled and created a political firestorm in the process. The amended bill now sought to repeal all the earlier comprehensive Master and Servant acts and to replace them with this new bill. It was motivated, the preamble stated, by the "doubts [that] have arisen concerning the interpretation of the [earlier] Statutes."[145] A very broad wage recovery clause appeared first. Then the clause covering breaches by workers was set forth:

> if any Servant, *Workman*, Labourer or *other person* shall contract to serve *or work* for any other person, and . . . shall absent himself or herself therfrom before the term of his or her contract *or before the work contracted to be performed shall be completed*, or shall be guilty of any other misbehaviour concerning such service or employment . . . [then if convicted by a justice of the peace up to two months in common gaol].[146] (emphasis added)

The language was comprehensive, although it is not at all clear that it would have accomplished more than the earlier bill would have. The amended bill was presented on March 13, 1844, just as the miners of Northumberland and Durham were preparing for their great strike of that year. When it became known that this bill was pending before Parliament,

---

[143] Ibid., 227. The bill continued to exempt domestic servants from coverage under the Master and Servant acts (226–27).

[144] Engels, *Condition of the Working Class*, 319. The Webbs were of the same view; see *History of Trade Unionism*, 185.

[145] *Parl. Papers* (1844), III:229.

[146] Ibid., 230–31 (clause 4). The bill did not require that contracts be in writing to be enforceable before a worker had actually entered his or her employment, as the 1823 act required. The bill did include provisions favorable to labor. Not only was there a broad wage recovery clause (clause 2); but maximum sentences were reduced to two months (clause 4); the process against workers was normally to commence by the issuance of a summons rather than an arrest warrant (clause 5) (a procedural change later enacted into law by Jervis's Act, 11 & 12 Vict., c. 43 [1848]); wage recovery against absentee employers was made easier (clause 6); the "Act for the More Effectual Recovery of Penalties, etc." was extended to wage recovery orders, reversing the decision in *Wiles v. Cooper* (clause 9); appeals to Quarter Sessions were to be allowed (clause 10) (the 1823 act had made the orders of justices final); and domestic servants were again to be exempted from coverage (clause 10).

labor organizers went around the country soliciting signatures for petitions. The potter's union and the coal miners in the north were especially active in the campaign mounted against the bill.[147] On May 1, 1844, when the bill was presented to Parliament for a vote, Thomas Duncombe, one of the few labor-friendly members of Parliament, rose to oppose it:

> [T]he measure was an invidious attempt to degrade and oppress the labouring classes. . . . A new principle was introduced, unknown to the Legislature of this country. The only legislation in reference to labour which had heretofore taken place, had been in respect to persons hired for a certain term, and the Legislature had given Magistrates power to fine or imprison persons who did not fulfill their contract, and there had certainly been instances of persons who had been imprisoned under these circumstances. *But there was no instance of power having been given to the Magistrates to send persons to the House of Correction for neglect or dereliction of duty in job or piece work. Now, it appeared they were about to put the two kinds of labour upon the same footing, and give the Magistrates the same power in cases of job and piece work, which they now possessed in the case of labour hired for a term.*[148] (emphasis added)

Duncombe was clearly wrong on the law. Job and piece work, at least in a number of the principal trades, had been explicitly covered by acts of Parliament. But it seems that there was a widespread impression among working people that this was not so. Duncombe said that he had upwards of 200 petitions opposing the bill, signed by hundreds of thousands of persons.[149] He went on to denounce the bill on grounds that would become very familiar during the campaign for the abolition of penal sanctions in the 1860s and 1870s, unequal treatment under the law. This bill represented "another instance of there being one law for the rich and another for the poor – one law for the employer and another for the employed."[150]

> Was this the way to keep the labouring classes in subjection? Was there no other medium except through the police and the treadmill? Were those the only resources to which the Secretary of State for the Home Department could appeal for affording security to the State? Were the treadmill and the policeman's stave the only ties the right hon. Baronet could think of to unite the labouring classes with their employers? He thought a better feeling and a stronger attachment of interest might be induced by kindness and good treatment, on the one hand, and by fidelity on the other.[151]

---

[147]   Webb and Webb, *History of Trade Unionism*, 185; Engels, *Condition of the Working Class*, 320.

[148]   Hansard's *Parl. Debates* (1844), 74, 519.

[149]   Ibid., 522–23.

[150]   Ibid., 521–22.

[151]   Ibid., 522.

Duncombe then made a threat, utilizing one of the few political resources that those who spoke for the laboring classes had available to them in this period:

> Let the House consider the state which many parts of the kingdom were now in. . . . Sir Augustus Henniker, as chairman of the Quarter Sessions for the county of Suffok [said] a short time ago . . . "that he did not believe the whole metropolitan police could put down incendiarism in that county, there was so much discontent and suffering prevailing among the labouring population." If this state of things had not yet extended to other parts of the country, it behoved the House to take care lest the passing such a law as this they did make the words of Sir Augustus Henniker apply to every manufacturing district in the kingdom.[152]

Mr. Bernal, in an even more questionable interpretation of the existing law, thought the bill objectionable because it would extend criminal liability to "every class of handicraft in the Kingdom. . . ."[153]

> [E]very operative engaged, no matter in what manufacture, would under this Bill be bound to remain any time provided by the contract in the Factory, or if he absented himself for a single day in the week would be liable to be brought before a magistrate for punishment and imprisonment.[154]

Sir James Graham responded in support of the bill. First, he described all the ways in which the bill would help working people. Then he came to the crux of the matter. In his opinion,

[152] Ibid.

[153] Ibid., 528. Recall that the 1823 act by its terms covered "*any* Artificer, . . . Handicraftsman . . . Labourer or other Person [who] contract[ed] . . . to serve . . . for any Time or Times," 4 Geo. IV, c. 34 (1823). No case had decided that the terms "artificer," "handicraftsman," or "labourer" were restricted only to the specific trades listed in the act, although an expansive reading of Lord Denman's opinion in *Kitchen v. Shaw*, 6 AD. & E. 729, 112 Eng. Rep. 280 (1837) might support such a view. "We find ourselves compelled to say that the *'other persons'* are not all persons whatever who enter into engagements to serve for stated periods, but persons of the same description as those before enumerated; and that the generality of the words must have been so restricted" (opinion of Lord Denman, 282; emphasis added). But another, and I think superior, reading of Lord Denman's opinion was that he was addressing only the term "other persons" in the 1823 act. *Kitchen v. Shaw* involved a domestic servant, and it had long been thought that such servants were excluded from the coverage of the acts. As to "servants," the acts only listed "servants in husbandry." Deciding that the term "other persons" did not bring a completely different kind of servant under the act was arguably quite different from saying that the categories "*any* Artificer, Handicraftsman, or Labourer" (emphasis added), which were specifically included in the act, only meant those in the specific trades listed. This was precisely Lord Ellenborough's position in *Lowther v. Radnor*.

[154] Hansard's *Parl. Debates* (1844), 74, 528.

the terms used in the Act of 20 Geo. II, c. 19 [1747] might fairly be considered to include job and piece work, and that it was a mere question of construction, and the whole and sole matter now in debate was whether the House of Commons would put a construction upon the words of that statute which should extend its operation to job and task work, notwithstanding an adverse decision by the courts of law.[155]

Mr. Gally Knight, one of the drafters of the bill, was of the view that the people had been misled:

[T]he opposition to this Bill arose from our having accidentally come across the meditated strike of the colliers – the great strike which was to have taken place throughout the whole of the North of England on the same day. Sir, I hold in my hand the proof of this: this newspaper contains the account of one of the earliest meetings which took place on this subject at Sheffield, where a delegate from Glasgow was introduced on behalf of the colliers, and on behalf of the colliers, besought the assembled operatives to do their utmost to defeat this Bill. And how did he engage them to oppose it? By reading to them a Clause which is already the law of the land, (the 4th Clause of this Bill,) and giving them to understand that it was entirely new matter, and levelled against the liberties of the working classes of every description – whereas the truth is, that this Clause is only re-enacted here because the Act in which it already exists is repealed by this Bill; and the only really new matter in this Bill is entirely in favour of the working classes.[156]

Another of the original bill's drafters gave a more balanced and accurate assessment of the current state of the law and of the changes intended by the original bill. Mr. Robert Palmer said that

An alteration in the law had become advisable, in consequence of some recent decisions of the Court of Queen's Bench. As the Bill now stood, it was very different from [the original bill] and he confessed he preferred the original Bill, as being more intelligible and more simple. It had been asked whether workpeople in factories and other places would be affected by the Bill? He believed that many cases of this kind were [already] provided for by special Acts of Parliament.[157]

[155] Ibid., 525.
[156] Ibid., 529.
[157] Ibid., 530–31.

On a vote, the bill was defeated. What seems most astonishing in all this is the state of uncertainty in Parliament and the country about the precise coverage of the existing master and servant law. The series of decisions that had come down from the King's (later Queen's) Bench beginning in 1827 had apparently created enough confusion about which kinds of workers the law actually covered so as to put the terms of existing law up for grabs, creating an opportunity for far-reaching, conflicting popular reinterpretations of existing law.

Lowther v. Radnor, decided at the beginning of the century, had left no doubt that the 1747 act covered task work and that the words of general expression in the act were meant generally. The language in the 1823 act was very similar to the language in the 1747 act. However, the decisions of the King's Bench in the intervening period had deprived *Lowther v. Radnor* of its vitality.[158] The defeat of the 1844 master and servant bill in Parliament could well be understood as parliamentary acquiescence in the court's construction of the statutes, a triumph for the working classes. But what precisely was the court's construction of the statutes? How far did it restrict the earlier statutes? Did it only exempt piece and task work under the 1823 act, or did it go further?

On the one hand, this entire episode may be seen merely as the culmination of a limited struggle to free piece workers (and only piece workers) from the full burdens of the Master and Servant acts, a struggle that had been launched by Peter Moore in 1823. In the 1844 debates, it was only the re-extension of the Master and Servant acts to piece and task workers following the Queen's Bench apparent restriction of earlier acts that created the political controversy. No one was heard to say that the entire apparatus of penal sanctions should be dismantled.

On the other hand, if one accepted the broadest possible interpretation of the Queen's Bench decisions, the one urged by Mr. Bernal, the Master and Servant acts would cover neither piece and task work nor contracts for a term in any but the eight listed trades (and given the apparent redun-

---

[158] The one expansive reading of the statute that I have found in this period was not related to piece or task work. It involved a designer who drew patterns that were later engraved on rollers and used in calico printing. He had been committed to the house of correction for breaching his five-year agreement. Brought up before the Queen's Bench under a writ of *habeas corpus,* he claimed to be an artist "of a higher grade," "not at all of the humble character of the persons enumerated" in the 1823 act and therefore not falling under the jurisdiction of the magistrates. Mr. Justice Williams found him to be either an "artificer" or "other person" within the terms of the act. *Ex parte Eli Ormerod,* 13 L.J. (n.s.) (mag. cases) 73 (1844). However, calico printer was one of the trades specifically listed in the act.

dancy in the list, perhaps fewer than eight).[159] As important as these listed trades were, such an interpretation would have been tantamount to partial repeal of penal sanctions under the guise of maintaining the status quo.

In this sense, the 1844 debates at once did and did not expand the struggle over the Master and Servant acts beyond the narrow terms in which it had been cast since the 1820s. The conflict over piece and task work was an old one that did not directly challenge the legitimacy of the acts with respect to contracts for a term. On the other hand, the debate did begin publicly to undermine the legitimacy of penal sanctions. If re-extending penal sanctions to certain categories of workers represented "oppression, tyranny, and degradation," and if consequently it was the right thing to try to restrict the current law through interpretation to as few workers as possible, the inevitable question would seem to be, Why did it not represent oppression, degradation and tyranny to subject *any* worker to penal sanctions? Part of the answer is to be found in the traditional belief that piece and task work were different from contracts for a term and that in the case of contracts for a term it was legitimate to hold people to their promises to work for a specified time. However, Mr. Bernal was even beginning to call this distinction into question.

This entire controversy had been set in motion by a conflict within the state between the judiciary and the legislature that the working classes moved to exploit. Engaging in that process also changed them. Their long-held view of the Master and Servant acts had been vindicated by acts of state, by decisions of the Queen's Bench. Now Parliament was trying to reverse these decisions, trying to re-extend the Master and Servant acts beyond what the court (and working people) thought legitimate. It was in the course of beating back this attempted re-extension of the Master and Servant acts under the guise of maintaining the status quo and upholding a traditional view of the acts that basic public attitudes toward these acts began to change. Nevertheless, this process was still at an early stage. In 1844 the working classes and their allies were actively engaged in a campaign to pass the Ten Hours bill, but no similar agitation was undertaken against penal sanctions. That would wait for nearly twenty more years.

In the meantime, having set this entire process in motion, in the 1850s the Queen's Bench began to reverse course, making matters even worse. In case after case, the court elaborated an expansive reading of the 1823 act, relying on the act's general words ("artificer," "handicraftsman," "contract to serve in any other manner," "or other person"), which had previously received a restricted reading, to certify that a broad range of workers was covered. By the early 1860s, the working classes could have been

---

[159] "Servant in Husbandry, Calico Printer, Miner, Collier, Keelman, Pitman, Glassman, Potter."

left with very little hope that the coverage of the acts would be restricted piecemeal through interpretation.

In 1852, the Queen's Bench heard an appeal from the County Court of Monmouthshire. A coal miner, one Weaver, had brought an action against Floyd, a coal contractor for whom he worked, claiming he was owed wages. The contractor moved to set off against the wage claim the value of goods he had supplied to the miner, arguing that the miner was not an "artificer" covered by the Truck Act. The County Court found for the miner and the contractor appealed.[160]

In many instances, coal mining was conducted through a system by which contractors and subcontractors would let from the owner a portion of a mine and would be paid according to the amount of coal dug. Contractors frequently employed subcontractors, who might actually do some of the mining themselves, but who also employed and paid other men under them. A variation on this system involved a group of miners taking an area of a mine to dig at a certain rate per ton and sharing out the proceeds among themselves, with the head man receiving a larger share. These subcontractors were known as butty colliers. In formalistic terms, the legal problem posed by this system was whether such butty colliers were "independent contractors" or a species of employee.

The question arose in two different legal contexts, under the Master and Servant acts, but also under the Truck Act of 1831.[161] The Truck Act had been passed to protect workers. The Master and Servant acts could also be used by workers to recover wages, but they simultaneously exposed workers to criminal liability for contract breaches. The problem for the courts was that since the two kinds of statutes were considered to be *in pari materia*,[162] a finding that a butty collier was not an "artificer" under the Truck Act could well mean that he was also not an "artificer" subject to punishment under the Master and Servant acts. That was the problem the Queen's Bench confronted in *Weaver v. Floyd*.[163]

Weaver, the miner, was not bound by the agreement to work any stated number of hours or to do any fixed amount of work, and he was free to employ other men to assist him. For four months he had one man working under him and during one month two men. He also performed labor personally, and he could only be dismissed or leave his service on a month's notice.[164] Was he a subcontractor not covered by the Truck Act,

---

[160] *Weaver v. Floyd*, 21 L.J. (n.s.) (Q.B.) 151 (1852), 151.

[161] 1 & 2 Will. IV, c. 37 (1831).

[162] See *Lawrence v. Todd*, 32 L.J. (n.s.) (mag. cases) 238 (1863), 241.

[163] 21 L.J. (n.s.) (Q.B.) 151 (1852).

[164] *Weaver v. Floyd*, 21 L.J. (n.s.) (Q.B.) 151 (1852), 151.

or was he an "artificer" covered by the act? The answer turned on whether he was contractually obligated to perform labor personally and whether it was for the labor he was being compensated. Were the tons of coal produced merely a means to measure how much he should be paid for his labor (piece work)? Or were they a means for measuring how much he was to be compensated for selling the commodity coal by the ton to the contractor? By highlighting the fact that he was obligated under the agreement to give a month's notice, the court concluded that he was personally obligated to perform manual labor for the contractor, was being paid for that personal labor, and hence was covered by the term "artificer" in the Truck Act.

There were at least three separate factors taken into account in determining whether a person was an "independent contractor" or a "servant." The first was whether he was obligated to perform labor personally. The second was whether the commitment to perform labor was exclusive. Here also the fact that notice to quit was required seemed crucial. A third consideration was not discussed by this court. The miner was being paid in part for the labor of other people, not merely for his own labor. He would compensate them out of the pay he received. Suppose they had produced more value for him than he compensated them for. If one profited by the labor of others, did that not make such a person a "contractor" rather than a "servant?"

What is surprising is that the Queen's Bench reached an altogether different result than the Court of Exchequer had reached several years earlier in the well-known case of *Riley v. Warden*[165] and that the Court of Common Pleas also reached the very next year in *Sharman v. Sanders*.[166] In both of these cases it was found that similarly situated subcontractors were not "artificers" under the Truck Act. In *Riley v. Warden*, Mr. Baron Rolfe was of the view that the Truck Act applied "to workmen and labourers who earn wages by their own personal labour, and not to those who, although they join in the work, derive a profit from the exertion of others."[167]

It was the Queen's Bench that saw most of the cases brought under the Master and Servant acts, and the logic of giving a broad reading to the term "artificer" in the Truck Act became apparent the very next year when the court had to deal with *In the Matter of George Bailey, In the Matter of John Collier*.[168] In that case two butty colliers had been committed to the house of correction under the 1823 Master and Servant Act. When

---

[165] *Riley v. Warden*, 2 Ex. 59, 154 Eng. Rep. 405 (1848).

[166] *Sharman v. Sanders*, 22 L.J. (n.s.) (c.p.) 86 (1853).

[167] *Riley v. Warden*, 2 Ex. 59, 154 Eng. Rep. 405 (1848), 410.

[168] 3 El. & Bl. 607, 118 Eng. Rep. 1269 (1854).

brought before the Queen's Bench on a writ of *habeas corpus*, they argued, among other things, that they should be discharged because there was no contract of service and the justice, therefore, lacked jurisdiction. Under their agreement, they said, they were free to work as much or as little as they pleased, and were paid only for what they did decide to produce; they were in the nature of subcontractors rather than servants. The Queen's Bench upheld the conviction.[169]

In 1856, the court was again confronted with an appeal from a wage claim brought in a county court in which the defendant had tried to set off the value of goods supplied to the plaintiff butty collier. Citing *Weaver v. Floyd,* the court declared in *Bowers v. Lovekin*[170] that the term "artificer" in the Truck Act did apply to butty colliers and the defendant should not be permitted a setoff. Mr. Justice Erle argued for a broad reading of the term "artificer" on the grounds that it helped to protect workers:

> It would not appear to me right to say that when a workman con-
> tracted to do work by the piece and made no other contract, that the
> act did not apply. To hold that it applied only where the workman
> engaged to give his personal labour would be, in effect, to repeal the
> Truck Act in almost all cases of contracts for work by the piece. The
> true construction of the act . . . is, that the act should apply to con-
> tracts for work by the piece when it is consistent with the contract
> that the party should work personally, and he has actually done
> so. We should look at the work done and the position in life of the
> parties.[171]

Both the 1747 and 1823 statutes extended wage recovery rights to the same categories of workers who were subjected to penal sanctions. A broad reading of these categories, even if the purpose were to broaden the scope of wage recovery rights, would inevitably also have broadened the

---

[169] Ibid., 1273–75.

[170] 25 L.J. (n.s.) (Q.B.) 371 (1856).

[171] *Bowers v. Lovekin,* 25 L.J. (n.s.) (Q.B.) 371 (1856), 374 (opinion of Mr. Justice Erle). The Exchequer opinions on this subject continued to be in conflict with Queen's Bench opinions just as they were on the subject of the permissibility of multiple imprisonments under the Master and Servant acts. In the 1864 case of *Sleeman v. Barrett,* 2 H. & C. 934, 159 Eng. Rep. 386, the Exchequer ruled that butty colliers were not artificers within the scope of the Truck Act. The lawyer arguing in favor of coverage under the act cited the earlier Queen's Bench decisions under the Truck Act and also pointed out that earlier decisions of the Queen's Bench had found butty colliers to be servants under the Master and Servant Act. "Butty colliers are uniformly dealt with under that statute [4 Geo. IV, c. 34 (1823)]: *In re Bailey* and *In re Collier,*" 390. But the court rejected this argument. In *Ex parte Allsop; Re Disney,* 32 L.T. 433 (1875), the scope of the decision in *Sleeman v. Barrett* was restricted; butty colliers were found to be "labourers or workmen" within the meaning of the bankruptcy act.

scope of penal sanctions. The same joining of broader wage recovery
rights with broader scope for penal sanctions also characterized the defeated 1844 master and servant bill. The Truck Act covered some of the
same categories of workers that were covered by the Master and Servant
acts. To the extent that a court read these categories broadly for the purpose of extending protections to workers, it would simultaneously be
opening these workers to the possibility of criminal prosecution under the
Master and Servant acts because the two acts were viewed as enacted to
serve similar purposes. Which was this court's primary motive, liberaliza-
tion or labor discipline? It makes little difference, because, regardless of
the motive, one of the inevitable consequences of liberal readings was to
extend criminal liability. One of the things that the 1844 debates showed
was that if there was to be a tradeoff between wage recovery and criminal
liability, working people preferred less criminal liability even at the ex-
pense of more difficult wage recovery.[172]

It is apparent that Mr. Justice Erle's attitude toward piece work represented a shift from earlier views.[173] Indeed, the year before Mr. Justice
Wightman, sitting in Bail Court, heard *Ex parte Gordon,* an application for
a *certiorari* to bring up a conviction under the 1823 Master and Servant
Act.[174] The decision he issued there placed in doubt the continued vitality
of *Hardy v. Ryle, The Queen v. Johnson, Lancaster v. Greaves,* and the reasoning
in *Kitchen v. Shaw* by resurrecting *Lowther v. Radnor.* Piece and task work
might yet fall squarely under the 1823 act.

The facts of *Ex parte Gordon* are important. Edward Gordon, a tailor,
contracted "to serve [John Scholefield] in his trade of a tailor in the capacity of a tailor, at certain wages, from thence to an indefinite time determinable by either contracting party on the said Edward Gordon finishing any

---

[172] See remarks of Mr. Bernal on the 1844 Master and Servant bill in Hansard's *Parl. Debates* (1844), 74, 528.

[173] In *Ingram v. Barnes,* 7 El. & Bl. 115, 119 Eng. Rep. 1190 (1857), a divided Exchequer Chamber (Erle, J., from the Queen's Bench dissenting) followed the Exchequer and Common Pleas decisions in *Riley v. Warden* and *Sharman v. Sanders* rather than the Queen's Bench decisions in *Weaver v. Floyd* and *Bowers v. Lovekin,* holding that a workman who hired other workmen to assist him in a project and was not expressly obligated to labor personally was not an "artificer" within the Truck Act. In 1859, Mr. Justice Erle became Chief Justice of the Court of Common Pleas and in 1863 adhered to the posi-tion he had laid out in his dissent in *Ingram v. Barnes,* finding that such a workman was an "artificer" within the 1823 Master and Servant Act. See *Lawrence v. Todd,* 14 C.B. (N.S.) 554, 143 Eng. Rep. 562 (1863).

[174] 25 L.J. (n.s.) (mag. cases) 12 (1855). The 1823 Master and Servant Act (4 Geo. IV, c. 34) made the orders of a single justice final. No appeals to Quarter Sessions were given. Ear-lier Master and Servant acts had allowed such appeals; see 20 Geo. II, c. 19 (1747) and 6 Geo. III, c. 25 (1766). On the other hand, the 1823 act did not expressly prohibit the is-suance of writs of *certiorari* as some earlier acts had; see 20 Geo. II, c. 19 (1747). Where

piece of work he might from time to time be engaged on."[175] This framing of the contract terms, of course, was an attempt to turn an engagement to do piece work without any fixed term of service into a contract for an indefinite term determinable on the completion of any piece of work. At the hearing Scholefield established that he was a tailor who employed many men, all of whom worked on his premises. Gordon had come to him as a journeyman some six weeks to two months before the breach for which he was being prosecuted. Gordon

> was employed by Scholefield to make sometimes trousers and sometimes waistcoats, as he was required; that he was paid wages at a certain price per garment, according to a list of prices agreed upon between the master and the men. The work performed was done in the complainant's shop. It was shewn further that Gordon could refuse work if he liked; if work was offered which he had not agreed to do; and also that if Scholefield had no work for Gordon to do when he applied he did not give him any. Scholefield further added, that his men did not work for other persons, and that if he found them working for others he should discharge them immediately.[176]

One must wonder, of course, whether these journeymen tailors actually did refrain from soliciting work from other tailors when Scholefield turned them away. Gordon's breach, which gave rise to this prosecution, was to have refused to finish a piece of work that he had begun. "He did not finish the waistcoat [upon which he had been working], and refused to do so, and said he was going to Sheffield. The Justice convicted Gordon, and directed him to be confined for fourteen days for the offence in the house of correction."[177]

Arguing against the application for the writ, Huddleston cited *Kitchen v. Shaw, Lancaster v. Greaves, Hardy v. Ryle*, and *Ex parte Johnson*, among others. In support of the application, Milward cited *Lowther v. Radnor* and *Blake v. Lanyon*. The question, Mr. Justice Wightman thought, was whether Gordon was a servant to Scholefield under the 1823 act. The 1823 act did not mention tailors specifically. "Gordon," Mr. Justice Wightman observed,

> was not to serve for any specific time nor for any specific job originally agreed upon, but he was to serve to do such work as he should

an act of the justices was declared final but no prohibition on *certiorari* had been included, the courts continued to exercise a supervisory authority by making the writ available; see John Orth, *Combination and Conspiracy: A Legal History of Trade Unionism, 1721–1906* (Oxford, 1991), 13–14.

[175] *Ex parte Gordon*, 25 L.J. (n.s.) (mag. cases) 12 (1855), 12–13.

[176] Ibid., 13.

[177] Ibid.

be set to do, and undertake to do, and he was to do it on the premises of his employer. The contract did not extend beyond any particular job he was engaged upon at any particular time, *but during that job, and until it was finished,* he was to work *exclusively* for his employer.[178] (emphasis added)

It seems clear that it is possible to construe almost any form of piece work as an exclusive arrangement during the time it takes to finish a single job. Citing *Lowther v. Radnor,* Mr. Justice Wightman concluded,

Gordon, therefore, is, I think, brought within the words of the statute as an "artificer or handicraftsman," "or other person," who had contracted to serve "for any time or times whatsoever or in any other manner." These last words, "in any other manner," seem to me very important. I think, therefore, that there was evidence here of such relation between the parties as would give the Magistrates jurisdiction.[179]

Over the next few years, the courts did not decide a series of difficult cases that may have placed earlier decisions in doubt, the way *Ex parte Gordon* did; rather, the issue of jurisdiction seems largely to have disappeared. A variety of workers who were not listed in the 1823 act was unthinkingly subjected to the act.

In 1858, one Charles Smith was convicted of aiding and abetting a handicraftsman,[180] George Thompson, by counseling and procuring him not to commence his service under a written contract he had made with James Hallett, a shipbuilder. Thompson had signed the contract for a term with Hallett "to serve him in the capacity or employment of a handicraftsman, that is, a shipwright . . . for a certain period not yet then elapsed."[181] Smith had been convicted of the aiding and abetting offence and imprisoned. He was brought before the Court of Exchequer on a writ of *habeas corpus.* The court refused to discharge him, finding that the magistrate had jurisdiction. However, the court could only reach this result if

---

[178] Ibid.

[179] Ibid., 14.

[180] Section 5 of Jervis's Act, 11 & 12 Vict., c. 43 (1848), made it an offence for any person to aid, abet, counsel, or procure the commission of any offence punishable on summary conviction. This section would seem to have criminalized enticement by a third-party employer as well as actions of worker activists who might encourage a worker to strike in breach of a contract. It is not clear out of which of these contexts this case arose. Because it involved failure to commence service rather than departure from service, however, it seems probable that it grew out of a situation where a second employer had tried to entice away Hallett's shipwright.

[181] *Ex parte Smith,* 27 L.J. (n.s.) (mag. cases) 186 (1858), 186.

an underlying offence was stated under the 1823 Master and Servant Act against Thompson for neglecting and failing to enter his service. It was assumed without more that such an offence had been stated by these facts. That Thompson was a shipwright, and that shipwrights were not mentioned in the 1823 act or 1766 act, made no difference. Thompson was a "handicraftsman" within the terms of the acts.

In 1859, two similar cases arose in which jurisdiction over the particular kind of workers who had contracted never became an issue. On January 4, 1859, Rider agreed with Wood and others that he would "serve them as an anchor-smith and artificer from that day, at certain specified prices, for an indefinite period determinable on either of the contracting parties giving to the other fourteen days' notice."[182] A dispute about the prices of the work arose, and after giving defective fourteen-day notice Rider and others left their work. The justices of the peace were of the opinion that Rider was guilty of an offence under the 1823 act and requested an opinion from the Queen's Bench on the validity of the notice.[183] The Queen's Bench thought the conviction might not be supportable if Rider believed that he was giving valid notice, but there seems to have been no question that the magistrates had jurisdiction over the contract of an "anchor-smith and artificer" under the 1823 act.[184] Nor did there seem to be any question that they had jurisdiction over the contract of "a boiler and gasholder maker" under that act.[185]

The case of Alice Taylor, which came before the Queen's Bench in 1862, was more interesting. Taylor was a weaver in a cotton mill. She had asked permission of the overseer to leave her loom during the day. He had given permission on condition that she find a substitute for her loom and that she return to work at 6:00 the next morning. Taylor did find a substitute but did not return to work the next morning. When she did return to work, she was told to leave, and when she tried to collect her back wages the overseer refused to pay. She brought her complaint before the justices of the peace under the 1747 act. At the hearing the company contended that the justices were without jurisdiction because Taylor had not proved that the hiring was for any definite period or for an indefinite period determinable on a definite notice. It seems likely, moreover, that she worked by the piece. The justices dismissed her complaint but sought the opinion of the Queen's Bench on the question of whether she should

---

[182] *Rider v. Wood,* 29 L.J. (n.s.) (mag. cases) 1 (1859), 1.

[183] The local magistrates were authorized to seek the opinion of the superior courts on questions of law arising in the exercise of their jurisdiction by 20 & 21 Vict., c. 43 (1857), perhaps to help them avoid actions for false imprisonment.

[184] *Rider v. Wood,* 29 L.J. (n.s.) (mag. cases) 1 (1859), 4.

[185] *Ashmore v. Horton,* 29 L.J. (n.s.) (mag. cases) 13 (1859).

have been responsible for proving a contract of service to bring the case within their jurisdiction.[186]

At the Queen's Bench, Taylor's lawyer quoted the following language from the statute: "other labourers employed for any certain time *or in any other manner*" (emphasis in original).[187] The lawyer for the company argued that unless there was a contract of service "for any definite period at all" (by which he must have meant either a contract for a fixed term or a contract for an indefinite term determinable on fixed notice), the justices had no jurisdiction under the decisions in *The Queen v. Johnson, Hardy v. Ryle,* and *Lancaster v. Greaves.*[188] The court rejected this argument. Mr. Justice Crompton thought that the justices did have jurisdiction in that Taylor "was clearly bound to stay with the respondents as servant during *some time or other*" (emphasis added).[189] Mr. Justice Wightman thought that, "It is not necessary that the hiring should be for any specific time" to give the justices jurisdiction.[190] The court had become quite casual about establishing the precise bounds of the master and servant relationship; indeed, it could almost be said to have lost interest in the fine distinctions that had been drawn earlier. If someone was employed as a wage earner doing manual work, the presumption seems to have become by the 1860s that the acts gave the magistrates jurisdiction.

The next year, a decision in the Court of Common Pleas revealed a similar attitude. In 1862, H. M. Lawrence & Co., shipbuilders, had contracted with Robert Todd (and six others), angle-iron smiths and platers, to work exclusively for the company to

> enter the service of the said H. M. Lawrence in order to execute the whole of the skilled and unskilled labour requisite to complete in every respect of the very best workmanship . . . the entire iron hull of the vessel now building in his yard . . . and for this purpose the said Todd (and six others) shall employ such skilled and unskilled assistants as the said H. M. Lawrence shall deem requisite in order to complete the said vessel with all dispatch, such assistants to be paid by the said Todd. . . . The said H. M. Lawrence shall pay the said

---

[186] *Alice Taylor v. Carr and Porter,* 31 L.J. (n.s.) (mag. cases) 111 (1862), 111–12. For a separate report of the same case, see 2 B. & S. 335, 121 Eng. Rep. 1098 (1862).

[187] *Alice Taylor v. Carr and Porter,* 31 L.J. (n.s.) (mag. cases) 111 (1862), 112.

[188] Ibid., 112–13.

[189] Ibid., 113.

[190] Ibid. The Law Journal reporter added a footnote to Mr. Justice Wightman's opinion, citing Mr. Justice Parke's opinion in *Lancaster v. Greaves:* "There may indeed be a service, not for any specific time or wages" (n. 6).

Todd (and six others), or any of them, for their joint account, for each and every ton weight of iron-work executed . . . by the said Todd (and six others) and their assistants, the sum of 5£.[191]

There were other stipulations in the contract that Todd should be subject to the rules of the yard and that the contract created a master and servant relationship between Lawrence and Todd (and six others).[192]

Sometime after the work was begun Todd and two of the six men refused to continue and willfully absented themselves from the shipyard, delaying the completion of the ship. An information was laid under the 1823 Master and Servant Act, but the magistrate was of the opinion that the agreement did not create such a relationship as to bring the workers within the scope of the act and declined to convict them.[193] He apparently thought that the relationship resembled contractor and subcontractor more than master and servant. The opinion of the Court of Common Pleas was then sought. "I have been searching to see where the difficulty was in holding that the respondent was liable to conviction under this section," Mr. Chief Justice Erle declared, "because an iron-plater is obviously both an artificer and a handicraftsman within the meaning of the act."[194] He went on:

> It is obvious also that the statute is, in its spirit, applicable to such a case as this. It was meant to protect persons who had heavy contracts to complete within a certain time, and to give them a summary remedy in case their workmen left them without a reasonable excuse. Under some circumstances a person employed to do a particular job would not be the servant of his employer, but not when the employment is such as in this case. It is much stronger than the case of the journeyman tailor, who only worked occasionally for his master by the job; and yet he was held to be within the act – *Ex parte Gordon*. Nor can it be held that the mode of payment, 5£. per ton, would prevent the employment being such a one as would bring the respondent within the act. The words of the section include service "for any time or times whatsoever, or in any other manner." There is no restriction whatever as to the mode of payment, or the kind of work which is to be done. . . . I find no substantial ground for hold-

ing that this respondent was not liable to the penalties imposed by this section.[195]

Mr. Justice Byles delivered a concurring opinion: "I ought to say that I rely on the authority of *Bowers v. Lovekin* [finding butty colliers to be "artificers" under the Truck Act] in giving this judgment. The Truck Act is *in pari materia* with the statute which we are now considering, and it is a distinct authority in support of the view which we are now taking."[196] Although the facts of this case were favorable for finding a master and servant relationship, it is significant that Chief Justice Erle appealed to the spirit of the 1823 act to support his decision. It appears as though the court had become much more casual about establishing the precise line between subcontractors and servants, bringing many of those who might earlier have been thought to be independent subcontractors within the scope of the Master and Servant Act.[197]

By 1866 as evidence was being given before the Select Committee on Master and Servant, which was investigating proposals to reform the Master and Servant acts, there was no hint that the coverage of the acts was a subject of continuing controversy. Of course, it would have been in the interests of working people on this occasion to emphasize the unqualified harshness of existing law. Nevertheless, the debates over the precise

---

[195] Ibid. In a separate report of the same case Mr. Chief Justice Erle's words are recorded somewhat differently: "That the spirit of the statute was intended to apply to such a case, is perfectly manifest. The appellant had no doubt contracted to deliver the ship completely finished and fitted by a given day; and this he could not reckon upon accomplishing unless he could be secure of the cooperation of his workmen, and he makes his contract with them accordingly. This is exactly the case for the application of the summary remedy provided by the statute; as, without some such check, his workmen might at any time frustrate all his arrangements. Two of the six persons parties to the agreement have wilfully absented themselves, without lawful excuse. It has been held that a man who was hired to do a particular job, – as a tailor to make a garment, – comes within the description of a labourer in this statute, – *Ex parte Gordon*, 25 L.J., M.C. 12: and there are many other cases to the same effect." *Lawrence v. Todd*, 14 C.B. (N.S.) 554, 143 Eng. Rep. 562 (1863), 567.

[196] *Lawrence v. Todd*, 32 L.J. (n.s.) (mag. cases) 238 (1863), 241. In this report of the case, the concurrence is attributed to Chief Justice Erle. But he had already delivered his opinion, and in the other report of the case this concurrence is attributed to Mr. Justice Byles; see *Lawrence v. Todd*, 14 C.B. (n.s.) 554, 143 Eng. Rep. 562 (1863), 567. The attribution to Mr. Justice Byles makes more sense under the circumstances, and I have attributed the concurring opinion to him.

[197] However, in the next year the Court of Exchequer adhered to its earlier decision in *Riley v. Warden* and found that butty colliers were not covered by the Truck Act, rejecting a line of Queen's Bench decisions. See *Sleeman v. Barrett*, 2 H. & C. 934, 159 Eng. Rep. 386 (1864). Such a decision, of course, could have meant that butty colliers were not prosecutable under the Master and Servant acts. There is no evidence, however, of such a result.

coverage of the acts that were so important in 1844 made no appearance in the 1866 testimony. When questioned about the scope of the acts, George Newton, a potter, answered: "Q. 36. The Act applies practically, does it not, to all trades? – Yes, there are a number of trades specified in the Act, but there is a very inclusive term, 'handicraftsman,' 'or other person,' who shall enter into any contract to serve. 37. It likewise specifies agricultural labourers? – They are not exempted. 38. The only exemptions are domestic servants? – Yes."[198] George Odger, a shoemaker working in the putting out system, testified that the 1777 act was commonly used against home piece workers to compel them to return work timely.[199]

By the early 1860s very little hope could have been left among working people that the courts would limit the scope of the Master and Servant acts through a process of interpretation or that piece work would not be treated in the same way as contracts for a term. On this issue, as well, by the 1860s the courts had produced an interpretation of the Master and Servant acts that not only was disadvantageous to working people in their own view but also represented a retreat from an earlier, more favorable position. Just at a time when labor was growing stronger, the common law courts left little doubt that the narrowly circumscribed issue of the proper treatment of piece work, which had been the subject of decades of struggle, would never be resolved favorably to labor in that forum.

PROCEDURAL PROTECTIONS
IN CRIMINAL PROSECUTIONS

One final set of issues followed a pattern similar to those discussed previously. Among other things, Peter Moore's 1823 bill tried to address the unfair treatment that workers often received at the hands of local magistrates. The bill proposed various procedural reforms that I have already discussed. Interestingly, the Moore bill would have made it impossible to attack proceedings before justices on the ground of want of proper form.[200] However, it was on just this ground that lawyers representing workers had great success during the 1840s in quashing convictions under the Master and Servant Act. At least during this decade, the common law courts used their supervisory powers to try to push the summary justice administered by the local magistrates in the direction of incorporating some of the procedural safeguards provided at common law to persons who were being criminally prosecuted.

---

[198] "Report from the Select Committee on Master and Servant," *Parl. Papers* (1866), XIII: Qs. 36–38.

[199] Ibid., Q. 1813.

[200] "A Bill for Repealing Several Acts," *Parl. Papers* (1823), II:305; see also White and Henson, *A Few Remarks on the State of the Laws*, 133–34.

The attacks were generally on the legal sufficiency of the warrants of commitment. In *Johnson v. Reid*, the warrant was found to be bad because it failed to state that the contract was in writing or that the service had been entered on. In the case of an oral contract, the service would have had to have been entered on for the 1823 act to give jurisdiction. Because the warrant had not stated that the contract was in writing, that the service had been entered on, or that the work had not been done, it was held to be insufficient to give jurisdiction.[201]

A large number of cases arose in 1844 as the great strike was prepared and launched in the coal fields of the north. As previously mentioned, W. P. Roberts began in early 1844 systematically to contest the convictions of miners. In the cases in the common law courts that I have found, the prisoners were brought before the court under writs of *habeas corpus*. In *The Queen v. Lewis*, decided on January 13, 1844, the warrants of commitment were found to be defective because in two cases they did not state the occupation of the worker. That was crucial for giving jurisdiction under the 1823 act. In a third case they failed to state that the evidence at the hearing had been given on oath.[202] The prisoners, miners, were discharged. In *In the Matter of Copestick*, decided in April 1844, the workman was brought up under a writ of *habeas corpus*. The warrant of commitment was again found to be defective in not stating the nature of the service undertaken, and the prisoner was ordered discharged.[203]

In *In the Matter of Isaac Tordoff*, also brought before the court under a writ of *habeas corpus* and decided in the same month, the justice of the peace had recited in the warrant of commitment that he had "convicted" Tordoff of the offence. The court treated the warrant of commitment as a conviction that required recitation of the facts that the evidence had been given on oath in the presence of the prisoner. Because those facts had not been recited, the warrant was found defective and the prisoner, a collier, was discharged. The court rejected the argument that this was a mere warrant of commitment that would be good if founded on a good conviction that must be presumed.[204] It did not decide whether a conviction was necessary at all under the 1823 statute, however. That statute only spoke of justices "committing" persons to the house of correction following a hearing to determine whether a worker had failed to fulfill a contract or had "been guilty of any other Misconduct or Misdemeanour" in the execution thereof.[205] If no conviction was necessary, and none had been made, what form would be required of a warrant of commitment?

---

[201] *Johnson v. Reid*, 7 L.J. (n.s.) (mag. cases) 25 (1840), 27.

[202] *The Queen v. Lewis*, 13 L.J. (n.s.) (mag. cases) 46 (1844), 47.

[203] *In the Matter of Copestick*, 13 L.J. (n.s.) (mag. cases) 161 (1844), 161.

[204] *In the Matter of Isaac Tordoff*, 13 L.J. (n.s.) (mag. cases) 145 (1844), 147.

[205] 4 Geo. IV., c. 34 (1823).

When the cases of John Gray and Hugh Blaney, colliers, were brought before Mr. Justice Patteson under a writ of *habeas corpus,* the lawyers who appeared in support of the commitment argued that no conviction was necessary under the 1823 act. They were of the view that a commitment under the act was in the nature of an order rather than a conviction and that "the same strict formalities are not required."[206] Mr. Justice Patteson reacted strongly:

> I do not regard mere terms in the least, for, whether this be an order or commitment, or conviction, I wish to know whether a Magistrate can order a man to be imprisoned for an offence, without shewing that he has heard the evidence on oath? I do not know whether the omission to set out the evidence has ever been objected to, but it would take a great deal to convince me, that where a statute gives a power to imprison, an instrument like this must not possess the requisites of a conviction.[207]

The warrant of commitment had recited that the justice "convicted" the prisoner. Mr. Justice Patteson was concerned that "here a party is to be deprived of his liberty, without the power of cross-examining the witnesses produced against him, under a statute of a highly penal character."[208] Mr. Justice Patteson then delivered his opinion:

> I myself cannot understand that, because an act of parliament is drawn, as, I am sorry to say, most of them are, imperfectly and loosely, and it is not stated, as it ought to have been, that the party might be brought before a Magistrate, and convicted by him, and that he should sentence him upon that conviction; that, because the act of parliament puts it altogether, and says, in general words, he may do this, therefore I am told it is not a conviction, but an order. . . . If an act of parliament says an offence shall be committed by certain acts, and a Magistrate shall have power to commit and punish for that offence, then I say, that any instrument by which the Magis-

---

[206] *Re John Gray and Hugh Blaney,* 24 L.J. (n.s.) (mag. cases) 26 (1844), 27. It had been decided in the eighteenth century that if a justice's adjudication resulted in an "order" rather than a "conviction," even if the order resulted in "severe penalties" as orders frequently did, it was not necessary for the justice to adhere to the formalities required for a conviction. *Dominus Rex v. Lloyd,* 2 Strange 996, 93 Eng. Rep. 992 (8 Geo. II), 993; and *Rex v. Bissex,* Sayer, 303, 96 Eng. Rep. 888 (1756), 889. The distinction between criminal convictions and administrative orders resulting in penal sanctions was not very clearly drawn in many of the statutes that the justices administered. It appears that the superior common law courts were beginning to try to impose such a distinction in the eighteenth century on the various kinds of summary adjudications that the justices were empowered by legislation to undertake.

[207] *Re John Gray and Hugh Blaney,* 24 L.J. (n.s.) (mag. cases) 26 (1844), 27.

[208] Ibid.

trate says the party was brought before him and *convicted,* is a conviction.[209] (emphasis added)

As such the warrant of commitment had to recite that evidence given before the justice had been given on oath while the accused party was present. The prisoner was ordered discharged.

In *In the Matter of John Hammond,* again involving a miner, the full Queen's Bench took this line of reasoning one step further. It required warrants of commitment to summarize the evidence actually given on oath in the accused party's presence if the warrant recited that the party had been "convicted." If the warrant recited that a party had been "convicted" then the warrant, as an instrument of conviction, must meet the strict requirements of such an instrument. Lord Denman declared that, "It appears to me that we are to deal with these documents as we find them, and that this warrant is also a conviction in the very terms of it. . . . [W]e have to deal with a document by which the party is deprived of his liberty, and that document does not shew that there is at present a good conviction to warrant his detention."[210] On the same day, June 1, 1846, the court also decided another *habeas* case. This case also involved a miner. An information brought against the miner had led to his commitment to the house of correction for three months at hard labor for breaching his contract. The court, finding that the information failed to state an offence because it failed to state that the miner had "unlawfully" absented himself from his service, ordered the prisoner discharged.[211]

In 1848 the tide began to turn. William Leigh, a collier, had been committed in 1844 for breach of contract by a Lancaster justice of the peace. On September, 17, 1844, he was discharged by *habeas corpus* and brought an action against the committing justice. The justice proceeded to draw up a conviction long after the commitment had taken place. The justice's liability turned on whether the warrant of commitment was defective and whether the later conviction could correct errors of form in the earlier commitment. The Exchequer Chamber[212] heard the case in May 1847 and issued a decision at the beginning of the following year. The decision found the warrant of commitment defective in that it had failed to state that "his contract to serve was in writing, or that the service was entered

---

[209] Ibid., 29.

[210] *In the Matter of John Hammond,* 15 L.J. (n.s.) (mag. cases) 136 (1846), 139.

[211] *In the Matter of Turner, Ollerton, and Others,* 15 L.J. (n.s.) (mag. cases) 140 (1846).

[212] The Exchequer Chamber was, at this time, the court to which appeals from the other superior common law courts (Queen's Bench, Court of Exchequer, Common Pleas) could be taken.

upon; one of those two circumstances being essential to give the Magistrate Jurisdiction to commit to hard labour."[213]

Although the decision was favorable to the miner, the opinion by Mr. Baron Parke left the door open to less rigorous future reviews of warrants of commitment. Mr. Baron Parke was of the opinion that in the 1823 statute "the legislature did not intend that there should be any other instrument to authorize the detention than a warrant of commitment founded upon a proper information by the Master or his agent; that no conviction properly so called, was required or authorized to be filed at the sessions."[214] He went on to say that "whether this be *an order, as, indeed, I think it is,* or be in the nature of a conviction, it being, as it seems to me, the only document the existence of which the legislature contemplated, the legality of the imprisonment must depend upon the legality and sufficiency of that instrument alone" (emphasis added).[215] If it was only an order, as Mr. Baron Parke believed, the warrant of commitment would not be held to the same strict standards of formality to which convictions were held.

---

[213] *Lindsay v. Leigh,* 17 L.J. (n.s.) (mag. cases) 50 (1848), 56.

[214] Ibid., 55. The problem of statutes, which spoke only of justices committing persons to the house of correction without also specifying that the person must first be convicted of an offence, was an old one:

> Most . . . authors of manuals [in the seventeenth century] believed that justices outside sessions had the power to commit a broad range of offenders to houses of correction. . . . [However, t]hese authorities believed individual justices could use houses of correction for custodial, but not punitive, purposes [i.e., could use them to hold persons until their cases were to be heard but not as punishment unless their cases had first been properly adjudicated]. In 1666, the King's Bench judges ruled that in the specific case of idle persons who lived above their station . . . offenders could be committed by an individual justice to a house of correction to be put to hard labor, but they could not be punished (whipped) until the case was tried at sessions. . . . To be punished, one had to be convicted of an offence, but did a mere commitment to a house of correction . . . by a justice acting outside sessions constitute a conviction? Several authors of manuals for justices appear to have believed that a commitment on [the vagrancy statute 7 Jac. 1 c.4] did constitute a conviction. . . . [And] on hearing an appeal of a commitment for "idle and disorderly" behavior in 1731, Justice Probyn ruled that such commitments were authorized by the [vagrancy] statute, and "the statute makes the conviction."

> Robert B. Shoemaker, *Prosecution and Punishment: Petty Crime and the Law in London and Rural Middlesex, c. 1660–1725* (Cambridge, 1991), 37–38. See *The King v. Talbot,* 11 Mod. 415, 88 Eng. Rep. 1122 (4 Geo. II) ("This is a bare commitment to the house of correction; the statute directs what is to be done with the person when there, therefore the statute makes the conviction," 1123).

[215] *Lindsay v. Leigh,* 17 L.J. (n.s.) (mag. cases) 50 (1848), 55–56.

Lindsay v. Leigh was followed in 1851 by the case of *In re Joseph Askew,*[216] in which a warrant of commitment was found to be defective in failing to state that the contract was in writing or the work entered on.[217] However, two years later the Queen's Bench began to turn hostile to claims that warrants of commitment had to recite a number of things that the court had previously held that they must recite. In *In the Matter of Geswood,*[218] brought before the Queen's Bench under a writ of *habeas corpus,* the court rejected the argument that to be good a warrant of commitment had to set out the evidence that was given before the justice.[219] In rejecting this argument the court relied not only on the reasoning of *Lindsay v. Leigh,* but also on section 17 of Jervis's Act (1848),[220] which had legislatively prescribed forms not only for convictions, and for orders, but also for warrants of commitment founded on convictions or on orders.[221] A warrant conforming to these legislatively prescribed forms, the court implied, would henceforth be considered sufficient. The forms did not require the recitation of evidence heard by a justice in a proceeding. The warrant in this case was nevertheless found defective in that it did not state that the worker's absence was "unlawful."[222]

Six months later the court went even further, holding a warrant of commitment good even though it did not recite that evidence had been given to the justice on oath and in the presence of the accused party. The warrant of commitment had stated in one place that the accused "was, this 10th day of December 1853 . . . duly convicted before me . . . of the said offence."[223] Lord Campbell declared that this warrant of commitment

> is not itself a conviction, but proceeds upon a prior conviction referred to in it. It does not, therefore, require the incidents of a conviction. No doubt there may be such a thing as an instrument which is both a conviction and a commitment under this statute, but this document is no such thing. *It is quite consistent with everything which appears here that there has been a good conviction* properly shewing that the evidence was taken on oath, and in the prisoner's presence. I therefore think the warrant is good on its face in all respects.[224] (emphasis added)

---

[216] 20 L.J. (n.s.) (mag. cases) 241 (1851).

[217] Ibid., 243.

[218] 23 L.J. (n.s.) (mag. cases) 35 (1853).

[219] *In the Matter of Geswood,* 23 L.J. (n.s.) (mag. cases) 35 (1853), 37–39 (opinions of Campbell, Ch. J., Coleridge, J., and Wightman, J.).

[220] 11 & 12 Vict., c. 43 (1848).

[221] Ibid. See Schedule of Forms appended to the statute.

[222] *In the Matter of Geswood,* 23 L.J. (n.s.) (mag. cases) 35 (1853), 37–39.

[223] *Ex parte Bailey, Ex parte Collier,* 23 L.J. (n.s.) (mag. cases) 161 (1854), 162.

[224] Ibid., 164.

Mr. Justice Wightman and Mr. Justice Crompton were of the view that a good previous conviction could be presumed.[225] These decisions left intact very little of the court's earlier decisions holding warrants of commitment defective when they failed to set out the evidence given before the justice or failed to state that the evidence had been given on oath and in the presence of the party accused. In 1858, in a *habeas* proceeding that challenged a warrant of commitment, the Court of Exchequer allowed a second warrant of commitment drawn up by the same justice to be substituted for the first admittedly defective one and then proceeded to find the later warrant sufficient.[226]

By 1860, the earlier successes that those representing workers had had in quashing convictions on the ground that warrants of commitment were defective had become harder to come by. The impulses that moved Lord Denman and Mr. Justice Patteson to provide workers with some of the protections granted under common law to those criminally accused seem largely to have disappeared. By 1860, labor found itself in much the same position with respect to all these narrowly framed issues. From a simple instrumental perspective, we should expect that sooner or later organized labor would move to adopt entirely new strategies for dealing with the Master and Servant acts. However, such an instrumental perspective does not entirely capture the profound changes that these long, though nonsystematic, legal struggles had produced. For as the courts were moving definitively to reject a labor-friendly view of the Master and Servant acts in the 1850s, they were simultaneously eroding the traditional rationales that had given penal sanctions whatever legitimacy they may have possessed in the eyes of laboring people. They had done so, moreover, just at a time when labor was becoming increasingly well organized, and was about to embark on a new period of militancy. How had the courts arrived at such a position?

Each of the issues I have discussed has its own history, but there are important common themes as well. Between the 1820s and 1840s, Parliament and the common law courts seem to have had quite different ideas about what the scope of the Master and Servant acts properly should be. On two occasions Parliament passed acts that were designed not only to extend the reach of the Master and Servant acts but to extend them in reaction to court decisions.[227] On another occasion, Parliament failed to pass an even more ambitious bill that would have reversed a decade of

---

[225] Ibid., 165.

[226] *Ex parte Smith*, 27 L.J. (n.s.) (mag. cases) 186 (1858), 188–89.

[227] 10 Geo. IV, c. 52 (1829) extended the 1823 Master and Servant Act to a range of workers listed in the 1777 act, and 6 & 7 Vict., c. 40 (1843) extended coverage to piece workers in a number of trades "whether such Contract or Engagement shall be to work or be employed for any Person exclusively, or for all or Part of his Time, or for specific Work, or otherwise." and whether the work shall be done "by himself or by any Person or Persons to be employed by or under him."

court decisions.[228] Parliament seems to have wanted to cover as many manual wage workers as possible, and it does not appear to have been particularly concerned whether a worker was a full-time employee for a term or a piece or task worker who had been engaged to do a particular job. It also does not seem to have cared whether the engagement was exclusive or whether the worker would employ and pay underworkers out of his wages. All of these worker situations would be covered under one or another of the Master and Servant acts. Parliament had pursued this policy fairly consistently since the eighteenth century. Only in the case of domestic servants did it arguably intend to exclude a type of manual wage worker. Even then, efforts were made early in the nineteenth century to try to bring domestic servants under the coverage of the acts.[229]

Parliament, it seems, held a view of the position of manual wage workers that was simultaneously more traditional and more modern than the one held by the King's Bench in the 1820s, 1830s, and early 1840s. Station in life, together with an agreement to provide labor services, had placed a worker in one of the various forms of traditional service that the laboring population could occupy. Traditionally, service might be for a term, or by the day, or it might be by the task or by the piece. Task work might call for the worker to supply the materials and tools himself and to employ others to assist him. All of these were considered forms of service. These views are reflected in several late eighteenth-century common law decisions. In *Hart v. Aldridge*[230] it was held that a common law action for enticement would lie in the case of a journeyman shoemaker who worked by the piece and left a pair of shoes unfinished when he went over to a second employer. Mr. Justice Aston was of the opinion that such an action would lie even in the case of a home worker who accepted work from more than one person: "[I]f he were employed to finish a certain number of shoes for a particular person by a fixed time, and a third person enticed him away I think an action would lie. . . . [T]he [master and servant] law inflicts a penalty upon workmen leaving their work undone."[231] In an 1806 case brought under the 1747 Master and Servant Act, Lord Ellenborough appears similarly to have relied on traditional understandings. A person hired to dig and stean a well and to employ and pay an assistant under him was a "labourer" covered by the Master and Servant Act:

---

[228] See "A Bill For Enlarging the Powers of Justices in Determining Complaints between Masters, Servants, and Artificers . . . ," *Parl. Papers* (1844) III:223 and 229.

[229] "A Bill for the Better Settling of Disputes between Masters and Workmen, and Also between Masters and Mistresses of Families and Menial and Domestic Servants," *Parl. Papers* (1801), I:389.

[230] 1 Cowp. 55, 98 Eng. Rep. 964 (1774).

[231] *Hart v. Aldridge*, 1 Cowp. 55, 98 Eng. Rep. 964 (1774), 965 (opinion of Aston, J.).

"Sopp was employed to do the work either by the day or the piece, and . . . Franklin assisted Sopp in the work, under the retainer of Sopp, and not of Mr. Lowther: a common practice with labourers as well in husbandry as in other business."[232]

Beginning in the eighteenth century, however, legal theorists and some judges began to feel impelled to try to systematize and rationalize the common law, which was increasingly viewed as having developed in a more or less *ad hoc* way. By the nineteenth century, this impulse was quite strong, and I think one can see it in the efforts the King's Bench made to try to develop a coherent theory of the master and servant relationship. The contract of service was a contract, but it was a distinct species of contract that established a "relation" between parties, a "relation" that gave one of the parties a certain legal control over the person of the other party. The legal incidents of this "relation" were different from the legal incidents of relations established between parties through other kinds of contracts. Other contracts left parties pretty much as they had been before the contract had been undertaken, juridical equals with limited contractual obligations toward one another enforceable through common law actions that mainly provided for the payment of money damages for breach.[233]

How could the peculiar legal incidents of this species of contract be rationalized? If a contract called for a worker to make his or her physical labor available to one employer exclusively for a term, then arguably that employer would have a claim to control that labor, and indirectly, the physical person of the worker, at least for certain purposes.[234] On the other hand, if this was the theory that justified the legal incidents associated with this species of contract, then what of agreements that did not call for the labor to be made available on an exclusive basis, agreements that did not call for the labor to be performed personally by the contractor, or agreements that called for part of the remuneration to be paid for labor done by others? It is difficult to see how any of these cases fit within the theory that purported to explain the peculiar legal incidents associated

---

[232] *Lowther v. Radnor*, 8 East 113, 103 Eng. Rep. 287 (1806), 290.

[233] It is important to remember, however, that even money judgments left the judgment debtor subject to possible imprisonment for debt at this time. However, imprisonment for debt was viewed as quite different from the penal sanctions imposed by the master and servant law; see Chapter 6.

[234] It seems also to have been considered significant that the labor promised was physical labor, rather than work that required the use of other faculties. Artificers, of course, performed both mental and physical labor, but it was the physical component of the labor that placed them firmly in the relationship. But see *Ex parte Eli Ormerod*, 13 L.J. (n.s.) (mag. cases) 73 (1844) (designer who invents and draws patterns used in calico printing is "artificer" within 1823 Master and Servant Act).

with "contracts of service," hence the restrictive reading of the language "contract to serve" in the Master and Servant acts elaborated by the King's Bench in the 1820s, 1830s, and early 1840s.

What changed in the 1850s? For one thing, court personnel changed. Lord Denman, the chief justice since 1832, retired in 1850 and was replaced by the more conservative Lord Campbell, who seems to have set a far different tone in the Queen's Bench. At the same time, the Chartist agitation of the late 1830s and the labor unrest of the hungry 1840s that accompanied the legal advances of those decades gave way in the 1850s to relative labor peace.[235] A period of stability offered the perfect opportunity for retrenchment. However, there was a good deal more to this process. Parliament, the common law courts, and working people all acted on one another through a complex process of circular causation. The decisions of the King's Bench legitimated the views of working people about the proper treatment of piece work under the Master and Servant acts, but called forth a reaction in Parliament that set off, in turn, an organized worker campaign to defeat a pending bill in Parliament. After the change in court leadership in 1850, there was time to reflect on the aggressive way in which labor had taken advantage of the earlier decisions of the court. Labor had in fact succeeded, with the decision in *The Queen v. Johnson*,[236] in having practically all piece workers excluded from coverage under the principal Master and Servant acts. It became apparent to the courts by the 1850s that matters had gotten out of hand, and the statutes certainly contained language to support broad coverage.

There was also an aspect of this reaction that derived from changing legal ideas about contract. As mentioned previously, from the mid-eighteenth century on a segment of the governing elites of England worked to establish personal agreements as the principal basis for market relations. Nevertheless, legal ideas about these agreements evolved significantly. As the process of legal systematization and abstraction proceeded, different species of agreements increasingly came to be viewed merely as different forms of the same thing: abstract, generalized contract. John Nockleby has described the course of these developments in detail.[237] He has shown that the actions for harboring and enticement that were originally restricted to the master and servant relation came to be abstracted and extended to a wide range of contracts by the middle of the nineteenth century. They gave rise to the general tort of interference with contractual

---

[235] Webb and Webb, *History of Trade Unionism*, 198–200, 224–25; see also R. K. Webb, *Modern England: From the 18th Century to the Present* (Toronto, 1970), 279–86.

[236] 7 L.J. (n.s.) (mag. cases) 27 (1839).

[237] "Tortious Interference with Contractual Relations in the Nineteenth Century: The Transformation of Property, Contract, and Tort," *Harvard Law Review* 93 (1980).

relations, as the master and servant relationship increasingly came to be viewed as just another form of contractual arrangement.[238] As just another contract, the authorities could provide whatever remedies for breach good policy dictated. In the case of labor agreements with manual wage workers, there were good policy reasons for thinking that only penal sanctions offered reliable enforcement. The traditional distinctions between service for a term and service by the piece or task no longer seemed significant as the focus of legal inquiry shifted to agreements pure and simple. An agreement was an agreement, whatever its particular terms. If Parliament concluded that a certain class of agreements (those of manual wage workers) should be enforced through penal sanctions, then the courts would find little difficulty in applying this remedy to this class of agreements.

At the same time, however, the process of abstraction made it easier to compare labor agreements with other contracts and naturally provoked the question: Why should this class of contracts be treated so differently from other contracts? As the tradition of understanding master and servant agreements as a distinct species of contract faded, it became more difficult to justify the unique remedies provided for the breach of these agreements. In the unitary universe of contract, those remedies began to seem more and more anomalous.

How the position the courts developed in the 1850s undermined another aspect of the traditional legitimization of penal sanctions has already been discussed. The doctrine that piece workers for a term were bound criminally by their agreements but that their employers were only obligated to provide them work when it was available[239] undercut the traditional notion that masters and servants owed each other an extensive set of reciprocal duties during the term of the service. This notion had played an important role in legitimizing penal sanctions in the eyes of working people. The idea that workers were bound criminally to their employment during the entire term (a captive workforce) at the same time that employers remained free to employ them as much or as little as they judged to be in their interests made penal sanctions seem much more like class legislation than it had when the obligations of one party appeared to be balanced by the obligations of the other party. How had the courts come to this?

During the 1820s, 1830s, and early 1840s, the common law courts adhered to the rule that there must be adequate consideration to support a promise to provide labor services exclusively to one employer for a term. If there was no such consideration in the form of a promise to provide

---

[238] Ibid.

[239] Where the employer had not expressly undertaken more extensive obligations.

work during the term, none would be implied and the contract would be unenforceable.[240] The judges could not have foreseen that this private law doctrine would become part of the public struggles between organized labor and employers in the 1840s and 1850s. The idea of freedom of contract, an increasingly popular idea with judges, seems to have played an important role in the judicial crafting of the initial doctrine. Freedom of contract required courts not to imply promises where parties had not explicitly made them. Courts should refrain from writing contracts for the parties. A more practical consideration supported this idea in the context of employment contracts. If an employer had not expressly promised to guarantee work or wages in lieu of work, it would have been unthinkable for the courts to imply such a promise. How could the courts insist that an employer keep a business running simply to provide work for his workers when it would have been economically foolhardy for him to have done so? The first case in which this doctrine was drawn into the struggles between workers and employers did not pose an especially difficult legal problem. In late 1843, when a coal miner[241] sought damages for the days he was not provided work during his contract term, the rejection of his claim was based solidly on precedent.[242] The employer had not explicitly promised to supply work.

However, when lawyers for labor began to argue that similar contracts were unenforceable under the Master and Servant acts because they lacked mutuality, the courts were confronted with a more difficult problem from the perspective of existing doctrine. That they rejected this claim as well in the 1850s, moving to change doctrine in the process, was the result of a number of circumstances. In addition to the relative labor peace of the 1850s and the change in court leadership, ideas about freedom of contract may also have played a role in this turn of events.

Lord Denman's first reaction to the argument had been: "I should be slow to say that any opinion of ours as to the validity of this contract, on the ground of public policy [private law doctrine of lack of mutuality], would prevent either party to it from being amenable to the summary jurisdiction provided for the breach of it, *when they have both voluntarily entered into it*" (emphasis added).[243] If a person made an agreement voluntarily he or she should be held to it. If it was a one-sided agreement, it was not up to the courts to protect competent adults from their poor decisions. What the courts required at this date was not that consideration should be adequate but merely that consideration in some form be found. At a deep

---

[240] *Young v. Timmins*, 9 L.J. (Exch.) 68 (1831).

[241] *Williamson v. Taylor*, 5 Q.B. 175, 114 Eng. Rep. 1214 (1843); for a separate report of the case, see 13 L.J. (n.s.) (Queen's Bench) 81 (1843).

[242] See, for example, *Young v. Timmins*, 9 L.J. (Exch.) 68 (1831).

[243] *In the Matter of Turner, Ollerton, and Others*, 15 L.J. (n.s.) (mag. cases) 140 (1846), 144.

level it was probably the idea that people should be held to the agreements they had voluntarily made, even if those agreements were sometimes foolish and one-sided, that was an important factor in moving the
court in a new direction in the 1850s.

There is a problem with this explanation, however. The courts ultimately based the enforceability of such contracts on the implied obligations of employers, an idea at odds with the main thrust of freedom of
contract. They had to imply such an obligation to find any consideration
to support the worker's agreement to be bound exclusively to one employer for a term. How can this development be explained? I think we
have to begin to concede at this point that the courts' position was based
on something more than ideas about freedom of contract. It was based on
judges' views about the thinkable and unthinkable when it came to running businesses and hiring workers. Two things seem to have been unthinkable: that courts could obligate employers to keep businesses running when trade was slack merely to provide work for workers and that
the contracts workers had voluntarily made might be unenforceable. The
combination of these two unthinkable propositions led the judges to re-
make doctrine when lawyers for workers began to press the issue, abandoning freedom of contract to impose a limited obligation on employers
to support the enforceability of such agreements against workers. Ironically, the ultimate result was the further erosion of one of the traditional
rationales for penal sanctions.

The relaxation in the 1850s of the strict scrutiny to which the courts
had previously subjected warrants of commitment can similarly be explained by a combination of changing social circumstances and changing
legal ideas. The social circumstances were discussed previously. The legal
ideas are associated with another aspect of the modernization of the common law, the easing of the insistence on strict adherence to arcane formalities. In the case of warrants of commitment, it was Parliament that promoted simplification,[244] but the courts seem to have been only too happy
to accommodate, at least in the case of summary criminal jurisdiction under the Master and Servant acts.[245]

It would have been difficult to predict in advance that the legal fortunes
of the Master and Servant acts would take all these twists and turns. Who
could have foreseen that the common law courts and Parliament would
become adversaries with respect to the Master and Servant acts in the
1820s, or that the courts would have authored a pro-labor reading of the
acts that became the basis for working class litigation and a working class
parliamentary campaign? Who could have guessed that the courts would
then reverse course to support parliamentary policy, a reversal that would

---

[244] See 11 & 12 Vict., c. 43, s. 17 (1848).

[245] *In the Matter of Geswood*, 23 L.J. (n.s.) (mag. cases) 35 (1853).

simultaneously undercut key rationales for penal sanctions that the courts had earlier played a role in constructing? These complicated twists and turns could not all have been anticipated before the fact. At the end of this long chain of events the practice of penal sanctions was left more socially vulnerable than it had been previously, a state of affairs that does not come as a complete surprise but that also could not have been completely predicted in 1844.

These interpretive struggles should be of interest to economic historians as well as legal historians of labor. Penal sanctions under the 1823 statute did not present a fixed rule or set of rules over this long period. Common law adjudication practically guaranteed that the rules would be in flux for much of the time. Sometimes they were altogether uncertain, at other times the courts clearly acted to change one or another aspect of previous legal practice. All of these circumstances might have affected at the margins the payoffs that workers and employers could expect in various dimensions of their negotiated relationship. If the justices of the peace were forced to provide an array of procedural protections to workers and employers were challenged in sessional hearings and on appeal by union lawyers, then a quick and inexpensive method for eliciting effort and controlling turnover may have become marginally more expensive for employers. As a result, their expected payoffs from its use would have had to have been recalculated. If piece workers not hired for a term were exempt from penal sanctions that might have affected at the margin the payoffs for both workers and employers of hiring or being hired by the piece, this would have made certain contractual forms marginally more attractive to employers and less attractive to workers or vice versa. If employers were faced with a choice between uncertainty over the criminal enforceability of their labor agreements and commitments to provide work during the contract term, then the expected payoffs from long-term piece work contracts might have been marginally less for them. If they were certain of their enforcement rights but could still suspend work when necessary, the marginal payoffs might have been greater. However, exactly the opposite might have been true of worker payoffs in these two situations.

What is certain is that by 1860, as a result of these interpretive struggles, the common law courts had remade the legal terrain on which the Master and Servant acts rested. This new ground was less favorable to labor but also offered weaker normative support for the continued existence of penal sanctions. Before discussing the campaign for radical reform of penal sanctions that labor undertook in the 1860s, however, I take a closer look at the evolving strategies employers and workers pursued as they negotiated and renegotiated their relationship in the shadow of penal sanctions. In Chapter 5 I examine the struggles between the two groups that were waged *under* the rule of penal sanctions and the changes those struggles helped to produce in working people.

5

Struggles under the Rules
Strategic Behavior and Historical Change in Legal Context

Modern free wage labor is generally taken to mean labor working under agreements that are determinable at will or that are not determinable at will but in which the legal system prohibits certain remedies for breach, particularly criminal sanctions and specific performance. To the extent that employment at will was adopted in any English trade during the nineteenth century, the practice rendered criminal sanctions for contract breach irrelevant.[1] We know something about employment at will in Britain during the 1860s from testimony given before the Select Committee appointed in 1866 to investigate possible reforms of the Master and Servant acts.[2] The Committee members took a special interest in the practice because for them it represented a kind of social experiment, wage labor markets operating without the benefit of penal sanctions. The Committee wanted to know, in essence, whether wage labor could be profitably maintained under a system in which penal sanctions were not available to employers as it considered possible reforms of the Master and Servant acts.

MINUTE CONTRACTS

The Select Committee learned that by 1866 "minute contracts" were widespread in the Scottish coal fields. Nearly 25,000 of the 35,000 Scottish coal miners were working under such contracts.[3] Where minute contracts had been adopted employers generally did not prosecute workers

---

[1] In theory, at least, it was possible to have punished breaches of contracts even under agreements at will if the breach had taken place before a party had terminated the relationship and if the breach itself was not viewed as an implicit termination of the relationship. Where employment at will had been adopted during this period in England, however, this does not seem to have occurred.

[2] The first such Select Committee had been appointed in 1865, but its mandate lapsed when a new Parliament was elected.

[3] Testimony of Archibald Hood, in "Report from the Select Committee on Master and Servant; Together with the Proceedings of the Committee, and Minutes of Evidence" (hereinafter "Select Committee on Master and Servant"), *Parl. Papers* (1866), XIII:Q. 1245.

under the Master and Servant acts.[4] The common understanding seems to have been that minute contracts were the practical equivalent of employment at will requiring no notice for termination or quitting.[5]

Scottish owners and managers who testified before the committee spoke of the clear benefits both to them and their workers of the minute contract system. They also testified that minute contracts were steadily gaining in popularity among Scottish mine owners. The solicitor for the Association of Mine Owners of Scotland, however, raised questions about how widespread those views actually were among employers: "I find a contrariety of views among employers upon that subject; even among mine owners I find those who think it is desirable to maintain a system of warnings, of a fortnight or a week, as the case may be, and who actually do maintain them."[6] Almost no English coal mines, however, worked under the minute contract system. Most used fortnightly or monthly contracts,[7] and in Durham annual contracts were the rule in 1866.[8] One witness testified that he did not know of any English colliery that worked on the minute contract system.[9] Another, however, gave evidence that in the Manchester area a few large English collieries "neither give nor require notice."[10] Unlike their Scottish counterparts, English employers who testified before the Committee all thought that minute contracts were beneficial to neither employers nor workers.

Minute contracts were clearly the norm in the Scottish coal mines by this time, although some Scottish employers didn't like them. English

---

[4] Testimony of Joseph Dickinson, Esq., before the "Select Committee on Master and Servant" (1866), XIII:Q. 2127

[5] But see Testimony of W. Burns, Esq., before the "Select Committee on Master and Servant" (1866), XIII:Q. 2327 (misnomer to call these contracts minute contracts; they are actually day contracts and as such may still be enforced under master and servant laws).

[6] Ibid., Q. 2322.

[7] I am using the terms "fortnightly" and "monthly" contracts loosely here to refer both to periodic contracts with definite terms and contracts of indefinite duration determinable on a definite period of notice; see Chapter 2.

[8] Testimony of J. Lancaster, Esq. (Chairman of the Wigan Coal and Iron Company and Vice President of the Mining Association of Great Britain), before the "Select Committee on Master and Servant" (1866), XIII:Q. 1461; Testimony of T. E. Forster, Esq. (manager of several collieries and President of the North of England Institute of Mining Engineers), before the "Select Committee on Master and Servant" (1866), XIII:Qs. 1551–54.

[9] Testimony of William Mathews, Esq. (owner of iron and coal works and President of the Mining Association of Great Britain), before the "Select Committee on Master and Servant" (1866), XIII:Q. 2514.

[10] Testimony of Joseph Dickinson, Q. 2114. See also Testimony of Alexander McDonald (agent for the miners of Scotland) before the "Select Committee on Master and Servant" (1866), XIII:Q. 568 ("I know that in one very large colliery in Lancashire they have adopted [minute contracts].").

mine owners, however, by and large refused to have anything to do with
the "minute" system. They insisted on using fortnightly, monthly, or annual contracts in their mines and continued vigorously to prosecute contract breaches.

Over the course of the nineteenth century, employment contracts generally became shorter, until, it is supposed, employment at will became the
rule in industrial employment. The explanation that has traditionally been
offered is that as labor became increasingly proletarianized the burdens of
contracts began to outweigh their benefits for employers. If a worker left,
he or she could easily be replaced by dipping into the large pool of workers
who were always in need of work. The existence of this pool meant that
the costs that accompanied contracts could be eliminated. Without a contract, workers could be sent back to the pool of the unemployed on a moment's notice, giving the employer a powerful disciplinary tool.

In fact, however, employment at will was far from being the norm in
England in the 1860s. It was actually a clear deviation from normal practice of the time. Most trades maintained contracts determinable on a fortnight's or month's notice. In Durham among coal miners annual contracts were the norm. In a number of trades, the "hiring" system in which
certain workers signed one-, two-, or three-year contracts continued to operate. The traditional explanation has only taken account of half the
story, leaving out the common situations in which labor was in short supply (to which contracts of various lengths, and their criminal enforcement, were a response), the interest employers had in preventing workers
from abandoning work without notice, and their interest in retaining the
disciplinary device of imprisonment for breaches of conduct at work.

Why then did some employers, in Scotland in particular, decide to give
up the benefits of the Master and Servant acts? Is the traditional story of
the natural rise of free labor true after all? If it is true, why did most
trades still maintain the requirement of a fortnight's or a month's notice in
the 1860s? Why did English mine owners continue to insist on the use of
either long contracts, short periodic contracts, or contracts requiring a period of a fortnight's or a month's notice to terminate and continue to enforce all these kinds of contracts through the criminal provisions of the
Master and Servant acts?

The Scottish owners and managers who testified all gave a pretty consistent account of why their works had adopted "minute contracts." The
testimony of the manager of the Shotts Iron Company is especially illumi-
nating:

2035. How do you find that [the] system [of minute contracts]
work[s]? – Very well with us.
2036. How long has it been in force in your works? – It is six years
since I introduced it into the Shotts Iron Works.

2037. What led you to introduce it? – I had some experience of the working of it . . . when I was at Messrs. Merry & Cunningham's works there. . . .

2040. What led to its being introduced into Messrs. Merry & Cunningham's works? – *There was a pretty long strike of the workmen; they stopped work without any warning whatever, and at the termination of that strike the masters gave notice, that as warnings did not seem to be held binding by the workmen neither would the masters hold them binding any longer, and therefore they would abolish the system of contract.* . . .

2043. Did [the men re-engage themselves] willingly [under this new system]? – No, they did not like it at first.

2044. What was the result; was it satisfactory to both parties? – Afterwards it was; *at first the best men did not like it at all, they did not like to be liable to be turned away at any time,* but after they got to see that such a power was never used by the masters, except to turn away bad men, they got quite reconciled to it, and *now they like it better than the old system.* . . . *[I]n the minds of some workmen it creates a feeling of independence; they feel that they are under no obligation to the employer, and that they can leave when they like.* . . .

2051. Was its introduction into the Shotts Iron Works the result of any strike? – No: so far as I can recollect, I think, in the first place there were *several men left without giving the necessary warnings that were required by the rules of the work at that time; and, in the second place, there was a case in which a workman proceeded against the company for refusing to pay him the same rate of wages that they had been previously paying him without giving him a fortnight's warning.* . . . The man lost his case, but *it was that case, and the men leaving without giving the necessary warning, that led me to introduce the system of no warnings.*

2052. You say that the men had been previously in the habit of leaving without warning; had many men in consequence of so leaving been prosecuted under the Acts we are considering? – As far as I can recollect, I do not think in all my experience as a manager, that I ever prosecuted a single man for leaving without warning.

2053. Practically, in your experience, as regards these Acts, they have been a dead letter? – yes, since I became the manager of the Shotts Iron Works.[11] (emphasis added)

Only the furnacemen and enginemen at the Shotts Iron Works continued to be required to give notice, "because they are in responsible places, and any one or more of them leaving on a sudden might put the company to very great inconvenience, besides entailing very serious loss and dam-

---

[11] Testimony of John Ormiston (manager of the Shotts Iron Works) before the "Select Committee on Master and Servant" (1866), XIII:Qs. 2035–53.

age."[12] Furnacemen and enginemen were required to give a week's notice. Another Scottish employer testified similarly that he had adopted the minute contract system in retaliation for a strike in which his men had stopped work without giving him the required warning. His men, he said, had not liked the new system at first because they felt less secure in their jobs.[13] He believed that minute contracts had also been adopted elsewhere in retaliation for strikes without warning.[14] Both of these witnesses testified that employers adopted the "minute" system after consulting among themselves and that frequently several employers adopted it at the same time:

> 2047. [I]t was arranged by the masters themselves.
> 2048. The masters of the district? – the masters of Ayrshire and Lanarkshire; I do not think they all went into the arrangement but Messrs. Baird, in Ayrshire, and Messrs. Merry & Cunningham, and some of the other Lanarkshire ironmasters, agreed to abolish warnings at that time.[15]

The labor witnesses who appeared before the Committee tended to support this account of the adoption of minute contracts in these Scottish industries. In almost every case, they said, it was introduced at the behest of management.[16] However, the labor witnesses also indicated that in certain cases workers had struck to retain minute contracts.[17]

> 627. The Trades unions then, in point of fact, have promoted a strike for the purpose of enforcing the minute system? – They have in one or two instances, I think; but the system was inaugurated by the employers, and the development of it has been carried on by the employers.
> 628. And the trades union, to a certain extent have endeavoured to force the system as well? – Yes; believing its effect to be beneficial.[18]

[12] Ibid., Qs. 2061–67. But in other collieries even the furnacemen and enginemen were on minute contracts, see testimony of Joseph Dickinson, Esq., Q. 2126.

[13] Testimony of Archibald Hood, Qs. 1231–35.

[14] Ibid., Qs. 1236–37.

[15] Testimony of J. W. Ormiston, Qs. 2047–48. See also Testimony of Archibald Hood, Q. 1231: "after [the strike], on meeting some of the neighbouring colliery owners, I told them I intended to abolish the warning system entirely; and after a few days' consideration, the owners of two of the principal collieries in the neighbourhood came to the same resolution."

[16] Testimony of Alexander McDonald, Qs. 505–6, 511. Testimony of Colin Steele (Scottish Iron Moulders Association, a trade union) before the "Select Committee on Master and Servant" (1866), XIII:Q. 714.

[17] Testimony of Alexander McDonald, Qs. 507–8, 623–28.

[18] Ibid., Qs. 627–28.

172 American Contract Labor and English Wage Labor

These witnesses also claimed that it had been the workmen who had pressured employers twenty-seven years earlier into changing from annual contracts to fortnightly and monthly contracts, when they had begun objecting to binding themselves for so long a period.[19] Scottish employers and labor witnesses all seemed to agree that minute contracts were beneficial to both sides. English coal mine owners, on the other hand, strongly disagreed. John Lancaster, a justice of the peace and chairman of the Wigan Coal and Iron Company, was unequivocally opposed to eliminating criminal sanctions or to moving to a minute contract system:

> 1457. You think in your own interests as well as the interest of those you employ, who might be entirely thrown out of their employment by a man leaving his work, you require the present law of master and servant? – I think so.
>
> 1458. Are you aware that in Scotland, out of 35,000 miners, 25,000 are under this system of minute contract? – I have read that in the evidence; I did not know it before. . . .
>
> 1460. [In previous years, a few mines in England had adopted the minute system], but the impression left on my mind was, that it brought an inferior class of population there; that they were more floating about.
>
> 1461. What is the length of your contracts generally? – A month is the longest contract that I know of; a fortnight is the general one.[20]

Another English mine operator testified that minute contracts would certainly work badly in his district: "I have 540 or 550 men cutting coal at Seaton Delaval; they cannot get all places alike, and if a man got balloted to a place which turned out a little worse than the next place, he would go off."[21]

English mine owners consistently argued that fortnightly and monthly contracts served the interests of workers. Although they were being more than a little disingenuous in doing so, some of their points were nevertheless well taken. John Lancaster testified that

> the men would prefer to have, in our case, fortnightly contracts, rather than be dismissed at a moment's notice; I think that great hardships might arise from that on both sides.
>
> 1464. Would not the men under hourly contracts be more under the control of the masters? – I think so.[22]

19   Ibid., Qs. 476–89.

20   Testimony of John Lancaster, Esq., before the "Select Committee on Master and Servant" (1866), XIII:Qs. 1457–61.

21   Testimony of T. E. Forster, Esq., before the "Select Committee on Master and Servant" (1866), XIII:Q. 1578.

22   Testimony of John Lancaster, Esq., Qs. 1463–64. See also Testimony of William Mathews, Esq., Q. 2517.

Another English mine operator testified that he did

> not know any district in which such a system [of minute contracts]
> would be liked; I do not think the men would be willing to adopt it.
> 1550. They would require greater security for the maintenance of
> their employment? – Yes.
> 1551. They have now the security of a month's notice? – Yes. . . .
> 1552. Have monthly contracts been in operation for any length of
> time? – Twenty-one years.
> 1553. Previously to that what were the contracts? – Yearly.[23]

Another English mine owner, asked about the "minute" system, replied
that "I cannot offer the Committee any evidence upon that point, because, as far as I am aware, there are no such contracts in England; a day
contract means no contract at all, in fact."[24] He went on to say that fortnightly contracts are "the most convenient" because "time is allowed for
the men to seek other employment, and a convenient time is allowed to
the master to seek other men."[25]

The testimony of a more impartial witness, an inspector of coal mines,
seems to support the Scottish employers' view. The miners, he said, were
reluctant at first to give up the security of fortnightly contracts, but once
minute contracts had been introduced they came to see the benefits in being freed from the threat of prosecution under the Master and Servant
acts.[26]

Certain labor witnesses who testified before the Committee adopted a
rhetorical strategy similar to the one employer witnesses used. They argued that minute contracts served the interests of employers. Although
they too were being somewhat disingenuous, their points also were generally well taken. Colin Steele, Secretary to the Iron Moulders' Association,
a trade union, testified that

> if a workman is unsteady, and an employer requires to give him a
> fortnight's warning, or a week's warning, it takes him some time to
> get quit of him, whereas, in minute's warnings he can be dismissed if
> he is doing anything that is improper, and the employer would be
> likely to get a person that would be more suitable to him.[27]

Other labor witnesses were more candid, offering a sense of the benefits to employees as well as to employers. William Dronfield, Secretary to

---

[23] Testimony of T. E. Forster, Esq., Qs. 1550–53.

[24] Testimony of William Mathews, Esq., Q. 2514.

[25] Ibid., Qs. 2515–17.

[26] Testimony of Joseph Dickinson, Esq., Q. 2121.

[27] Testimony of Colin Steele, Q. 715. See also Testimony of Alexander McDonald, Q. 470
(if an employer must give notice, a worker "after the warning, might do him a vast
amount of injury").

the organized trades of Sheffield (an amalgamation of trades unions), observed that the shorter the contract the better off were both employer and employee:

> [S]o far as the employer is concerned, he would, in the event of the falling off of work, be able to dispense with a large staff of hands in half the time, supposing the notice were a fortnight instead of a month, and in that case it would be an advantage to him; and with respect to the men, they would be at liberty a fortnight sooner in the event of a better situation offering itself. In my own trade I know a number of instances where better situations offered, and employers generally have refused to let the men go under the month . . . and in consequence of that the men have lost the other situation, because the employer there would not wait.[28]

Another labor witness, William Evans, testified that in the prosperous state the pottery trade was then in, long contracts worked against the interests of workers. The "long period of the agreement takes from the workman the power of raising the price of his labour."[29] He admitted that in the then-current state of the pottery trade, day contracts would be disadvantageous on balance to employers, but that they would also bring some benefits:

> The probability is that such a system, placing the workman in an independent position of that kind, leaving the master to discharge him if he were a bad or inattentive, or careless workman, would work well; the best skilled and most attentive man would have the best price, and would be retained longest in his employment, but the employer would often suffer loss and inconvenience from such sudden changes.
> 1424. And the employer would have it in his power to part sooner with a bad servant? – Yes. In the United States there is no law to force any compensation for neglect of duty; all the redress the master has is to discharge the man if he is a careless workman.[30]

One labor witness made it clear that in Scotland, where the "minute" system had been introduced, workers would never agree to go back to working under contracts that required a month's notice before leaving. He was asked, "[h]ave you ever known an instance of any mine-owner or lessee who had adopted the system of minute or day contracts, reverting

---

[28] Testimony of William Dronfield before the "Select Committee on Master and Servant" (1866), XIII:Q. 810.

[29] Testimony of William Evans before the "Select Committee on Master and Servant" (1866), XIII:Q. 1410.

[30] Ibid., Qs. 1423–24.

to the former system of fortnightly or monthly contracts? – The men would not submit to monthly contracts now."[31] The same witness attributed the refusal of English coal mine owners to adopt the minute system to "the prejudices that exist on the part of the employers, who have not had before them perhaps the beneficial effects of the adoption of the system."[32]

However, there is also evidence that employers sometimes tried to reimpose annual contracts in trades in which fortnightly or monthly contracts had been the practice for many years. In the pottery trades, which were experiencing a labor shortage in the years 1864–1866, employers began to insist on annual contracts and the workers resisted.[33] In the coal fields in the north of England, employers began to try to reimpose annual contracts in 1863.[34] In Northumberland the miners were well organized and fought off the effort, but in Durham the owners prevailed, in part, it seems, because they were able to take advantage of a temporary labor surplus.[35] Annual contracts remained in effect in Durham until 1872, when the labor shortages of that year made it possible for the miners to force the owners to eliminate the annual bond.[36]

Ironically, it had been the masters in the northern coal fields who had first abandoned annual contracts in 1844 in the course of a long and bitter strike. "The coal owners had introduced a monthly bond to strengthen their position, for they thought by this monthly bond to get clear of any one who took a part in the union."[37] In the 1860s the northern miners fought against reintroduction of the annual bond, but in 1844 they had done everything in their power to try to retain long contracts. At a general meeting of the miners held in June 1844, a resolution was adopted: "That in the opinion of this meeting, the master's *monthly* agreement is calculated to break up our union and destroy our liberties as Englishmen, therefore this meeting pledges itself to resist it by all legal and constitutional means" (emphasis added).[38] One of the grievances of the workers who went out on strike in 1844, to which the employers' monthly bond was a response, was that they were subject to fines under

---

[31] Testimony of Alexander McDonald, Qs. 501–2.

[32] Ibid., Q. 569.

[33] Testimony of William Evans, Qs. 1375–82, 1404–10.

[34] Richard Fynes, *The Miners of Northumberland and Durham: A History of Their Social and Political Progress* (1873; reprint Sunderland, England, 1923), 206.

[35] Ibid., 246. Unemployment was higher in 1863 than it would be during the following three years; see Table 2.1.

[36] Ibid., 219, 235, 237–38.

[37] Ibid., 62.

[38] Ibid., 77.

the annual contract for missing a single day's work, "but the masters often laid the men idle without any compensation at all, and as they were bound to them for a whole year as their servants, it was reasonable they should find them constant employment or wages."[39] In a strike that had taken place thirteen years earlier, in 1831, the miners had similarly insisted that because the pit bond bound both sides for a full year, it should guarantee them minimum earnings throughout the term.[40]

In 1844, the mine owners adopted monthly contracts that offered no minimum work or earnings guarantees, but many of the miners had not yet given up hope of winning back longer contracts.[41] Ironically, in light of their later staunch opposition to annual contracts, in 1854 the miners of Durham bargained for the reintroduction of an annual bond. The yearly contract was brought back in Durham "at the miners' request – during the boom of 1854, when coalowners also conceded a guarantee of minimum employment under the bond. The reintroduction, [however,] was neither widespread nor effective."[42] As late as 1854 the Durham miners seem to have been more interested in securing long contracts with earnings guarantees and enforcing employer obligations under those contracts than in continuing to work under contracts that allowed them to leave employers on shorter notice. As late as the 1850s, at least some Durham miners seem to have accepted the legitimacy of being bound by long contracts enforced through penal sanctions as long as their masters were similarly bound to find work or wages in lieu of work for them during the term.[43]

After the masters in the northern coal fields introduced monthly contracts in 1844, it quickly became apparent that those contracts also held certain benefits for workers and certain disadvantages for their employers: "If the monthly bond gave the owners the privilege of turning men off they wished to get rid of, the men took the same advantage and were frequently giving in their notice and leaving, and thus the owners were never sure of the pits working with any regularity or any degree of permanency."[44] Although Durham miners sought to reintroduce an annual

---

[39] Ibid., 67.

[40] Ibid., 18. See also James A. Jaffe, *The Struggle for Market Power: Industrial Relations in the British Coal Industry, 1800–1840* (Cambridge, 1991), 105, 115, 155–56. The annual contract from 1843 is reproduced in the appendix to Fynes's book, 291–96.

[41] Roy Church, *The History of the British Coal Industry, 1830–1913: Victorian Pre-eminence* (Oxford, 1986), 261.

[42] Ibid.

[43] There may have been opposition to long contracts among Scottish coal miners, however, as early as 1839. Testimony of Alexander McDonald, Qs. 474–90.

[44] Fynes, *Miners of Northumberland and Durham*, 134.

bond in 1854 and achieved some success,[45] by 1863 they too had come to be adamantly opposed to yearly contracts.[46]

Let us conclude by offering one final bit of testimony. A South Staffordshire iron and coal works owner, who was also a justice of the peace, testified during the 1866 hearings that

> There has been a great complaint on the part of the workmen with regard to committing men to prison for breaches of contract, or, in other words, visiting a civil offence with a criminal punishment. There has been a very prevalent impression of injustice on the part of the workmen on that score; and not only so, but the stipendiary magistrates of my district, who have generally had to deal with those cases, are under the same impression, that it is hardly right to visit a civil offence with a criminal punishment. There has therefore been considerable disinclination on the part of the magistrates to commit, as well as on the part of the prosecutors to have the men committed.[47]

This testimony must be taken with a grain of salt because South Staffordshire was among the districts that had the highest prosecution rates between 1857 and 1875.[48] Nevertheless, it may reflect real pressures that had begun to be brought by the workers against employers, raising the intangible costs of prosecutions. The result in South Staffordshire may have been stubborn enforcement of the acts in the face of worker resistance, but perhaps in Scotland the added costs of prosecutions made employers more reluctant to use the Master and Servant acts.

The preceding testimony, although based heavily on the experiences of only one industry (mining), can be used to draw up a kind of generic balance sheet of the benefits and costs of minute and longer contracts to workers and employers. My conclusions may not be equally applicable to other trades, but the factors discussed are general enough to support the expectation that they may be. This is a complex calculation that depends on the weighing of a number of competing variables.

---

[45] Church, *History of the British Coal Industry*, 261.

[46] Ibid., 219.

[47] Testimony of William Mathews, Q. 2423.

[48] Daphne Simon, "Master and Servant," in *Democracy and the Labour Movement: Essays in Honour of Dona Torr*, ed. John Saville (London, 1954), 194; D. C. Woods, "The Operation of the Master and Servants Act in the Black Country, 1858–1875," *Midland History* 7 (1982): 97. See also *Judicial Statistics of England and Wales* (London, 1857–1875).

I. *Low Unemployment*

Employers, Minute Contracts: Costs – Penal sanctions were not available and the threat of dismissal under these labor market conditions was generally not very powerful. If employers needed labor they would be reluctant to use threats of dismissal. There was therefore little overall power to discipline the labor force under these circumstances. Worker threats to leave were more powerful, and there were potentially high turnover and agency costs. Retention of key workers was a problem. Upward pressure was exerted on wages from all of these sources.

Benefits – It was possible to get rid of workers quickly if there was a sudden downturn in trade or if workers became troublesome in various ways.

Workers, Minute Contracts: Costs – There was no employment security in the event trade suddenly fell off.

Benefits – The power to leave immediately was of great benefit where other employers were seeking workers and offering higher wages. Workers were not subject to criminal punishment and were free to shop their labor around, provoke a bidding war, and get the best wage.

Employers, Long Contracts: Costs – On the other hand, a system of long contracts enforced criminally would not have benefited employers who had not already secured the labor they needed. Long contracts would have deprived them of free access to the labor market. Criminal sanctions would have interfered with their ability to bid workers away from other employers. In many cases, long contracts also committed employers to give work or wages even if trade suddenly took a downturn. Even where employers made no such promise, from the 1830s until the late 1840s they could not be certain such contracts would be enforceable. More important, where they failed to make such a promise, that failure might in itself become a controversial subject in labor relations. Each time a contract was negotiated the topic would come up, and depending on the state of the labor market and the state of worker organization, owners would either concede or refuse to concede such guarantees.[49] Moving to short contracts might mean that the workers would be less invested in pressuring so aggressively for such guarantees, given that the relationship would then be a short-term one determinable on a month's or a fortnight's notice. Long contracts also reduced an employer's ability to get rid of workers who became labor agitators, a concern of mine operators, as evi-

---

[49] In the northern coal fields the 1831 annual pit bond contained earnings guarantees; the 1832 bond did not. The guarantees were reintroduced in 1838 and became a prime issue in the 1844 strike. See Church, *History of the British Coal Industry*, 260–61.

denced by both employer and labor sources. Following the 1831 strikes in the north, "Henry Morton, Lord Durham's agent explained that [under the annual pit bond] while he could dismiss 'deputies', who were lower ranking supervisory personnel, with impunity, he had to wait until 'next year [to] have an opportunity of proscribing all those infamous Rogues, the Ranter Preachers – and other bad characters.'"[50] Richard Fynes offers a similar account of employer anxieties concerning the annual bond during the 1844 conflict.[51]

Benefits – To the extent that an employer already had the labor he wanted, he would have benefited enormously from long contracts enforced through criminal sanctions in tight labor markets. They served as a way to discipline his labor force at a time when dismissal was not a substantial threat, reducing turnover and eliciting effort during such periods, generally tying down his workforce and keeping its wages from being bid up. Strikes during the term were breaches of contract and could be punished with a prison sentence.

Workers, Long Contracts: Costs – There was the threat of up to three months on the treadmill for shirking or for premature departure. Workers were unable to shop their labor around for better offers. Wages were limited to those negotiated for however long the contract ran, in the face of rising wages in the trade. No strikes were allowed during the term.

Benefits – Workers would have employment security and perhaps some earnings security for the term, depending on the contract and the state of the law at the time. This was not of great value while the labor market was tight but offered a hedge against economic downturns.

Employers, Fortnightly and Monthly Contracts: Costs – Wage stabilization and turnover cost reduction probably were not as good as under long contracts. It was not possible to get rid of workers immediately, as under minute contracts.

Benefits – Penal sanctions were available. This was a powerful method for eliciting effort in tight labor markets when the threat of dismissal was less effective. Such discipline was not available with minute contracts. These contracts reduced turnover costs by allowing for orderly replacement of workers. There was probably some wage stabilization by comparison to minute contracts. Guarantees of employment or earnings security were either eliminated or reduced, and there was less exposure in the

---

[50] Jaffe, *Struggle for Market Power*, 101. This kind of problem could be reduced if an employer could obtain a contract clause permitting him to terminate the relationship on shorter notice.

[51] Fynes, *Miners of Northumberland and Durham*, 62.

event of a downturn than under long contracts. It was possible for employers to permanently reduce the workforce more quickly than under long contracts and to get rid of labor agitators more quickly than under long contracts. No strikes were allowed without a period of notice.

Workers, Fortnightly or Monthly Contracts: Costs – There was a threat of up to three months on the treadmill for shirking or departure without notice. No strikes were allowed without a period of notice. Workers were not free to accept a new job at higher wages until they worked out their notice. There was not much employment security in the event of an economic downturn, and workers could be let go after two weeks or a month.

Benefits – Workers were not subject to instant dismissal except for just cause. They had to be given a term's notice for dismissal, which was a little more employment security than under minute contracts. They had time to find a new position. Workers were better able to take advantage of a tight labor market to raise wages than under long contracts.

On balance, it would appear that minute contracts would probably not have been as good for employers as longer contracts during periods of low unemployment, but employers would have been divided on this question. Some would also have had an interest in unobstructed access to labor markets. In the case of workers, minute contracts would generally have been more beneficial than other contracts while labor markets remained tight. Conversely, employers probably would have benefited on balance from long contracts in tight labor markets, and workers would have been relatively worse off under such contracts, at least as long as those market conditions continued. Fortnightly and monthly contracts would have fallen somewhere in between, except that they would have exposed workers to the possibility of three months on the treadmill and conversely would have continued to give employers an effective way to reduce turnover and elicit effort in tight labor markets.

II. *High Unemployment*

Employers, Minute Contracts: Costs – No penal sanctions were available. Employers would experience a loss of labor and/or payment of higher wages should trade suddenly pick up.

Benefits – The threat of dismissal was powerful to elicit effort. Employers could quickly adjust the size of the workforce to changes in trade without long-term obligations. They could recruit labor at the lowest going rate.

Workers, Minute Contracts: Costs – The threat of dismissal was a powerful disciplinary device. Workers had no employment or earnings security.

Benefits – Workers were not subject to being sent to the house of correction for up to three months. They were not tied to an employer should the economy suddenly improve.

Employers, Long Contracts: Costs – In many cases employers had to continue to provide work or wages in lieu of work while trade was depressed. The threat of instant dismissal was not available except for just cause.

Benefits – The disciplinary device of penal sanctions was available. There would be a reliable labor supply at established wages should the economy suddenly improve.

Workers, Long Contracts: Costs – Workers were subject to up to three months on the treadmill for breaches of conduct or for premature departure. They were stuck with old wage terms should the economy suddenly improve and wages begin to rise.

Benefits – Workers had employment security and more or less extensive earnings security for the term, depending on the particulars of the contract and the state of the law at the time.

Employers, Fortnightly or Monthly Contracts: Costs – There was no instant dismissal without just cause. There was also a lag of a period's notice in adjusting the size of the workforce, as well as a lag of a period's notice in adjusting wages downward or securing cheaper labor from the market. Employers were exposed to wage pressures and turnover should trade improve.

Benefits – Penal sanctions were available for shirking or for departure without notice. No strikes could take place without notice. The threat of dismissal after notice was still available. There were limited or no guarantees about providing work or wages in case trade remained poor or declined further.

Workers, Fortnightly or Monthly Contracts: Costs – Workers were subject to penal sanctions. There could be no strikes without notice. Workers faced a lag of a term's notice to accept higher wages should trade improve. Employment and earnings security were limited to a term's notice.

Benefits – Workers were not subject to instant dismissal without just cause. They had some time to secure a new position. There was some employment and earnings security, by comparison to minute contracts. There was a lag in downward pressure on wages.

In general, during economic downturns minute contracts would have served the needs of employers well, except that they would have had to give up the disciplinary device of imprisonment. At the same time, while such labor market conditions prevailed minute contracts meant no job security for workers. The threat of instant dismissal became a powerful disciplinary device. Under these conditions, long contracts provided benefits to workers such as limited or more extensive employment and earnings security and no instant dismissal except for just cause. However, under long contracts workers would also have been subject to criminal punishment. While labor markets were slack long contracts would not have been as beneficial to employers as minute contracts, except for the fact that under long contracts they would continue to have the benefit of penal sanctions. Monthly and fortnightly contracts would have given employers greater employment flexibility and also the benefit of penal sanctions.[52]

THE MOVEMENT TOWARD SHORTER CONTRACTS

In the face of these opposing and crosscutting considerations, I'd like to try to explain the general movement towards shorter contracts, but the retention of long contracts in certain cases, by using a nontechnical, game theoretical approach to analyze developments.[53] The various customary lengths of service in particular trades (yearly, fortnightly, monthly, or minute) can be understood as multiple, unstable equilibria in the bargaining relationship between employers and workers. Prior to the 1840s, many English and Scottish coal miners worked under annual contracts. As long as both sides adhered to that practice in good times as well as bad, both sides would have shared in the benefits as well as the burdens of long contracts to a greater or lesser extent, and this might have constituted an equilibrium. Because of the competing considerations that the parties had to take into account, however, this equilibrium might have been highly

---

[52] Some workers, of course, would have wanted to take the opportunity afforded by labor shortages to sign long contracts to gain employment security, and some employers may have been tempted by a labor surplus to tie their workers down with long contracts to secure a labor supply in anticipation of future tight labor markets, as in the case of the Durham mine owners in 1863.

[53] On the recent use of game theory in history, see Avner Greif, "Economic History and Game Theory: A Survey" (Stanford Working Papers, 1997), and "Micro Theory and Recent Developments in the Study of Economic Institutions Through Economic History" (Stanford Working Papers, 1996); see also Michael Huberman, *Escape from the Market: Negotiating Work in Lancashire* (Cambridge, 1996), Chapter 5. Compare David M. Kreps, *Game Theory and Economic Modelling* (Oxford, 1990), 87: "I contend that the major successes [in game theory] have come primarily from formalizing common-sense intuition in ways that allow analysts to see how such intuitions can be applied in fresh contexts and permit analysts to explore intuition in and extend it to slightly more complex formulations of situations."

unstable. Even small changes in behavior or attitudes might have generated enough pressure to destabilize the practice.

By *equilibrium* I mean a widespread practice in a trade of using contracts of a certain length, where neither side is pressing for a change, and where both sides are satisfied enough with the balance of costs and benefits of the particular contract length.[54] These equilibria represented delicate balances of competing considerations in which the parties' calculations depended in part on tastes that were a product, among other things, of background ideas. Employers derived benefits from yearly contracts but were also subject to some costs.[55] The same was true for workers. How the benefits and costs were calculated and balanced depended in part on the value placed on each. How much value was placed on employment security and on long-term employment itself, for example, depended in part on ideas. One English coal owner testified that he rejected the idea of employment at will because he was afraid that it would lead to a working population that was, as he put it "more floating about."[56] Traditional ideas about contracts and social imbeddedness seem to have played a role in his calculation of the benefits of monthly and fortnightly contracts as opposed to minute contracts. Similar ideas affected the calculations of workers.

These equilibria were unstable because small changes in the relationship could lead parties to recalculate the fine balance of their payoffs and to press for a change. Every contract length held benefits and costs for both parties. Which was emphasized, and in what quantum, determined how each party would react to a proposed change in contract length. In mining, workers, in most cases, seem to have wanted to retain the status quo until a change had been introduced. Then they began to appreciate

[54] It's important to understand that this particular sharing of costs and benefits only involves the costs and benefits of different contract lengths. I am not addressing the many other contract terms that determined to a large extent how equitably the joint product of capital and labor was divided between the two. On equilibrium defined as a form of satisficing, see Kreps, *Game Theory*, 180 n.29. ("Another rationalization, suggested by models of retrospection and concomitant inertia in behaviour, is that the individual may settle for a 'satisfactory' course of action because its consequences are well known and understood; to break from a routine might result in an increase in strategic uncertainty (how will others respond?), which is judged to be unworthwhile if the 'expected gains' are small. Notions of aspiration levels, arrived at by early experience and then rarely shifted, come into play. . . . If we look not for exact equilibria but only for almost or epsilon-equilibria, the set of what is an equilibrium in certain contexts expands enormously.")

[55] Employers worked very hard to try to have it both ways; see Chapter 4. They attempted to limit their exposure under long contracts in various ways – no work guarantees, short notice to terminate a long agreement – while insisting that their workers were criminally bound for the entire term. However, they never succeeded in completely eliminating the costs of long contracts.

[56] Testimony of John Lancaster, Qs. 1457–61.

that there were benefits for them associated with the change as well as costs, and employers began to appreciate that there were costs as well as benefits. After the change had taken place, the parties sometimes switched sides. At first, many coal miners opposed shorter contracts as an attack on their employment security. Later they fought for shorter contracts or employment at will and against the reintroduction of annual contracts. Once a change had occurred, experience of the new practice sometimes led to changes in the tastes of the parties, altering their calculations of the balance of the costs and benefits of different contract lengths.[57] Many miners, for example, seem to have come to value the benefits of short contracts much more once they had worked under them. By the 1860s a real shift in the attitudes of miners seems to have taken place. Many more seem to have become willing to live with less employment security (or to doubt that long contracts brought much earning security) in order not to be bound criminally for long periods of time.

Equilibrium positions were upset when small changes in the relationship led one party (usually) to decide that on balance its interests would be better served by changing to contracts of a different length. In mining, employers were the initiators of change in most cases. Sometimes both sides agreed on the proposed change. More often one party resisted the proposed change. A new equilibrium was established when the stronger party had had its way but the weaker party had come to conclude that it derived substantial benefits from the new contract length and was won over to the practice.

According to testimony before the Select Committee, in 1839 the Scottish miners began to object to being bound for so long a term as a year. This early change in attitude among Scottish miners may have been enough to tip the balance in the direction of fortnightly or monthly contracts because, depending on their provisions, yearly contracts would also have exposed employers to some economic risks. Employers could eliminate many of these risks simply by conceding the demands of miners and moving to short contracts. In moving to fortnightly or monthly contracts they would not have been giving up the benefits of the Master and Servant acts.

In the northern English coal fields, the shift from annual to monthly contracts was initiated by mine owners and resisted by the men, although a similar underlying process appears to have been at work. In the early 1840s labor relations deteriorated again in the northern coal fields after a period of relative stability. In 1844 the workers launched a great strike. Among other things, they were striking for the benefits to which they

---

[57] James G. March, "Bounded Rationality, Ambiguity, and the Engineering of Choice," in *Rational Choice,* ed. Jon Elster (New York, 1986), 154. ("[A]ctions and experience with their consequences affect tastes. Tastes are determined partly endogenously.")

believed they were entitled under annual contracts. Because the workers had agreed to work for an entire year, the owners should live up to an obligation to give them a minimum amount of work or wages in lieu of work during the entire year.

These demands, and the growing militancy of workers, tipped the mine owners into abandoning the annual bond in favor of monthly contracts. They sought to accomplish at least two things by embracing these contracts. First, under monthly contracts they could get rid of troublesome union organizers more quickly. Second, it would be easier to avoid earnings guarantees where the agreement only created a potentially short-term relationship between the parties. They also could secure these advantages without having to give up the benefits of the Master and Servant acts. These considerations led mine operators to recalculate the payoffs to them of annual as opposed to monthly contracts. The workers resisted the change because yearly contracts held benefits for them that they were reluctant to give up, particularly employment (if not always earnings) security. Indeed, in 1854 the Durham miners used the bargaining leverage they gained in a tight labor market to force the owners to promise to restore annual contracts with guarantees of minimum earnings.

Once the change to monthly contracts had taken place, however, many miners began to enjoy the greater liberty that went along with a shorter notice period, and employers began to see that monthly contracts sometimes made it difficult for them to hold labor when they needed it most. Once again, as long as both parties adhered to the practice through the full trade cycle, there would have been a sharing of the benefits and burdens of monthly contracts, and this too may have constituted an unstable equilibrium.

In the late 1850s Scottish miners took advantage of a temporary labor shortage to press various demands on mine owners. The result, apparently, was to destabilize the settled practice of using monthly contracts in Scotland. Scottish mine owners testified that it had been long strikes taken without the required warning that had moved them to abolish warnings altogether in this period. One manager testified that individual miners leaving without warning and a miner's suit against the company for contract breach had pushed him into adopting minute contracts. Scottish owners and managers shifted to minute contracts, it appears, because they had come to feel that miners had upset the delicate sharing of the benefits and burdens of short contracts. They were refusing to be bound by the required warnings yet simultaneously insisting that employers fulfill their obligations under the contract. For employers who were reluctant to try to enforce contracts by using the Master and Servant acts, for one reason or another, the change to minute contracts made sense.

Scottish mine operators tried to introduce the new system in groups so that their relative competitive position would not be compromised as they shifted to employment at will. The change to employment at will also seemed to constitute an equilibrium in which the benefits and burdens of contracts at will would be shared over the course of the trade cycle. Moreover, labor witnesses testified that this was an equilibrium the Scottish coal miners would resist changing. They were now adamantly opposed to ever working again under monthly contracts.

Because the Master and Servant acts were still in effect, however, mine operators faced with strikes without warnings still had an alternative to employment at will. They could adhere to fortnightly or monthly contracts and move vigorously to enforce the legal duties of workers by prosecuting them under the acts. Maintaining such contracts meant that they retained a powerful weapon against strikes without warning and a powerful disciplinary device in the pits. Mine operators, by making liberal use of the Master and Servant acts, could decide to defend fortnightly and monthly contracts against actions that might undermine them, and this is what many English mine operators chose to do.

In the 1860s, English mine operators in the north pursued yet a third strategy. Beginning in 1863, they tried to reintroduce annual bindings as a way of reasserting control over their workforce. Long contracts enforced through criminal sanctions gave them a powerful weapon, tying workers down criminally for an extended period. However, by the 1860s English miners in the north wanted nothing further to do with annual contracts and resisted the change.

After 1844, British mine operators had at least three options: defend the status quo of fortnightly or monthly contracts, shift to minute contracts, or move to restore long contracts. Why the different options would have been exercised along national lines is difficult to say. Durham, in the far north of England, where annual contracts were reintroduced in 1863, was only a short distance from Scotland, where minute contracts were the norm by this time. Perhaps Scottish employers were less inclined to use the English master and servant laws; perhaps Scottish miners were less willing to abide by English legislation. Perhaps the memory of their recent serfdom had led the Scots to agitate for shorter contracts earlier and had stiffened their resolve to resist even short contracts by the 1860s.[58] On the other hand, perhaps it was because Scottish miners were less well organized and Scottish mine operators less worried about the impact of possible strikes.[59]

---

[58] Serfdom among Scottish coal miners had only been abolished by Parliament between 1775 and 1799. See Christopher A. Whatley, "'The Fettering Bonds of Brotherhood': Combination and Labour Relations in the Scottish Coal-mining Industry, c. 1690–1775," *Social History* 12 (May 1987) for an analysis of this process.

[59] Church, *History of the British Coal Industry*, 738.

By the 1850s, these options were not all equally palatable to either workers or mine operators. Defending the status quo of fortnightly or monthly contracts or shifting to minute contracts seem to have provoked less resistance on both sides than attempts to reintroduce long contracts. The Durham mine operators reluctantly agreed to restore annual contracts in 1854 while labor markets were tight, but when unemployment increased the mine operators defected, bringing back short contracts without guarantees. When the mine operators reassessed their position in 1863 and decided to reintroduce annual contracts, the northern miners had also reassessed their position and resisted the long contracts. Workers in the pottery trade also opposed the reintroduction of annual contracts in the 1860s.

Hence, by the 1850s it had become easier to bring about change in one direction than in the other. A shift from longer contracts to shorter contracts provoked less opposition than attempts to reverse direction and restore longer contracts. Because of this lack of perfect reversibility a decision to shift to monthly, fortnightly, or minute contracts for short-term strategic reasons might well have been difficult to change later on. Employers had reasons for wanting on occasion to adopt short contracts or minute contracts to counter actions of their workers, which they often interpreted as defection from the established terms of the relationship. When worker attitudes grew more hostile to long contracts, employer strategic behavior and changed worker tastes reinforced one another and led to a steady drift toward shorter contracts. In Scotland by the early 1860s this process had led to the widespread adoption of employment at will in coal mining, but in England mine operators stopped at monthly and fortnightly contracts and in some cases tried (with only mixed success) to reverse direction by bringing back annual contracts.[60] Under both kinds of agreements English employers continued to enjoy the considerable benefits of the Master and Servant acts.

EFFECTS OF CHANGES IN THE LAW

The changed legal rule about mutuality that the courts had adopted in the early 1850s may have played a role in stabilizing the use of contracts in England. If a legal rule had forced employers to choose between contracts containing earnings guarantees and contracts at will, they may well have calculated that the downside exposure of contracts with guarantees

---

[60] This discussion, it should be emphasized, applies to contract lengths widely adopted in trades or industries as a whole, not to the practice of negotiating individual agreements with highly skilled workers. Long contracts negotiated with individuals remained common in many trades throughout the period.

was too risky, and moved during economic downturns to a system of at-will employment. Because of the change in the rule in the early 1850s they did not have to face this choice. They could continue to use contracts enforceable through criminal sanctions but simultaneously remain free from the risks involved in earnings guarantees. The new rule may have led them to press workers harder for short contracts without earnings guarantees, and perhaps even on occasion for long contracts without earnings guarantees when that seemed especially advantageous. On the other side, the changed legal rule may have contributed to making long contracts, and even short contracts, that much less attractive to working people.

It is possible that the minute contracts that some Scottish employers had adopted by this time constituted a stable equilibrium. Scottish labor witnesses testified that the men working under minute contracts would never submit to monthly contracts again. It seems likely, moreover, that the use of minute contracts in Scotland played a role in destabilizing the use of criminally binding contracts in England. I present evidence in Chapter 6 that by the 1870s many workers in both countries had come to embrace minute contracts as a way of escaping liability under the Master and Servant acts. In addition, by the 1870s some working people had come to refer to men "hired" to serve under long contracts as "slaves."[61] It seems likely that the campaign to reform the Master and Servant acts that labor launched in 1863 helped to educate English workers about Scottish practices. In the process it may also have helped to accelerate the shift in worker tastes away from long contracts and toward minute contracts, precisely because the latter did not subject workers to criminal liability.

It is important to understand that the various equilibria, and the pressures that operated to destabilize them, were products in part of the background legal rules then in effect. But for the repeal in 1824 to 1825 of the earlier Anti-combination acts, labor might not have been able to organize well enough to destabilize earlier equilibrium positions. It is clear that the new law made a significant difference on the ground. A period of intense worker organizing followed passage of the 1824 act.[62] In the 1840s, the coal miners of Durham and Northumberland frequently cited the 1825 legislation as they began to organize their first permanent unions.[63] The 1825 legislation represented a fundamental change in the ground rules, le-

---

[61] Woods, "Operation of the Master and Servants Act in the Black Country," 103 and n. 25.

[62] See Sidney Webb and Beatrice Webb, *The History of Trade Unionism* (London, 1920), 104–5; John Orth, *Combination and Conspiracy: A Legal History of Trade Unionism, 1721–1906* (Oxford, 1991), 82; E. P. Thompson, *The Making of the English Working Class* (New York, 1966), 520.

[63] Fynes, *Miners of Northumberland and Durham*, 65, 116.

galizing labor organizations for the first time. But for the repeal of wage
setting legislation earlier in the century, labor might not have found it necessary to organize so aggressively to press for higher wages. By 1844,
English miners were proclaiming: "That it being the lawful and inherent
right of every working man in the kingdom to obtain the best possible
price for his labour, [we avow our] intention and determination to procure, individually and collectively [higher wages] and to abstain from
working until such remuneration be obtained."[64] If it had not been for the
timely change in the rule about mutuality in labor agreements, many
English employers might not have continued to find even short, criminally binding contracts economically advantageous over the course of the
trade cycle.

British workers became more powerful over the first decades of the
nineteenth century as they reinterpreted the promise of English liberty
and began to organize. The repeal of earlier Anti-combination acts in
1824 to 1825 aided their organizing efforts significantly. As workers grew
stronger, although they were far from being the equals of their employers,
they began to upset the terms of the earlier relationship. The strategic behavior in which employers engaged to counter worker actions sometimes
involved shifting to shorter contracts. However, once this step had been
taken it became difficult for either party to reverse, and the relationship
moved by fits and starts to shorter term equilibria involving a different
sharing of benefits and burdens over the trade cycle. When some Scottish
employers began to embrace minute contracts, that step not only became
difficult to reverse but created a tantalizing example for workers throughout Britain, and may have provided one of the motives for the campaign
to reform the Master and Servant acts, which was initiated in 1863.

Employer interests with respect to contract lengths did not cut in one
direction only; nor did worker interests. The movement toward shorter
contracts must be understood as a dynamic process in which the opposing and crosscutting interests of both sides, and the struggles between
them in the context of a particular set of legal rules and of changing attitudes, all played a role.

The equilibria discussed above were not only a product of the background legal rules but also interacted dynamically with those rules. Labor
practices and legal rules operated on one another through an intricate
process of circular causation.[65] The repeal of wage setting legislation and
the adoption of the Combination Act of 1825 were among the important

---

[64] Ibid., 58, from the resolution of the coal miners of Durham and Northumberland during
the strike of 1844.

[65] Duncan Kennedy, "The Stakes of Law, or Hale and Foucault!" *Legal Studies Forum* 15
(1991): 334–35.

factors that made it simultaneously necessary and possible for labor to organize well enough to upset initial equilibria. Once large numbers of workers had begun to serve under fortnightly, monthly, or minute contracts, they began to develop a taste for the greater liberty and independence that short contracts brought. They could leave their work on relatively short notice if they served under a monthly or fortnightly contract and enjoyed even greater liberty and independence under minute contracts. The change in the rule about mutuality undermined one of the traditional rationales for penal sanctions and contributed to workers having less of a financial stake in contracts of any length.

It seems clear that a sea change took place by the early 1860s in worker attitudes toward long contracts and toward criminal penalties to enforce those contracts. Whereas many workers appear to have accepted the legitimacy of long contracts and their penal enforcement into the 1850s, demanding only that their employers be held to reciprocal obligations, by the early 1860s workers seem to have come more generally to resist the idea of long contracts. Not only had they developed a taste for the greater freedom short contracts offered, but they had also learned that they could not rely on long contracts for earnings security during economic downturns. A change in legal rules had placed the state's imprimatur on the employer practice of binding workers criminally for a long term without offering them earnings guarantees. Of course workers could still bargain for such guarantees, but the new rule made it easier for employers to avoid such obligations. At the same time, employers seem to have become less interested in long contracts, except when they faced an immediate labor shortage, under which conditions long contracts made little sense for labor.

The strategic behavior related to contract length that both sides engaged in over several decades seems to have led to the emergence of minute contracts as the most stable contractual form. The sharing of the economic burdens and benefits of minute contracts over the trade cycle did not depend on the parties remaining loyal to the terms of the relationship but was accomplished through exit.[66] Minute contracts might also have become the most stable contractual form for another reason. They were the only type of contract in which labor, by now quite sensitive about legal subordination, could feel that it faced employers on a plane of legal equality, neither party being subject to the degradation of the criminal law as part of the employment relation. By this time contracts of any length frequently did not offer workers enough financial advantage to offset this increasingly oppressive disadvantage. Nevertheless, English employers and many Scottish employers stubbornly clung to fortnightly, monthly, or

---

[66] On "exit," see Albert O. Hirschman, *Exit, Voice, and Loyalty: Responses to Decline in Firms, Organizations, and States* (Cambridge, Mass., 1970).

longer contracts in the 1860s because they derived significant benefits from these contractual arrangements under the Master and Servant acts. In an abstract sense, employment at will may have become the most stable contractual form by this time, but it was not one most employers were prepared to embrace while they still could avail themselves of the contract remedies contained in the Master and Servant acts.

Most of these changes took place just beneath the surface of British political life. However, in 1863 a new chapter opened in the history of penal sanctions. A group of Scottish trade unionists launched a campaign to radically reform the Master and Servant acts. They lobbied parliament for a change in the basic ground rules of wage work, demanding that worker criminal liability for contract breaches under the Master and Servant acts be radically restricted or entirely eliminated. It is to that part of the story I turn next.

6

Struggles to Change the Rules

In 1863 a small group of Glasgow trade unionists launched a campaign to promote basic reform of the Master and Servant acts.[1] It has been argued that this campaign was initiated by Scottish rather than English workers because the Master and Servant acts operated more harshly in Scotland than in England. In England, after passage of Jervis's Act in 1848,[2] magistrates had the option of summoning workers to proceedings rather than immediately issuing a warrant for their arrest; by the 1860s it was common for English justices to do so. Jervis's Act, however, did not apply to Scotland, and there, master and servant cases still began with the arrest of the worker. However, the story cannot have been this simple. For one thing, by this time tens of thousands of Scottish workers were no longer, as a practical matter, subject to the Master and Servant acts, working as they did under the minute contract system. Ironically, however, rather than assuage discontent with the Master and Servant acts, the minute contract system may have exacerbated it by making it clear that a world of wage work without penal sanctions was not only conceivable but practical.

It took three months of internal debate for the Glasgow unionists to arrive at a set of demands. Finally, the group agreed that three basic changes were necessary. First, all cases should be tried in the County Courts in England and before the sheriffs in Scotland rather than before local magistrates, whose membership was drawn so heavily from the employing classes. Second, only a civil action should be available to parties for breaches of labor contracts, and it should begin, as civil actions did, with the issuance of a summons. Third, the only remedy for contract breach should be money damages.[3] However, according to Daphne Simon, at this stage of the campaign, the trade unionists were prepared radically to compromise these principles:

> The feelings of the delegates were all against the law: they called it a cruel relic of feudal barbarism, burned with indignation at its dis-

---

[1] Daphne Simon, "Master and Servant," in *Democracy and the Labour Movement: Essays in Honour of Dona Torr,* ed. John Saville (London, 1954), 173.

[2] 11 & 12 Vict., c. 43 (1848).

[3] See Simon, "Master and Servant," 174.

crimination against their class, and longed for complete equality. But their ideas made them hesitant about demanding that equality and doubtful of being able to win it. They were uncomfortably conscious of the plausibility of the masters' favourite argument that the workman must be imprisoned because he would so seldom have the resources to pay damages. So they added an amendment to their resolution on damages providing for imprisonment up to three months if damages were not paid within three days, and they expressly explained this amendment on their opponents' ground that it would "prevent workmen breaking their contracts with impunity."[4]

After developing their proposals, the Scottish group wrote to the Home Secretary asking for the introduction of reform legislation. Sir George Grey refused to commit himself. In response, the trade union group began to organize a broad campaign among trade unionists in both England and Scotland and succeeded in gaining wide support from union members.[5] The delegates to a London conference to promote reform held in 1864 began the process of lobbying members of Parliament.[6] J. M. Cobbett, an MP and a son of the Radical William Cobbett, agreed to introduce a reform bill based on the unionists' demands, but these demands were now somewhat changed from the original ones outlined in Glasgow. One change was of particular significance because it was ultimately to find its way into the 1867 reform act. The unionists now proposed that judges in master and servant cases be given the power to order the performance of a contract or to annul it.[7] Only if an order of performance was disobeyed could damages be awarded, and these damages were to be recoverable through distress warrants. Imprisonment was not to be available.[8] The strategy here seems to have been to try to meet the anticipated objection of employers that damages would be an insufficient remedy while simultaneously maintaining the civil nature of the proceeding by substituting a civil remedy, an order of performance, for the criminal remedy of imprisonment. The proposal, however, was still vulnerable to the objection that should a worker not have sufficient property to satisfy a damage judgment, an order of performance would be worthless. If such an argument were made, the unionists would be back where they had started, facing the contention that the inability of workers to pay damages made imprisonment an indispensable remedy. In the meantime, the unionists had introduced into the mix the idea that courts should be given the power to order the performance of labor agreements.

---

[4] Ibid.

[5] Ibid., 175–77.

[6] Sidney Webb and Beatrice Webb, *The History of Trade Unionism* (London, 1920), 251–53.

[7] Simon, "Master and Servant," 178 n. 2.

[8] Ibid.

The bill sponsored by Cobbett received a first reading and then was withdrawn. By the next year, 1865, the movement for reform had gained enough support in the country and among members of Parliament that Sir George Grey felt obliged to receive a deputation of trade unionists and fourteen members of Parliament. Only Cobbett, among the MPs, argued for the immediate introduction of reform legislation. The rest merely asked Grey to appoint a Select Committee to study the need for reform, and he was only too happy to slow reform down by obliging.[9] The Select Committee on Master and Servant met relatively briefly in 1865 before Parliament was dissolved.[10] Cobbett lost his seat in the elections. In the next year the Association of Working Men, a group promoting reform, approached Lord Elcho to move for the reappointment of the Select Committee, which he did on March 22, 1866.[11] In May 1866 the members of the Committee were appointed, with Lord Elcho as chairman.[12] The Select Committee heard testimony from both labor and employer witnesses and in July 1866 issued its report, with the testimony of the witnesses appended.[13]

The Committee's report concluded that the present law "is objectionable," and suggested several changes:

1. all cases should henceforth be publicly tried, in England, before two or more magistrates (not, as the workers had wanted, before a County Court);
2. a summons rather than an arrest warrant should be issued in the first instance;
3. "punishment" in the first instance should be by fine (rather than by imprisonment), but on failure to pay the fine, by distress or by imprisonment (not, as the workers had wanted, by an order of performance in the first instance followed by damages and distress, if necessary, but not "punishment" either by imprisonment or fine);
4. the magistrates should have the power to order the contract performed, and, if necessary, to order the party to find security for doing so (an idea originating with the workers);

[9] Ibid., 179. For appointment of the Select Committee in 1865 and nomination of its members, see Hansard's *Parl. Debates* (1865) CLXXVIII:col. 956.

[10] Simon, "Master and Servant," 179. See also "Report from the Select Committee on Master and Servant Together with the Proceedings of the Committee and Minutes of Evidence" [hereinafter "Select Committee on Master and Servant"], *Parl. Papers* (1865) VIII: June 15, 1865.

[11] Hansard's *Parl. Debates* (1866) CLXXXII:col. 816.

[12] Ibid., col. 817.

[13] "Select Committee on Master and Servant," (1866) XIII: July 30, 1866.

5. in "aggravated" cases of contract breach that caused injury to persons or property, the magistrates should have the power of punishing by imprisonment immediately (not the complete elimination of imprisonment the workers had wanted); and
6. arrest of wages in Scotland to pay fines should be abolished.[14]

The core of the argument that labor had been making in the 1860s was that penal sanctions violated one of the basic principles of the liberal state, that all persons were entitled to equal treatment under law. The appeal to equality under law assumed two slightly different forms. In the first place, the specific terms of the Master and Servant acts were said to treat employers and workers unequally. Workers were only given a civil remedy for the contract breaches of their employers, whereas their employers enjoyed a criminal remedy against them. As a purely formal matter, this objection might have been met and penal sanctions simultaneously preserved simply by giving workers a criminal remedy against their employers. When this way out of the normative challenge was suggested, however, employers failed to greet it with much enthusiasm.[15] This was not really the result that workers would have wanted in any case. Increasingly, the equality under law argument was framed as an argument that disputes over labor contracts should be treated in the same way as disputes over all other contracts, as purely civil matters.

LORD ELCHO'S REFORM BILL

In March 1867 Lord Elcho formally asked Mr. Walpole, the Home Secretary in the new Conservative government, to bring in a bill for the reform of the Master and Servant acts. Lord Elcho said that the Select Committee that he had chaired the previous year had concluded in its report that "the present state of the law was objectionable."[16] "The law," he said,

as it at present stood, was this – that a servant, if he broke a *civil* contract, was liable to a *criminal* prosecution, and might be imprisoned with hard labour. Such a state of law as this was harsh, unjust, and un-called for – and required remedy at the hands of Parliament.[17] (emphasis added)

---

[14] Ibid., iii.

[15] Hansard's *Parl. Debates* (1867), CLXXXVII:col. 1610 ("The men, [Mr. Fawcett] believed, would not object to aggravated breaches of contract on their part being treated as criminal offences, if aggravated breaches of contract on the part of the masters were similarly dealt with"); see also Simon, "Master and Servant," 183.

[16] Hansard's *Parl. Debates* (1867) CLXXXV:col. 1259 (March 1, 1867).

[17] Ibid.

The Home Secretary claimed that he was not in a position to bring in a bill immediately. Believing that reform could not wait, in April Lord El-cho introduced his own bill as a private member's bill.[18] He reiterated that

> [a]s the law now stood a breach of contract, which ought to be viewed and which the Committee viewed as a civil offence, was treated criminally. That was the real grievance of which the em-ployed class complained. . . . It was therefore proposed by the Bill that there should be equality between the employed and their em-ployers – that breaches of contract, as a rule, should be treated as civil offences.[19]

Lord Elcho had prepared the ground for the introduction of his bill as carefully as he could. He had, he said,

> been in communication both with men and masters on that subject, and a Bill had been drawn up first by the men, and afterwards sub-mitted to the masters. The present measure . . . was mainly based on the Resolutions of the Committee of last year; and both masters and men were agreed in the main on its provisions.[20]

Although the bill supposedly was based on the Resolutions of the Select Committee as well as consultations with men and masters, it implicitly re-jected several key resolutions of the Select Committee that would have de-prived proceedings under the act of their purely civil character. The Elcho bill instead seems to have attempted to make such proceedings as nearly civil in nature as seemed politically possible in the circumstances.

The bill did not give labor the jurisdictional forum it had wanted, the County Courts, but it did require that two justices of the peace adjudicate complaints at Petty Sessions, not, as formerly, one justice of the peace pos-sibly out of sessions. The bill also restricted the grounds of complaint to "neglect or refusal to fulfill any contract of service," or to "breaches or non-performance of labor contracts."[21] This was an effort to bring the lan-guage of the master and servant law into line with notions of contract as purely civil in nature. What the Elcho bill omitted was the "misconduct or misdemeanor" language of earlier Master and Servant acts.

The Elcho bill also made available to employers for such contract breaches a set of essentially civil remedies: in the first place, an order of performance, and in the magistrates' discretion, an order to find sufficient security for performance; or, in the alternative, an order annulling the

---

[18]   Ibid., cols. 1261–62; and Hansard's *Parl Debates* (1867), CLXXXVI:cols. 1059–60 (April 2, 1867).

[19]   Hansard's *Parl. Debates* (1867), CLXXXVI:cols. 1059–60 (April 2, 1867).

[20]   Ibid., col. 1060.

[21]   *Parl. Papers* (1867), IV:5–14 (Bill 105).

contract. In addition, damages or compensation could be awarded, recoverable by distress if necessary. If an order of performance was disobeyed, or damages were not paid, then the defendant's property could be distrained against for the purpose of paying off the damage judgment. No direct remedy was made available for failure to fulfill an order of performance. Up to this point, the remedies followed pretty closely those that labor had asked for in its 1864 bill. However, if the property distrained against was insufficient to pay the damages or compensation awarded, Lord Elcho's bill provided that the party could be committed to the house of correction or to the common gaol for up to three months, but without hard labor.[22] This provision did not represent a radical departure from contemporary procedure in civil actions, because in ordinary civil cases, imprisonment of judgment debtors who failed to pay damage awards could still be obtained. The main differences were that ordinary debtors were not normally sent to the house of correction and that they could in many cases secure their release if they were insolvent.[23] Lord Elcho's bill also withheld the power to "punish" by fine, merely authorizing awards of damages or compensation as in civil actions. In the circumstances, given that imprisonment for debt had not at this time been abolished, Lord Elcho's bill came very close to making master and servant proceedings civil in nature.

The bill was equally friendly to labor in its handling of the criminal side of the issue. The "Report of the Select Committee," delivered the previous year, had made the suggestion that in addition to "simple" breaches of contract, for which fines followed by distress or imprisonment should be available, a second category of contract breach should be established: "aggravated cases of breach of contract, causing injury to person or property," in which magistrates could punish immediately with imprisonment.[24] Not only did Lord Elcho's bill withhold the power to "punish" by fine for "simple" breaches, it also went some distance toward rejecting altogether the idea that contract breaches in and of themselves should ever result in criminal punishment. In an apparent effort to preserve the civil nature of the proceedings, the bill established an entirely separate procedure for criminal prosecutions and indicated that such prosecutions should only be based on acts that were already criminal under the general criminal law. Part III of the bill provided that where

> *the Injury to the Person or Property* of the Party or Parties [resulting from the breach or nonperformance of a contract of service] has been *wilfully and maliciously inflicted so as to amount to a Criminal Act,* and not to be

[22] Ibid., 11–12.

[23] "An Act for the Relief of Certain Insolvent Debtors," 54 Geo. III, c. 28 (1813).

[24] "Select Committee on Master and Servant," (1866) XIII:iii.

remedied by pecuniary Compensation . . . the said Justices . . . shall send the Case for Trial before the Court of Criminal Judicature at the Quarter Sessions of the Peace. . . . [and the party shall there] be tried according to the legal and accustomed Mode of Procedure of such Court against Criminals and Offenders, and upon Conviction the said Offender or Offenders *shall and may be sentenced to such Punishment as by Law is awarded for Crimes and Misdemeanors of the like Nature.*[25] (emphasis added)

Lord Elcho had gone some distance toward making proceedings for contract breach entirely civil in nature, seemingly limiting criminal prosecutions to acts that were defined as criminal independently of the Master and Servant acts. However, he had not gone the whole way. If a particular act committed by a worker against persons or property was already a crime, what need was there for this section?[26] As the section was worded, it did in fact create a distinct criminal offence because the injury had to flow from a breach of contract that, therefore, was made an element of a new offence created by the bill. Nevertheless, as imperfect as the clause was, it went a good deal further, both procedurally and substantively, toward addressing labor's main grievance than did the Select Committee's suggestion that local magistrates should have the power to imprison workers immediately for "aggravated" contract breaches "causing injury to persons or property."

In Parliament Lord Elcho's bill met with a good deal of resistance, principally of two kinds. There were those members, a majority of those who spoke, who agreed that "the present state of the law was very unsatisfactory,"[27] that reform was necessary, and that masters and men should, in principle, stand on the same footing.[28] However, almost all of those who thought reform necessary and who spoke for the *principle* of equal treatment thought that Lord Elcho's bill had gone too far. They were of the opinion that the bill would have to incorporate exceptions to the principle to deal with special circumstances and that these required the retention of the penal features of the traditional law. Mr. Pease, for example, said that

[t]hough he had a strong objection to the power of imprisonment, there were some cases in which it would be advisable to preserve that power. There was the case of protecting workmen from the strikes of

---

[25] *Parl. Papers* (1867), IV:5–14 (Bill 105), 13.

[26] This point was made in Parliament in a debate over the bill. Hansard's *Parl. Debates* (1867), CLXXXVII:col. 1608 (remarks of Mr. Henley, June 4, 1867).

[27] Hansard's *Parl. Debates* (1867), CLXXXVII:col. 1603 (remarks of Mr. E. Potter, June 4, 1867); see also remarks of Mr. G. Clive, col. 1604; and Mr. Pease, also col. 1604.

[28] See the June 4, 1867, debate over Lord Elcho's bill, Hansard's *Parl. Debates* (1867), CLXXXVII:cols. 1603–12.

their fellow workmen which was provided for by the dread of imprisonment. A colliery employing large numbers of men and a great deal
of shipping might be stopped by the strike of an engineman. A thou-
sand men might thus be thrown out of work.[29]

Mr. Alderman Salomons said that

> he must express his approval of the Bill. It was founded on reciproc-
> ity of principle between master and servant. By the present law, the
> master was responsible civilly – the servant criminally. [Nevertheless]
> [i]n all cases where, by the Act of the servant, any injury was inflicted
> upon the master which could not be compensated by fine, an option
> of imprisonment . . . ought still to be left.[30]

Mr. Bruce said that he

> agreed with the principle of the Bill. . . . Under ordinary circum-
> stances, a breach of contract between workman and employer might
> be easily dealt with as a merely civil offence. But there were cases in
> which the act of a servant in breaking his contract involved much
> more than an offence to his master. It involved a loss of employment
> to a vast number of his fellow workmen, the interruption of work,
> the payment of heavy damages to third parties and the infliction of
> an amount of evil altogether disproportionate to any possible remedy
> which could be exacted from servants. An illustration of that oc-
> curred in his own neighbourhood a few years ago. A haulier, em-
> ployed in hauling coal out of a colliery, was dismissed for improper
> conduct. . . . Without any notice the remaining hauliers, about eight
> in number, in that colliery struck work, and the consequence was
> that a large colliery, employing between 200 and 300 colliers, was
> stopped, every workman lost his wages, the coal owners were unable
> to deliver the coal at the port, and had to pay for demurrage and de-
> lay; and all that arose through the summary and peremptory act of
> those hauliers. Under the Bill, how would they have been dealt
> with? A summons would have been taken out against them, and
> they might have been compelled to fulfil their contract, that was, to
> return to their work. But what remedy was that? The evil had al-
> ready been done, and an interruption of work for a week had taken
> place.[31]

Although conceding the abstract principle that masters and men should
stand on the same ground, most of those who supported reform did not

---

[29] Ibid., col. 1605 (remarks of Mr. Pease).

[30] Ibid., col. 1607 (remarks of Mr. Alderman Salomons).

[31] Ibid., col. 1609 (remarks of Mr. Bruce).

think that even the power to order the performance of labor contracts would suffice to meet the requirements of employers. Workers would never be able to compensate masters for the substantial costs of lost production that could flow from strategic contract breaches. The only recourse was to try to deter such behavior altogether by exacting a high price from workers who committed such acts, and the only way that could be done was by retaining penal sanctions.

A second, smaller group spoke against even the principle of reform. Mr. Liddell, for example, said that he

> could not agree that the House would do well to adopt the whole principle of the present Bill. That principle was the abandonment of the punitive process against the workman and the doing away with the deterrent effect of the present law.[32]

Mr. Jackson asked,

> Was a man, having charge of an engine at a pit's mouth, who got drunk and ran away to be dealt with merely as a debtor, though he might leave 400 or 500 fellow workmen below in enforced idleness and in cruel uncertainty for six or seven hours? It was the knowledge that under the existing law he would be dealt with very differently, which kept such a man from getting drunk and running away.[33]

It was Mr. Liddell's view, moreover, that the principle of equal treatment was not in fact violated by the current master and servant law. The respective positions of masters and servants were so different that they legitimately required different treatment. "It was all very well to talk of equalizing the law between master and servant," Mr. Liddell said "[b]ut . . . the responsibility of maintaining discipline rested with the master alone, so that in no sense could their respective positions and obligations be considered equal."[34]

In his preliminary negotiations Lord Elcho had gotten the representatives of the workers to agree to his bill, but the Mining Association representing masters had raised objections. Lord Elcho had nevertheless gone forward with the bill.[35] It is the strong objections of the masters that are reflected in the June 4, 1867, debate. It is not surprising that as the bill was amended in committee it began to take a form more closely resembling the resolutions passed by the Select Committee the previous year, which had preserved much more of the existing law.

---

[32] Ibid., col. 1606 (remarks of Mr. Liddell).

[33] Ibid., col. 1611 (remarks of Mr. Jackson).

[34] Ibid., col. 1607 (remarks of Mr. Liddell).

[35] Ibid., col. 1612 (remarks of Lord Elcho).

At the same time, however, many members spoke of the pressing need for reform. Why was there a widespread feeling that reform of the Master and Servant acts was now necessary? The answer must be found in the pressure that labor was able to bring to bear on ruling elites. This pressure was essentially of two kinds: disruptive activity that imposed costs on employers and disruptive argument that exposed the hypocrisy of a polity ostensibly based on liberal principles. The power of the threats and the power of the arguments depended on one another. To the extent that the arguments were not successful in harnessing the authority of basic norms in making the case for reform, the power of the threat was reduced. Disruptive activity could then be characterized as mere coercion, not as legitimate grievance, and might be met with direct counterforce. To the extent that the power of the threat was insignificant, the effectiveness of the argument would be reduced. If labor wasn't causing trouble, their arguments could simply be ignored.

In the political context, labor's argument had great power. It resonated deeply with the widely held liberal belief that whatever material inequalities there might be, everyone was entitled to equal treatment under the law. But what were the threats that complemented this argument and helped to give it political bite? Members of Parliament were concerned about two problems in particular. First, they thought reform would remove one of labor's main grievances and thereby "promote a better understanding between employers and employed."[36] "The fact," Mr. Samuelson said,

> that the present law was not enforced in the districts where textile manufactures were carried on was an argument for its abolition. It was said to be necessary in the mining districts, on the ground of there not being in many cases a cordial understanding between masters and workmen: but the present law was one cause of that misunderstanding, for we could not expect trades unions to change their policy as long as this ground of complaint existed. . . . He could not see why a source of irritation like this should not be removed at once.[37]

In the minds of some members of the employing classes the deep discontent of the workers with the Master and Servant acts was one important source of the hostile labor relations that raised production costs. In

---

[36] Ibid., col. 1605 (remarks of Mr. Pease).

[37] Ibid., cols. 1605–06 (remarks of Mr. Samuelson). The Master and Servant acts actually continued to be used in the textile trade in Lancashire down to 1866. See H. I. Dutton and J. E. King, "The Limits of Paternalism: The Cotton Tyrants of North Lancashire, 1836–54," *Social History* 7 (January 1982): 66–67 and the prosecutions cited in Chapter 2, n. 117.

their view, these costs had begun to outweigh the benefits the law offered to employers. There was a second threat, however, that certain members of Parliament took especially seriously. They were concerned that if the present law were not reformed the workers would take steps to render it a nullity in practice by embracing the minute contract system. This would be bad, not only because it would mean that the Master and Servant acts had been eliminated de facto, but also because masters would then be deprived of the considerable benefits they derived from contracts. Reform was necessary if contracting and contract enforcement were to survive as an integral part of wage labor. Lord Elcho said that "[i]t was most desirable that the breach of contract should be made the subject of a civil action. In Scotland there were 35,000 miners, and 25,000 did not serve under this law."[38] Mr. Samuelson thought that

> [a]s long as the present law existed no workman who respected himself would enter into a long contract. Whatever trades unions might think or say to the contrary, it was desirable that contracts between masters and men should be of considerable duration. . . . [T]he law as it at present stood was both unjust and impolitic.[39]

The weight of sentiment in Parliament seems to have been in favor of throwing the workers a sop, salving their psychic wound in an effort to restore labor peace. Concede the principle that men and masters should stand on the same ground, but retain in the details of the legislation as much of the old penal system as possible, a system that many employers still viewed as indispensable to the proper functioning of markets based on wage labor.

The representatives of the workers who continued to be involved in negotiations over amendments to Lord Elcho's bill were pressured into accepting this compromise partly by the weakness of their position in Parliament, partly by their desire to get almost any kind of reform legislation passed, and partly by their own lack of conviction that penal sanctions were an unqualified evil.[40] John Proudfoot, new Secretary to the Glasgow Committee, took part in these negotiations. The bill had gone into committee, he wrote, "with a great many proposed alterations and amend-

---

[38] Hansard's *Parl. Debates* (1867), CLXXXVII:col. 1611 (remarks of Lord Elcho).

[39] Ibid., col. 1606 (remarks of Mr. Samuelson).

[40] See, for example, Testimony of Thomas Winters (manager of a working man's benefit society) before the "Select Committee on Master and Servant," (1866) XIII:Q. 1220: "Others have expressed the opinion that the workman should only be prosecuted criminally where life was imperilled? – I do not know about that; where a man is thrown out of work, and his family wants bread through the misconduct of another, I think the law ought to have a hold upon the man who caused it." See, in general, Simon, "Master and Servant," 174 ("They were uncomfortably conscious of the plausibility of the masters' favourite argument that the workman must be imprisoned because he would so seldom have the resources to pay damages"); see also 185, 187.

ments. . . . After very considerable discussion, both with his Lordship [Elcho] and some of the lawyers in the House, we felt obliged to give way. . . . Otherwise the Bill might be endangered by the opposition."[41] In a quite literal sense the new ground rules were the negotiated result of a struggle between masters and men. The outcome of these negotiations could not have been known in advance. It is possible that labor could have won better terms; Lord Elcho's original bill might have been enacted. However, it is also possible that labor could have done worse and gotten no reform legislation at all. At this time there were relatively few voices in Parliament speaking on labor's behalf, and although the trade unions were not happy with the results, for the most part they seem to have accepted them. During the next few years, conflict over the Master and Servant acts was suspended.

THE MASTER AND SERVANT ACT OF 1867

The amended bill that became law in August 1867 retained much more of the traditional law than had Lord Elcho's initial bill. To begin with, the "misconduct and misdemeanor" language of earlier acts had been added back in as grounds for complaint. Second, failure to obey an order of performance or an order to find security for performance in the case of "simple" breaches could now result in immediate imprisonment. Third, "simple" breaches could now be "punished" with a fine. In addition, imprisonment could always follow failure to pay a fine or damages, distraint having been eliminated as an intermediate step. But the most important change was that a category of "aggravated" breaches "causing injury to persons or property" that could lead directly to imprisonment was now part of the legislation. Given that this vague formulation left room to imprison a worker directly under almost any circumstances, it could hardly be claimed that the master and servant law had been fundamentally transformed. In the new law, two justices could adjudicate not only "simple" breaches but "aggravated" breaches as well.

As discussed in Chapter 2, between 1868 and 1871 the number of prison sentences for contract breach fell substantially, but on average 500 workers were still being imprisoned each year. Before the reform bill had been passed approximately 1,500 workers a year had been imprisoned. However, throughout the early 1870s local magistrates were also issuing orders of performance. In 1872 and 1873 a booming economy and growing labor militancy led to an increase in prison sentences again; approximately 750 workers were imprisoned in each of these years, about half the pre-reform number, but still a healthy figure.[42] Throughout the early 1870s, moreover, the total number of annual prosecutions brought under

---

[41] *Glasgow Sentinel,* July 6, 1867, quoted in Simon, "Master and Servant," 187.

[42] See Chapter 2, note 133, for sources and statistics.

the reformed Master and Servant Act actually exceeded the number brought annually before the law was changed.[43]

Nevertheless, the Reform Act of 1867 did alter the status quo. For one thing, fines became the norm in both descriptive and prescriptive senses of the term, and imprisonment became an exception that required justification. This represented a genuinely new departure. For another, adoption of the principle that labor agreements ought to be treated as civil matters made a difference, even though that principle received mainly symbolic implementation in the 1867 act. The legitimacy of the principle having been conceded, the hand of labor was strengthened in future struggles over the acts. It would be relatively simple to demonstrate just how far the details of the 1867 statute deviated from its promise and to expose the crude hypocrisy with which it had been fashioned. There is one final matter that has not been much commented on but that deserves our attention. The 1867 act abolished arrest of wages in payment of fines, a process that had previously been available in Scotland. This must be counted a curious development in the new law. If one was serious about enforcing contracts against propertyless workers, why would one give up one of the better pecuniary holds over such persons, wage garnishment? One answer has to be that for various reasons arrest of wages was seen as more troublesome and less effective than penal sanctions, and if it were implemented it might fatally weaken the argument for penal sanctions. If arrest of wages had been available throughout Great Britain it would have been much more difficult to make the argument that workers lacked the means to pay fines or damages and consequently that penal sanctions were indispensable. One owner of an iron and coal works in South Staffordshire testified in 1866 before the Select Committee on Master and Servant that he was unalterably opposed to arrest of wages:

> Supposing [a] man [who had been fined] left his employment and went out of the district, would you approve of following his wages? – No, I am not an advocate for the following of a man's wages. There are plenty of means of obtaining justice without that. What I understand by following wages is this, giving notice to a new employer to stop that man's wages on your behalf. If I received a notice from a previous employer to stop a man's wages I would not stop them. I would be no party to a quarrel between the previous employer of that man and the man himself.
>
> You think, for all parties, imprisonment would be better? – I think it would.[44]

---

[43] See Table 2.1.

[44] "Select Committee on Master and Servant," (1866), XIII:Qs. 2521–22.

All of the employers who testified were opposed to arrest of wages. The only arguments in favor of preserving the process came from some labor witnesses, who were divided on this point. A number of them also opposed arrest of wages.[45] The united front that employers presented on this issue, together with the divisions among labor witnesses, made it an uncontroversial matter to abolish arrest of wages in Scotland in the 1867 law. Indeed, the same whig rhetoric of progressive upward movement through ever more enlightened stages of historical development that Lord Elcho used to denounce penal sanctions[46] was capacious enough to be used against a practice that today we consider a perfectly modern pecuniary remedy against poor debtors, wage garnishment. "The arrest of wages in Scotland for the payment of fines ought to be abolished," Mr. Powell said. He "hoped the House would very shortly . . . sweep the arrest away, as a relic of a past age, and unworthy of the time in which they lived."[47] Apparently, which practices would turn out to be authentic "feudal relics" and which faux "feudal relics" could not be predicted, because that determination depended on the unpredictable judgments of future generations. If a practice was not revived in the future, it could be definitively judged a feudal relic after enough time had passed, but it was only possible to make this judgment accurately after the fact. By looking backward after the fact, "feudal relics" always inevitably disappear.

In 1867 an even more significant change took place in the ground rules of British life. The second reform act, passed in that year, extended the parliamentary franchise to town artisans.[48] "The electorate was doubled [as a result of the act], and in towns the working classes gained a majority."[49] The trade unions were not slow to try to make use of the new dispensation, urging their members to register to vote and to vote only for those parliamentary candidates who would support trade union demands.[50] In 1869 another rule change also occurred that is important for our story: "An Act for the Abolition of Imprisonment for Debt"[51] was passed by Parliament.

---

[45] See "Arrestment of Wages" in the index of "Select Committee on Master and Servant" for citations to the testimony on arrest of wages and for pro and con summaries of that testimony.

[46] "This harsh law was really a remnant of serfdom" (remarks of Lord Elcho), Hansard's *Parl. Debates* (1867), CLXXXVII:col. 1611 (June 4, 1867).

[47] Ibid., CLXXXV:col. 1261 (remarks of Mr. Powell, March 1, 1867).

[48] The Reform Act of 1867, of course, has its own complicated history. See, among others, F. B. Smith, *The Making of the Second Reform Bill* (Cambridge, 1966); Frances E. Gillespie, *Labor and Politics, 1850–1867* (New York, 1966); and Maurice Cowling, *Disraeli, Gladstone, and Revolution: The Passing of the Second Reform Bill* (London, 1967).

[49] R. K. Webb, *Modern England: From the 18th Century to the Present* (Toronto, 1970), 326.

[50] Webb and Webb, *History of Trade Unionism*, 274.

[51] 32 & 33 Vict., c. 62 (1869).

The process of causation in social and political life is extraordinarily complicated. Sometimes gains in one domain place groups in a position to achieve gains in other domains. Sometimes gains in one domain lead to a reaction in other domains. Responding in part to the growing power of organized labor, the Liberal government in 1871 moved to change the statutory rules.[52] It enacted the Criminal Law Amendment Act. The new legislation broadened the statutory definition of conduct that constituted criminal coercion by workers in the course of trade disputes. "[I]ts effect was to make almost all the traditional forms of action necessary for a successful strike (such as peaceful picketing) a crime and, if done by several men in concert, a criminal conspiracy."[53] In this case the reaction produced a counterreaction. The Parliamentary Committee of the new Trades Union Congress launched a campaign to have the new act repealed. At the same time, it began to call for the repeal "of all penal legislation bearing on trade disputes," renewing the struggle over penal sanctions for contract breach that had been suspended since 1867.[54]

It is important to understand that neither labor nor the governments of the period singled out the rule authorizing penal sanctions for breaches of labor agreements as somehow uniquely involving the freedom or unfreedom of workers. It was viewed by both sides as just another rule, constituting a single aspect, albeit a significant aspect, of the larger legal background that structured the power relationships between employers and workers. Its status in this regard was no different from the rules about bargaining tactics in trade disputes that were the subject of a simultaneous struggle. Indeed, the issues of penal sanctions for breaches of labor agreements and the legitimate scope of union bargaining activities were viewed as so similar by contemporaries that when the newly elected Conservative government had a Royal Commission appointed in 1874 to study the labor question, the charge of that Commission was to "Inquire into the Working of The Master and Servant Act, 1867 [and] The Criminal Law Amendment Act." It was not until later that the issue of penal sanctions for breaches of labor agreements was sanctified as an issue standing apart, involving the core freedom of workers, and was placed in an altogether different category from the issue of how extensive the legal liberties of trade unions ought to be in the struggle for life, which remained a subject over which men of good faith could continue to disagree.

---

[52] The Criminal Law Amendment Act codified, in the main, a number of earlier judicial decisions adverse to labor.

[53] Simon, "Master and Servant," 189; see also Webb and Webb, *History of Trade Unionism*, 279–83.

[54] Webb and Webb, *The History of Trade Unionism*, 285.

After 1867, a few men affiliated with the labor movement ran for Parliament,[55] but after the passage of the Criminal Law Amendment Act trade union interest in direct electoral action accelerated. In the general election of 1874, thirteen independent labor candidates stood for Parliament, and two, Alexander Macdonald and Thomas Burt, became the first labor members of the House of Commons.[56] This marked a crucial turning point in the fortunes of labor. Henceforth it would have a direct voice, however weak, in the corridors of power.

To complement the political campaign, labor also undertook an ideological campaign. Frederic Harrison, a lawyer long associated with the labor movement, wrote a tract that picked up where the previous campaign for reform of the master and servant laws had left off. It was a grievous violation of the principle of equality under law, he argued, for labor agreements to be treated so differently from all other civil contracts. Unequal treatment of workers and employers made the law flagrantly class biased. "The Act of 1867," he wrote, "was an important gain to the working classes, and was intended by its promoters as a measure of justice and equality. But it did not do its work completely, and the time has come to amend it. Its main object was to abolish the immoral and one-sided principle that made the contracts of workmen enforceable by imprisonment. But it really let in that principle again by a side wind."[57]

> Imprisonment for breach of civil contract is a flagrant exception to ordinary [contract] rules. . . . It is contrary to the whole current of modern legislation. What is the ordinary course of civil law? A breach of contract, as such, is the subject of a civil remedy. It may be redressed by an action for damages, or a suit in chancery. But, in either case, it is not regarded as a crime. It forms a right of action, a subject of litigation not for criminal prosecution. . . . To fail in paying £10,000 at the date agreed, [is] a subject for a lawsuit. To miss a day's work [is] a matter for prison.[58]

Harrison went on to argue that the ordinary remedy for contract breaches was damages, even where a breach involved large sums of money and had adverse effects on the public:

---

[55] Ibid., 287.

[56] Ibid., 289–90.

[57] Frederic Harrison, "Tracts for Trade Unionists: Imprisonment for Breach of Contract or the Master & Servant Act," in *1868, Year of the Unions: A Documentary History*, ed. Edmund Frow and Michael Katanka (New York, 1968), 141. For the context in which these tracts were published, see Webb and Webb, *History of Trade Unionism*, 286.

[58] Harrison, "Tracts for Trade Unionists," 141–42.

The contracts of commercial and ordinary affairs often involve very great interests. Men are ruined, and families are desolated every day by deliberate breach of solemn engagements. When a contractor puts bad material in a bridge or a ship, he risks the lives of hundreds. The overtrading of a few speculators may bring on a national panic, and the jobs of a knot of directors cause more suffering than a bad winter. Now a breach of contract of this class amounts morally to a public crime, but where no penal statute is broken it is absolutely unpunished. . . . The sudden loss of the workman's labour may often be a serious matter, but it is preposterous to pretend that it can approach in consequence to the stoppage of a bank.[59]

It was crucial, however, that labor meet the argument that because workers might not be able to pay damages, an employer simply had to have some recourse.[60] Harrison made two points in this regard. First, he argued that in many contract cases not involving workers, a merchant or a shopkeeper would possess no assets and leave the damaged party without an effective remedy for breach. Why should workers be treated differently?

Contracts are broken a hundred times a day by men whom it is no use to sue. And a Bill to make all breaches of contract alike punishable with imprisonment would be received with a storm of ridicule. . . . Merchants and shopkeepers would appear in crowds at the Old Bailey. And without any fraud, without any criminal conduct, other than neglecting a civil contract to pay money, bankrupts and insolvents would repent at leisure under three months of gaol.[61]

Second, Harrison argued that workers contracted with numerous people other than their employers in the normal course of their lives. None of these other people enjoyed a criminal remedy for worker contract breaches:

The baker and grocer who supplies the workman with goods on his contract to pay has no such remedy. A baker who is £2 out of pocket

<hr>

[59] Ibid., 142–43.

[60] In testimony given in 1866 before passage of the 1867 Master and Servant Reform Act, labor witnesses had stressed that circumstances had changed: Many working people now participated in union benefit funds that gave them a vested stake in the community and incentives to perform their contracts. In many cases, unions would now pay fines or damages for breaches of contracts, undermining the argument that such actions were futile in the case of workers. A few employer witnesses agreed with the latter point, but judged its significance differently. See "Select Committee on Master and Servant" (1866), XIII:Qs. 1841–51, 1874, 1944, 2423.

[61] Harrison, "Tracts for Trade Unionists," 148. "An Act for the Abolition of Imprisonment for Debt. . ." had been passed in 1869; see n. 51.

cannot carry a workman before a magistrate, and give the man three months of gaol. Why should the employer, who loses £2 by the man's absence from work, be able to do so?[62]

Arguing in the early 1870s, Harrison did not mount a similar attack on the power to order the specific performance of labor contracts. On the contrary, he saw that power as part of the solution rather than as part of the problem. "A breach of contract, as such, is the subject of a civil remedy," he wrote. "It may be redressed by an action for damages, or a suit in chancery. But, in either case, it is not regarded as a crime. . . . [T]he worst that can befall [the defendant] is the payment of damages or the performance of his contract, with costs."[63]

It is important to keep in mind that in the 1870s the direct influence of labor in Parliament was still quite limited. Labor primarily relied on the extra-parliamentary power of the trades unions, the electoral power that it had begun to exercise at the margins in the delicate electoral balance between the two major parties, and the power of labor arguments based on widely accepted liberal norms. Writing about this period, the Webbs were of the opinion that

> [e]ven after 1867 [the] followers [of labor] formed but a small minority of the electorate, whilst the whole machinery of politics was in the hands of the middle class. Powerless to coerce or even to intimidate the governing classes, they could win only by persuasion. . . . [In agitating for repeal of the Criminal Law Amendment Act] [t]hey insisted only on the right of every Englishman to bargain for the sale of his labour in the manner he thought most conducive to his own interests. What they demanded was perfect freedom for a workman to substitute collective for individual bargaining, if he imagined such a course to be for his own advantage. Freedom of association in matters of contract became, therefore, their rejoinder to the employers' cry of freedom of competition.

> It is clear that the Trade Unionists had the best of the argument. It was manifestly unreasonable for the employers to insist on the principle of non-interference of the State in industry whenever they were pushed by the advocates of factory legislation, and at the same time to clamour for the assistance of the police to put down peaceful and voluntary combinations of their workmen. The capitalists were, in short, committed to the principle of *laissez-faire* in every phase of industrial life, from "Free Trade in Corn" to the unlimited use of labour of either sex at any age and under any conditions: and what

---

[62] Harrison, "Tracts for Trade Unionists," 149.

[63] Ibid., 141–42.

the workmen demanded was only the application of this principle to the wage contract.[64]

Having conceded in principle in 1867 that labor agreements should be treated as civil in character, those who wished to defend the status quo were placed in an embarrassing position after 1871. They were forced to argue that the 1867 act had not deviated in the main from the principles of civil actions, but that to the extent it had, these departures were justified by the profoundly different circumstances surrounding labor agreements.

THE EMPLOYERS AND WORKMEN ACT OF 1875

Following the general election of 1874, a Conservative government took office, and in an effort to redeem electoral pledges it announced that a Royal Commission to study the labor laws was to be appointed. A biographer of Disraeli has commented that "[a]s a result of the [Reform] Act of 1867 it was electorally necessary to make some concession to working-class demands, and it may be that the Conservatives after 1874 were more ready to do this than the Liberals after 1868."[65]

Labor had hoped that, having contributed to the Conservative victory in 1874, it would be rewarded with the immediate repeal of the Criminal Law Amendment Act. When instead a Royal Commission was appointed, labor took it as an indication that it had been betrayed, that the labor question was being shelved. The unions refused to participate in the Commission's proceedings.[66] Eventually, one of the two independent labor members of Parliament, Alexander Macdonald, was persuaded to serve on the Commission.[67]

If the appointment of the Royal Commission was a disappointment, its report must have been even more of one. It called for only minor changes to the 1867 Master and Servant Act, and for the rest developed an elaborate rationalization for keeping the act's main provisions as they were. The ground of debate, however, was now narrowly circumscribed. Everyone agreed that disputes over labor contracts should, as a rule, be treated as purely civil in character.

[64] Webb and Webb, *History of Trade Unionism*, 293–94.

[65] Robert Blake, *Disraeli* (New York, 1967), 553.

[66] Webb and Webb, *History of Trade Unionism*, 290.

[67] "Ultimately Alexander Macdonald, M.P., allowed himself to be persuaded to serve, together with Tom Hughes; and George Shipton, the Secretary of the London Trades Council, Andrew Boa, the Secretary of the Glasgow Trades Council, and a prominent Birmingham Trade Unionist gave evidence." Ibid.

The Commission reported that labor had raised two main objections to the 1867 act's treatment of "simple" contract breaches. First, it was inappropriate for the act to empower magistrates to impose fines for contract breaches. Only damages and compensation were appropriate. Second, and more important, imprisonment for failure to obey an order of performance or an order to find security for performance or for failure to pay a fine or damages was for the same reason highly objectionable. Since the passage of the Act for the Abolition of Imprisonment for Debt in 1869, it was argued, a judgment creditor could not have a judgment debtor imprisoned unless the debtor possessed resources but refused to pay.[68] The same rule should apply in master and servant proceedings.[69]

For the most part, the Commission thought that these objections lacked merit. Their report did concede that "simple" breaches of contract "should be divested of all character of criminality" and therefore recommended "that the power of the magistrate to impose a fine . . . , where compensation cannot be assessed, should be taken away."[70] The report also recommended that the language that authorized complaints on the grounds of "misdemeanor or misconduct" should be removed as similarly belonging "to the domain of the criminal law."[71]

Aside from these few changes and one other, the report strove to justify the provisions of the 1867 act covering "simple" breaches. "It is, in the first place, to be observed," the report stated, "that as regards orders for the fulfillment of the contract . . . , the basis of the [objection] fails. The mode in which courts having jurisdiction to order specific performance enforce their authority in case of disobedience is by imprisonment. There is therefore nothing exceptional in the application of this remedy in case of disobedience here."[72]

The report did agree that the power to imprison for failure to pay damages for breaches of contract was at this date "more or less anomalous" because in the case of "the non-payment of damages for the breach of any other contract, [imprisonment] would not in the absence of proof of means of payment, be available."[73] However, according to the Commission, this anomaly was completely justifiable given the unique circumstances surrounding labor contracts. The Commission employed an old

<hr/>

[68] 32 & 33 Vict., c. 62 (1869).

[69] "Second and Final Report of the Commissioners Appointed to Inquire into the Working of the Master and Servant Act, 1867, The Criminal Law Amendment Act, 34 & 35 Vict., c. 32, and for Other Purposes," *Parl. Papers* (1875), XXX:10.

[70] Ibid., 11.

[71] Ibid.

[72] Ibid.

[73] Ibid. See "An Act for the Abolition of Imprisonment for Debt," 32 & 33 Vict., c. 62 (1869).

argument once again to do service in defense of penal sanctions, presenting it with great conviction and passion:

> That the breach of [a labor] contract on the part of a person in the
> employ of another may involve a serious, and where it is accompa-
> nied by the concurrent action of others a ruinous, loss to the em-
> ployer, beyond the immediate loss arising from the loss of profit on
> the work contracted for, by exposing him to liability for the breach of
> some contract into which he may have entered, while the loss to the
> workman will be limited to a temporary loss of employment, is obvi-
> ous. It is equally so that the remedy by an action for damages by the
> employer by reason of any such loss, must be nugatory as against the
> workman, who, in the great majority of instances, has no resources
> beyond the wages he earns by his labour nor has he property by sei-
> zure of which the damages awarded could be realized. . . . [T]o take
> away the power of imprisonment on non-payment of compensation
> awarded for breach of contract, would be to enable the workman to
> break his contract with absolute impunity. . . . Being, generally speak-
> ing, dependent on his labour alone, the workman disposed to leave
> his contract unfulfilled, can only be restrained from doing so by be-
> ing made liable to imprisonment.[74]

The one change that the Commission would recommend on the question of imprisonment for "simple" contract breaches following failure to
pay damages was that imprisonment should not be in the house of correction "where, of course, the restraint is greater and the discipline far more
strict but [in] the prison, or department of a prison, to which persons imprisoned for debt are usually committed."[75]

The "aggravated" breach section of the 1867 act had elicited even
stronger objections than the "simple" breach section. This section permitted magistrates to imprison immediately for "aggravated" contract violations. The commissioners did consider that the loose wording of the section had led magistrates, in certain cases, to abuse their authority,
imprisoning workers for what amounted to "simple" contract breaches.
But they thought the remedy was to tighten the language of the section,
not to eliminate imprisonment for "aggravated" breaches. However, here
they had to concede that the "aggravated" breach provision did depart
from the principles of civil actions. The question for the commissioners

---

[74] "Second and Final Report of the Commissioners Appointed to Inquire into the Working
of the Master and Servant Act, 1867, The Criminal Law Amendment Act, 34 & 35 Vict.
c. 32, and for Other Purposes," *Parl. Papers* (1875), XXX:10.

[75] Ibid., 11.

was "whether it is not justified and called for by the special circumstances and the necessity of the case."[76] Needless to say, they found that it was:

> In all these cases we have in the first place a wrongful act, wilfully and deliberately committed by the party breaking his contract. He is both legally and morally in the wrong; for, independently of legal obligation, common honesty, as well as justice, require that engagements once entered into shall be honestly fulfilled. The mere breach of such an obligation should not, indeed, suffice to bring a person committing it within the reach of the penal law. But when to an act, wrongful in itself, the fact is added that serious injury and mischief are contemplated by the wrong doer as about to result from it, and are, in fact, likely to result from it, it becomes a question whether, for the prevention of the serious mischief which such a violation of contracts would be likely to occasion, a breach of contract accompanied by such circumstances of aggravation should not be brought within the scope of the penal law. There might be less reason for making such a breach of contract penal if pecuniary compensation commensurate to the injury caused could be recovered. But here, again, we must assume that in the vast majority of instances pecuniary compensation is out of the question; and the object of the law must therefore be rather to deter dishonest and unprincipled men from breaches of contract for which they are unable to atone by making compensation. . . . *The law is exceptional, but it is justified by the necessity of the case, and the serious mischief and inconvenience which would arise from such engagements being broken.*[77] (emphasis added)

Only Alexander Macdonald dissented from the official report of the Commission. In that dissent, Macdonald argued, a little obscurely, that "specific performance of time contracts should . . . be limited. Imprisonment [should] be used only to compel specific performance of the contract in the ordinary legal way, and to compel payment of damages [when the defendant had resources] but not as a punishment for poverty."[78] He also argued that the "aggravated" breaches section "ought to be entirely removed," [79] but his was a lone voice on the Commission.

Even at that date, many in the ruling elite continued to feel that penal sanctions were functionally indispensable for employers of waged labor. They were only prepared to do more of what they had done in 1867:

---

[76] Ibid., 12.

[77] Ibid.

[78] Ibid., 28.

[79] Ibid.

rearrange details to make proceedings look a little more like civil actions while at the same time preserving as much of the old penal system as possible. On February 17, 1875, the date the Royal Commission's report was issued, it was far from certain that they would not succeed in shoring up the penal sanctions system just as they had in 1867. Labor would howl in protest no doubt, but that had happened before, and there was no reason to believe that the storm could not be weathered as it always had been before. Up to this point even those who represented labor had not called for the elimination of orders of specific performance. That issue did not even appear to be on the table.

When the Conservative government decided to introduce legislation, however, the Home Secretary, Richard Assheton Cross, argued in the Cabinet that this legislation should go well beyond the recommendations of the Royal Commission. The rest of the Cabinet apparently disagreed, believing that token concessions to labor would be enough. Disraeli supported his Home Secretary against the rest of the Cabinet, and Cross was given leave to develop more far-reaching proposals.[80] The legislation Cross initially introduced, however, did not represent the total break with the past that it has been characterized as. What Cross sought to do was to produce a bill that resembled the bill Lord Elcho had initially introduced in 1867.[81] Just as Lord Elcho had, Cross proposed to separate the civil and criminal aspects of contract disputes. Cross went further, however. He introduced two entirely separate pieces of legislation to address the two aspects of the problem. One piece, the Employers and Workmen Bill, was to be entirely civil. The other, the Conspiracy and Protection of Property Act, was to be entirely criminal.

On the civil side, Cross's bill echoed Elcho's earlier bill in eliminating both "fines" and the language of "misconduct or misdemeanor." But whereas Lord Elcho's Bill gave as remedies specific performance and damages, followed by distraint to pay damages and imprisonment if damages were not paid, Cross's bill proposed to modify these remedies in two ways. Addressing the issue of specific performance, Cross was led to say (for the first time in the context of the Master and Servant acts so far as I am aware) that specific performance was not an appropriate remedy in the case of contracts for personal services:

> There is another question which has been very much pressed upon our notice, not simply by the Report of the Commissioners, but also

[80] Blake, *Disraeli*, 555.

[81] In introducing the legislation Cross said, "According to [Lord Elcho's] original Bill there might be an order for fulfilment of the contract, or it might be annulled, compensation might be assessed for injury, and wilful and malicious injury was made a crime indictable at Quarter Sessions. In the progress of the Bill changes were introduced, and when it became law it had assumed a different complexion." Hansard's *Parl Debates* (1875), CCXXIV:col. 1671 (June 10, 1875).

by everyone who has written upon this subject. They have all thought that contracts could be enforced, as in the Court of Chancery, by an order of specific performance. It is extraordinary what a number of persons have written and have said that; but the obvious answer is that the Court of Chancery never does enforce contracts; it has always steadily refused to do so. Therefore, to order specific performance is not possible.[82]

The Liberal member for the University of London, Robert Lowe, went even further as he praised the Home Secretary for exposing the utter falsity of popular views about specific performance. Specific performance, he argued (and this is also a first as far as I am aware), turned contracts of hire into slavery:

> The right hon. Gentleman deserved great credit for having exploded altogether the doctrine of the specific performance of the labour contract which was founded on an entire misapprehension of the practice of the Courts of Equity. If a Court would refuse to order Mr. Kean to act Richard III. continuously, because it would involve a succession of efforts no man could be called upon to make, was it not monstrous that a Court should claim to compel a man to do a particular thing for a year? It would be introducing a principle of slavery utterly inconsistent with the genius of our laws and institutions, and for which no precedent or parallel could be found in the law of England.[83]

Even as Lowe was rewriting English legal history, placing the final touches on the modern myth of free labor, Cross could not quite get himself to go the whole way. He could not give up the idea that some remedy beyond damages was still necessary. If it could not be specific performance per se, then perhaps it could be a version of the pre-1867 practice of offering workers the choice of returning to their work or facing the consequences for which the legislation otherwise provided.

Cross inserted a clause that allowed a worker to avoid an award of damages by entering an agreement to return to work and giving security for performance. "The security shall be an undertaking by the defendant to perform his contract, subject on non-performance to the payment of a sum to be specified in the undertaking."[84] If a worker failed to obey the

---

[82] Ibid., col. 1677.

[83] Ibid., CCXXV:col. 659 (June 28, 1875). Mr. Tennant also thought that specific performance was inappropriate, but on the older ground that "it was in the very nature of a contract of personal service that it could not be specifically enforced. Even if it could be enforced, he conceived that far more harm than good would result from forcing an unwilling workman to return to employment" (cols. 670–71).

[84] "A Bill to Enlarge the Powers of County Courts in Respect of Disputes between Employers and Workmen . . . ," *Parl. Papers* (1875), II:101, 102.

order of performance that he had now agreed to be bound by and failed
to pay the sum specified, he could be committed to prison for up to a
month.[85] To understand why any worker might be tempted to enter into
such an agreement, it is necessary to understand the alternative remedy
that workers faced under Cross's bill. As Cross had promised, this alternative was the civil remedy of damages. However, just as Lord Elcho's bill
had included the civil remedy of damages, followed by distraint, followed
by imprisonment for failure to pay the damages, because civil process at
that time still authorized the imprisonment of judgment debtors, Cross's
civil remedy of damages must be understood against the background of
the new civil process that had been established by the 1869 Act for the
Abolition of Imprisonment for Debt. That act authorized County Courts
to order the payment of small debts of up to £50 in installments, and if it
could be shown that a debtor had the resources to pay any installment but
failed to do so, then that debtor could still be imprisoned for up to six
weeks.[86]

Robert Lowe described how this procedure might well lead to the imprisonment of workers following awards of damages. In the County
Courts, he pointed out, judges

> had the power of ordering the defendant to pay by installments, and
> if he made default in any instalment and it could be proved that he
> had had money in his hands, no matter what other claims he might
> have had to meet, he was liable, if he did not pay, to be imprisoned;
> the payment might be divided into seven instalments, and the defen-
> dant was liable to be imprisoned upon all of them.[87]

Cross's bill extended these powers to courts of summary jurisdiction
(including sessions of the peace), which were authorized to hear disputes
over labor contracts involving up to £10 in damages.[88] Above £10, such
disputes had to be taken to the County Courts. To avoid a damages
award, which might be followed by an order to pay in installments,
which might be followed by six weeks' imprisonment for failure to pay
any installment where it could be shown that a worker had had money
(wages) in his hands, a worker might well agree to return to work and
give security to perform that promise, exposing himself to the possibility
of a month's imprisonment for failure to perform and to pay the security
specified.

The debate in Parliament proceeded altogether differently than the debate over Lord Elcho's bill had eight years earlier. Where in 1867 Lord

[85] Ibid.

[86] See 32 & 33 Vict., c. 62, s. 5 (1869).

[87] Hansard's *Parl. Debates* (1875), CCXXV:col. 660 (June 28, 1875).

[88] "A Bill to Enlarge the Powers of County Courts," 101, 102, 104.

Elcho's proposals had run into a storm of resistance on the ground that they were too liberal, now the weight of sentiment in Parliament was that Cross's bill had not gone far enough. It seems that once the Conservative government decided to move beyond the proposals of the Royal Commission, that decision opened the floodgates in Parliament. In an effort to curry favor with the newly enfranchised segments of the working classes, Liberals now competed with Conservatives to press for genuine implementation of the principle that disputes over labor contracts should be treated as purely civil in nature.

Two significant objections to Cross's bill were raised. The first was that his substitute for specific performance permitted imprisonment even where a defendant did not have the means to pay. This was a deviation from the civil process established by the 1869 Debtor's Act, which allowed imprisonment only where a debtor had the means to pay but refused. This objection was raised strenuously by numerous members.[89] Mr. Lowe went further, arguing that the process established by the 1869 act, which could still lead to imprisonment for small debts, should itself be eliminated.[90] The second objection was raised by the independent labor members, Alexander Macdonald and Thomas Burt. They wanted to deprive the local magistrates of all jurisdiction in labor contract disputes and to have all disputes heard by the County Courts.[91] In the end, Mr. Assheton Cross gave way on the specific performance clause but not on the forum clause. On July 16, he offered an amendment that allowed a worker to avoid a damages award by agreeing to return to work and finding a third-party surety for performance. For failure to perform the agreement, the surety would forfeit the specified amount and would then "have the same right to recover the money against the defendant which the master originally had."[92] The terms of the 1869 Act for the Abolition of Imprisonment for Debt, however, remained part of the Employers and Workmen Bill when it became law.

Imprisonment for breach of a labor agreement, or more precisely imprisonment for a judgment debt flowing from breach of a labor agreement, could still occur after the 1875 act had passed, but only after a number of steps had first been taken: an initial damages award, followed by an order to pay that award in installments, followed by a failure to pay any installment where it could be shown that the defendant had the resources

---

[89] Hansard's *Parl. Debates* (1875), CCXXV:cols. 651–52 (Lord Robert Montagu, June 28, 1875); col. 673 (Mr. Mundella, June 28, 1875); cols. 1332–36 (Mr. Mundella, Mr. W. F. Forster, Sir Henry James, Lord Robert Montagu, Sir William Harcourt, Mr. Lowe, July 12, 1875).

[90] Ibid., cols. 660–61 (Mr. Robert Lowe, June 28, 1875).

[91] Ibid., CCXXIV:col. 1687 (Mr. Macdonald, June 10, 1875); CCXXV:col. 681 (Mr. Burt, June 28, 1875).

[92] Ibid., CCXXV:col. 1590 (Mr. Assheton Cross, July 16, 1875).

to pay. Perhaps it was the cumbersomeness of this process that in the end discouraged its use by employers and led to the effective end of imprisonment following breaches of labor agreements, rather than, as popular belief would have it, as a result of the final elimination of this remedy by the 1875 act itself.

To the great chagrin of labor, the act also continued to give jurisdiction over labor disputes up to £10 to courts of summary jurisdiction, which were presided over in many places by justices of the peace. The Employers and Workmen Act introduced sweeping changes into the adjudication of disputes over labor agreements, but it cannot be said to have marked a complete break with the past. The legal changes it introduced, when considered in detail, look more like substantial incremental changes than like the legal revolution they have often been thought to be. Nothing could make this clearer than the survival in the Conspiracy and Protection of Property Act of criminal sanctions for certain breaches of labor agreements. Before discussing the criminal side of Cross's proposed legislation, there is one other clause of the civil act that merits further attention.

During the debates over the 1867 Master and Servant reform act, a number of MPs expressed the view that penal sanctions were not used among textile manufacturers to enforce their labor agreements.[93] This turns out not to have been true. Lancashire textile manufacturers were still using penal sanctions to enforce labor contracts as late as 1866.[94] At the same time, they were also enforcing some of these contracts in the American style, by withholding wages that a worker could lose if he or she was absent from or left work without giving the required notice.[95] By forcing workers to choose between remaining for the contract term and obeying all factory rules or losing the wages they needed so badly, mill owners found that they could effectively enforce the labor agreements of their wage workers in this way as well.

[93]   Ibid., CLXXXV:col. 1260 (remarks of Mr. E. Potter, March 1, 1867); CLXXXVII:cols. 1604–05 (remarks of Mr. E. Potter, and Mr. Samuelson, June 4, 1867). Daphne Simon reached a similar conclusion in "Master and Servant," 190.

[94]   For examples of prosecutions in Lancashire textile mills in 1865 and 1866, see Chapter 2, n. 117.

[95]   See, for example, *Mary Taylor v. Carr and Porter*, 30 L.J. (n.s.) (mag. cases) 201 (1861); *Alice Taylor v. Carr and Porter*, 31 L.J. (n.s.) (mag. cases) 111 (1862). There were several different legal bases for wage loss. One was the common law entirety doctrine, which provided that no wages were due an employee who left or wrongfully breached his or her agreement before completing an entire term, even if the term were a week; see, for example, *Walsh v. Walley*, 9 L.R. (Queen's Bench) 367 (1874). Technically, loss of wages in these cases was not forfeiture because the wages had never legally been earned in the first place. Forfeiture of wages was also possible where employees worked under express contract provisions calling for forfeiture of back wages if they failed to give the required notice before leaving or otherwise breached the labor agreement.

When Cross's Employers and Workmen Bill was being amended in committee, Mr. Mundella, an old friend of labor, introduced an amendment that would have prohibited this practice in the case of women and children. This was another difficult choice (along with the choice between remaining or being imprisoned) that employers should no longer be permitted to force workers under contract to make. When introducing the amendment, Mr. Mundella said

> that in textile manufactories a very large percentage of those employed were women and children. These latter were often subjected to the operation of certain printed rules of a harsh and arbitrary character, the effect of which was to forfeit whatever wages might be due to them should they be absent from illness or in any other way transgress the regulations. He could, if necessary, mention 50 cases of this kind. In one case a woman who had lost her husband in the night, being unable in consequence to go to work before 7 instead of 6 o'clock in the morning, she forfeited 10 days' earnings which were due to her, and on the case coming before the magistrates they said the case was a very hard one but they had no power in the matter.[96]

Although Mr. Mundella withdrew his amendment, it was later added back into the bill in the House of Lords.[97] The 1875 act, consequently, contained the following provision:

> In the case of a child, young person, or woman subject to the provisions of the Factory Acts, 1833 to 1874, any forfeiture on the ground of absence or leaving work shall not be deducted from or set off against a claim for wages or other sum due for work done before such absence or leaving work, except to the amount of the damage (if any) which the employer may have sustained by reason of such absence or leaving work.[98]

In the minds of many workers, the two kinds of hard choices that employers could no longer force certain workers to make as they decided whether to continue at their labors were not perceived as so different that

---

[96] Hansard's *Parl. Debates* (1875), CCXXV:col. 1340 (amendment offered by Mr. Mundella, July 12, 1875).

[97] Ibid., CCXXVI:col. 546 (August 5, 1875), and "Lords Amendments to Employers and Workmen Bill," *Parl. Papers* (1875), II:119.

[98] "Employers and Workmen Bill," 38 & 39 Vict., c. 90, s. 11 (1875). In 1876, the common law courts applied the entirety doctrine to partially negate the effect of this clause. *Gregson v. Watson*, 34 L.T. 143 (1876), held that under the rules of one textile mill women operatives were not entitled to compensation for partial weeks of work, their wages not being apportionable within each week. Accordingly, this loss of wages did not fall under the "wages due" clause of the statute. However, in 1880 the courts retreated from this position in *Warburton v. Heyworth*, 6 Q.B.D. 1 (1880).

labor offered under one choice was viewed as unfree whereas labor offered under the other was viewed as its opposite, free. Labor moved to get rid of both kinds of hard choices, because both operated in varying degrees to coerce the fulfillment of personal services agreements. Only as a result of the interpretation placed on the 1875 act by ruling elites would these two different kinds of hard choices begin to be thought of as creating two qualitatively different forms of labor.

THE CONSPIRACY AND PROTECTION OF PROPERTY ACT OF 1875

When Cross introduced the Employers and Workmen Bill, which was to deal with the civil side of labor contract disputes, he also introduced a separate criminal bill, the Conspiracy and Protection of Property Act, which would continue to subject certain breaches of labor agreements to criminal punishment. In one clause, the bill covered specific categories of workers, water and gas workers, and criminalized contract breaches that threatened the delivery of these services. Another clause covered breaches of contracts of service or hiring more generally. In the form in which it was enacted into law, this clause provided:

> Where any person *wilfully and maliciously breaks a contract of service or hiring, knowing or having reasonable cause to believe that the probable consequences of his so doing, either alone or in combination with others, will be* to endanger human life, or cause serious bodily injury, *or to expose valuable property* whether real or personal *to destruction or serious injury,* he shall on conviction thereof by a court of summary jurisdiction, or on indictment as herein-after mentioned, be liable either to pay a penalty not exceeding twenty pounds, or to be imprisoned for a term not exceeding three months, with or without hard labour.[99] (emphasis added)

Cross justified the clause in the following terms:

> Take, for instance, the case of any man who wilfully with his hands strikes a blow at any property belonging to another, and inflicts an injury to that property maliciously and aware what the consequences would be, that offence falls within the existing law. Now, a man may do precisely the same injury with his feet as he does with his hands when he walks away from his work, knowing at the same time that injury to the property will ensue. We therefore, propose to place such an offence in the same category as that where a workman strikes a blow at property with the hand and injures it. These two cases, we think, may be put under the criminal law.[100]

[99] "Conspiracy and Protection of Property Act," 38 & 39 Vict., c. 86, s. 5 (1875).

[100] Hansard's *Parl. Debates* (1875), CCXXIV:col. 1676 (remarks of Mr. Assheton Cross, June 10, 1875).

During the debate over Cross's bill Thomas Burt demanded to know "whether, under that clause, an act was to be regarded as criminal simply because of the large amount of the damage done: if so, that was a dangerous principle to lay down."[101] A month later, the Lord Chancellor answered Mr. Burt's question in the affirmative:

> On a former occasion [one of the Lords] mentioned a case in which a workman in charge of iron in smelting works left it while it was in a liquid state the consequences of which was that the furnace had to be taken down, and an expense of some £2,000 was incurred by the employer. He (the Lord Chancellor) believed that a person acting as the workman described by his noble Friend had done would come within the clause, and he was confirmed in that belief by the opinion of persons more conversant with the criminal law than he was. The law would infer motive in such a case. It was quite true that a penalty of £20, or three months' imprisonment, inflicted on the offender would not compensate the employer, but it would not be possible to afford him adequate pecuniary compensation by any enactment in a Bill such as this; and, moreover, the penalty proposed by the Bill was exactly the same as that now in force under Lord Elcho's Act [the 1867 Master and Servant Act].[102]

Lord Montagu and Robert Lowe objected to the clause on the ground that if an act is a crime it should be a crime whether or not the person is under contract and regardless of his status in life. The criminal law should impose legal duties as widely and generally as possible. Making breach of a labor contract an element of the crime smacked of class or special legislation, singling workers out for degrading treatment, just as in the past. Lord Montagu argued that

> to break a civil contract was a civil act, and we had no right to inquire into the intention. In the case of a minute contract, a man at the pumping engine of a mine might walk away without notice, immense damage might be done to property, and yet the act would not be a criminal one. But if there was a contract for a week, the man who should do the same act would commit a crime, and to agree to do so would be conspiracy.[103]

Robert Lowe went further:

> He wished to suggest as a principle the making of our legislation as wide and general as possible, and he was disposed to agree in the

---

[101] Ibid., CCXXV:col. 681 (remarks of Mr. Burt, June 28, 1875).

[102] Ibid., CCXXVI:col. 165 (remarks of the Lord Chancellor in the debate over the "Conspiracy and Protection of Property Bill," July 29, 1875).

[103] Ibid., CCXXV:col. 656 (remarks of Lord Robert Montagu, June 28, 1875).

view of the right hon. Gentleman that some punishment should follow desertions of duty involving serious consequences. It seemed to him that if a man by a wilful breach of duty deprived a town of gas and water or placed human life in danger . . . or if he endangered property of considerable value, it was quite right and fair that he should come within the dominion of the law. He submitted, however, that faults of that kind could be committed by other people besides workmen and that it was not wise to limit the punishment to working people, and thus put a kind of stigma upon them. Supposing, for instance, that a contractor for gas or waterworks the construction of which involved the supply or non-supply of a whole district, or possibly the lives of a number of people, failed from mere negligence to set his men to work, and mischief followed, there was no law to punish him; but if one of his workmen had absconded and damage followed as a consequence, such workman would be liable to heavy punishment. . . . If the right hon. Gentleman [extended the coverage of the clause in this way], he would be making a very reasonable concession to a not unnatural feeling of sensitiveness and jealousy on the part of the working classes, who objected strongly to be made the subject of special legislation.[104]

The clause, however, was enacted as Cross had proposed it, and became part of the Conspiracy and Protection of Property Act. Contract breach could still give rise to criminal punishment under certain circumstances. Because he analyzed these situations in the traditional way, Cross framed this legislation in terms of criminal punishment for labor contract breaches, failing on the criminal side, as he had on the civil side, to break totally with the past. According to later views, what was to be punished in these kinds of situations was not contract breach but a kind of industrial sabotage, effected by leaving a key position in industry or transport suddenly without advance notice and with the knowledge that it would lead to loss of life, injury to persons, or destruction of property.

THE CAUSES AND CONSEQUENCES OF REFORM

It is important to ask what led Parliament to go as far as it did in 1875. The answer lies in a combination of factors, all of which can be viewed as kinds of threats labor posed to the existing order of things and to which reform was a strategic response. First, it was widely believed that the Conservative Party had been helped into office by the votes of the newly enfranchised segments of the working classes, and the Conservative govern-

---

[104] Ibid., col. 662 (remarks of Robert Lowe, June 28, 1875).

ment was striving to make good on some of its electoral promises. This effort set off a competition with the Liberal Party for the votes of the working classes, votes that might just shift, at the margins, the electoral balance between the two major parties in a number of constituencies. Each side began to vie with the other to meet labor's demands within limits established by a new consensus over what the legitimate grievances of labor were (labor agreements should be treated as purely civil matters) and how they should be addressed.[105] This new consensus was itself partly the result of the long ideological campaign that labor had waged.

As in 1867, a number of extra-parliamentary threats bolstered labor's position in these political negotiations. The early 1870s were a period of low unemployment and of great labor militancy. Labor developed a self-confidence it had not shown in 1867. The trade union movement, which had cooperated with the Select Committee appointed to investigate the labor laws in 1865 and 1866, refused to cooperate with the Royal Commission in 1874. The direct costs to employers of labor discontent were now higher, hence the incentives were greater for going along with a reform that might reduce discontent. Robert Lowe thought that reform legislation "would do great good by soothing passions and conciliating those who believed they had conflicting interests."[106] It would serve "as a proof that Parliament was anxious as far as it could to meet their [the working classes'] wishes and to conciliate their feelings, and it might have some effect in toning down an acerbity which now existed. They all wished to restore harmony and unity among all classes."[107] Mr. Mundella said he knew of two strikes in Wales "which had cost £6,000,000, [but which] might have been settled in three or four hours if wisdom and moderation, instead of a spirit of antagonism had at first prevailed."[108]

Labor members and supporters also hinted darkly that other, even more serious threats waited in the wings should labor grievances fail to be addressed. Mr. Mundella said that

> he had with him an extract from a foreign journal, which stated that every foreign working man was a Socialist and desired to be a Robespierre. But you would not find a Socialist or Internationalist in the United Kingdom. Why was that? Because our workmen had strong common sense and respect for property, and all they wanted was that masters and workmen should stand on equal bases of right.[109]

---

[105] See, for example, the remarks of Sir Charles Forster, June 28, 1875, ibid., cols. 671–72.

[106] Ibid., col. 658.

[107] Ibid., col. 664.

[108] Ibid., col. 674.

[109] Ibid.

Thomas Burt argued that

> [t]he workingmen of this country were loyal, but their allegiance was strained to the greatest possible extent when [the] House passed laws that were not in harmony with the highest moral sense and intelligence of the community.[110]

Alexander Macdonald

> felt perfectly confident that [the Home Secretary] . . . was desirous of giving fair play to the working man; and he believed the right hon. Gentleman had not in the remotest corner of his mind any intention of interfering with trades unions – he was equally sure the Government collectively had no such intention, *because they would not dare in the present state of things to interfere with them.*[111] (emphasis added)

There was still another threat that militant labor posed, however, and there were those in Parliament who argued that if this threat weren't countered through reform, the Master and Servant Act would be rendered irrelevant in any case. Labor had found an escape from penal sanctions by opting for minute contracts whenever possible. Tight labor markets in the early 1870s placed labor in a strong position to insist on minute contracts more often. If one wished to preserve a waged labor system in which contracts continued to play a role in creating a stable workforce, making labor contracts tolerable to workers by altering contract remedies was an absolute necessity. Cross asked:

> What was the consequence of [the present state of the law that criminalized labor contract breaches]? The men said they would not take any contract which would subject them to such ignominy; and many of their contracts were rather implied than expressed by the payment of wages at certain times. They would not enter into any contract beyond the day, hour, or minute. If the law remained as it was, that state of things would become more general than it was. If there was any great struggle between masters and men, it would make no difference to the men whether they left on Saturday or Wednesday; and so long as the present law existed they would leave on Saturday night without saying a single syllable and not go back on Monday morning. Thus they found out the way of escaping the criminal laws, and the result would be only to increase the ill-feeling which already existed.[112]

---

[110] Ibid., col. 682.

[111] Ibid., col. 666.

[112] Ibid., cols. 677–78 (remarks of Assheton Cross, June 28, 1875).

His views were echoed by Lord Montagu, who went further, however, urging a highly traditional view of the benefits of contracts for a term. "The effect [of criminalizing labor contract breaches]," he argued,

> would be to induce working men to get rid of all contracts and have only minute contracts. In connection with the point, let them remember there was not more than a day's consumption of edibles in London. The locomotive engine-drivers all made minute contracts. They could leave at any time, and produce danger and inconvenience to the public. . . . [The minute contract system] was adopted at present by miners, ironworkers, engineers, and the building trade – which included joiners, masons, carpenters, plumbers, and plasterers – and shipbuilders, and in the Nottingham textile trades when a man finished his warp. It would be to the advantage of the State to have long and, if possible, permanent contracts, so that we might not have a nomad population.[113]

Labor members of Parliament, on the other hand, were of an altogether different mind, arguing that minute contracts were a good thing for both employers and workers, and demonstrated, moreover, that penal sanctions were totally unnecessary in wage labor markets. Whatever the complex origins of the minute contract system in the dynamics of struggle between workers and employers in earlier decades, by the 1870s labor had become a powerful advocate of minute contracts. Alexander Macdonald

> was of opinion that there was no necessity for penalties for breaches of contract – the system of "minute contract" which had been adopted in many of the largest manufacturing establishments in this country with great advantage to all the parties concerned proved this. He hoped the time would come when in all our large industrial establishments work would be carried on on that condition. Under a minute contract an incompetent or vicious workman could be immediately got rid of instead of being able to continue in an establishment for some weeks or months to the annoyance of his employer. A minute contract would also, on the other hand, enable a workman instantly to leave the employment of an unjust master. The minute contract produced perfect respect in both parties, and put them both in a position of perfect independence. The employer refrained from doing wrong to his workman, because he knew that the man might leave him at any moment, and, on the other hand, the working man refrained from doing wrong to

---

[113] Ibid., cols. 657–58 (remarks of Lord Montagu, June 28, 1875).

his master, because he knew that he could get rid of him at any moment.[114]

The popularity of minute contracts among working people had grown since the 1860s, not only because of a secular trend toward greater and greater distaste of penal sanctions, but also because of some short-term factors. The early 1870s were years of very low unemployment, and under such conditions minute contracts were of great economic benefit to working people. The spread of minute contracts was one of the factors that led ruling elites to soften their position on the Master and Servant acts. In trades that had already adopted "minute contracts," the Master and Servant acts would have been rendered irrelevant, and employers would have had little incentive to agitate for their retention, but minute contracts had not been adopted everywhere. More trades still adhered to short contracts of a week, fortnight, or month, and in these, penal sanctions continued to be useful to employers, as prosecution statistics in the early 1870s make clear. In certain trades employers even engaged in struggles to try to lengthen contract periods.

However, in trades that maintained the practice of short contracts, the growing militancy of labor under conditions of labor scarcity altered the calculus of employers. They were confronted with a dilemma, and in deciding which horn to embrace found their collective response divided. If penal sanctions were successfully defended, labor would continue to have strong incentives to bargain for minute contracts in more and more trades, and it was feared workers would increasingly be in a position to obtain them. If they did, then employers would not only have effectively lost the benefits of penal sanctions in any case but also the benefits many of them believed they derived from short contracts. The choice appeared to be between defending penal sanctions and possibly losing both penal sanctions and short contracts, or conceding on the question of penal sanctions and retaining the benefits of contracts. Employers must have found it difficult to present a unified front under these circumstances. Some may have opted to defend penal sanctions with the hope that they could prevail in a struggle to force workers to accept contracts for a term. but others may have opted for reform, calculating that this would be a surer way of preserving the practice of short contracts. The latter seems to have been the view of Cross and Montagu, although Cross may have been using this argument merely for political purposes. He may well have believed that the contract system could not be saved in any case.

With the employing classes divided on the continuing need for and desirability of penal sanctions, the proponents of reform found it possible to

---

[114] Ibid., col. 668 (remarks of Alexander Macdonald, June 28, 1875); see also cols. 672–73 (remarks of Mr. Mundella arguing the benefits of short contracts, June 28, 1875).

carry the day. However, it was only because there was now a powerful movement to change the rules, built on the political and organizational strengths of labor, the effectiveness of their arguments, and their determination to circumvent the rules if they could not be changed, that Parliament was confronted with this Hobson's choice. Without the determined opposition of labor, penal sanctions could have been preserved for the benefit of any industries that wished to maintain criminally binding contracts.

In retrospect, of course, it appears clear that the reformist way out of the dilemma was no way out at all. Once reform of contract remedies had reduced the ability of employers to enforce labor agreements, they would have less incentive to enter contracts for a term, even if labor had then wanted them.[115] It seems likely that the outcome of reform would only be to speed up the movement to employment at will, bringing about the very result that reformers had tried to avoid: the demise of both penal sanctions *and* binding contracts.[116]

The spread of employment at will and the elimination of penal sanctions went hand in hand under these circumstances, but neither was the inevitable outcome of the modernization of industry, the simple result of employers moving to replace costly and antiquated legal coercion of labor with the efficient discipline of the market. Both employment at will and the abolition of penal sanctions were the outcomes of long and complex economic and political struggles between workers and employers within modern market society, struggles that were themselves the result of changes in legal ground rules that had occurred earlier in the nineteenth century. These changes in legal ground rules created both the conditions and the framework for the struggles that were to have as *their* outcome the adoption and spread of employment at will in a few industries and changes in workers' views of long contracts, followed by further changes in basic ground rules, the extension of the suffrage, and later, after further political and economic struggles, additional changes in the ground rules: the practical elimination of penal sanctions for most contract breaches, followed by a further spread of employment at will.

---

[115] Of course, to the extent that the common law entirety doctrine or express contractual provisions exposed workers to loss or forfeiture of back wages for departure without the required notice or for dismissal for misconduct, employers still had a remedy that could make short contracts useful to them. For a discussion of the entirety doctrine and wage forfeiture in this period, see M. R. Freedland, *The Contract of Employment* (Oxford, 1976), 126–36, 227–33. There appears to have been less use of this device in Britain than in the United States, perhaps because the British had had penal sanctions available for so long.

[116] By the early twentieth century there was a widespread belief that the contracts of manual workers were terminable at will; see Freedland, *Contract of Employment*, 145. Cf. F. Meyers, *Ownership of Jobs – A Comparative Study* (Berkeley, Calif., 1964), 21 (1867 and 1875 reforms halted the movement to contracts of employment terminable at will).

Before the fact, reform was far from inevitable. The Royal Commission had produced an elaborate rationale for retaining the status quo, and the Cabinet had endorsed this view just weeks before Cross introduced his legislation. If Cross had decided not to pursue radical reform just then, or if Disraeli had not supported Cross, or if for any other reason the Cabinet/Royal Commission view had prevailed, radical reform probably would not have occurred in 1875.

In arguing for reform, Cross felt the need to assure Parliament that his reforms did not represent a stab in the dark, a social experiment that had never been tried anywhere else before, with unknown consequences. He pointed out that all the major European countries had long had contract laws that were similar to the law only then being contemplated by Parliament and that these countries had not unduly suffered as a result. In 1873 and 1874, the Home Office had conducted a study, soliciting reports on the master and servant laws in various foreign countries. As reform of the English law was being considered in Parliament, the "Copy of All Reports on the Law of Master and Servant in Foreign Countries Transmitted to the Home Office in 1873 and 1874" was printed as a *Parliamentary Paper*.[117] Cross was apparently basing his comments on these reports. He contended, a bit deceptively in light of what the reports actually said, that

> Foreign nations are a long way ahead of us in this matter. In Italy, France, Belgium and Germany there is absolute equality and all these matters have for a long time been treated as civil contracts. We are therefore taking precisely the same step which has already been taken by foreign nations, and we shall be in no worse a position as regards these contracts than any of those nations.[118]

However small a role it may have played in convincing ruling elites to go along with reform, one factor was that similar practices had already been successfully tried in other countries. The French Civil Code, adopted following the French Revolution, had long prohibited the specific enforcement of contracts of personal service. Prussia had repealed penal sanctions for contract breaches in the case of factory workers and journeymen (but not other types of wage workers) in 1869 for its own reasons. These developments in other places must be added to the factors that have to be considered in explaining the British reform of 1875.

Citing foreign precedents strengthened the argument for reform in Britain in more than one way. It showed not only that such an experiment

---

[117] *Parl. Papers* (1875), LXII (April 26, 1875).

[118] Hansard's *Parl. Debates* (1875), CCXXIV:col. 1679 (remarks of Assheton Cross, June 10, 1875).

could work but also that reform was not in fact much of an experiment at all. It was already the norm in much of Europe, and in enacting reform Britain was merely joining the modern European mainstream. To the extent that "modern" also had prescriptive connotations, citing these foreign precedents strengthened the case for reform as well. Reform, being modernization, was a good thing.

The universe of factors that might contribute to bringing reform about in any country, and which from the historian's perspective might explain reform in retrospect, changed each time reform legislation was enacted, or was defeated, somewhere else in any society that was vaguely comparable to the one in which a similar struggle was taking place. The outcomes of struggles in some places often became a factor in similar struggles in other places, used as precedent both descriptively and prescriptively by one side or the other in struggles to change or defend the status quo. Once the British had enacted their legislation in 1875, that development itself created a new factor that assumed a life of its own, exerting its own causal influence on future struggles for reform elsewhere.

Social conditions constantly change in large and small ways. New developments are constantly added to the mix of factors at work, and small changes in conditions after the passage of only short periods of time can produce radically different outcomes. In 1867 only limited reforms were adopted in Britain, but eight years later much more thoroughgoing reform was enacted. Numerous domestic developments had changed the parallelogram of forces operating in British life. One nondomestic factor was that, in 1869, Prussia moved to decriminalize contract breaches for its factory workers. This must have placed some additional pressure, however slight, on British elites. If rigid, authoritarian Prussia could take this step, it would be somewhat awkward for the liberty-loving British to be seen as balking at a similar measure.

When Cross introduced his legislation he began to reshape the justification for doing away with penal sanctions. Up until that time, the debate had centered largely on labor's argument and the responses to that argument. Labor's chief complaint was that the Master and Servant acts were class legislation singling out working people as a different, inferior species who were not the legal equals of every other British subject. The grievance was framed in terms of a fundamental liberal principle: All people were entitled to equal treatment under law. There was also a practical side to the unequal treatment argument, as evidenced by Alexander Macdonald's comments about minute contracts. Under the old master and servant laws employers had a qualitatively different kind of weapon available to them than workers did. What labor wanted was for the same kind of weaponry to be available to both sides. Macdonald had no trouble with the threats an employer could make under minute contracts to let a worker go for bad behavior because workers could use the same type of threat against an employer:

> The employer refrained from doing wrong to his workman, because he knew that the man might leave him at any moment, and, on the other hand, the working man refrained from doing wrong to his master, because he knew that he could get rid of him at any moment.[119]

The rhetorical focus of labor's campaign for reform was equal treatment at law, driven by a desire to eliminate class legislation. Thomas Burt thought "that until very recently the House considered that the working man belonged to a different order and required different laws from those which applied to other classes."[120] This was no longer acceptable.

PENAL SANCTIONS AND FREEDOM

In the course of the debate over reform Assheton Cross, with the assistance of Lord Elcho, moved to reframe the justification for eliminating penal sanctions. Equal treatment under law was still a component of this new rhetorical strategy, but the two began to emphasize a second theme as even more important: individual freedom from coercion. They also began to associate this individual freedom from coercion with freedom of contract. "The ancient law with reference to the relations between master and servant," Cross said, "did not promote freedom of contract in any way, the Laws as originally laid down were very oppressive and restrictive." [121] This was certainly true of the pre-eighteenth-century legislation, which required laboring people to enter contracts and to enter contracts of a certain length, and which dictated that wages were to be set by the local magistrates or by Parliament. However, these features of the master and servant laws had been repealed in the early nineteenth century. Were penal sanctions for breaches of contracts whose terms had been voluntarily established by the parties also an infringement of freedom of contract? Cross was a little cagey on the question but did create the impression that penal sanctions, being a residue of the ancient law, could be viewed in a similar way. He said that all objections to the 1867 act "may be traced to what the Act retains of the character of our ancient law that forbade freedom of contract for service; and this Act although it mitigates the ancient law in many ways, still retains a criminal character."[122] His proposal, he

---

[119] Ibid., CCXXV:col. 668 (remarks of Alexander Macdonald, June 28, 1875).

[120] Ibid., cols. 680–81 (remarks of Thomas Burt, June 28, 1875).

[121] Ibid., CCXXIV:col. 1669 (remarks of Assheton Cross, June 10, 1875).

[122] Ibid., col. 1672.

said, was that "the whole of the old law, so far as it is coercive, shall be swept away."[123]

There was a tactical reason for this rhetorical reframing of the issue. Freedom of servants from coercion by their masters was linked to freedom of individual will, which was linked to freedom of contract, which was further linked, in Cross's and Elcho's formulation, to freedom from coercion by fellow workers. Cross was proposing to retain the Criminal Law Amendment Act at this stage of the parliamentary deliberations and took the opportunity created by his proposed elimination of penal sanctions to buttress that other position. "When we declare there shall be absolute freedom of contract between master and workman," he said,

> we are also of opinion that there must be equal freedom of contract between workman and fellow-workman. If a workman is entitled to make a contract with his master as he might make a contract for his bread . . . or anything else, if he breaks his contract he is to be as free from his fellow-workmen as from his master. There is to be no infringement by Parliament on his liberty as regards his master, and there must be no coercion on his free will by his fellow workmen or bodies of his fellow-workmen. He must have precisely the same liberty as anyone else in this country; and therefore we come now to consider what must be done in the case of the Criminal Law Amendment Act.[124]

Cross went on to say that we "do not propose to make any alteration in the Criminal Law Amendment Act of 1871."[125] Lord Elcho echoed Cross's refrain:

> He would conclude by saying that it appeared to him that the Government was now acting rightly in putting master and servant upon an equality before the law and in carrying out absolute freedom not only between master and servant, but between workman and workman. . . . [O]ne thing was absolutely necessary – namely, to secure the absolute freedom of individuals, and not to allow any one class or any individuals of any class to interfere with the freedom of others.[126]

In the June 28, 1875, debate, Cross concluded his remarks by saying that

> as there was to be absolute freedom of will between master and servant, he (Mr. Cross) said there should be absolute freedom between

[123] Ibid., col. 1674.

[124] Ibid., col. 1679.

[125] Ibid., col. 1682.

[126] Ibid., CCXXV:col. 666 (remarks of Lord Elcho, June 28, 1875).

a man and his fellow-servant – a man should work if he liked, he should not work if he did not like; he should belong to a trades union if he liked, but should not be compelled to belong to a trades union. He believed the great object of all good government in England . . . [was] that there should exist, so far as was consistent with general public order, the greatest amount of individual freedom of action it was possible to attain.[127]

Several points need to be made about this reframing of the issue of penal sanctions in terms of individual freedom. First, from the modern perspective, it is a little surprising that it happened so late in the day, that freedom was not always the primary ground of the debate. Up until almost the last moment it simply wasn't, and it is now a little easier to understand why. For one thing, there was a large tactical advantage for labor in framing its attack on penal sanctions in terms of legal equality and class oppression rather than in terms of individual liberty.

In addition, linking repeal of penal sanctions to freedom of contract was not an easy thing to do. In essence, Cross was saying that freedom of contract included a kind of freedom to break contracts, in that only less effective remedies would henceforth be authorized to enforce contracts for personal services. Behind this reconceptualization actually lay a decision to restrict freedom of contract in the interests of promoting freedom of person, two liberal values that stood in some tension with one another. To the extent that freedom of contract was absolute, one should be free to contract away one's personal liberty. If one was not free to contract away one's personal liberty, then freedom of contract was, to this extent, restricted – in favor of freedom of person. Some trade-off between the two values was necessary if both were to be simultaneously maintained. By redefining freedom of contract to include a freedom to break contracts subject only in many cases to the payment of damages, Cross was smoothing over this contradiction. In the process, he was also proposing a completely modern understanding of free labor and its relationship to free contract. Free labor was free by virtue of the fact that the performance of promised labor services, even in the case of completely voluntary agreements, could not be enforced through penal sanctions or specific performance because that would represent an unacceptable infringement on individual liberty. Such a restriction on contract remedies, in this view, should nevertheless not be characterized as a restriction on freedom of contract, but rather as an expression of freedom of contract, the freedom to enter, then break, then re-enter contracts freely.

---

[127] Ibid., col. 678 (remarks of Assheton Cross, June 28, 1875).

This was only half of Cross's conception of free labor. The other half was that free labor could not be "coerced" by fellow workers. This view was more than the passing fancy of one man. As late as 1891, the

> *Economist* noted . . . that "the general labour controversy is going largely to turn upon the respective rights and duties of free labourers and unionists" – free labourers being defined as all those who wished to make their own independent contract with their employers regardless of the trade-union position.[128]

All the parties could agree on half of Cross's redefinition of free labor, but the other half would be vigorously contested and would ultimately fail to become a part of the modern understanding of free labor. The half that was not contested soon became the standard view of penal sanctions. Penal sanctions (and specific performance) were singled out as contract remedies that coerced labor and uniquely interfered with the freedom of individual workers. Other coercive contract remedies, such as losing wages for absences or lateness, did not come to be characterized in the same way, even when they were legislatively prohibited. They were not thought of as coercing the performance of labor in the way that penal sanctions and specific performance were now thought to do. These other coercive pecuniary contract remedies continued to be part of the purely voluntary universe of free contract.

Parliament ultimately repealed the Criminal Law Amendment Act in 1875 and changed the legal rules governing bargaining tactics in trade disputes, enhancing the economic power of labor. At the same time, it enacted the Employers and Workmen Act (38 & 39 Vict., c. 90), together with the Conspiracy and Protection of Property Act (38 & 39, Vict., c. 86), which eliminated in most cases criminal sanctions for contract breaches.

[128] John Saville, "Trade Unions and Free Labour: The Background to the Taff Vale Decision," in *Essays in Labour History,* ed. Asa Briggs and John Saville (London, 1967), 319.

7

Freedom of Contract and Freedom of Person

The traditional account of the rise of free labor is backwards. The advent of freer markets in England during the late eighteenth and nineteenth centuries did not produce "free labor," but rather, by modern standards, a form of "coerced" contractual labor, similar to, although less harsh than, the contract labor used in the colonial periphery. For English elites who worked to make markets freer during this period, penal sanctions were an integral aspect of reform, guaranteeing that markets organized on the basis of private agreements would function properly. When they possessed the political power to do so, the English employing classes enacted and used penal sanctions to enforce the contracts of wage workers. It was only as a result of the greatly increased power of labor later in the nineteenth century that the regime of contract rules we refer to as modern free labor was fought for and enacted into law.

Modern free labor in England must be seen as a product of labor's struggle to improve its position in a market society. In general, labor pursued three broad strategies of legal reform, which admittedly were not always consistent with one another. First, labor worked to enact rules that would increase its bargaining power by giving it legal permission to engage collectively in a broader range of activities designed to bring employers to terms. Second, labor supported rule changes that would improve the main alternatives to wage labor by establishing, for example, social insurance programs, unemployment compensation, and old age pensions. Third, labor also supported efforts to restrict freedom of contract in certain areas through the passage of, for example, maximum hours and minimum wage legislation. We must place the repeal of penal sanctions in this last category, as a successful effort on labor's part to restrict freedom of contract by limiting the contract remedies legally available to employers. Modern free labor in England was a product of the growing power of labor within a free market society. It constituted, and still constitutes, a clear limitation placed on freedom of the market in the interests of reducing the coercion to which wage workers were subject.

CONTRACTS OF SLAVERY

This story has not been fully told before, it seems, because of the common misconception in the United States that modern contract rules have been in effect in England for centuries. Benno Schmidt, in an influential article describing the legal background of the early twentieth-century United States Supreme Court peonage decisions, wrote, for example, that

> the long-accepted position of Anglo-American criminal law is that an individual breaching a contract should not be subject to criminal penalties. There are many reasons of principle and policy behind the tradition. It has been thought inappropriate to employ the moral stigma of the criminal law for contractual nonperformance. . . . [I]t is economically efficient to permit contract breach where the cost of performance exceeds the value of performance. . . . *All in all, the jurisprudence of criminal law indicates that to treat breach of a labor contract as a crime would be a stark and dubious deviation from tradition.*[1] (emphasis added)

We now know that this conclusion is simply wrong.

A second reason this story has not been fully told is that many lawyers and historians believe that modern free labor is an expression of freedom of contract rather than a limitation upon it and therefore is in an altogether different category than minimum wage or maximum hours legislation. As a practical matter, of course, the repeal of penal sanctions did *not* reduce freedom of contract. Penal sanctions, being part of the criminal law, were not formally waivable by contracting parties.[2] In other words, they were a mandatory, state-imposed term that the parties were not formally free to contract around. The scope of the freedom of contracting parties to make their own contract terms was not reduced by the repeal of such a mandatory term. After repeal parties could not contract *for* penal sanctions, it is true, but before repeal they could not expressly contract *out of* penal sanctions.

From another perspective, however, the repeal of penal sanctions does represent an important restriction on the scope of freedom of contract. If we begin from the principle of perfect freedom of contract, in which one is free to contract for a stricter remedy or a less strict remedy for breach of

---

[1] Benno C. Schmidt, Jr., "Principle and Prejudice: The Supreme Court and Race in the Progressive Era. Part 2: The Peonage Cases," *Columbia Law Review* 82 (1982): 705.

[2] Although not formally waivable, they could be waived informally where, for example, an employer adopted a practice of not criminally enforcing contracts, perhaps to make the firm more attractive to workers, a form of nonpecuniary competition for labor. There were cases in which a firm adopted a self-conscious policy of not using the master and servant laws. See Testimony of John Ormiston before the "Select Committee on Master and Servant," *Parl. Papers* (1866), XIII:Q. 2052.

contract, then limiting parties to less strict remedies represents a narrowing of freedom of contract. Moreover, it represents a kind of restraint on alienation.[3] Before repeal of criminal sanctions one could transfer what amounted to a "property" right in one's labor.[4] After repeal one could only create a "liability" right in purchasers of one's labor.[5] One was, in effect, restrained from alienating the property one possessed in one's labor.

In practice, freedom of contract was never absolute. The legitimate scope of freedom of contract was always an issue in the formation and maintenance of free markets. Even during the high point of laissez-faire liberalism in England, there was one category of labor contracts that constituted a clear exception to the principle of perfect freedom of contract. English law considered contracts of slavery null and void. Legal commentators have expended a great deal of effort over the years analyzing whether this restraint on freedom of contract can be justified, but the clear consensus, in the middle of the nineteenth century was that freedom should not include the freedom to alienate one's freedom. The refusal to recognize contracts of slavery is a corollary of this principle.[6]

Less attention has been paid to the question of what precisely makes a labor contract a "contract of slavery." John Stuart Mill mentioned two factors in his discussion of contracts of slavery in *On Liberty*, written in 1859.

[3] In recent years a few law and economics scholars have begun to recognize this fact and to treat it as a problem again. See, for example, Stewart E. Sterk, "Restraints on Alienation of Human Capital," *Virginia Law Review* 79 (March 1993); and Christopher T. Wonnell, "The Contractual Disempowerment of Employees," *Stanford Law Review* 46 (November 1993). Other legal scholars, however, would tend to see these restraints on alienation as an example of beneficial "incomplete commodification," which helps to preserve the prerequisites for a human life decently lived. On the incomplete commodification of modern labor, see Margaret Jane Radin, *Contested Commodities: The Trouble with Trade in Sex, Children, Body Parts, and Other Things* (Cambridge, Mass., 1996), 108–10.

[4] Anthony T. Kronman, "Specific Performance," *Chicago Law Review* 45 (1978): 352. ("The right to positively enjoin a promise . . . may be viewed as an entitlement protected by a property rule.")

5 This statement may not be strictly true. A contract remedy such as loss of back wages may be a severe enough sanction to be called a "property" rule. On the distinction between liability rules and property rules, see Guido Calabresi and A. Douglas Melamed, "Property Rules, Liability Rules and Inalienability: One View of the Cathedral," *Harvard Law Review* 85 (1972); see also I. Ayres and E. Talley, "Solomonic Bargaining," *Yale Law Journal* 104 (1995): 1036–37. ("In some contexts, the law attempts to impose sanctions that are severe enough to deter all nonconsensual takings. The protection of entitlements with such severe sanctions is what Calabresi and Melamed called 'property' rules. In other contexts, the law requires nonconsensual takers to pay an amount of damages that is set not to deter all takings but rather to compensate the entitlement holder for the loss of the entitlement. The protection of entitlements with these less severe sanctions is what Calabresi and Melamed called 'liability' rules. Restraining orders, specific performance clauses, and certain types of punitive sanctions represent 'property' protections, while expectation damages . . . [is an] example of 'liability' protection.")

[6] John Stuart Mill, *On Liberty*, ed. David Spitz (New York, 1975), 95.

One was the length of the engagement ("engagements which involve personal . . . services should never be legally binding beyond a limited duration of time"[7]). The second was the power to withdraw ("there are perhaps no contracts or engagements, except those that relate to money or money's worth, of which one can venture to say that there ought to be no liberty whatever of retractation"[8]). Whether Mill believed that both factors must be present to make a labor contract a contract of slavery is not known. However, he does not seem to have considered absence of the power to withdraw[9] in combination with an agreement to serve for a month or even several years sufficient, since he seems not to have considered English wage labor agreements of the period "contracts of slavery."

It is now possible, however, to understand why by the 1870s English workers were calling persons "hired" under multiple-year contracts from which they could not withdraw "slaves," and this raises an important point. The category of "contract of slavery" can be enlarged or shrunk depending upon the length of the period of engagement that is taken to be "beyond a limited duration." It can also be enlarged or shrunk depending on whether the presence of both factors or one factor alone is sufficient to render a labor agreement a "contract of slavery." It can be enlarged or compressed depending upon what the power to withdraw is taken to mean. At one extreme, if the power to withdraw were interpreted to mean the power to walk away from an agreement free from any adverse legal consequence, then any labor agreement enforceable through any legal remedy would have to be considered, strictly speaking, a "contract of slavery." Perhaps this is just another way of saying that at bottom the freedom to enter legally binding contracts stands in contradiction to the ideal of perfectly free labor. Perhaps employment at will approaches the ideal of perfectly free labor, but only if we choose to ignore a range of extracontractual coercive pressures operating on workers to enter and remain in wage labor relationships.

The ban on self-enslavement has been justified in numerous ways, but

> [o]ne rationale . . . has been that it is a second-best device for preventing certain forms of deception and duress that cannot be attacked more directly. If we assume that in most cases a person would not contract into slavery unless he were illegitimately compelled to do so, but that such compulsion is difficult to detect . . . a flat prohibition against such agreements may be the only administratively feasible way of preventing illicit coercion.[10]

---

[7] Ibid.

[8] Ibid.

[9] It seems likely that Mill would have regarded penal sanctions as preventing withdrawal.

[10] Anthony T. Kronman, "Paternalism and the Law of Contracts," *Yale Law Journal* 92 (1983): 777.

The logic of this rationale for voiding contracts of slavery, however, switches the focus of the inquiry from the length of service and power to withdraw from a "voluntary" contract to the conditions under which such a contract has been entered. It assumes, in effect, that the harshness of the contract terms in themselves indicate that entry into the contract could not possibly have been "voluntary." One implication of this view is that there is no meaningful distinction between "contracts of slavery" and "slavery." Contracts of slavery can never be genuinely voluntary and should therefore be classified as involuntary servitude. In a number of cultures in earlier times, it was an accepted practice for the very poor who were at risk of starvation to enter into contracts of slavery with a powerful patron. If we accept the above rationale for the rule against self-enslavement, it would have to be the case that a contract signed by someone faced with this difficult choice was entered into involuntarily. "Economic" coercion in such a case would be viewed as having given rise to involuntary servitude.

The issue of whether a contract has been entered into voluntarily or involuntarily suffers from the same logical difficulty discussed at some length in the Introduction. It is not possible, as a logical matter, to distinguish difficult choices that give rise to "voluntary" decisions to contract from difficult choices that give rise to "coerced" decisions to contract. In any case, this book does not primarily focus on the issue of "voluntary" or "involuntary" *entry into* labor contracts. I am mainly concerned with the issue of *withdrawal from* presumptively "voluntary" labor agreements. Can certain contract enforcement mechanisms by themselves turn voluntary labor agreements into contracts of slavery because they interfere with withdrawal? If so, which ones? Depending on the answers to these questions the category of contract of slavery can be enlarged or reduced, and depending on whether it is enlarged or reduced, the scope of freedom of contract will have been enlarged or reduced with it.

When English labor succeeded in having penal sanctions for contract breach largely eliminated in 1875, that act established the regime of contract rules that constitute the *practice* of modern free labor. However, the main argument labor made for this reform, that penal sanctions violated the principle of equal treatment under law, makes up only part of the modern *conception* of free labor. The core of the modern conception, that penal sanctions alone are enough to turn "contracts of labor" into "contracts of slavery" because they prevent withdrawal, seems to have been developed in England only after ruling elites began to take the prospect of this new regime of contract rules seriously. In the decades following 1875 Cross's rhetorical reframing of the issue won wide acceptance as common law judges and legal commentators began to reinterpret the rule against specific performance of personal services contracts (and by implication penal sanctions) as a rule designed to prevent contractual slavery. Specific performance, they began to say, was a remedy for contract breach that could "turn contracts of service into contracts of slavery."[11] "An agreement to serve," Maitland wrote in his 1909 lectures on Equity, "can not be specifically enforced, otherwise men might in effect sell themselves into slavery."[12] This position is on the cusp of the modern legal *conception* of free labor:

> From a [modern] legal point of view, it is not the length of service that makes a contract of employment self-enslaving, nor is it the nature of the services to be performed; even a contract of short duration that calls for the performance of routine and unobjectionable tasks is a contract of self-enslavement and therefore legally unenforceable if it bars the employee from substituting money damages for his promised performance. . . . Whatever its other terms, an employment contract is enslaving if it gives the employer a right to compel specific performance of the agreement.[13]

As a result of the successful struggle of organized labor to repeal penal sanctions for contract breaches, the category of "contracts of slavery" was greatly enlarged and the scope of freedom of contract reduced. This limitation on the freedom of the market, put into place as a result of the exertions of labor, is the origin of modern free labor in England.

FREE LABOR

The term "free" labor is a shorthand way of expressing a complicated societal judgment that employers should not be permitted to force laboring people to make certain difficult choices as they decide whether to perform their labor agreements. During much of the nineteenth century, English wage labor was sometimes elicited by forcing wage workers to make a kind of difficult choice we today consider an incident of "coerced" labor. Hardly anyone alive in England at the time, however, would have considered English wage labor "coerced." From this perspective, it becomes meaningless to speak of the rise of free labor as such because free labor is a political and moral conclusion (or a legal or constitutional one) rather than a thing, a conclusion, moreover, that is subject to revision. Modern "free" labor is defined essentially by the moral and political judgment that penal sanctions and specific performance should not be permitted to en-

---

[11] Fry, L.J., in *De Francesco v. Barnum*, 45 Ch. D. 430 (1890), 438.

[12] Frederic William Maitland, *Equity, Also the Forms of Action at Common Law* (Cambridge, 1916), 240.

[13] Kronman, "Paternalism and the Law of Contracts," 778–79.

force "voluntary" labor agreements because those remedies turn contracts for labor into contracts of slavery.

It has been one of my goals up to this point to examine the history of one kind of difficult choice that came to be delegitimized in England over the course of the nineteenth century as a result of labor's struggles. It was moved from the category of difficult choice that could be presented to elicit "free" labor into the category of threat that produced "contracts of slavery." Modern "free" labor is the product of these struggles, but it is important to keep in mind that modern "free" labor continues to classify a range of other contract remedies that present other difficult choices as legitimate pressures that lead to "voluntary" rather than "coerced" labor. From the modern perspective, for example, damages for contract breach are entirely unproblematical. They can never "coerce" the performance of labor. Penal sanctions and specific performance, which do coerce the performance of labor, and damages, which do not coerce the performance of labor, however, do not exhaust the possible remedies for contract breach that the law may give or to which contracting parties can agree. There is any number of other enforcement mechanisms, including negative injunctions and wage forfeiture. The law must take a position on each of them. Do they illegitimately coerce the performance of labor, or are they legitimate remedies available for breach of voluntary labor agreements, even if they do tend to pressure the purveyor of services into performing the agreed-upon labor?

In the twentieth century, English chancery courts confronted just this question with respect to negative injunctions and ended up driving a line through the remedy of negative injunction itself. Some negative injunctions presented to the breaching party such harsh choices that they were the equivalent of specific performance and would coerce the rendition of labor services. Other negative injunctions would present difficult choices that would merely "tempt" the party to continue to perform labor services. The definitive statement of this position was issued in *Warner Brothers Pictures Incorporated v. Nelson*,[14] in which Warner Bros. sued Betty Davis, asking the court to issue a negative injunction prohibiting her from practicing her profession during the contract term with anyone other than the plaintiffs. Mr. Justice Branson declared that

> the court, true to the principle that specific performance of a contract of personal service will never be ordered, [will never] grant an injunction in the case of such a contract to enforce negative covenants if the effect of so doing would be to *drive* the defendant either to star-

[14] 106 L.J. Rep. 99 (King's Bench Division, 1937). My analysis of this case draws heavily on Robert Hale, *Freedom through Law: Public Control of Private Governing Power* (New York, 1952), 191.

vation or to specific performance of the positive covenants."[15] (emphasis added)

In Davis's case a negative injunction would not force her to choose between starvation and performance of labor services. It would only force her to choose between a highly remunerative career and some other less remunerative job, say $1 million as an actress versus $15,000 as a waitress. In the eyes of the law, this choice between disagreeable alternatives, performance versus a low-paying job, was not so harsh as to coerce the performance of her labor services. It was merely harsh enough to "tempt" her to perform:

> It was also urged that the difference between what the defendant can earn as a film artist and what she might expect to earn by any other form of activity is so great that she will in effect be *driven to perform* her contract. . . . The defendant is stated to be a person of intelligence, capacity and means, and no evidence was deduced to show that, if enjoined from doing the specified acts otherwise than for the plaintiffs, she will not be able to employ herself both usefully and remuneratively in other spheres of activity, though not as remuneratively as in her special line. She *will not be driven, although she may be tempted,* to perform the contract, and the fact that she may be so tempted is no objection to the grant of an injunction.[16] (emphasis added)

Here the legal line separating difficult choices that coerce labor from difficult choices that merely "tempt" free labor was drawn, an arbitrary line drawn through a continuum of coercive pressures that can be brought to bear to enforce contracts for personal services.

TOWARD A NEW HISTORY OF FREE LABOR

The story of English wage labor in the nineteenth century makes necessary a revision of the conventional wisdom about the history of wage labor in the metropolitan core. Wage labor, it turns out, is a form of contractual labor that may be legally constructed in a variety of different ways. In nineteenth-century England it took a form that by modern standards would place it in the category of "coerced" labor. The binary opposition free/coerced labor is itself an historical artifact, a product, in its fully rationalized form, of the Scottish and Continental enlightenments. The changing judgments made over time as to precisely what coercive pres-

---

[15] *Warner Bros. Pictures Incorporated v. Nelson,* 106 L.J. Rep. 99 (King's Bench Division, 1937), 100.

[16] Ibid., 102.

sures place a particular labor practice in the one category or the other are similarly historical and regional conventions. What the story of nine-teenth-century English wage labor makes clear, however, is that during this period employers pursued their economic interests by having their wage workers sign binding labor agreements that were then strictly en-forced against them.[17] The inclination to use and strictly enforce contracts seems to have characterized the behavior of employers throughout the metropolitan core during this period. Which contract enforcement mecha-nisms could actually be used in any particular place, however, was a com-plicated matter that turned in large measure on the legal, political, social, and cultural rules and norms of the place and on the outcome of struggles over these rules and norms.

The labor victory in abolishing penal sanctions and restricting other ef-fective contract remedies in England accelerated the movement toward employment at will, as binding contracts became less attractive to employ-ers who were mainly left with relatively expensive, cumbersome, and inef-fective remedies for contract breach. Employers were forced to operate within this new constraint, but within this constraint they did devise other, perhaps less satisfactory, kinds of contractual arrangements to con-trol turnover and monitoring costs.[18]

Was the English experience typical of the evolution of wage labor over the nineteenth century and into the twentieth century throughout Europe? In other words, was wage labor characterized by a fairly uniform linear development during this period, even if this development was dif-ferent than the one we have been taught to see? We know too little at this time to arrive at firm conclusions, but a tentative answer is, yes and no. What seems to have been true is that nineteenth-century employers of wage labor saw contracting and contract enforcement as an important ele-ment of the proper functioning of labor markets, but precisely what en-forcement mechanisms they used depended on the local political, legal, and cultural context. I discuss the American case in detail in the next chapters, but as far as other European states are concerned I can only of-fer the outline of an answer. Common patterns did exist, but there was also a great deal of diversity based on local practice. It is unlikely that a single explanation will be able to account for the changes that took place in labor practices over time, although an increasingly powerful labor movement, together with the extension of the suffrage, may have been crucial factors in many places.

---

[17] Employment at will, of course, is also a form of contract, but when I use the term "con-tract" in the text I mean a contractual relation that is not determinable at will.

[18] For a summary of the modern literature on these arrangements, see Mark Kelman, "Pro-gressive Vacuums," *Stanford Law Review* 48 (April 1996): 980.

France and Belgium

Following the French Revolution, France enacted its well-known Civil Code. Article 1780 of that code denied courts the power to order workers to perform their agreements.[19] It is not clear precisely what the rationale for the rule was, but unlike England, France did not supplement this prohibition on the specific enforcement of contracts for personal services with criminal legislation subjecting workers to penal sanctions for breaches of labor agreements. In this respect the nineteenth-century French regime of contract rules established a legal form of wage labor that was less coercive than English wage labor.

Nevertheless, like their English counterparts, French governing elites were of the view that freer wage labor markets could not be expected to operate properly unless labor contracts could be enforced. As a consequence, French workers began to be required to carry a "livret," a work passport that they took from job to job. The effectiveness of the livret law has been much debated, but in theory these work books served as

> work passports for the registration of hirings, dismissals, and debts. Laborers remained free to contract the best conditions they could with employers. But once hired, they could not go elsewhere until the employer returned their *livret* to them with written indications that they had fulfilled all obligations under the contract. It was understood that the obligations would usually include obeying work rules of the kind once enforced by the guilds and giving advance notice of one's intention to quit. If a laborer quit before having paid back all advances on wages made by the employer, then the debt could be registered in his *livret* and paid off by a lien of 20 percent on future earnings. *[Minister of the Interior] Chaptal's justification [1802] for these measures. The market could not work if there were no means to ensure that engagements once undertaken would be carried out.*[20] (emphasis added)

Penal sanctions and the "livret" both represented attempts to enforce, in different ways, the labor agreements of British and French workers in their respective freer post-revolutionary worlds. The law requiring work-

---

[19] Michael Sonenscher, *Work and Wages: Natural Law, Politics and the Eighteenth-Century French Trades* (Cambridge, 1989), 367; see also "Copy of All Reports on the Law of Master and Servant in Foreign Countries Transmitted to the Home Office in 1873 and 1874," in *Irish University Press Series of British Parliamentary Papers, 1865–75* (Shannon, Ireland, 1968), XVIII:544.

[20] William Reddy, *The Rise of Market Culture: The Textile Trade and French Society, 1750–1900* (Cambridge, 1984), 71–72. See also Alberto Melucci, "Action Patronale, pouvoir, organisation. Règlements d'usine et contrôle de la main-d'oeuvre au XIXe siècle," *Mouvement Sociale* 97 (1976): 143–44; cf. Sonenscher, *Work and Wages*, 368; Arthur Louis Dunham, *The Industrial Revolution in France, 1815–1848* (New York, 1955), 201–2.

ers to carry "livrets" was only repealed in 1890.[21] It is not clear whether repeal had been argued for on the ground that the "livret" illegitimately "coerced" the performance of labor contracts, or on some other ground, or whether it was not necessary to mount any argument because the requirement was no longer observed in practice. It is also not clear what role French labor may have played in bringing about changes in practice and in law, and it is not clear what range of contract remedies remained available to employers after the "livret" law had been eliminated.

As late as 1874, Belgian law contained a similar requirement:

> Every workman employed in a factory or a workshop must be provided with a "livret," certifying his entrance and departure, as well as the fact of his having fulfilled his engagements towards his master. The workman who has received an advance of wages, or contracted an engagement to work for a certain time, cannot send in his "livret" before having acquitted his debt of labour, and fulfilled his engagements, if his master insists on it. . . . [A Royal decree of 1854] obliges the workman to have a "livret" in proper form, under penalty of a 26 to 200 francs fine, and an imprisonment of from one to fourteen days. But it must be observed that the legality of the [decree] in this respect has been contested by the tribunals. [A bill to make livrets optional is now pending before the Chamber of Representatives.][22]

Prussia

Unlike the French and the Belgians, but like the British, the principal German state, Prussia, did have legislation criminalizing breaches of labor agreements, and this legislation too had been adopted as part of the project of making markets freer. Penal sanctions for labor contract breaches were seen as necessary for the continued stable functioning of labor markets as traditional constraints were relaxed. "Freedom of trade" (Gewerbefreiheit) was introduced into Prussia in 1845 by the Industrial Law (Gewerbeordnung) of that year.[23] This liberal, free market reform mandated that the relationship between masters and their journeymen in the arti-

[21] "Copy of All Reports on . . . Master and Servant," 544–45. On repeal, see Melucci, "Action Patronale, pouvoir, 143.

[22] "Copy of all Reports on . . . Master and Servant," 535–36. This report was compiled by the British in 1873 and 1874 and referred to by Assheton Cross in his speech introducing the 1875 Employers and Workmen reform bill.

[23] "Gesetzsammlung für die Königlichen Preußischen Staaten 1845" [hereinafter "PGS"], Gewerbeordnung 41–78 (1845). Freedom of trade, however, was repealed four years later, in 1849, and not reestablished in Prussia until the Industrial Law of 1869, enacted by the North German Confederation.

sanal sector, and between factory workers and their employers in the expanding industrial sector, should henceforth be governed by contracts freely negotiated by the parties.[24] For breach of these contracts, however, factory workers, journeymen, and other wage workers were subject, under the 1845 reforms, to penal sanctions, including prison. The law declared that "Journeymen, helpers, and factory workers, who leave work without permission and without legal justification, or are guilty of shirking, or gross disobedience or insistent obstinacy, are to be punished with a fine up to twenty Thalers or prison up to fourteen days."[25] These sanctions are less harsh than the sanctions imposed by English law. For one thing, prison was not mandatory; the adjudicating official could impose a fine instead. The maximum prison term of fourteen days also was considerably shorter than the three-month maximum authorized by English law. Penal sanctions for contract breaches by factory workers were eliminated by the Industrial Law (Gewerbeordnung) of 1869,[26] in the newly formed North German Confederation.

This rule change, however, only covered factory workers. Servants, tenant laborers (Gesinde), and "such workpeople as have engaged themselves for any particular agricultural or forest work" continued to be subject to penal sanctions for breaches of their agreements until the twentieth century.[27] As late as July 1874, moreover, a measure was pending in the Reichstag to change the 1869 Industrial Code back "and particularly to subject to reprehensive measures any illegal breach of contract on the part of industrial workmen."[28] Not until the revolutionary upheaval that brought the Weimar Republic into being following World War I were the last of these penal sanctions for contract breaches eliminated.[29] Obviously, the history of penal sanctions in Prussia and Germany shares features with the history of penal sanctions in England and with the history of contract enforcement in France and Belgium. Just as obviously, however, it is also a history peculiar to the German states. The combination of factors that explain the crucial details, why certain rules were changed at one time and other rules were changed much later, was likely to have been different from the combination of factors that explain the timing and implementation of rule changes in other European states.

[24] "PGS," 1845, *Gewerbeordnung,* §§ 134, 145.

[25] Ibid., § 184.

[26] "Bundesgesetzblatt des Norddeutschen Bundes, 1869," *Gewerbeordnung* no. 26, 245–82, § 154.

[27] "Copy of All Reports on . . . Master and Servant," 545–46.

[28] Ibid., 545.

[29] Shearer Davis Bowman, *Masters and Lords: Mid–19th Century U. S. Planters and Prussian Junkers* (Oxford, 1993), 234 n. 17.

Denmark, Norway, and Switzerland

Coercive fines followed by imprisonment for nonpayment were available to enforce contracts in Denmark as late as 1874.[30] In Norway, the police could punish servants who left without notice by fining them or imprisoning them for a few days upon application from their employers.[31] In Switzerland,

> [a]ccording to the Factory Laws of Basel Town, the work in hand must be completed before the piece-worker can leave the service of his employer. In 1870, 46 workmen of a silk factory left their work unfinished at a moment's notice, on the refusal of their employer to grant a certain increase of wages they had demanded. Their master instituted a suit against them before the Civil Tribunal for damages, whilst the police authorities called upon the workmen to answer for the breach of contract. They were condemned in the civil court to return to their work, and pay damages; and in the police courts to a fine of five francs per head. Such a decision, I am informed, could never have been arrived at in the Canton of Berne.[32]

In other parts of Switzerland, workers were required to carry a traveling or work book that they had to exhibit before receiving factory employment.[33] According to the 1873 report to the Home Office, the law of many cantons, towns, and communes continued to subject *servants* to criminal penalties for breaching their agreements, although these penalties may not have been enforced for many years.[34]

Obviously, there is a great deal still to be learned about the use of a range of coercive contract enforcement devices in Europe. The story is an enormously complicated one, involving local police regulations as well as national legislation. What roles a broadened suffrage and an activist labor movement may have played in the elimination of such devices are among the questions that remain to be answered.

The Colonies

Turning from England and Europe to the colonial periphery it is with an entirely new perspective. Throughout the colonies of the British Empire, master and servant legislation authorized criminal sanctions for labor contract breaches. Although in many cases this legislation was not directly

[30] "Copy of All Reports on . . . Master and Servant," 547.

[31] Ibid., 551.

[32] Ibid., 554.

[33] Ibid.

[34] Ibid., 556–57.

copied from the British Master and Servant acts, and differed in detail from colony to colony, it is ultimately to British domestic assumptions about contract enforcement that this colonial legislation must be traced. Just as the origins of the criminal enforcement of labor contracts in the colonial periphery can be traced back to the contractual practices and beliefs of the core, so can the gradual elimination of such colonial legislation. Changes in basic beliefs about contract enforcement in the metropolitan core ultimately also led to campaigns to change the law in the periphery, but in numerous cases this did not happen immediately. Indeed, long after penal sanctions had been eliminated in England, new statutes, and in some cases municipal ordinances, were still being passed and enforced in colonies and dominions of the British Empire.

Ontario, Canada, adopted penal sanctions for labor contract breaches in the first half of the nineteenth century. This legislation was repealed in 1877, shortly after the British repealed penal sanctions at home.[35] In New South Wales, Australia, repeal of penal sanctions seems to have taken place earlier, in 1858,[36] but in the Cape Town Colony in Africa they remained in place until well into the twentieth century.[37] Indentured servitude in Britain's Caribbean colonies only ended during the second decade of the twentieth century.[38] In India a Master and Servant act authorizing criminal punishment for contract breach remained in effect as late as 1935.[39] In the Dutch East Indies, penal sanctions were widely enforced through the 1920s and remained on the statute books until 1947.[40] In 1958, the International Labour Office found that penal sanctions were still used, although not widely, in several British territories in Africa: Kenya, Rhodesia, Swaziland, Bechuanaland, and Basutoland.[41]

---

[35] Paul Craven, "The Law of Master and Servant in Mid-Nineteenth-Century Ontario," in *Essays in the History of Canadian Law*, ed. David Flaherty (Toronto, 1981), I:199.

[36] Adrian Merritt, "The Historical Role of Law in the Regulation of Employment – Abstentionist or Interventionist?" *Australian Journal of Law & Society* 1 (1982): 61.

[37] Robert Ross, "Emancipations and the Economy of the Cape Colony," *Slavery & Abolition* 14 (April 1993): 131, 142.

[38] Hugh Tinker, *A New System of Slavery: The Export of Indian Labour Overseas, 1830–1920* (London and New York, 1974), 334–66; and K. O. Laurence, *A Question of Labour: Indentured Immigration into Trinidad and British Guiana, 1875–1917* (New York, 1994), 432–83.

[39] Paul E. Baak, "About Enslaved Ex-slaves, Uncaptured Contract Coolies and Unfree Freedmen: Some Notes about 'Free' and 'Unfree' Labour in the Context of Plantation Development in Southwest India, c. 1824–1962" (Paper presented at the Conference Free and Unfree Labour, International Institute of Social History, Amsterdam, The Netherlands, January 1994), 13–14.

[40] Margo Groenewould, "Towards the Abolition of Penal Sanctions in Dutch Colonial Labour Legislation," *Itinerario* 10, no. 2 (1995): 78–79, 81, 83.

[41] Ibid., 86.

Once Europeans had changed their basic attitudes about their own contractual practices, British and European anti-slavery movements could begin to make some headway with the argument that colonial penal contract practices were merely another form of slavery.[42] In the twentieth century, the International Labour Organization, established by the League of Nations after World War I, began to play an important role in the effort to eliminate the penal enforcement of labor agreements everywhere in the world. The first time the ILO formally took up the question of penal sanctions, the positions staked out by the Employer and Worker Groups reproduced in certain respects the earlier English experience.

In 1929, the issue of "forced labor" came before the International Labour Conference. One critical question was how forced labor was to be defined. Was contract labor to be considered "forced labor?"

> It was suggested . . . that a more satisfactory definition of forced labour might be attained if, in addition to postulating the possibly nonvoluntary character of the forced worker's entry upon his task, the fact that *he cannot withdraw himself from it voluntarily* be also part of the definition. Otherwise, it was asserted, much forced labour would escape from the scope of a Convention on the subject.[43] (emphasis original)

"Any analogy between forced labour and such contracts was forcibly denied by one member of the Employers' Group who pointed out that in the Dutch East Indies every care was taken to ensure that workers understood the terms of their contracts before signing them, and who declared that in any well-administered colony no contract implying a real constraint should be possible."[44] The "Workers' Group," in the face of this resistance, put forward and argued for a resolution calling for a study of contract labor "with a view to the question of [its] complete abolition being placed on the Agenda of one of the next Sessions of the International Labour Conference with the shortest possible delay."[45] In 1939, the first conference on penal sanctions was held, and the resulting convention urged that penal sanctions be "abolished progressively and as soon as pos-

---

[42]   See, for example, Katharine Coman, "The History of Contract Labor in the Hawaiian Islands," *Publications of the American Economic Association, Third Series* 4 (August 1903): 485, 533 ("Penal enforcement of a labor contract is inconsistent with the trend of modern labor legislation. It suggests slavery."). See her discussion of changes in American and European law over the nineteenth century, 539–40.

[43]   International Labour Conference, *Forced Labour*, Questionnaire I (Fourteenth Session, Geneva, 1929), 10.

[44]   Ibid., 11–12.

[45]   Ibid., 42.

sible."[46] In 1955, the ILO finally adopted a convention that called for the abolition of all penal sanctions within one year.[47] That convention came into force in 1958.[48]

From being an unquestioned aspect of contractual labor in England, in some European countries, and throughout the colonial empires established by them in the nineteenth century, penal sanctions gradually fell into disfavor nearly everywhere over a long period from about 1870 to about 1955. The English experience, at least, suggests that this development may have had more than a little to do with the growing political and economic power of labor in the English and European worlds.

In the next chapters, I examine the American case as a way of beginning to develop a detailed, comparative account of the legal conditions of nineteenth-century wage labor that will identify common patterns but also recognize the diversity of contractual practices in different countries. In the northern United States, penal sanctions were not, in the main, available after the 1830s. Nevertheless, penal sanctions were not finally declared unconstitutional under the United States Constitution until the first decade of the twentieth century and were used extensively in southern states in the decades following the Civil War. They were also used against merchant seamen until late in the nineteenth century and, to a much more limited extent, against lumbermen and miners working in remote locations in a few northern states during the first decade of the twentieth century. Even in the northern states that refused to allow penal sanctions in the nineteenth century, binding labor contracts and labor contract enforcement was still an important feature of wage labor. In that case, however, the allowable range of contract enforcement devices was more limited than in England. The chief enforcement mechanism was wage forfeiture.

---

[46] International Labour Conference, *Penal Sanctions for Breaches of Contract of Employment*, Report VI(2) (Thirty-eighth Session, Geneva, 1955), 16–18.

[47] Ibid., 18.

[48] See Convention No. 104, in *International Labour Conventions and Recommendations, 1919–1981* (Geneva: International Labour Office, 1982), 856.

PART TWO

"Free" and "Unfree" Labor
in the United States

8

"Involuntary Servitude" in American Fundamental Law

The question of the use and legality of penal sanctions to enforce labor contracts in the United States is a complicated one. Before the mid-eighteenth century, statutes in a number of American colonies subjected "hired" as well as imported workers to penal sanctions for breaches of their labor contracts.[1] Over the course of the eighteenth century these provisions began to disappear from the colonial codes, leaving immigrant indentured servants as the only adult white contractual labor still subject to penal sanctions.[2] The reasons for the disappearance of penal sanctions to enforce the contracts of hired workers remain unknown. Whatever explanations may be developed, however, must simultaneously account not only for the disappearance of these remedies in the case of hired labor but also for their continued use in the case of imported labor.

By 1800 wage work in the United States was different than it was in England, at least for adult white native-born workers. The agreements of these wage workers could not be enforced through penal sanctions or specific performance. However, penal sanctions to enforce the contracts of imported indentured servants continued to be legal and to be used in the United States until the 1830s. Significant numbers of servants were im-

---

[1] Massachusetts, Rhode Island, Maryland, Virginia, North Carolina, and South Carolina are among the colonies in which there is evidence that "hired servants" could be compelled to perform their agreements. See Robert Steinfeld, *The Invention of Free Labor: The Employment Relation in English and American Law and Culture* (Chapel Hill, N.C., 1991), 47–51; see also Christopher Tomlins, *Law, Labor and Ideology in the Early American Republic* (Cambridge, 1993), 243 n. 51, 248–52.

[2] There was one significant exception, seamen. The contracts of sailors on private vessels could be criminally enforced until the twentieth century. Richard Morris was of the view that penal sanctions continued to be used against some white workers in Maryland beyond the 1830s (although his evidence seems inconclusive) and against free blacks there even longer; see "Labor Controls in Maryland in the Nineteenth Century," *The Journal of Southern History* 14 (August 1948): 391–92. Binding out convicted criminals to terms of service with private parties (distinct from the later practice of convict leasing), Morris found, was also quite common in nineteenth-century Delaware; see "The Course of Peonage in a Slave State," *Political Science Quarterly* 65 (June 1950): 245–48.

ported, on and off depending on international conditions, until about 1820. During the following decade fewer and fewer servants were imported; around 1830 the last ones entered the United States. By the later 1830s all had completed their service. Thereafter, the treatment accorded to European workers imported into the United States under contracts was brought into line with the treatment long accorded to American wage workers. By the late 1830s, neither the agreements of adult white American wage workers nor those of adult imported European contract laborers were enforced through penal sanctions or specific performance.

The reasons for this basic change in the treatment of imported contract labor must be sought in a combination of factors, including the growing identification of indentured servitude with black slavery at a time when black slavery was under attack in the North; a radicalism among white wage workers flowing from the ideology of the Revolution that led them to attack the enforcement of the contracts of imported white workers in the 1820s; and the early expansion of the suffrage in many states, which gave American workers political clout wage workers elsewhere did not possess.[3] After the 1830s, penal sanctions played no role in the lives of adult white wage or contract workers in the United States. Indeed, in many circles, the idea of penal sanctions to enforce labor contracts became unimaginable because they were thought to transform ordinary labor contracts into contracts of slavery.

Two things need to be said about this nineteenth-century American form of wage labor, however. First, the absence of penal sanctions and specific performance did not mean that contract enforcement was not an important issue during the first two-thirds of the century for employers and in the law. Like the English and Europeans, nineteenth-century American employers also seem to have believed that the enforcement of labor contracts was crucial to the proper functioning of wage labor markets. However, in contrast to England and Prussia, the remedy that American contract law allowed them, and on which they primarily relied to enforce labor agreements, was wage forfeiture.[4]

Second, the absence of penal sanctions in the North in the case of white adult workers did not mean the end of the use of penal sanctions for contract breach against all workers in the United States. People of color were subjected to penal sanctions for labor contract breaches in a number of places in the United States and its territories throughout the nineteenth century, as were merchant seamen. It is to that part of the story of penal sanctions for contract breaches in the nineteenth-century United States

---

[3] See Steinfeld, *Invention of Free Labor*.

[4] I am using "wage forfeiture" loosely here to refer not only to "forfeiture" of wages legally earned but also to wages lost under the entirety doctrine that the worker technically had not earned at all because he had failed to fulfill a contractual condition precedent.

that I turn first, before considering contract enforcement against white wage workers in the North.

THREE INTERPRETATIONS OF "INVOLUNTARY SERVITUDE"

The legal history of penal sanctions for the enforcement of labor contracts in the United States in the nineteenth century is inseparable from the story of the northern rejection of black slavery. Following the Revolution, northern states from New England to Pennsylvania all either abolished slavery outright or enacted statutes for its gradual abolition.[5] One of the issues that had to be confronted as they did so was whether labor contract enforcement devices like penal sanctions would continue to be legal. This issue arose because in a number of jurisdictions where slavery had been outlawed slave owners sought to retain the labor services of their bondsmen by signing them to long contracts enforceable through penal sanctions or specific performance. The principal source of nineteenth-century American law on the question of the legal permissibility of these kinds of contractual practices came from courts sitting in several states that were carved out of the old Northwest Territory, as they interpreted the language of the Northwest Ordinance of 1787. That Ordinance had declared: "There shall be *neither Slavery nor involuntary Servitude* in the [Northwest] territory otherwise than in the punishment of crimes, whereof the Party shall have been duly convicted" (emphasis added).[6] The 1787 Ordinance covered an area encompassed by the present states of Ohio, Michigan, Indiana, Illinois, and Wisconsin. The question of the permissibility of penal sanctions and specific enforcement of labor contracts became a question of "fundamental law"[7] as the Ordinance, passed by Congress in 1787, was enacted to provide a framework of government for the territory and for any states carved out of the territory. As a question of "fundamental law," the permissibility or impermissibility of penal sanctions became a question of whether penal sanctions or specific per-

---

[5] The process of emancipation, however, took a surprisingly long time. See Ira Berlin, *Many Thousands Gone: The First Two Centuries of Slavery in North America* (Cambridge, Mass., 1998), Chapter 9; see also Joanne Pope Melish, *Disowning Slavery: Gradual Emancipation and "Race" in New England, 1780–1860* (Ithaca, N.Y., 1998).

[6] *The Northwest Ordinance,* Art. VI (1787).

[7] I use the term "fundamental law" rather than "constitutional law" here because the Northwest Ordinance, on which a good deal of the jurisprudence dealing with the interpretation of "involuntary servitude" was based before the Civil War, was not, strictly speaking, a constitution. It had been enacted by Congress in 1787 as a statute but had come to assume a juridical status more akin to a constitution. The question of whether it could bind the peoples of the territory in perpetuity was the subject of heated debate in several territories carved out of the original one during the period in which these territories sought statehood and first drafted state constitutions.

formance to enforce labor agreements turned labor agreements into the "involuntary servitude" prohibited by the Ordinance. After the Civil War, the language of the Ordinance was incorporated into the Thirteenth Amendment to the United States Constitution, which prohibited "slavery" and "involuntary servitude" everywhere in the nation, and the question of the permissibility of penal sanctions became a question of United States constitutional law.

When examining the early interpretations of the term "involuntary servitude," however, it is important to keep one thing in mind. Adult white indentured servants were still being imported into the United States in 1787, and would continue to be imported in significant numbers, on and off, until 1820, and in smaller numbers until at least 1830. It seems likely that the framers of the Northwest Ordinance would have considered these contractual arrangements to be "voluntary," rather than the "*involuntary* servitude" against which the Ordinance was directed.

As the question was addressed in the new states carved out of the Northwest Territory, it was presented in an entirely different context. The issue arose as a result of the desire of southerners moving into the new territories[8] to bring slaves with them even though the Ordinance had clearly prohibited slavery in the territories. At least to begin with, several territorial legislatures seemed disposed to try to accommodate these desires by passing legislation that authorized the indenting of black persons brought into the territories.

Three separate and distinct constitutional traditions interpreting the term "involuntary servitude" emerged from this situation. In 1800, Ohio was separated from the rest of the Northwest Territory.[9] Two years later a convention held in the territory adopted a proposed state constitution. In 1803 Ohio was admitted to the union as a new state. The legislation that Congress passed in 1803 to enable Ohio to become a state required that the constitution of the new state "not [be] repugnant to the ordinance of . . . 1787."[10] It is a provision of the Ohio constitution of 1802 that established the first of the three interpretations of the term "involuntary servitude." Section 2 of that constitution's Bill of Rights provided that

[8] Over time, several territories were carved out of the old Northwest Territory as other parts of the original territory were admitted to the union as new states.

[9] Strictly speaking, the 1800 division did not separate Ohio from the rest of the Northwest Territory, but rather separated the Northwest Territory (Ohio) from the rest. The balance of the original Northwest Territory was renamed the Indiana Territory and consisted of the present states of Indiana, Illinois, Wisconsin, and part of Michigan. On this first division, therefore, the Northwest Territory properly so-called was reduced in extent to encompass what would become the state of Ohio in 1803, and part of what would later become the state of Michigan. See Robert M. Taylor, Jr., ed., *The Northwest Ordinance, 1787: A Bicentennial Handbook* (Indianapolis, Ind., 1987), maps 8–9.

[10] Quoted in John Codman Hurd, *The Law of Freedom and Bondage in the United States* (Boston, 1862; New York, repr. 1968), II:116, n. 2.

There shall be neither slavery nor involuntary servitude in this State otherwise than for the punishment of crimes, whereof the party shall have been duly convicted, nor shall any male person arrived at the age of twenty-one years, or female person arrived at the age of eighteen years, be held to serve any person as a servant under the pretence of indenture or otherwise, *unless such person shall enter into such indenture while in a state of perfect freedom, and on condition of a bona fide consideration, received or to be received. . . . Nor shall any indenture of any negro or mulatto hereafter made and executed out of the State, or if made in the State, where the term of service exceeds one year, be of the least validity, except those given in the case of apprenticeship.*[11] (emphasis added)

This provision of Ohio's constitution focused in general on the moment of *entry into* a contractual relationship. If entry into a binding labor agreement was "voluntary" and for good consideration, that was enough to take it out of the category of "involuntary servitude." Lack of a power to withdraw from the relationship during the contractual term did not apparently change "voluntary service" into "involuntary servitude" under the Ohio constitution. In the case of black people, however, a further requirement was added, that the contract be only of a relatively short duration, no longer than a year. The implication here, of course, must be that even a voluntary agreement could become slavery or involuntary servitude if the relationship went on for too long. If the relationship endured for only a relatively short period, less than a year, then the absence of the power to withdraw – that is, the availability of penal sanctions to enforce the agreement – did not transform the relationship into slavery. In this tradition, therefore, the length of the term of service, rather than the kinds of contractual remedies available for breach, was the crucial factor in determining whether a *voluntary* agreement had been transformed into involuntary servitude or slavery.[12]

This jurisprudential tradition, which focused on the need to limit the length of terms of service in labor agreements to preserve the personal liberty of workers, persisted through the nineteenth century and into the

---

[11] Ibid.

[12] Of course, this provision could also be interpreted to mean that it was only the combination of a lack of power to withdraw together with a lengthy term of service that turned a voluntary agreement into involuntary servitude. In this view, neither duration of service nor harsh contract remedy alone could turn voluntary contracts into involuntary servitude. They could do so only when they occurred together. The Ohio Constitution did not seem to reflect a similar concern in the case of the contracts of white adults, for whom no constitutional limit was placed on the length of voluntary contracts for service. This silence likely reflected the absence of a problem arising from adult whites indenting themselves for long terms of service, a problem that was quite real in the case of black people brought into the territory.

twentieth. In 1872, California added a provision to its Civil Code declaring that, "A contract to render personal service, other than a contract of apprenticeship . . . cannot be enforced against the employee beyond the term of two years from the commencement of service under it."[13] This provision was enacted at a time when negative injunctions were not available under California law even to enforce contracts for unique or exceptional services.[14] The focus of the concern for employees was the length of service in and of itself even where the remedy for breach was only damages. In 1919, undoubtedly under pressure from the increasingly powerful motion picture industry, California made negative injunctions available in the case of contracts for unique or exceptional services, and in 1930, undoubtedly under pressure from the same source, extended the maximum length of service to seven years. When Warner Bros. sought to extend Olivia De Haviland's service beyond seven years by interpreting the statute in a particular way, the California Appeals Court rejected their argument. At the same time the court held that the statute, which did in fact restrict freedom of contract, was properly enacted as an exercise of legislative authority to promote the public welfare and as a proper exercise of the police power:

> It is safe to say that the great majority of men and women who work are engaged in rendering personal services under employment contracts. Without their labors the activities of the entire country would stagnate. Their welfare is the direct concern of every community. Seven years of time is fixed as the maximum time for which they may contract for their services without the right to change employers or occupations. Thereafter they may make a change if they deem it necessary or advisable. There are innumerable reasons why a change of employment may be to their advantage. . . . As one grows more experienced and skillful there should be a reasonable opportunity to move upward and to employ his abilities to the best advantage and for highest obtainable compensation. . . . The power to restrict the right of private contract is one which does not exist independently of the power to legislate for the purpose of preserving the public comfort, health, safety, morals and welfare. The power to provide for the comfort, health, safety and general welfare of any or all employees is granted to the Legislature by article XX, section 17½ of the state Constitution. . . . Under the same principles, a law of Louisiana limiting the term of personal service contracts was upheld as a proper exercise of the police power and an expression of state policy.[15]

[13] As quoted in *De Haviland v. Warner Bros. Pictures*, 67 C.A. 2d 225 (1944), 229.

[14] Ibid., 233.

[15] Ibid., 235–36.

This first tradition played a relatively minor role in the conflicts over the interpretation of the term "involuntary servitude" that were to be played out over the nineteenth century and into the early twentieth. The other two constitutional traditions that were produced in states carved out of the old Northwest Territory proved to be much more important.

When Ohio was separated from the Northwest Territory in 1800, the rest of the territory became the Indiana Territory. In 1805, the Michigan Territory was separated from the Indiana Territory, and the Indiana Territory came to consist of the present states of Indiana, Illinois, and Wisconsin.[16] In 1807, the Indiana territorial legislature, dominated at that moment by the pro-slavery faction in the territory, enacted legislation making it relatively easy for slave owners to bring slaves into the territory by having them sign indentures obligating them to serve their masters for twenty or forty years or longer. The act provided that any person owning a slave who was over fifteen years old could bring that slave into the territory and within thirty days

> go with the same before the clerk of the court of common pleas of the proper county, and in the presence of said clerk, the said owner or possessor shall determine and agree to and with his or her negro or mulatto, upon the term of years, which the said negro or mulatto will and shall serve his or her said owner or possessor, and the clerk is hereby . . . required to make a record thereof. . . . If any negro or mulatto removed into this Territory . . . shall refuse to serve his or her owner as aforesaid, it shall and may be lawful for such person, within sixty days thereafter to remove the said negro or mulatto to any place, which by the law of the United States, or territory, from whence such owner or possessor may or shall be authorized to remove the same.[17]

In 1809, the Indiana Territory was divided. The new Indiana Territory consisted of an area that would become the present state of Indiana. The rest of the territory was renamed the Illinois Territory and consisted of the present states of Illinois and Wisconsin.[18] The Indiana territorial legislation of 1807 continued to apply in the Illinois Territory after it was separated from Indiana in 1809.[19] In addition, although the first Illinois state constitution, adopted in 1818, changed the law regarding indentures, adopting verbatim the Ohio provision already discussed, it also grand-

[16] See Taylor, *Northwest Ordinance, 1787,* map 10.

[17] Francis Philbrick, ed., *The Laws of Indiana Territory, 1801–1809* (Springfield, Ill., 1930), 523–24.

[18] See Taylor, *Northwest Ordinance, 1787,* map 11.

[19] Hurd, *Law of Freedom and Bondage in the United States,* II:132.

fathered indentures entered into before the adoption of the constitution under the earlier 1807 territorial legislation.[20]

In 1828, a case brought by a black woman against her master for assault, battery, wounding, and false imprisonment came before the Illinois Supreme Court.[21] The defendant answered the action by saying that he was legitimately holding the woman pursuant to an indenture she had signed in 1814 under the territorial legislation of 1807. The indenture committed her to serve him for a term of forty years, and he was merely enforcing its terms.[22] In deciding whether the territorial legislation of 1807, under which the indenture had been signed, complied with the prohibitions on slavery and involuntary servitude contained in the Northwest Ordinance, the Illinois high court produced one of the two interpretations of "involuntary servitude" that would dominate constitutional jurisprudence on the question for the next three-quarters of a century.

The Illinois high court framed its analysis in terms of whether a laboring agreement had been *entered into* "voluntarily." If it had, then legal enforcement of the resulting agreement through specific performance or penal sanctions did not change the labor from voluntary to involuntary. The labor was "voluntary" because the worker had "voluntarily" agreed to perform it. All that was involved was the enforcement of a contract freely entered into.[23] In 1843, this interpretation of the term "involuntary servitude" was confirmed by the Illinois Supreme Court. In a concurrence in *Sarah v. Borders,* Justice Thomas declared that Illinois law on the subject of the indenting of black persons

> simply holds parties, who being free to contract, had voluntarily done so, to a specific performance of their contract. It operates on no other indenture than such as "were entered into without fraud of collusion," and these being good and valid, even under the compact [i.e. the Northwest Ordinance], as not imposing upon the person indentured involuntary servitude, it does not, and was not intended to, confirm indentures originally void [as having been entered into as a result of fraud or coercion].

---

[20] Hurd, *Law of Freedom and Bondage in the United States*, II:132–33. When Illinois became a state in 1818, the Wisconsin portion of the Illinois Territory was separated from Illinois and joined to the Michigan Territory, which then came to encompass the present states of Michigan and Wisconsin. See Taylor, *Northwest Ordinance, 1787,* map 13.

[21] *Phoebe, a Woman of Color, v. Jay*, 1 Ill. (Breese) 268 (1828). "The number of negroes held in Illinois under the indenture system gradually decreased. In 1830 there were only seven hundred and forty-six. This was due to deaths, removals from the State, expiration of indenture contracts." N. Dwight Harris, *The History of Negro Servitude in Illinois and of the Slavery Agitation in That State, 1719 1864* (1904; New York, repr. 1969), 52.

[22] *Phoebe, a Woman of Color, v. Jay*, 1 Ill. (Breese) 268 (1828).

[23] Ibid.

[In seeking to invalidate an indenture, a plaintiff] may . . . allege fraud, misrepresentation, or *coercion* in procuring the execution of such indenture or contract, and under the Constitution, as he would have been under the compact, the plaintiff will, on sustaining such allegation, by proof, be entitled to a discharge from further servitude.[24] (emphasis added)

Given the long history of indentured servitude in America and the common practice of using penal sanctions to enforce labor contracts in Europe, the Illinois court's view of "involuntary servitude" was probably quite widely shared at the time. The Illinois rule did leave unresolved the question of how harsh the terms of a "voluntary" labor agreement would have to be before the agreement would be considered a contract of slavery and impliedly prohibited by the absolute prohibition on slavery contained in the Ordinance. Under the Illinois rule, any state of servitude short of outright slavery could apparently be entered into in conformity with the Ordinance as long as it was done "voluntarily."

Under the Illinois rule the court did have to face the question of precisely what circumstances rendered a decision to sign an indenture "voluntary" or "involuntary" in the first place. In *Phoebe v. Jay*,[25] the Illinois Supreme Court held that the territorial legislation of 1807 violated the Ordinance's prohibition on "involuntary servitude," but only because it sanctioned the enforcement of agreements that had been *involuntarily entered into*. The court entertained no doubt that the 1807 territorial legislation confronted black people with a difficult choice (sign the indenture or be returned to slavery in another state) that necessarily made their decision to sign an indenture a "coerced" decision that gave rise to "involuntary servitude." "I conceive that it would be an insult to common sense," Justice Lockwood wrote for the court, "to contend that the negro, under the circumstances in which [s]he was placed, had any free agency. The only choice given [her] was a choice of evils."[26] What other difficult choices might "coerce" a person into entering a labor relation "involuntarily" remained to be explored.

Even though in Illinois the specific enforcement of a forty-year labor agreement did not render the labor involuntary as long as the agreement had been entered into voluntarily, a very different interpretation of "involuntary servitude" was developed by the Indiana Supreme Court.

---

[24] *Sarah, a Woman of Color, v. Borders*, 4 Scam. 341 (Ill., 1843), 347 (concurrence of Justice Thomas).

[25] 1 Ill. (Breese) 268 (1828).

[26] Ibid., 270. The Illinois high court did not void the indenture in this case on that ground, however. It found that the provision of the Illinois constitution grandfathering indentures entered into under the territorial legislation had operated as a modification of the Northwest Ordinance because Congress had voted to admit Illinois into the union under a constitution containing this provision.

Shortly after Indiana was separated from Illinois in 1809, the anti-slavery faction in Indiana gained the upper hand and repealed the territorial legislation of 1807 authorizing the indenting of slaves within thirty days after they were brought into the Indiana Territory.[27] In June 1816, Indiana adopted a constitution and in December of the same year was admitted to the union. The Indiana constitution prohibited slavery and involuntary servitude and declared that no "indenture of any negro or mulatto hereafter made and executed out of the bounds of this State [was] of any validity within this State." Since the territorial legislation authorizing the indenting of black people within the state had been repealed in 1810, and the constitution invalidated all indentures entered into outside the state, any decisions about an indenture entered into after the adoption of the constitution would have to be made on the basis of common law.

In October 1816, just months after the Indiana constitution was adopted, Mary Clark, "a woman of color," "voluntarily" signed an indenture with her master obligating her to serve him for a period of twenty years.[28] Several years later she sought to be released from her obligations. She sued out a writ of habeas corpus, claiming that she was being detained illegally by her master.[29] Her master defended by arguing that she was being properly held under the indenture she had "voluntarily" signed. A lower court rejected her suit, but on appeal to the Indiana Supreme Court she was released from her service.[30] The court, in a far-reaching opinion issued in 1821, established the second main constitutional interpretation of the term "involuntary servitude." The court declared that

> [w]hile the [woman] remained in the service of the obligee without complaint, the law presumes that her service was voluntarily performed; but her application to the Circuit Court to be discharged from the custody of her master, establishes the fact that she is willing

[27] There were actually two separate 1807 territorial acts governing the indentures of black people. One, Chapter XLVIII, authorized the enforcement of indentures against black people who had been brought into the territory already under a contract to serve another. The second authorized the indenting of slaves brought into the territory within thirty days after their arrival (Chapter LXIV). This latter legislation was the subject of the dispute in *Phoebe v. Jay*. In 1810 Indiana repealed the second piece of legislation absolutely but the first piece of legislation only prospectively, so that those who had signed indentures out of state before repeal could still be held to their indentures in state. What the constitution of 1816 did was to declare invalid any indentures entered into out of state, the indenturing legislation covering in-state indentures having been absolutely repealed by the 1810 act. See Philbrick, *Laws of Indiana Territory,* 463 and 523–24; and Hurd, *Law of Freedom and Bondage in the United States,* II:126–27.

[28] *The Case of Mary Clark, a Woman of Color,* 1 Blackf. 122 (Ind. 1821), 122–23.

[29] Ibid., 122.

[30] Ibid., 126.

to serve no longer; and, while this state of the will appears, the law can not, by any possibility of intendment, presume that her service is voluntary. . . . The fact then is, that the appellant is in a state of involuntary servitude; and we are bound by the Constitution, the supreme law of the land, to discharge her therefrom.[31]

Her master, therefore, was not entitled to hold her against her will even though she had "voluntarily" obligated herself to stay with him for twenty years.[32] Neither was he entitled to ask the state to specifically enforce the agreement against her. "Many covenants," the court said,

> the breaches of which are only remunerated in damages, might be specifically performed, either by a third person at a distance from the adversary, or in a short space of time. But a covenant for service, if performed at all, must be personally performed under the eye of the master; and might, as in the case before us, require a number of years. Such a performance, if enforced by law, would produce a state of servitude as degrading and demoralizing in its consequences, as a state of absolute slavery; and if enforced under a government like ours, which acknowledges a personal equality, it would be productive of a state of feeling more discordant and irritating than slavery itself.[33]

Under the Indiana interpretation, labor became "involuntary servitude" the moment a person wanted to leave the relationship but was prevented from doing so either by the physical restraint of his or her employer or by a judicial decree of specific performance. Here, the legal right to withdraw from the labor relationship at any time the laborer wished marked the boundary between "free labor," and "involuntary servitude." The use of the legal remedies of specific performance (and by implication, penal sanctions) to enforce even a "voluntary" labor agreement turned the labor into "involuntary servitude." The issue implicitly left unresolved by the Indiana interpretation was whether a labor contract could be enforced through *any* legal remedy at all consistent with the prohibition of "involuntary servitude."[34] The rule brought to the surface a fundamental problem with liberal commitments to freedom, which contained a basic,

---

31 Ibid., 125–26.

32 Ibid., 125.

33 Ibid., 124–25.

34 Just a few years after issuing the opinion in *Mary Clark's Case,* Justice Holman of the Indiana high court ruled that a farm worker *was* subject to wage "forfeiture" under the entirety doctrine. This represented an implicit decision that to force a worker to choose between loss of several months of back wages and performance of his contract would not create a condition of "involuntary servitude." See *Cranmer v. Graham,* 1 Blackf. (Indiana) 406 (1825).

unresolvable contradiction between a commitment to liberty of person and a commitment to liberty of contract. Liberty of person under the Indiana interpretation required that one's contractual liberty be restricted, insofar as one could no longer freely alienate one's labor irrevocably by contract.[35]

These opposing interpretive traditions, generated in the 1820s by the conflict over slavery in the Northwest Territory, persisted in American constitutional law throughout the nineteenth century. Surprisingly, a definitive choice between the two was not made by the United States Supreme Court until the twentieth century. This is not to say that both views enjoyed equal popularity in the wider culture. It is fair to say that throughout the North by the late 1830s, labor practices and ideas conformed, in the main, to the view set forth by the Indiana court. However, only a few court opinions inscribed this view in constitutional law. One was rendered by the Massachusetts Supreme Judicial Court in 1856.

Tyler Parsons brought an action against Abby Trask and Others for enticing away his servant, Elizabeth Lycka. In 1840 Lycka had signed an indenture with Parsons promising to serve him for a period of five years, and she then accompanied him from Sweden to take up her duties with his family in Massachusetts. Two years later she left to go to work for Trask, and Parsons sued Trask for enticement. Enticement was a recognized action at Massachusetts common law at the time,[36] but the Massachusetts Supreme Judicial Court was completely unsympathetic to the plaintiff's claim under a contract like this one, whose aim was to establish a kind of indentured servitude. "It is, in substance and effect, a contract of servitude," the court said, "with no limitation but that of time":[37]

> Such a contract, it is scarcely necessary to say, is against the policy of our institutions and laws. If such a sale of service could be lawfully made for five years, it might, from the same reasons, for ten, and so for the term of one's life. The door would thus be opened for a species of servitude, inconsistent with the first and fundamental article of our Declaration of Rights, which, *proprio vigore*, not only abolished every vestige of slavery then existing in the Commonwealth, but rendered every form of it thereafter legally impossible.[38]

Although the Indiana/Massachusetts view that specific or penal enforcement of voluntary labor agreements amounted to "involuntary servi-

---

[35] On this contradiction, see Guyora Binder, "Substantive Liberty and the Legacy of the Fuller Court" (Unpublished manuscript, 1980), § VI. (30.); and Frank H. Knight, *Freedom & Reform: Essays in Economics and Social Philosophy* (1947; repr.: Indianapolis, In., 1982), 78–79.

[36] *Boston Glass Manufactory v. Binney*, 21 Mass. (4 Pick.) 425 (1827).

[37] *Parsons v. Trask*, 73 Mass. (7 Gray) 473 (1856), 478.

[38] Ibid.

tude" or "slavery" was a view that dominated the law and practice of labor relations in the northern states before the Civil War, the Illinois tradition continued to have its proponents as well.

In 1850, at the invitation of President Zachary Taylor, New Mexico
adopted a constitution by an overwhelming majority of its voting inhabitants.[39] The constitution prohibited slavery and involuntary servitude,
but its definition of involuntary servitude was the Illinois one:

> [N]o male person shall be held by law to serve any person as a ser-
> vant, slave or apprentice, after he arrives at the age of twenty-one
> years; nor female in like manner, after she arrives at the age of eigh-
> teen years; *unless they be bound by their own consent after they arrive at such
> age,* or are bound by law for punishment of crime.[40] (emphasis
> added)

At the time the constitution was adopted, New Mexico had not been
formally established as a territory by Congress but was still being ruled
by a military governor, and the constitution never went into effect. However, it did reflect the sentiments of the voting inhabitants of New Mexico,
and once a territorial government had been established, the territorial legislature seems to have followed the basic principles laid down in the earlier constitution. In 1852, the territorial legislature passed a statute declaring that

> All contracts, voluntarily entered into between masters and servants,
> agreeing and designating the kind of service, the salary, and the time
> such service shall continue, whether any money shall have been
> given or received in advance or not, both parties shall be compelled
> to comply with the contract without power to rescind it [except on
> three narrow grounds].[41]

In commenting on this legislation, in a case in which the return of a peon
was being sought, the New Mexico Supreme Court observed that

> By this [legislation a servant] must abide by and fulfill his agreement
> according to its terms, whether he owes or does not owe, pays or
> does not pay. Unless he can get his master's consent to rescind or
> prove some one of the causes specified to procure a cancellation, he
> may be prosecuted for a failure and so may the master, and the ser-

---

[39] Jack Rittenhouse, ed., *Constitution of the State of New Mexico, 1850* (Houston, Tex., 1965),
viii; and Richard Hofstadter, William Miller, and Daniel Aaron, *The American Republic to
1865* (Englewood Cliffs, N.J., 1959), 495.

[40] Rittenhouse, *Constitution of the State of New Mexico, 1850*, 14 (Declaration of Rights, Article
I, Sec. 1).

[41] Quoted in *Jaremillo v. Romero*, 1 N.M. 190 (1857), 204.

vant compelled to a compliance by a fine and imprisonment. . . . It appears clear that the legislators were determined that by no means should either of the parties escape the consequences of their own voluntary engagements.[42]

In England in 1857, at the same time that the New Mexico high court delivered this opinion, such a characterization of penal sanctions for breaches of labor agreements would have been largely uncontroversial. But in the northern United States, where the Illinois/New Mexico view of "involuntary servitude" represented a distinctly subordinate tradition, in large measure because penal sanctions had come to be so inextricably associated with attempts to circumvent prohibitions on slavery, this position could give rise to a firestorm.

In 1860, the U.S. House of Representatives attempted to nullify all New Mexican territorial statutes that provided for the penal enforcement of labor agreements on the ground that they "establish[ed], protect[ed], or legalize[d], involuntary servitude, or slavery,"[43] but the legislation failed to pass the Senate. In the course of the debate over the bill, Southerners argued that the New Mexican legislation was no more objectionable than the English law of master and servant, to which it was compared.[44] When Congress passed an act to encourage immigration, the northern view of contractual servitude was inscribed in that legislation, leaving employers without a criminal remedy to enforce the contracts of imported workers.[45]

One might think that the Civil War would have laid the interpretive question definitively to rest, but even that cataclysm failed permanently to resolve the question. Following the war, Congress did make efforts to write the Indiana/Massachusetts view of "involuntary servitude" into the Constitution of the United States. The Thirteenth Amendment, adopted in 1865, prohibited slavery and "involuntary servitude" except as punishment for a crime. In 1867, pursuant to its power to enforce the Amendment, Congress passed the Anti-peonage Statute. By its terms the statute voided all laws that enforced "the *voluntary* or involuntary service or labor of any persons *as peons*, in liquidation of any debt or obligation, *or otherwise*" (emphasis added).[46] The statute seemingly did extend the Thirteenth Amendment prohibition on "involuntary servitude" to "voluntary" labor relationships.

---

[42] Ibid., 205.

[43] Hurd, *Law of Freedom and Bondage in the United States*, II:211 n. 1.

[44] House, *Slavery in the Territory of New Mexico*, 36th Cong., 1st sess., 10 May 1860, H. Rept. 508, Serial 1069, 32–33 (from the minority report dissenting from the Judiciary Committee's favorable report of the bill).

[45] See Chapter 1.

[46] 14 *United States Statutes* 546, sec. 1.

However, even though by its terms the prohibition applied throughout the United States and its territories, it was restricted to "peonage," an institution that might be thought to occur only in former Spanish colonies. In any case, the act did not seem to include the full range of master and servant relationships. Moreover, in the very effort to make clear that it was extending the coverage of the Thirteenth Amendment to "voluntary" labor relationships, the statute undermined itself by using language that preserved the idea that there could be such a thing as "voluntary servitude." It did not make clear that all servitude, whether voluntarily undertaken or not, was "involuntary servitude." In the event, the Thirteenth Amendment simply prohibited "involuntary servitude," and as an effort to include the penal enforcement of voluntary labor contracts in that term, the Anti-peonage Act was flawed and ambiguous. As a result, it did not in fact resolve the jurisprudential conflict over the interpretation of the term "involuntary servitude." The Illinois/New Mexico interpretive tradition did not disappear after the Civil War. Although it remained subordinate to the Indiana/Massachusetts view, it continued to inspire court decisions upholding the constitutionality of legislation establishing penal sanctions to enforce "voluntary" labor agreements.

The lack of a definitive constitutional resolution of the interpretive question may help to explain why the U.S. Army, and in certain cases agents of the Freedmen's Bureau, could believe that they were introducing a "free labor" system into the South after the Civil War despite the fact that in numerous cases they provided for the criminal enforcement of the labor contracts of former slaves who came under their jurisdiction.[47]

Following the Civil War, a number of the southern states enacted Black Codes, which also contained provisions, among others, for the criminal punishment of labor contract breaches. Coming from southerners, rather than from northern occupation forces, these efforts were greeted in the North as nothing less than attempts to reestablish slavery, and most of the codes were repealed or withdrawn, although some of the early laws survived.[48] With one eye on possible northern reaction, in the 1880s Southerners began again to fashion a new set of laws calling for criminal punishment, in most cases not directly for breach of labor contracts but rather for acceptance of advances followed by failure to work out one's time.

---

[47] Eric Foner, *Reconstruction: America's Unfinished Revolution, 1863–1877* (New York, 1988), 55, 166–67. Later Reconstruction governments, however, which embraced the more common northern conception of free labor, resisted the pressure of planters who wanted legislation enacted to enforce the performance of labor contracts (372–73).

[48] William Cohen, *At Freedom's Edge: Black Mobility and the Southern White Quest for Racial Control, 1861–1915* (Baton Rouge, La., 1991), 28–37; see also Foner, *Reconstruction*, 199–200. When they attempted to justify these laws in the face of northern reaction, some Southerners pointed out that they "had been modeled on army and Freedmen's Bureau labor regulations." Foner, *Reconstruction*, 208.

These so-called false pretense statutes proliferated in the 1880s and 1890s, and they were not the only penal contract enforcement legislation that Southerners enacted in these years. Other legislation made it a crime for one to fail to inform a new employer that he or she had abandoned a contract with the previous employer. Another made it a crime for an employer to hire any worker who was already under contract to another employer but had left the original employer before fulfilling the contract term.[49] The constitutionality of this legislation would be tested during the early twentieth century, and I discuss these decisions later in this chapter.[50] At this juncture, it is merely important to understand that the Illinois view of "involuntary servitude" continued to have surprising vitality in late nineteenth-century law.

In 1889, the South Carolina Supreme Court ruled that a state law that imposed criminal sanctions for labor contract breaches did not violate the constitution's prohibition on "involuntary servitude":

> If the general assembly sees proper to make the violation of a particular species of civil contracts a criminal offence, we are unable to discover in the provisions of the constitution anything which forbids such legislation. No person is required to enter into such a contract unless he chooses to do so; and if he does so, he must take the consequences affixed by the law to the violation of a contract into which he has voluntarily entered. . . . We are unable to discover any feature of "involuntary servitude" in the matter. Everyone who undertakes to serve another in any capacity parts for a time with that absolute liberty which it is claimed that the constitution secures to all; but as he does this voluntarily, it cannot be properly said that he is deprived of any of his constitutional rights; and if he violates his undertaking he thereby of his own accord subjects himself to such punishment as the law making power may have seen fit to impose for such violation.[51]

It is tempting, of course, to dismiss this decision as southern rationalization, but there were other judicial decisions dating from the same period

[49] To be liable to criminal punishment under these statutes, the second employer had to have had notice of the first contract.

[50] I do not mean to offer a comprehensive legal description of the system of southern peonage during the late nineteenth and early twentieth centuries. That has been done ably elsewhere. See, for example, Cohen, *At Freedom's Edge;* Daniel Novak, *The Wheel of Servitude: Black Forced Labor after Slavery* (Lexington, Ken., 1978); Benno Schmidt, "The Peonage Cases," *Columbia Law Review* 82 (1982). What I mean to do here is to point out that the constitutional status of various penal devices to enforce voluntary labor contracts had not been definitively resolved even as late as 1900.

[51] *State v. Williams,* 32 S.C. 123 (1889), 126.

rendered outside the South that suggest that this view of penal sanctions was more widespread at the time than we might have suspected.

In 1898 the United States annexed Hawaii, which became a territory in 1900. Even while the islands remained an independent kingdom during most of the nineteenth century, Americans exercised enormous influence over the development of Hawaiian institutions.[52] It was Americans, primarily, who developed the commercial agriculture of the islands, the sugar cane and pineapple plantations, and devised the labor practices and laws that sustained this agriculture. Much of the labor for these industries was supplied by contract laborers, originally native Hawaiians but later imported from a variety of countries around the globe.

The first Master and Servant acts enforcing these labor contracts were apparently adapted from American laws governing merchant seamen, which made the breach of shipping articles a criminal offence.[53] As the whaling industry became less important and commercial agriculture more important, the seamen's law was adapted to agricultural work. Acts were passed that provided for the penal enforcement of labor contracts. In the meantime, under the influence of American ideas of good government, the kingdom of Hawaii began to adopt written constitutions.[54] Article XI of the 1864 and 1887 constitutions declared that "involuntary servitude, except for crime, is forever prohibited in this Kingdom. Whenever a slave shall enter Hawaiian territory, he shall be free."[55]

The adoption of these constitutional provisions should come as no surprise given that transplanted New Englanders were an important component of the non-native governing elite in the kingdom. Many of the Hawaiian Supreme Court justices appointed during the second half of the century had been trained at northern U.S. law schools.

In 1891, a Japanese contract laborer challenged the penal enforcement of his labor contract under the existing master and servant law, arguing that it violated the Hawaiian constitution's prohibition of "involuntary servitude."[56] The opinion of the court upholding the legislation was written by Chief Justice Albert Francis Judd. Judd had been born in Honolulu but was educated at Yale College and Harvard Law School, from which he received a law degree in 1864. He had become Chief Justice in 1881.[57] Judd wrote for the court,

---

[52] Ralph S. Kuykendall and A. Grove Day, *Hawaii, a History: From Polynesian Kingdom to American Commonwealth* (New York, 1948), 193.

[53] Katharine Coman, *The History of Contract Labor in the Hawaiian Islands* (New York, 1903), 9.

[54] Ralph S. Kuykendall, *Constitutions of the Hawaiian Kingdom: A Brief History and Analysis* (Honolulu, 1940), 7–8.

[55] Quoted in *Hilo Sugar Co. v. Mioshi,* 8 Haw. 201 (1891), 203.

[56] Ibid.

[57] A. Grove Day, *A Biographical Dictionary: History Makers of Hawaii* (Honolulu, 1984) (entry under Albert Francis Judd).

A fair and honest contract to work for another willingly and freely made with a knowledge of the circumstances, cannot be said to have created a condition of involuntary servitude. The contract which creates the state or condition of service, if it is voluntary when made and the conditions and circumstances unchanged, except that the mind of the one who serves is now unwilling to fulfill it, is not by that fact changed into a contract of involuntary servitude forbidden by law. If the contract is lawful and constitutional in its inception, it does not become illegal or unconstitutional at the option of one of the parties to it. . . . Our labor contract system is not slavery.[58]

Perhaps this decision should not really be surprising. It was, after all, delivered by a white male upholding labor laws that were primarily enforced against people of color[59] on the agricultural periphery of the American empire, laws, moreover, as he himself put it, "upon [which] our agricultural enterprises rest in great measure."[60]

Should the opinions of the South Carolina and Hawaiian courts be dismissed in this way? Or did they in fact reflect a more widely held understanding of "involuntary servitude" that only disappeared later, and partly as the result of twentieth-century Supreme Court decisions rejecting it? In 1891, when Judd delivered his opinion, the United States Supreme Court had still not faced the question of whether penal sanctions to enforce labor agreements turned a voluntary arrangement into the "involuntary servitude" prohibited by the Thirteenth Amendment. When it did for the first time, in 1897, a majority of the court adopted not the Indiana/Massachusetts interpretation of the term "involuntary servitude," but the Illinois/New Mexico/South Carolina/Hawaii interpretation. The Indiana/Massachusetts view would ultimately triumph in the twentieth century, but at that time it found support only in Justice Harlan's dissent.

Robertson v. Baldwin arose when several merchant seamen were arrested for deserting their ship in Oregon before it had completed its voyage, in breach of the contract they had signed to perform the duties of seamen during the entire voyage. The men were held until the ship was ready to sail, and then they were placed on board against their will. They refused to perform their duties, and when the ship returned to San Francisco, they were charged with refusing to work in violation of a federal statute gov-

---

[58] *Hilo Sugar Co. v. Mioshi,* 8 Haw. 201 (1891), 205.

[59] Hawaiian contract laborers did include some workers imported from Portugal, Germany, and Scandinavia. Coman, *History of Contract Labor in the Hawaiian Islands,* 27–33.

[60] *Hilo Sugar Co. v. Mioshi,* 8 Haw. 201 (1891), 204.

erning merchant seamen.[61] They sued out a writ of *habeas corpus* asking that they be freed from their confinement, arguing that the federal statute under which they were being held violated the "involuntary servitude" provision of the Thirteenth Amendment.

The court upheld the validity of the statute on two grounds. The first, broader ground is the more interesting one. The validity of this statute, Justice Brown wrote for the court,

> depends upon the construction to be given to the term "involuntary servitude." *Does the epithet "involuntary" attach to the word "servitude" continuously, and make illegal any service which becomes involuntary at any time during its existence; or does it attach only at the inception of the servitude, and characterize it as unlawful because unlawfully entered into?* If the former be the true construction, then, no one, not even a soldier, sailor or apprentice, can surrender his liberty, even for a day; and the soldier may desert his regiment upon the eve of battle, or the sailor abandon his ship at any intermediate port or landing, or even in a storm at sea. . . . *If the latter, then an individual may, for a valuable consideration, contract for the surrender of his personal liberty for a definite time and for a recognized purpose, and subordinate his going and coming to the will of another during the continuance of the contract;* – not that all such contracts would be lawful, but that *a servitude which was knowingly and willingly entered into could not be termed involuntary. Thus, if one should agree, for a yearly wage, to serve another in a particular capacity during his life, and never to leave his estate without his consent, the contract might not be enforceable for the want of a legal remedy, or might be void upon grounds of public policy, but the servitude could not be properly termed involuntary. Such agreements for a limited personal servitude at one time were very common in England [citing the 1823 English master and servant act]. . . . The breach of a contract for personal service has not, however, been recognized in this country as involving a liability to criminal punishment, except in the case of soldiers, sailors and possibly some others, nor would public opinion tolerate a statute to that effect.*[62] (emphasis added)

---

[61] Richard Morris has estimated that between 1861 and 1893 a total of 708 American and foreign merchant seamen were committed to the Baltimore jail for violating their shipping articles by deserting their ships. The commitment of merchant seamen to the Baltimore jail for contract breach before the Civil War was also common. Richard Morris, "Labor Controls in Maryland in the Nineteenth Century," *The Journal of Southern History* XIV (August 1948): 393–95. Between 20 and 50 percent of the arrested seamen in Baltimore were African Americans, but in Oregon and California, where the *Robertson* case arose, the Sailor's Union of the Pacific had no black members. At the time the case arose in 1895 it came as a shock to the seamen because the arrest of coastal sailors for breach of their agreements in the Pacific northwest "had not happened within the memory of any of the coasting sailors." Hyman Weintraub, *Andrew Furuseth: Emancipator of the Seamen* (Berkeley, Calif., 1959), 113, 35.

[62] *Robertson v. Baldwin*, 165 U. S. 275 (1897), 280–81.

The majority correctly saw that criminal punishment for labor contract breaches was not nearly as anomalous as many people in the United States thought. It cited recent English law as a way of vindicating its choice of freedom of contract over freedom of person, its resolution of that unresolvable dilemma within liberalism. The court also placed its decision on a second ground. "[T]he [Thirteenth] amendment," Justice Brown wrote, "was not intended to introduce any novel doctrine with respect to certain descriptions of service which have always been treated as exceptional," merchant mariners constituting one of these exceptions.[63] In a blistering dissent, Justice Harlan offered this reply to the court's opinion:

> The condition of one who contracts to render personal services in connection with the private business of another becomes a condition of involuntary servitude *from the moment he is compelled against his will* to continue in such service. He may be liable in damages for the nonperformance of his agreement, but to require him, against his will, to continue in the personal service of his master is to place him and keep him in a condition of involuntary servitude.[64] (emphasis original)

Harlan raised the specter that

> If congress under its power to regulate commerce with foreign nations and among the several states, can authorize the arrest of seamen who engaged to serve upon a private vessel, and compel him by force to return to the vessel and remain during the term for which he engaged, a similar rule may be prescribed as to employés upon railroads and steamboats engaged in commerce among the states. . . . Again, as the legislatures of the States have all legislative power not prohibited to them . . . why may not the States, under the principles this day announced, compel all employés of railroads engaged in domestic commerce, and all domestic servants, and all employés in private establishments, within their respective limits, to remain with their employers during the terms for which they were severally engaged, under penalty of being arrested by some sheriff or constable, and forcibly returned to the service of their employers?[65]

---

[63] Ibid., 282.

[64] Ibid., 301.

[65] Ibid., 302–03. Even Harlan, however, was ambiguous about whether penal sanctions for contract breach would, in and of themselves, violate the amendment: "Even if it were conceded – a concession to be made only for argument's sake – that it could be made a criminal offence, punishable by fine or imprisonment or both, for such employés to quit their employment before the expiration of the term for which they agreed to serve, it would not follow that they could be compelled, against their will and in advance of trial and conviction, to continue in such service" (302). After being arrested and held in jail

For more than a decade Southerners had passed legislation to penally enforce labor contracts, but rarely had this legislation punished contract breaches directly. More often, subtle subterfuges were used. False pretense statutes, for example, punished a worker who accepted advances and then failed to fulfill his or her contract. The gist of the legislation ostensibly was to punish fraud rather than to criminalize breaches of labor contracts. These laws had apparently been written this way primarily to circumvent state constitutional restrictions on imprisonment for debt.[66] However, they also may have been written this way to avoid further northern meddling. Under the logic of *Robertson v. Baldwin*, such subtlety would be unnecessary, at least with respect to any prohibition contained in the Thirteenth Amendment to the Constitution of the United States. Southerners, where they were not otherwise constrained by their own

in Oregon for sixteen days, when the ship was ready to leave, Robertson and his shipmates were "placed on board . . . *against their will;* [and on ship] they refused to 'turn out' in obedience to the orders of the master" and were arrested again when the ship reached San Francisco. It seems to have been the fact that they were placed on board "against their will" that clinched the case for Harlan. It appears that it was arrest followed by "compulsion" to return to service that he objected to, apparently failing to see that compulsion in the form of a coerced consent could be elicited on the basis of the threat or actuality of imprisonment without additional force being necessary. (I can send you to jail, or keep you in jail, unless you *agree* to go back to work.)

[66] See, for example, *Lamar v. The State*, 120 Ga. 312 (1904) (constitutionality of Georgia's false pretense statute challenged as violation of state constitution's prohibition of imprisonment for debt. "If the act prescribes a punishment for a simple violation of a contractual obligation, it is beyond the power of the General Assembly. But if its purpose is to punish for fraudulent and deceitful practices, it is valid, even though the fraud or deceit may arise from the failure to comply with a contractual engagment," 313. Statute held valid, 314); and *State v. Williams*, 150 N.C. 802 (1909), involving a statute making it a misdemeanor for a sharecropper to take advances and then willfully abandon his crop but not mentioning fraud held unconstitutional on ground that the state constitution prohibited imprisonment for debt. "In order to convict, the State must show to the full satisfaction of the jury something more than obtaining the advances, a promise to pay for the same, and a breach of the promise. Nothing else being shown, *these facts would constitute only a breach of contract and for this the defendant could not be prosecuted criminally.* The jury must be fully satisfied of an element of fraud in the transaction," 803 (emphasis added). See also *Ex parte Hollman*, 79 S.C. 9 (1908) (South Carolina's agricultural contract labor law struck down. "[W]e cannot avoid the conclusion that the statute in question provides for imprisonment for debt without proof of fraud, and, therefore attempts to deprive the citizen of one of the personal rights guaranteed by the Constitution of the State" (13).) These courts seem to have assumed that damages were the only "natural" consequence of contract breach. Hence, a statute that provided for imprisonment following contract breach must be imprisoning for the debt. This conclusion is not at all self-evident. The English imposed criminal sanctions for contract breach completely independently of civil actions. It was civil actions that gave rise to imprisonment of judgment debtors in England, not criminal prosecutions. Criminal prosecutions often led to imprisonment under the Master and Servant acts, but it was not imprisonment for failure to pay a judgment debt, it was directly for the act of breaching a contract. Imprisonment for debt could be completely independent of criminal punishment for labor contract breaches.

constitutions, might feel free to attack the problem of labor contract enforcement directly. Harlan, a Southerner himself, may well have realized that the majority's opinion could help clear the way for this kind of legislation in the South.

The majority opinion in *Robertson v. Baldwin* makes apparent that the interpretive tradition developed in Illinois during the 1820s still possessed great vitality at the close of the nineteenth century, long after the Civil War. At the time *Robertson v. Baldwin* was decided in 1897, there were, in effect, two systems of contract law governing labor agreements in the United States. The southern one bore similarities to the contract system that had been in effect in Prussia and England[67] not too many years earlier. The northern one, in which neither specific performance nor penal sanctions were available for labor contract enforcement, had a long history, and was supported by its own constitutional tradition that harked back to a decision of the Indiana high court. Under these two constitutional traditions, both systems could make out a plausible claim that they were "free labor" systems based on "free contract."

The truth seems to have been that the majority in *Robertson v. Baldwin* did not believe that its decision applied beyond merchant seamen. This is interesting in and of itself, given that *Robertson v. Baldwin* was brought to the Supreme Court as a test case mounted by the seamen's union.[68] The decision produced a strong reaction among organized seamen. As the *San Francisco Examiner* put it: "According to the highest tribunal which can pass on the matter, the difference between a deep-water sailor and a slave is $15 per month."[69] Union leaders immediately launched a campaign in

---

[67] It is clear that the southern system was much more brutal and more comprehensive than the English or Prussian ones. Southern law not only contained false pretense statutes, statutes to punish criminally enticers of labor, and statutes to punish abandoning a contract to go to work for a second employer without informing the second employer that one had abandoned a previous contract, but also criminal surety statutes, which authorized one person to pay a convicted criminal's fine and then to sign a labor contract with that person to pay off the fine, a contract criminally enforceable by the court, and statutes that authorized the leasing out of convicts. This comprehensive legal system of labor coercion supported by ubiquitous private violence went considerably beyond the systems in effect in nineteenth-century England or Prussia. The point here is only that aspects of the southern system bore a resemblance to English legal practice with respect to wage work earlier in the century. In the *United States v. Reynolds*, 235 U.S. 133 (1914), the U.S. Supreme Court struck down the Alabama criminal surety statute, declaring the criminal surety system to be a violation of the Peonage Act and the Thirteenth Amendment. Convict leasing, however, was never declared unconstitutional, although in a number of southern states the practice was dropped by the third decade of the twentieth century in favor of state-run chain gangs. See Benno Schmidt, "Peonage Cases," 651 n. 20, 676 n. 112.

[68] Weintraub, *Andrew Furuseth*, 35.

[69] Quoted in ibid.

Congress to have the federal statute amended. Under intense pressure from the union, Congress did give the seamen half of what they wanted, amending the statute in 1898, but only eliminating criminal penalties for desertion in American ports, not for desertion in foreign ports.[70] The seamen's union continued to lobby Congress on and off for complete repeal of penal sanctions for more than a decade until, in the LaFollette Seamen's Act of 1915, they finally achieved what they had been seeking.[71] The seamen's victory was primarily symbolic by this time, however, given that ship owners had for the most part stopped invoking penal sanctions long before *Robertson v. Baldwin* ever arose. One lesson of the case, however, was that as long as such sanctions remained on the books, they could always be called into action again if ship owners should come to find it advantageous.

THE PEONAGE CASES AND CRIMINAL PUNISHMENT FOR LABOR CONTRACT BREACHES

The seamen pursued their goal of repeal exclusively through the legislature even after the Supreme Court had begun to hand down its first peonage decisions. In *Clyatt v. United States* (1905), decided only eight years after *Robertson*, the court seemed finally to decide between constitutional traditions, apparently adopting the Indiana interpretation of the term "involuntary servitude." Justice Brewer, writing for the court, declared,

> Peonage is sometimes classified as voluntary or involuntary, but this implies simply a difference in the mode of origin, but none in the character of the servitude. The one exists where the debtor voluntarily contracts to enter the service of his creditor. The other is forced upon the debtor by some provision of law. But peonage, however created, is compulsory service, involuntary servitude. . . . A clear distinction exists between peonage and the voluntary performance of labor or rendering of services in payment of a debt. In the latter case

---

[70] Ibid., 43. After failing to eliminate all penal sanctions for breaching merchant seamen in its 1898 amendment of the Seamen's Act, Congress did prohibit penal sanctions and specific performance to enforce Hawaiian labor contracts in 1900, in the Organic Act by which Hawaii was made a territory of the United States: "[N]o suit or proceedings shall be maintained for the specific performance of any contract heretofore or hereafter entered into for personal labor or service, nor shall any remedy exist or be enforced for breach of any such contract except in a civil suit or proceeding instituted solely to recover damages for such breach. *Provided further that the provisions of this section shall not modify or change the laws of the United States applicable to merchant seamen*" (emphasis added). *U.S. Statutes at Large* XXXI, ch. 339, "An Act to Provide a Government for the Territory of Hawaii," ch. I, sec. 10, 144.

[71] Weintraub, *Andrew Furuseth*, 120–21, 134.

the debtor, though contracting to pay his indebtedness by labor or service, and subject like any other contractor to an action for damages for the breach of contract, can elect at any time to break it, and no law or force compels performance or a continuance of the service.[72]

Several points need to be made about the *Clyatt* decision. First, although the language quoted above was broad enough to cover laws that imposed penal sanctions for labor contract breaches, the Court was not making a decision about that kind of legislation in *Clyatt*. *Clyatt* was a prosecution of individuals for returning other individuals to peonage. The question of whether penal sanctions imposed by state law for contract breaches established "involuntary servitude" still remained to be decided by the Court. Second, the *Clyatt* court did not overrule *Robertson*. Rather, it read the second ground of that decision as the rule of the case, and allowed it to stand. "We need not stop to consider," Justice Brewer wrote, "any possible limits or exceptional cases, such as the service of a sailor [citing *Robertson v. Baldwin*]."[73]

The ambiguous constitutional status of penal sanctions, even after the *Clyatt* decision, is evident in a Fourteenth Amendment opinion delivered by Justice Harlan. In *Adair v. United States,* decided in 1908, the Supreme Court struck down a federal statute that made it a criminal offence for an employer to require a worker not to join a union or to threaten to fire or fire a worker for joining one, on the ground that such legislation represented an unwarranted interference with freedom of contract. In the course of delivering the court's opinion, however, Justice Harlan wrote the following:

> Of course, if the parties by contract fix the period of service, and prescribe the conditions upon which the contract may be terminated, such contract would control the rights of the parties as between themselves, and for any violation of those provisions the party wronged would have his appropriate civil action. *And it may be – but upon that point we express no opinion – that in the case of a labor contract between an employer engaged in interstate commerce and his employé, Congress could make it a crime for either party without sufficient or just excuse or notice to disregard the terms of such contract, or to refuse to perform it. In the absence, however, of a valid contract between the parties controlling their conduct towards each other and fixing a period of service, it cannot be, we repeat, that an em*ployer is under any legal obligation, against his will, to retain an employé in his personal service any more than *an employé can be compelled,*

[72] *Clyatt v. United States,* 197 U.S. 207 (1905), 215.

[73] Ibid., 216.

against his will, to remain in the personal service of another.[74] (emphasis added)

Even if the *Robertson* court believed that its decision did not extend beyond merchant seamen, in the years after *Clyatt* was decided, some Southerners appealed to *Robertson* as a precedent for upholding the constitutionality of state laws penally enforcing labor contracts. In *State v. Murray*, decided by the Louisiana Supreme Court in 1906, the Court upheld the validity of Louisiana's false pretense statute on the ground that the legislation covered labor contracts of an exceptional nature exempt from the Thirteenth Amendment, citing the recent *Clyatt* opinion approving *Robertson* for this proposition. The U.S. Supreme Court, it said, had "recognized in the Legislature the power to make unlawful and punish criminally an abandonment by an employé of his part of labor *in any extreme cases* (emphasis added)."[75]

In *Ex parte Hollman*,[76] the attorney general of South Carolina attempted to defend the constitutionality of the state's agricultural contract labor law in state court by arguing in part that "imprisonment for the failure to perform personal service has been sustained by the Supreme Court of the United States in the case of *Robertson v. Baldwin*."[77] The South Carolina Supreme Court replied: "This is true; that case does hold constitutional an act of Congress authorizing punishment by imprisonment of deserting sailors. But the Constitution of the United States contains no provision against imprisonment for debt."[78] The court went on to strike down the statute as a violation of the state constitution's prohibition on imprisonment for debt.[79] Later in the same opinion, it also rejected the contention that it was possible "to bring contracts with agricultural laborers, such as that now under discussion, within the special cases referred to by Justice Brewer" in his *Clyatt* opinion. In this respect, the court reached a different conclusion from the one reached by the Louisiana court just two years earlier. Nevertheless, it is important to understand that even after the U.S. Supreme Court handed down its decision in *Clyatt*, *Robertson* was still being cited to try to establish the constitutionality of southern statutes

---

[74] *Adair v. United States*, 208 U.S. 161 (1908), 175–76.

[75] *State v. Murray*, 116 La. 655 (1906), 660.

[76] 79 S.C. 9 (1908).

[77] *Ex parte Hollman*, 79 S.C. 9 (1908), 18. This is a quotation from the court's opinion summarizing the attorney general's argument. A similar argument was attempted in a Federal District Court case for the District of South Carolina challenging the constitutionality of the same law. See *Ex parte Drayton*, 153 Fed. 986 (1907), 993–95.

[78] *Ex parte Hollman*, 79 S.C. 9 (1908), 18–19.

[79] Ibid., 19.

that imposed, directly or indirectly, penal sanctions for breaches of labor contracts.

Although the U.S. Supreme Court had still not definitively settled the issue by 1908, three years later, when it handed down its decision in *Bailey v. Alabama,* it did. In *Bailey,* the Supreme Court struck down Alabama's false pretense statute as violating the Anti-peonage Act and the Thirteenth Amendment. Justice Hughes, building on the *Clyatt* opinion, declared that the Anti-peonage Act "necessarily embraces all legislation which seeks to compel the service or labor by making it a crime to refuse or fail to perform it."[80]

Evidently the Supreme Court was of two minds on the question of the penal enforcement of labor agreements. When it came to their use against helpless black people in the South, with its history of slavery but also with its distance from northern labor relations, they felt inclined to invoke the Indiana tradition, which had, after all, first been developed in a similar context. The peonage cases that found their way before the Supreme Court had been initiated by federal authorities and did not grow out of an indigenous movement of black workers. The people responsible for the attack on southern peonage were progressives, committed to protecting the weak by reforming government and the legal system.

When the question of penal sanctions was posed outside the context of southern labor relations, however, as a theoretical matter of contract law or in a hypothetical northern context, northern elites seemed to view the question as much more difficult. However conceptually difficult it might be, the problem could only be posed as an abstract question when it came to northern labor relations. Political and social realities had long ago settled the question in the case of the vast majority of northern wage workers because, as the *Robertson* court put it, "public opinion would not tolerate" an effort to impose penal sanctions widely on the waged population.

The decision in *Robertson* indicates nevertheless that the Illinois/New Mexico view of "involuntary servitude" still survived in the North. It still offered employers, wherever political conditions permitted and circumstances gave them good economic reasons to want to enforce labor contracts,[81] a normative and legal foundation to support the passage of penal legislation to enforce labor contracts. During the first decade of the twentieth century, perhaps emboldened by southern legislation and by the

---

[80] *Bailey v. Alabama,* 219 U.S. 219 (1911), 243.

[81] Naturally, the employer interest in enforcing labor contracts after advances was greater, all other things being equal, than it was where no advances were given. Still, the state of employer interests alone did not determine what remedies would be available for contract breaches in such cases. In the 1860s, the federal law to promote the importation of contract laborers had not authorized penal sanctions, even though employers had to give transportation advances. The political and ideological conditions in Congress at the time foreclosed that possibility.

Robertson decision, the legislatures of three northern states enacted false pretense labor contract statutes of their own,[82] aimed at enforcing the labor agreements of white workers who had received transportation advances to remote lumbering or mining sites. Many but not all of these workers would have been immigrants. Minnesota enacted such a statute in 1901,[83] followed by Michigan in 1903,[84] and Maine in 1907.[85] We know that in Maine the statute was enforced. Rural justices of the peace committed numerous men to jail or sent them back to the woods to work out their contracts in the years following passage of the act.[86] One rural justice said that he alone had heard fifty or sixty cases since the act was passed.[87] In most cases prosecution was used as a way of getting men back to work. Nine out of ten cases were settled once the worker agreed to work out his time.[88]

In his dissent in *Bailey v. Alabama*, Oliver Wendell Holmes showed just how deeply vexing the question really was, and suggested that the majority had arrived at their opinion only because of the particular social context in which the case arose:

> We all agree that this case is to be considered and decided in the same way as if it arose in Idaho or New York. Neither public document nor evidence discloses a law which by its administration is made something different from what it appears on its face, and therefore the fact that in Alabama it mainly concerns the blacks does not matter.[89]

He went on to explain just how problematical the majority's opinion was: "The Thirteenth Amendment," he wrote,

> does not outlaw contracts for labor. That would be at least as great a misfortune for the laborer as for the man that employed him. For it certainly would affect the terms of the bargain unfavorably for the

---

[82] The framing of these statutes in terms of fraud rather than of contract breach may have helped to make them more morally and politically palatable, even though in the case of the Minnesota statute, as in the case of the similar Alabama statute, a presumption of fraud was raised simply by accepting an advance and then not working for long enough to repay it. 1901 Gen. Laws Minn., ch. 165, 212–13.

[83] Ibid.

[84] Mich. Comp. Laws, §§ 408.582–408.583.

[85] Me. Rev. Stat., ch. 128, § 12 (1917).

[86] John Clifton Elder, "Peonage in Maine" (Manuscript report sent to the Attorney General of the United States), National Archives, Record Group #60, Dept. of Justice File #50-34-0, 13–21.

[87] Ibid., 13.

[88] Ibid., 15–16.

[89] *Bailey v. Alabama*, 219 U.S. 219 (1911), 245–46.

laboring man if it were understood that the employer could do nothing in case the laborer saw fit to break his word. But any legal liability for breach of contract is a disagreeable consequence which tends to make the contractor do as he said he would. Liability to an action for damages has that tendency as well as a fine. If the mere imposition of such consequences as tend to make a man keep to his promise is the creation of peonage when the contract happens to be for labor, I do not see why the allowance of a civil action is not, as well as an indictment ending in a fine. . . . I do not blink the fact that the liability to imprisonment may work as a motive when a fine without it would not, and that it may induce the laborer to keep on when he would like to leave. But it does not strike me as an objection to a law that it is effective. If the contract is one that ought not to be made, prohibit it. But if it is a perfectly fair and proper contract, I can see no reason why the State should not throw its weight on the side of performance.[90]

Holmes was correct, of course: All contract remedies operate to enforce agreements by presenting a breaching party with a choice between performing and some disagreeable alternative. To the extent that a party decides to perform labor to avoid the unpleasant alternative, that party may be said to have chosen the lesser evil "voluntarily" or to have chosen it under "coercion." Either characterization is available, but once we decide to characterize such a choice as "coerced," as the majority did in the case of criminal penalties, then there is no logical ground for saying that any similar choice is "voluntary." The logical conclusion is that labor contracts cannot be enforced through any legal remedy at all consistent with the prohibition on "involuntary servitude."

---

[90] Ibid., 246–47. Holmes had apparently changed his mind on this question. In *The Common Law*, published thirty years earlier, Holmes had written that the common law

> has the advantage of freeing the subject from the superfluous theory that contract is a qualified subjection of one will to another, a kind of limited slavery. It might be so regarded if the law compelled men to perform their contracts, or if it allowed promisees to exercise such compulsion. If, when a man promised to labor for another, the law made him do it, his relation to his promisee might be called a servitude *ad hoc* with some truth. But that is what the law never does. . . . It is true that in some instances equity does what is called compelling specific performance. But, in the first place, I am speaking of the common law, and, in the next, this only means that equity compels the performance of certain elements of the total promise which are still capable of performance. . . . The only universal consequence of a legally binding promise is, that the law makes the promisor pay damages if the promised event does not come to pass. In every case it leaves him free from interference until the time for fulfilment has gone by, and therefore free to break his contract if he chooses (300–1).

Even with the careful qualifications written into these paragraphs, it is difficult to square Holmes's words with his dissent in Bailey.

Although Holmes was correct about all this, it does not seem to have bothered the majority in *Bailey,* who blithely ignored the coercive effects of money damages for contract breach, presenting them, in fact, as the opposite of "compelled" performance. "A clear distinction exists," Justice Hughes wrote, quoting *Clyatt,* "between peonage and the voluntary performance of labor or rendering of services in payment of a debt. In the latter case the debtor, though contracting to pay his indebtedness by labor or service*, and subject like any other contractor to an action for damages for breach of that contract, can elect at any time to break it, and no law or force compels performance or a continuance of the service"* (emphasis added).[91]

It is of course also true, as Holmes recognized, that certain alternatives to performance are less unpleasant than others, and fewer people will tend to choose to continue performance when confronted with them. However, the performance of those who choose to avoid these unpleasant alternatives by rendering the labor service is no more "voluntary" than the labor service of those who choose to perform to avoid the unpleasant alternative of prison. The decision of the majority is, from a logical standpoint, arbitrary, a decision to draw a line through a continuum and to call certain decisions to perform labor under certain kinds of threats "voluntary" and other decisions to perform labor under other kinds of threats "involuntary." In fact, the decision as to where to place such a line is not a decision about where coercion begins or ends in labor relations but a moral and political decision about what kinds of difficult choices we should continue to allow certain people to force other people to make, as the latter decide whether to continue to render personal services. For most courts this simply became a matter of saying that nonpecuniary remedies, physical violence, bodily confinement, and state imprisonment, were impermissible, whereas pecuniary remedies should always be permitted. On the other hand, for a few courts this decision seems to have been more complicated. It appears to have involved a judgment that even pecuniary remedies might fall on the other side of the line if the alternative to continued labor that they presented was harsh enough.

Bailey v. Alabama placed criminal penalties for breaches of labor contracts on one side of the line and ordinary money damages on the other, but the political and moral grounds for doing so were not laid out in *Bailey.* It may have been that these grounds were unpalatable enough to be left unarticulated. In several lower federal court peonage opinions issued before *Bailey,* however, the grounds on which line drawing rested were laid out in some detail. For one thing, judges writing in the lower courts made clear that this interpretation of the Anti-peonage Act and of "involuntary servitude" under the Thirteenth Amendment entailed an important restriction on freedom of contract. Federal District Court Judge

[91] *Bailey v. Alabama,* 219 U.S. 219 (1911), 243.

Thomas Jones of Alabama, giving instructions to a grand jury hearing cases under the Anti-peonage Act, wrote that

> The first step to create a condition of peonage is taken when the debtor or person agreeing to perform "service or labor" contracts that it may thereafter be coerced, against his will, by dominion over his person and liberty. . . . Under the [anti-peonage] statute a person may neither agree nor volunteer to be held to a condition of peonage, or to be coerced into subjection to such a condition. In the legal sense . . . such agreements are involuntary in their inception since the law forbids consent, and therefore treats the agreement as having been made involuntarily."[92]

In a charge to another grand jury considering indictments under the Anti-peonage Act, Judge Trieber of the Eastern District of Arkansas made clear that

> [t]he fact even that the laborer entered into that contract voluntarily and with full knowledge of the conditions of his employment is no excuse, for the law says that no person shall enter into such a contract, and, if he does, it shall be null and void.[93]

In the same grand jury charge, Judge Trieber laid out a political justification for these restrictions on freedom of contract. The first step was to characterize severe contract remedies for breaches of voluntary labor agreements as creating a kind of slavery. Even granting this characterization, why should people not be free to contract into a temporary servitude? Why should they not be free to choose temporarily not to be free if in their estimation it advanced their interests? Judge Trieber's answer was a good one, but also unsettling. People who contract away their freedom only do so involuntarily, in most cases, when economic necessity compels them to take this step. In other cases, they do so out of ignorance, not understanding the true range of their options. If these are not reasons enough to restrict freedom of contract, one final reason decides the question. Allowing these kinds of contractual arrangements would place our political system in jeopardy because they are fundamentally incompatible with basic rights of citizenship, particularly the right of suffrage. For this part of his argument, Trieber drew on an old republican tradition in American political thought:[94]

---

[92] *Peonage Cases*, 123 Fed. 671 (M.D. Ala. 1903), 680.

[93] *Peonage Cases*, 136 Fed. 707 (E.D. Ark. 1905), 709.

[94] See Robert Steinfeld, "Property and Suffrage in the Early American Republic," *Stanford Law Review* 41 (1989).

Congress recognized that in a government like ours – a republic – such a system of peonage was more dangerous to the safety of our republican institutions than slavery itself was, for a slave was property, and possessed none of the rights of citizenship, could not vote, and had no voice in the administration of the affairs of the nation. On the other hand, the peon, although practically a slave as long as he was indebted to his master or employer, without the privilege of changing his vocation or leaving his master . . . yet possessed all the rights of citizenship, including the right of franchise. To permit such a condition was deemed dangerous, as in the course of time it might happen that a very large number of people, compelled by their necessities, perhaps, or through ignorance or greed, might thus sell themselves to masters, and thereby come absolutely under their control, and yet, by reason of the privilege of the right to vote, in which they would probably be controlled by their masters, have a sufficient voice in the selection of the officials to determine the result of an election. In addition to that, such a condition might enable men of large wealth to obtain gradually a control of thousands of people – some by reason of their poverty, and others by reason of their ignorance – and thus establish a system in this country wholly incompatible with the principles upon which this government was founded.[95]

In the peonage cases, the Supreme Court created the modern constitutional standard for free labor by rejecting an earlier constitutional tradition that had defined "free" labor differently. This decision was forced on the court by the perceived need to combat southern efforts to *reimpose* a form of servitude on black people, a judgment based at bottom on the view that it was only because black people were compelled by the combined effects of political and economic powerlessness and by a lack of other better alternatives that they ever agreed to work under these conditions in the first place.

Later on the U.S. Supreme Court offered an additional rationale for these restrictions on contract remedies, one that English labor activists also relied on in the nineteenth century. Mr. Justice Jackson wrote in *Pollock v. Williams* that

in general the defense against oppressive hours, pay, working conditions, or treatment is the right to change employers. When the master can compel and the laborer cannot escape the obligation to go on,

---

[95] *Peonage Cases*, 136 Fed. 707 (1905), 707–08. See also the jury charge of the Federal District Court judge for the District of South Carolina. Judge Brawley observed that "the intention of the [anti-peonage] legislation was to abolish this system wherever it prevailed, and to prohibit its extension or establishment in any state or territory *where the conditions were such as to make it probable or possible that an ignorant and helpless population might be induced to submit themselves to a degrading and oppressive system*" (emphasis added). *United States v. Clement*, 171 Fed. 974 (1909), 975.

there is no power below to redress and no incentive above to relieve a harsh overlordship or unwholesome conditions of work.[96]

A right of exit may indeed represent a formidable check on the abuse of power, as long as the extra-contractual alternatives to continuing in the job are better than the terms under which the work is offered. However, if those alternatives are worse than the conditions of work, then the absence of formal legal remedies to strictly enforce a contract may make no difference in the real power of a worker to leave. Hence, there is a certain circularity in the above arguments when taken together. If a worker would not enter a harsh contract except because of economic necessity that presented the worker with a choice that was worse than the choice of entering the harsh labor relation, then merely eliminating a strict contract remedy to enforce that relation will have done nothing to reduce the pressure on the worker to continue to suffer the terms of that relationship, because the pressure arises not from any contract remedy but from the original difficult "economic" circumstances to which the worker continues to be subject.

Nevertheless, the circularity is not total, because to the extent that non-waivable, strict contract remedies force workers to choose between not working at all and working under strictly binding contracts, the elimination of strict remedies will in many situations increase workers' real power of exit and will in fact often operate as a check on the most egregious abuses of power in employment relations.

It is to these kinds of moral and political judgments that we trace the origins of the modern constitutional definition of free labor in this country, just as we must trace the origins of modern free labor in England to a political and moral victory of the laboring classes.

Modern free labor did not arise as the result of the spread of liberal ideas or the diffusion of "free" markets based on "free" contract. It is the result of a difficult political and moral resolution of fundamental conflicts within liberalism, a political and moral resolution of the liberal paradox of coercion and consent, and simultaneously of the contradiction between liberal commitments to freedom of contract and freedom of person. Modern free labor does not represent the pure expression of freedom of contract. On the contrary, it is constituted by a regime of contract rules that restricts freedom of contract by prohibiting workers from entering strictly binding contracts for the sale of their labor.[97] Other resolutions of these fundamental conflicts were possible, leading to regimes of free contract like those in England and Prussia or Illinois during the first two-thirds of the nineteenth century. Only political events and changing moral stand-

[96] *Pollock v. Williams,* 322 U.S. 4 (1944), 18.

[97] Binder, "Substantive Liberty," § VI. (30.); and Knight, *Freedom & Reform,* 78–79.

ards led to the line being drawn as it was in American constitutional law during the early years of the twentieth century. A broad suffrage, together with a longstanding association of contractual servitude with black slavery and a revolutionary commitment to formal equality, had led to a similar line being drawn for the majority of northern waged workers, in law and practice, more than a century earlier.

RESTRICTIONS ON OTHER CONTRACT REMEDIES

The decision that penal sanctions for contract breaches should be placed on one side of the line and ordinary damages on the other left unresolved the question of what should be the law's attitude toward a host of other possible contract enforcement mechanisms. On which side of the line should the law place a negative injunction, one prohibiting a sports superstar from playing with any team other than his present one? The disagreeable alternative to continuing to render labor services is to take up another calling in which the remuneration may be a small fraction of one's current salary. Is this alternative disagreeable enough to make the decision to play out the contract "involuntary servitude?" Suppose a negative injunction is phrased to prohibit a party from working anywhere other than for his or her present employer. The disagreeable alternative to performance would be living on welfare, if one could qualify, or perhaps starving. Is *this* alternative disagreeable enough to make the decision to continue in employment "involuntary servitude?" Under modern law, negative injunctions are constitutionally permitted. What about the case of an employer withholding a month's pay, payable only if a worker completes his contract term?

Questions of this sort were presented to a number of southern courts during the early decades of the twentieth century as they considered the constitutionality of a number of other penal statutory provisions devised by southern legislatures to enforce labor contracts. Two kinds of laws in particular raised these questions. One made a person under contract subject to criminal punishment if he or she abandoned the contract and took work with a third party without telling that party that he or she had failed to fulfill the first agreement. The second kind of law sometimes worked in conjunction with the first, at other times alone. It subjected to criminal punishment any employer who knowingly gave work to a person who had abandoned an earlier contract.

In *Toney v. Alabama,* decided in 1904, the Alabama Supreme Court ruled unconstitutional an Alabama statute of the first kind. This statute and decision are particularly interesting because the coercion to perform a labor agreement under this law did not come solely from a threat of imprisonment but from a threat of imprisonment in combination with a threat of starvation. The statute ostensibly punished failure to inform a new employer that one has just broken one's earlier contract, not the mere failure to perform the contract. As a result the statute forced the following hard choice on an individual contemplating breach of a labor agreement: (1) work out your time under the contract, (2) face imprisonment if you leave without telling your new employer that you have broken your old contract, or (3) reveal the breach to a new employer and face the substantial likelihood that you will not be offered work, given that employers who knowingly give you work may themselves be subject to criminal punishment.

Perhaps because the choice offered was not simply between imprisonment and continued labor, the court did not strike down the act on the ground that it created a condition of involuntary servitude. Instead, it struck down the statute on the ground that it violated the Fourteenth Amendment. Significantly, this interpretation of the Fourteenth Amendment's guarantee of freedom of contract became an important aspect of the modern constitutional notion of free labor, even where it has not been explicitly articulated as it was in *Toney v. Alabama*. Freedom of contract is here defined to include the right to break earlier labor contracts (subject to payment of damages), because without this right one's freedom to contract for the sale of one's labor would be impermissibly restricted. It makes no difference that one's own actions are the source of this kind of restriction on freedom of contract, the result of earlier exercises of one's freedom of contract. One's present freedom of contract cannot be restricted by earlier exercises of that freedom. Freedom of contract is both expanded and contracted by this definition. On the one hand, one is free to contract over and over again as often as one wishes, regardless of previous contracts. On the other hand, freedom of contract is restricted in the sense that one is not free to bind oneself irrevocably by an earlier agreement even if one wishes to do so. "Because of the restrictions it purports to place on the right to make contracts for employment and concerning the use and cultivation of land," the Alabama Court wrote, "this act is wholly invalid."[98] The Supreme Court of Mississippi reached a similar conclusion about a similar Mississippi law in 1912,[99] but it also found that the statute forced workers to choose between alternatives that were disagreeable enough to make any resulting labor involuntary servitude.[100]

The second kind of statute with which southern courts dealt presented an even more interesting situation. In the North, enticement, or interference with contractual relations, continued to be a valid action at common law. In the South, in many states, the common law action had been crimi-

---

[98] *Toney v. The State*, 141 Ala. 120 (1904), 125.

[99] *State v. Armstead*, 103 Miss. 790 (1912), 798.

[100] Ibid.

nalized, so that third-party employers were subject to criminal punishment for enticing away any worker already under an exclusive contract to another employer. Commonly, these enticement statutes included, as the common law action sometimes also did, the act of "harboring" as well as "enticing" a worker. The difference between "harboring" and "enticing" was that in "harboring" a third-party employer need not have persuaded a worker to break his or her previous agreement. He need only have offered that person work after the worker had already of his or her own volition and without encouragement from the third party left a former employer in breach of a previous labor agreement. Because these statutes subjected third-party employers, not the worker, to criminal punishment, it may well be asked how they could be thought to have coerced *the worker* into performing his or her labor agreement involuntarily. The answer again lies in the way the law attempted to structure the alternatives facing workers under contract. If no other employer would hire you because he feared criminal prosecution, you as a worker would be confronted with the following set of disagreeable alternatives: (1) work out your time or debt or (2) face the real likelihood of not being able to find any other gainful employment. One important way in which "harboring" differed from "enticement" is that "enticement" only covered a limited subset of all employers, those who had actively solicited a contract breach. "Harboring" applied to all possible future employers who had notice of the previous contract.

In 1919, the South Carolina Supreme Court, reversing a jury award of damages to one employer who had sued a second employer, announced that the passage of the Thirteenth and Fourteenth amendments had superseded and annulled the common law action of "harboring."[101] The common law action, it was held by the court, violated the Thirteenth Amendment's prohibition of "involuntary servitude":

> If no one else could have employed Carver during the term of his contract with plaintiff, after he elected to break that contract, without incurring liability to plaintiff for damages, the result would have been to coerce him to perform the labor required by the contract; for he had to work or starve. The compulsion would have been scarcely less effectual than if it had been induced by the fear of punishment under a criminal statute for breach of his contract, which was condemned as violative of the thirteenth amendment. . . . The prohibition is as effective against indirect as it is against direct actions and laws – statutes or decisions – which, in operation and effect, produce the condition prohibited.[102]

[101]   *Shaw v. Fisher,* 113 S.C. 287 (1920).

[102]   Ibid., 292.

Two things are particularly interesting about this decision. First, the court found that the disagreeable alternative of starvation (which may plausibly be characterized as an extreme pecuniary sanction) was nevertheless sufficiently disagreeable so that any labor rendered under the threat of it must be considered "involuntary servitude." Second, the liability for damages to which the common law subjected third-party employers was sufficiently coercive to create the threat of starvation in the first place. It was not necessary to threaten third-party employers with fine or imprisonment to create the real likelihood that the alternative facing a worker would be to work out the contract or starve. The pecuniary liability of third-party employers was apparently enough.

A similar case was presented to the Mississippi Supreme Court in 1927. A Mississippi statute subjected third-party employers to a fine of not less than $25 nor more than $100 plus liability for the repayment of all advances made by a former employer if they hired a worker knowing that that worker was already under contract to another employer. The court held that the "knowingly employ" provision of the statute violated the Thirteenth Amendment and should be read out of the statute:

> [D]uring the continuation of the contract of employment, the laborer would be compelled [by the operation of this provision] to render services, or, if he abandoned it, the hand of every man must be against him, and he cannot seek employment elsewhere without penalizing the party who employs him. In other words, by practical application, the mind of the laborer would not be free to breach his contract, as in all other lines of endeavor and commercial enterprises. He must "stay or starve," because no one could employ him until he had made investigation and found that such laborer or tenant had good cause to leave the leased premises, because the employer or landlord had first breached the contract. . . .
>
> [Quoting the opinion in an earlier Mississippi Supreme Court decision, the court continued] "Under the Thirteenth Amendment, it is doubtful whether any statute can be enacted which would have the effect of abridging or destroying the right of a person to abandon employment (subject to civil liability), as such would apparently constitute him an involuntary servant or engaged in servitude against his consent."
>
> [This opinion] is in line with what appears to be the view of the supreme court of the United States, that a laborer may breach his contract (subject only to civil liability), and one may thereafter deal with him as a free man.[103]

[103] *Thompson v. Box*, 147 Miss. 1 (1927), 12–14.

These decisions draw the line at a point that is similar to the one drawn by twentieth-century English equity courts as those courts determined the legitimate scope of negative injunctions. In both cases, forcing a worker to choose between starvation and continued labor was placed on the other side of the line, judged to create "involuntary servitude" in the United States and to illegitimately "drive" a worker to perform labor in England. If it was to continue to be available to employers, a labor contract remedy could apparently only be effective up to a point, according to some courts. Beyond that point, even if the sanction only exposed a worker to a pecuniary loss and not to physical violence or loss of liberty, it might still be judged to create contractual slavery. There are two important points about this position. First, it vividly demonstrates just how practically and conceptually difficult it is to maintain a strict line between free and unfree labor based on the notion that nonpecuniary pressures produce unfree labor while pecuniary pressures cannot.[104] Second, it makes clear that the line drawn even by these courts left sufficient room to allow employers to present workers with certain disagreeable alternatives to continued performance that could involve severe pecuniary loss and could operate quite harshly and quite effectively to pressure the performance of labor agreements.

[104] The difficulties involved in strictly maintaining this distinction became apparent to members of the U.S. Supreme Court in a case presented to them in the late twentieth century. See *United States v. Kozminski*, 487 U.S. 931 (1988), 958 n. 5. "Although it is heartening that the Court recognizes that strange environs and the lack of money, maturity, education, or family support can establish the coercion necessary for involuntary servitude, labeling such coercion 'physical' is at best strained," (concurring opinion of Justice Brennan).

9

Labor Contract Enforcement in the American North

Binding wage labor contracts[1] offered nineteenth-century English employers significant economic benefits, but contracting was only a useful strategy for reducing turnover and monitoring costs if employers were able to enforce contracts quickly and cheaply.[2] But for this ability to enforce contracts simply and cheaply, employers would have had to pursue cost reduction in other ways, and the contract system would not have assumed the importance it did in English wage labor relations. In the northern United States, a summary criminal remedy to enforce labor contracts was not normally available against native-born white adult wage workers at any time during the nineteenth century.[3] This very real constraint, however, did not eliminate the value to northern employers of using binding contracts with wage workers, largely because they had available a reasonable substitute for penal sanctions, wage forfeiture.[4] Wage forfeiture made

---

[1] I include in the term "binding contracts" those for a fixed term, for example, for a year or two years, which terminate at the conclusion of the period unless explicitly renewed; periodic contracts, for example those from week to week or month to month, which automatically renew at the end of each term unless a period's notice is given for termination; contracts of indefinite duration that could be terminated by giving some period of notice such as a week, a fortnight, or a month; and contracts to do or make some thing. All these contracts subjected workers to criminal sanctions for breach. Only contracts determinable at will (so-called minute contracts in England) did not.

[2] Clearly, the intensity of an employer's economic interest in controlling turnover and monitoring costs through contracts and contract enforcement varies depending on numerous factors, including the kind of labor the employer requires and the state of the labor market. In slack labor markets employers have less need to control turnover and monitoring costs, especially in the case of unskilled workers. Nevertheless, rules making labor contracts easily enforceable are desirable because they make it possible for employers to use contracting and contract enforcement in the numerous market conditions in which it is beneficial.

[3] For details and exceptions, see Chapter 8.

[4] I use the expression "forfeiture" here to include loss of wages under the entirety doctrine for failure to perform a contractual condition. In one sense this is not "forfeiture" because the condition precedent to the employer's obligation to pay wages has not been met, and legally, as a result, no wages can be forfeited because none have been earned.

labor contract enforcement inexpensive and effective. Because wage forfeiture was available in the United States, contracting could play a role in nineteenth-century American wage labor relations not completely unlike the one it played in English wage labor relations. The American practice had the added virtue that it was less vulnerable to the charge that it turned contracts of service into contracts of slavery, even though it confronted wage workers, depending on the circumstances, with a very disagreeable alternative to continued performance.

ENTIRETY

In England, the system of penal sanctions had been established by Parliament. In the United States, state legislatures were not prepared in most cases to follow a similar course, perhaps because of the broadened suffrage legislators confronted. However, there were a set of English common law rules that carried none of the political baggage that penal sanctions had come to carry in America by this time that could serve similar purposes, perhaps nearly as well. Before 1850, these rules were adopted by the common law courts in every state but one that considered the question.[5] This common law doctrine held that as a general matter contracts of service for a term or to perform task or piece work would be construed as entire and no wages would be owed to a worker who had voluntarily abandoned the contract before completing the term or task.

There were two related aspects of the doctrine of "entirety." First, where a contract for a stated term of service or to do specific work made no explicit provision as to the times wages would be due and owing, the contract was construed to be entire both as to service and payment. The worker was viewed as having promised to work for one entire term or until he or she had completed the prescribed tasks, and the employer was viewed as having promised to make one entire payment for the worker's one entire performance. Second, these promises were construed to be dependent, so that an employer's obligation to make good on his promise to pay depended on a worker's first fully performing the prescribed service.

[5] The single exception was New Hampshire; see *Britton v. Turner*, 6 N.H. 61 (1834). Precisely when the American judiciary first adopted these rules is a matter of dispute. Peter Karsten, "'Bottomed on Justice': A Reappraisal of Critical Legal Studies Scholarship Concerning Breaches of Labor Contracts by Quitting or Firing in Britain and the U.S., 1630–1880," *The American Journal of Legal History* 34 (1990), argues that they were brought over from England during the colonial period and operated continuously from then through the nineteenth century, although lower courts may not always have used them. Christopher Tomlins, *Law, Labor, and Ideology in the Early American Republic* (Cambridge, 1993), 270–78, is of the opinion that they were a more recent import, not embraced by American judges until the nineteenth century. Because few eighteenth-century judicial opinions were reported, we may never have a definitive answer. On the uses of entirety, see also Wythe Holt, "Recovery by the Worker Who Quits," *Wisconsin Law Review* (1986).

Because the employer's obligation to pay one entire payment was dependent on a worker performing the promised service completely, if a worker failed to do so, the employer was under no legal obligation under the contract to make good on his promise to make the one entire payment. Under this construction of a contract a worker could make no claim under the contract for wages for partial performance. If labor contracts had been construed as divisible rather than entire, at least where no express provision had been made as to the times wages were due and owing, then workers might well have been able to maintain actions on the contract for wages, based on their performance of divisible units of the contract.

The entirety doctrine typically worked as follows. If an agricultural laborer agreed to work for a farmer for a year at $20 a month or $240 for the year, and the worker quit after working ten full months, the contract was construed to be entire, unless the employer had expressly agreed *to pay the $20 a month to the worker at the end of each month.*[6] Full performance by the worker was considered a condition that had to be fulfilled before an employer was obligated to pay any wages under the contract. The worker was entitled to recover nothing under the contract for his ten months of service. No claim could be maintained that he was entitled to a divisible part of the contract price for ten months of labor. The employer was viewed as having bargained for twelve full months of service, and not for anything else, and it was for twelve full months of service that he had agreed to pay $240 at the conclusion of the term.

In the case of agricultural labor, one rationale for finding entirety in this situation was that the parties had not expressly prescribed how to apportion the wages, and it was simply impossible for a court to do so. The value of farm labor was obviously different in February than it was in June, July, or August. Simply dividing $240 by twelve would not reflect these large seasonal fluctuations in the value of the labor, even if the parties *had* spoken loosely of $20 a month. The payment of $240 was for one indivisible package, the total value of the labor in July and August as well as in February.

It is important to understand that "entirety" in this sense was primarily a rule of construction authorizing judges to read into labor contracts terms and conditions to which the parties had not explicitly agreed. Where a labor contract explicitly called for periodic wage payments to be made during the term of service, the courts of the period normally enforced an employer's contractual obligation to pay those wages. In *White v. Atkins*, for example, White had agreed to run Atkins's farm for a year and "to have $150, one hundred and fifty dollars, per year, *payable monthly,* if he

---

[6] See, for example, *Reab v. Moor*, 19 Johns. (N.Y.) 337 (1822); *Davis v. Maxwell*, 53 Mass. (12 Met.) 286 (1847).

wishes"[7] (emphasis added). Chief Justice Lemuel Shaw wrote for the Massachusetts Supreme Judicial Court that

> [t]he contract of plaintiff was, no doubt, for an entire year's service; but the performance of this entire contract was not a condition precedent to the plaintiff's right to recover any thing, because the plaintiff was, at his option, entitled to receive his pay monthly.[8]

In a case where the contract expressly called for the monthly payment of wages, a worker who quit after working ten full months would be legally entitled to collect ten months of back salary under the contract. The employer in turn would be entitled to bring a suit for damages for the worker's breach of his promise to serve twelve full months but would not be entitled to a forfeiture of the monthly wages for the ten full months of service performed.[9] The courts, therefore, generally treated labor contracts as "divisible" if the contract explicitly provided for "divisibility."

There were two basic situations in which the courts treated labor contracts as entire: where the contract expressly said that it was entire, that is, that no wages would be due unless the entire term of service had first been completed,[10] and, perhaps more important, where no explicit provision had been made as to the times wages were to be payable. In the second case entirety was the default rule where parties had failed expressly to provide for the payment of wages.[11]

---

[7] *White v. Atkins*, 62 Mass. (8 Cush.) 367 (1851).

[8] Ibid., 370.

[9] Ibid., 370–71. A worker, however, would not be entitled to wages for any portion of a month worked; the worker's completion of a full month's service was a condition that had to be fulfilled before the employer incurred any obligation under the contract to pay a month's wages (370). The monthly units were indivisible. As a result, even in this case a worker could forfeit up to a month's wages. Shaw wrote, "[t]he performance of a year's service was necessarily independent, and could not be a condition precedent to a monthly payment within the year. But as the monthly payments were to be made for services actually to be done, the performance of a month's service was condition precedent to the right to demand a month's wages, and these, therefore, were dependent stipulations" (370).

[10] For examples of such agreements, see *Hair v. Bell*, 6 Vt. 34 (1834) (plaintiff to work for defendant as a joiner for a year "and at the expiration of the time to pay him one hundred and eighty dollars," 34); *Philbrook v. Belknap*, 6 Vt. 381 (1834) (plaintiff to work for defendant for three years "at eight dollars a month . . . but if plaintiff left the defendant before the end of the three years, unless in case of sickness, plaintiff to have nothing for his labor," 384); and *Fenton v. Clark*, 11 Vt. 557 (1839) ("The plaintiff commenced working for the defendant on the nineteenth of September, 1837 under a contract to work for four months at $10 per month, and to receive no pay until he had worked the four months," 557).

[11] *Davis v. Maxwell*, 53 Mass. (12 Met.) 286 (1847) ("There is no time fixed for the payment [in the contract], and the law therefore fixes the time; and that is, in a case like this, the period when the service is performed. It is one bargain; performance on one part

Two different but related considerations are involved when we think about these rules. First, in the case of express agreements that no wages are to be due until the worker has fully performed the agreement, courts faced the question whether they should enforce such agreements. These kinds of agreements exposed workers to what in most cases amounted to penalties or forfeitures for breach of contract. Under many modern periodic wage payment statutes employers and ordinary employees simply cannot make such agreements because employers are subject to non-waivable duties to pay their employees wages on a regular, short periodic basis. In addition, courts today normally refuse to enforce contractual penalties or forfeitures. In other words, it is doubtful that courts today would enforce express agreements of this kind in the case of ordinary wage work. As to the second situation, where the rule of entirety supplied, as a rule of construction, contract terms to which the parties had not expressly agreed, the rule made it possible for employers to enter contracts for a term without having to negotiate for wage forfeiture in advance. It was undoubtedly easier for employers in many cases not to have to deal explicitly with the sticky issue of wage forfeiture at the time the agreement was being negotiated. Merely omitting from the agreement any mention of the payment of wages entitled the employer to wage forfeiture and to threaten wage forfeiture during the term of the agreement.

If a contract was entire, full performance by the worker was a condition for recovering any wages under the contract. Anything short of full performance meant wage forfeiture. It was obvious, therefore, that if a worker voluntarily left his job during the term of service he forfeited his back wages. However, the same generally held true if he should be dismissed by the employer for good cause during the term.[12] Under the strictest version of the English rule, a worker forfeited his wages even when he failed to complete his term of service because of sickness or

---

and payment on the other; and not part performance and full payment for the part performed," 290). Even where an employer actually paid wages to a worker periodically during the term, courts frequently held that this course of dealing was not enough in itself to establish that the parties intended to make compensation under the agreement divisible, in the absence of an express agreement to do so. See *M'Millan v. Vanderlip*, 12 Johns. (N.Y.) 165 (1815); but see also *Thorpe v. White*, 13 Johns. (N.Y.) 53 (1816) (the giving of a promissory note to an employee by employers worked a modification of the previously "entire" contract, and the note for wages for partial performance could be enforced); and also *Thayer v. Wadsworth,* 36 Mass. 349 (1837) (plaintiff entitled to have jury decide whether defendant's practice of paying wages at regular intervals sustained his contention that the agreement expressly called for the periodic payment of wages, 353–54.)

[12] Some American jurisdictions made a distinction between dismissal and abandonment, allowing a worker to recover in *quantum meruit* when he had been dismissed but not when he had abandoned. See *Byrd v. Boyd*, 4 McCord 246 (S.C. 1827). However, in other jurisdictions entirety applied in both situations. See, for example, *Lantry v. Parks*, 8 Cow. (N.Y.) 63 (1827), 64, quoting Lord Ellenborough in *Spain v. Arnott*, 2 Stark. 256 (1817).

death.[13] This strict liability rule was later relaxed in most jurisdictions in the United States, making clear that it was voluntary misbehavior that was the proper target of wage forfeiture, not the mere failure to perform a condition. When the New York Court of Appeals decided not to adopt the strict English rule, it explained its decision as follows:

> There is good reason for the distinction which seems to obtain in all the cases, between the case of a willful or negligent violation of a contract and that where one is prevented by the act of God. In the one case, *the application of the rule operates as a punishment to the person wantonly guilty of the breach and tends to preserve the contract inviolable;* while in the other, its exception is calculated to protect the rights of the unfortunate and honest man who is providentially and without fault on his part prevented from a full performance.[14] (emphasis added)

In the case of entire contracts, then, if a worker was either fired for what was viewed as good cause or quit without good cause during the term, he or she normally forfeited any back wages that had been withheld. Therefore, the disagreeable alternative to obeying an employer's orders during the term or continuing to work for the entire term was to lose one's back wages, amounting in some cases to the value of many months' labor.

Although "entirety" was, strictly speaking, a set of rules for interpreting obligations under contracts, the term has also come to be understood more broadly as including a set of rules about when a worker might recover the value of labor he or she had conferred on the employer off the contract in a quasi-contractual action of *quantum meruit* for the reasonable value of the worker's services. Not surprisingly, the rules governing recovery in actions of *quantum meruit* were as unfavorable to workers as the rules governing formal contract obligations. The two sets of rules reinforced one another. An action in *quantum meruit* proceeds on the ground that a worker has conferred valuable benefits on an employer and in fairness should be compensated for the reasonable value of his or her labor regardless of any explicit agreement between the two; otherwise the employer would be unjustly enriched. In nineteenth-century American courts, where a contract was found to be entire a worker who quit without good cause or was fired for good cause normally could not claim any compensation for the value of services he or she had bestowed on the employer in an action of *quantum meruit*.[15] Workers in this situation, therefore, could recover neither on nor off the contract.

---

[13] *Cutter v. Powell,* 6 Term R., 320 (1795).

[14] *Wolfe, Executor v. Howes,* 20 N.Y. (6 Smith) 197 (1859), 201.

[15] Numerous decisions allowed a worker to maintain an action of *quantum meruit* where his or her failure fully to perform was the result of illness. In some cases, it is difficult to

A clear judicial policy lay behind these rules. The modern legal view of contract is that a contracting party should, in most cases, have the option either of performing the contract or paying damages. That was not the view of most early nineteenth-century American judges. They believed that the law should enforce the performance of contracts, at least labor contracts. Parties to contracts should not be free to choose whether to perform or pay damages; their undertakings obligated them to perform and the law should establish policies that would make them do that. A right to bring a suit for damages was a totally inadequate remedy in most cases. It is this policy that lay behind these rules, and judges sometimes said as much.

In *M'Millan v. Vanderlip* (1815)[16] the court, for example, observed that "[t]he general practice, in hiring laborers or artisans, is, for 6 or 12 months . . ." and but for the entirety rule an employer would be left "the poor resort of a suit for damages. The rule contended for holds out temptations to men to violate their contracts."[17] The following language from *Lantry v. Parks,* decided by the New York Supreme Court in 1827, reflects a similar attitude:

> [A] party who enters into a contract, and performs part of it, and then, without cause, and without the agreement, or fault of the other party, *of his own mere volition, abandons the performance,* he cannot maintain an action, on an implied assumpsit, for the labor actually performed. Of course, he cannot sue on the express contract. . . . [I]f there was *a wanton desertion of the defendant's service* without his fault, the plaintiff was guilty of a violation of the contract.[18] (emphasis added)

In *Stark v. Parker* (1824), Justice Lincoln wrote for the Massachusetts Supreme Judicial Court that

> *Courts of justice are eminently characterized by their obligation and office to enforce the performance of contracts,* and to withhold aid and countenance from those who seek through their instrumentality, impunity or excuse for the violation of them. And it is no less repugnant . . . that a party who deliberately and understandingly enters into an engagement and voluntarily breaks it, should be permitted to make that very engagement the foundation of a claim to compensation for ser-

tell whether the court was allowing a *quantum meruit* or suggesting that the contract would be divisible when sickness prevented full performance and divisibility was feasible. See *Fenton v. Clark,* 11 Vt. 557 (1839); *Fuller v. Brown,* 51 Mass. (11 Met.) 440 (1846); and *Fahy v. North,* 19 Barbour (N.Y.) 341 (1855).

[16] 12 Johns. (N.Y.) 165 (1815).

[17] Ibid., 167.

[18] *Lantry v. Parks,* 8 Cow. (N.Y.) 63 (1827).

vices under it. . . . *It is not sufficient that [a worker] has given to the party contracted with, a right of action against him.*[19] (emphasis added)

In 1852, the Maine Supreme Court endorsed the *Stark v. Parker* rule, observing that "[i]f it were permitted to the laborer to determine the contract at his pleasure, no well founded reliance could be placed at any time, upon a due observance of it."[20]

It was well understood that the effectiveness of the "entirety" rule in enforcing the performance of contracts was achieved through the imposition of a "penalty" or "forfeiture" on workers. Sometimes it was judicial exponents of the rule who pointed this out, but more often it was judicial opponents of the rule or those who felt ambivalent about it.

In 1839, the Vermont Supreme Court pointed out that "to hold that there can be no recovery [for the value of labor conferred on an employer on or off the contract] operates as a forfeiture and in the nature of a penalty."[21] In 1843, Justice Isaac Redfield, writing for the same court, explained the court's decision to exclude one class of labor contracts, those to do specific work, from the operation of the entirety rule:

> There is no doubt, that, in all contracts, where, by the terms of the contract, either express or implied, entire fulfillment is a condition precedent to any right of action, no recovery, whatever, can be had for part performance. . . . Forfeitures are always odious, both at law, and in equity. *Conditions precedent are in the nature of forfeitures,* and for many years, the courts, both in this country, and in England, have inclined so to construe contracts as to avoid them [citing *Britton v. Turner*].[22] (emphasis added)

Before the 1850s, only the New Hampshire Supreme Court allowed workers to bring a *quantum meruit* action for the reasonable value of their services when they had willfully abandoned contracts for a definite term of service. A close look at *Britton v. Turner*, in which the New Hampshire court first laid down this rule, reveals that what lies behind the decision is a different view of the law's role in enforcing contracts. Justice Parker

---

[19] *Stark v. Parker*, 19 Mass. (2 Pick.) 267 (1824), 271.

[20] *Miller v. Goddard*, 34 Me. 102 (1852), 106.

[21] *Fenton v. Clark*, 11 Vt. 557 (1839), 561.

[22] *Booth v. Tyson*, 15 Vt. 515 (1843), 517–18. However, not all judges held this view. Some maintained that no forfeiture was involved. Failing to fulfill a condition precedent merely meant that no wages legally accrued. "If the plaintiff agreed to labor for the defendants for one year, for instance, and left their service at the expiration of six months, without cause, she could not maintain an action for the services actually rendered, not exactly on the ground of a forfeiture, but in consequence of the non-performance on her part of the special contract." *Rice v. Dwight Manufacturing Co.*, 56 Mass. 80 (1848), 87.

wrote for the court that "[i]f a person makes a contract fairly he is entitled to have it fully performed, and if this is not done he is entitled to damages." [23] A contracting party, Parker maintained, is entitled to performance or to damages, but that is all, and in most cases the entirety rule results in the employer receiving "by reason of the breach of contract by the [worker] a sum . . . utterly disproportionate to any probable not to say possible damage which could have resulted from the neglect of the [worker] to continue [to serve for the entire term]."[24] Parker said of the new New Hampshire rule that it binds "the employer to pay the value of the service he actually receives, and the laborer to answer in damages where he does not complete the entire contract."[25]

According to A. W. B. Simpson, for many centuries the common law of contract reflected a tension between two ideas:

> On the one hand we have the idea that the real function of contractual institutions is to make sure, so far as possible, that agreements are performed; the institution of the penal bond and the practice of the courts in upholding such bonds exemplified this idea. On the other hand we have the idea that it suffices for the law to provide compensation for loss suffered by failure to perform agreements. This second idea is not, of course, necessarily incompatible with the pursuit of the aim of encouraging contractual performance, but it is bound to impose a limitation upon the enthusiasm with which that aim is pursued, and there can well be contexts (for example, contracts for personal service) in which a positive value is attached to the right to break the contract so long as the defaulting party is made to pay compensation. Now if securing performance is the aim to be pursued, the use of penalties *in terrorem* of the party from whom performance is due is the natural and obvious technique. . . .
>
> The penal bond for securing performance was a sophisticated form of self-pledge. . . . The provision of security for performance is still a common practice today, but the general triumph of the compensatory principle has radically altered its character.[26]

Today, in most cases, contracts only entitle parties to performance or damages at the option of the breaching party. In the case of labor contracts, a version of this principle has been constitutionalized.[27]

---

[23] *Britton v. Turner*, 6 N.H. 481 (1834), 494.

[24] Ibid., 487.

[25] Ibid., 494.

[26] A. W. B. Simpson, *A History of the Common Law of Contract: The Rise of the Action of Assumpsit* (Oxford, 1975), 123–24.

[27] For details, see Chapter 8.

However, during the first half of the nineteenth century a majority of American judges seem to have believed, in the case of labor contracts for a term especially, that the role of the law should be to enforce performance of the labor, insofar as that was possible. Except for New Hampshire, no court adopted the position that workers should only be obligated to perform or to pay damages at their option.[28] Even the New Hampshire court was more ambivalent on this question than we may have supposed. The entirety rules that the courts enforced were an expression of these judicial views.

The story of "entirety" is more complicated than this simple picture suggests. The tension Simpson identifies in the English common law of contract can be discerned in courts on both sides of the entirety issue. On the one hand, even the decision of the New Hampshire court in *Britton v. Turner* was carefully qualified. Justice Parker made clear that *Britton* only rejected entirety as a default rule, a rule of construction when the parties had made no explicit agreement as to the time wages were to be paid. If the parties had expressly agreed that no wages would be earned until the service was complete, under *Britton* a worker could still make no claim for back wages either on or off the contract.[29] (In Vermont, at least, I have found a number of such agreements.)

A few years after *Britton,* the New Hampshire court itself expressed deep reservations about that decision. In *Hartwell v. Jewett,*[30] decided only four years after *Britton,* the court ruled that although a worker might maintain an action in *quantum meruit* for the reasonable value of labor conferred on an employer where the worker had quit before completing his term of service, the worker was not entitled to commence his suit until the contract term was over. Hartwell began work for Jewett on November 14, 1833, and served under a contract for a year. He worked until May 7, 1834, "when he left without any sufficient reason."[31] Jewett refused to pay him wages for the time he had worked, and Hartwell commenced an action against him on June 3, 1834. The New Hampshire Supreme Court ruled that a nonsuit should be entered against the plaintiff for having commenced his suit prematurely, that is, before the expiration of the term of service. Justice Upham, writing for the court, took a swipe at *Britton* as he justified the court's decision:

> It is desirable not to give the temptation of a payment of ready money, instead of a delayed payment, to those who already have,

---

[28] I discuss the interesting position of the Vermont Court below.

[29] *Britton v. Turner*, 6 N.H. 481 (1834), 493–94.

[30] 9 N.H. 249 (1838).

[31] Ibid., 249.

perhaps, too much encouragement, at least all they deserve, to faithlessness in fulfillment of their contracts.[32]

Even New Hampshire doctrine continued to be shaped in part by the idea that contract law should aim to enforce the performance of labor agreements, not merely to offer compensation for damages once breach had occurred. In *Hartwell* the court drew back from an unqualified endorsement of the idea that contracts should give the breaching party the option of performing or paying damages. New Hampshire contract doctrine continued to be shaped in part by the idea that the law ought to assist in the enforcement of the performance of labor contracts. Under the *Britton* rule, moreover, it was always possible for an unsympathetic judge or auditor to find that the damage to the employer from the worker's breach fully equaled the value of any labor performed, leaving the worker to recover nothing.[33] How often this may have happened would be difficult to tell. In the end, even the New Hampshire court did not completely embrace the compensation principle, but rather suspended labor contract doctrine between the two principles of performance and compensation.

On the other side of the issue, the Vermont Supreme Court embraced "entirety"[34] in its early decisions but by the late 1830s had begun to recognize the importance of the competing consideration that the rule could lead to the unjust enrichment of employers. Jones leased land from Dyer, and the two agreed that the lessee might clear as much land as he pleased and that the landowner would pay him $2.75 per acre. The agreement specified precisely how the work was to be done, and when a dispute arose between the two, it became clear that the work had not been performed according to the contract. Could the lessee nevertheless collect for the reasonable value of the labor off the contract? The Vermont Supreme Court ruled that he could. Even though the question arose in the case of a particular kind of labor agreement, one which called for specific work to be done rather than for service for a term, the reasoning of the court could easily have applied to agreements for a term. Justice Isaac Redfield wrote that

> where from the nature of the contract it is impossible to put the parties *in statu quo*, as where A builds a house or wall on B's land, or as in the present case, where labor has been performed on [lessor's] land by [lessee], from which [the landowner] will and must derive some benefit and which cannot be transferred to [lessee], the party entitled to it, it has been held that the party performing the labor

---

[32] Ibid., 252.

[33] See *Laton v. King*, 16 N.H. 280 (1848), in which the New Hampshire Supreme Court reversed the decision of an auditor who had awarded nothing to a plaintiff on this ground.

[34] See, for example, *Hair v. Bell*, 6 Vt. 35 (1834); and *Philbrook v. Belknap*, 6 Vt. 383 (1834).

might recover so much only as the labor is worth to the party who
must have the benefit of it. This rule is adopted *ex necessitate,* to prevent one party gaining an unconscionable advantage over the other.
. . . [T]he laborer is entitled to his own labor, or its product, where it
is in such a shape that he can carry it away. In this case he cannot.
Hence the rule has been adopted that the laborer may recover as on
a *quantum meruit,* or in strictness what the labor is worth to the defendant and no more. Otherwise the party benefitted would owe no
equivalent, and the party laboring would be without all remedy.[35]

It is obvious that workers who served for a term also could not in most
cases take back the benefit of labor conferred on an employer. A few years
later the Vermont court in fact allowed a worker, who had failed to complete his term of service because of illness, to recover on a *quantum meruit.*
In this case, the contract had expressly provided that no wages would
be owed until the plaintiff had worked out the entire term. Although the
facts of the case involved illness as an excuse, the court's opinion contained language that suggested it might soon be abandoning "entirety"
completely:

> [*Lantry v. Parks,* a New York case,] furnishes a practical illustration of
> the manifest injustice which may be done, under the rule that there
> can be no apportionment in the case of hired laborers for a given pe-
> riod. It is not the object of the law to punish the party for a violation
> of his contract, but to make the other party good for all damages he
> may sustain by such violation. . . . Under the doctrine that the con-
> tract is entire, and its performance a condition precedent, the result
> is, that if the laborer fails to fulfil his contract, but for a single day, he
> forfeits all that he has done, and in case of what he esteems maltreat-
> ment, he must submit to it, or leave his employer, not only subject to
> answer for such damages as may be sustained, but even at the peril
> of forfeiting all former earnings, in case it should be found by a jury
> of his country, that he left the service without sufficient cause. This
> forfeiture may be ten, or even an hundred fold, more than suffi-
> cient to compensate for all damages arising from a violation of the
> contract.[36]

However, in the following years the court continued to enforce "entirety" in the case of labor agreements to serve for a definite term.[37] After
Hartwell v. Jewett, New Hampshire labor contract doctrine constituted a
kind of compromise between the competing considerations of perfor-

---

[35] *Dyer v. Jones,* 8 Vt. 205 (1836).

[36] *Fenton v. Clarke,* 11 Vt. 557 (1839), 561–62.

[37] *Brown v. Kimball,* 12 Vt. 617 (1839); *Ripley v. Chipman,* 13 Vt. 268 (1841).

mance and compensation. In 1843, the Vermont court adopted its own version of a compromise between the two principles. In *Booth v. Tyson*, Justice Isaac Redfield wrote an opinion that acknowledged the contradictions between the two principles. He attacked the "harshness and severity, if not injustice" of the "entirety" doctrine, and accused it of creating forfeitures that are "always odious both at law and in equity."[38] But Redfield did not go on to repudiate the "entirety" rule completely, merely to limit it to one class of labor agreement, those for a specific term. Entirety should continue to apply in the case of contracts for a term, Redfield ruled, "partly upon the ground of strict [prior] authority, and [partly because] such contracts are incapable of apportionment – not being of a uniform nature."[39] In the case of other classes of labor contracts, those to perform a particular task or to perform piece work, workers should be able to recover for partial performance if the contract was susceptible to apportionment, and in *quantum meruit* otherwise.[40]

Booth involved an iron worker who had agreed to mold pieces for 150 iron stoves. The work was to be done using the employer's furnace. The workman was to be paid so much for each piece of work. He left before completing all the pieces for the required number of stoves, but his employer kept and used the pieces he had completed. When the iron worker sued for wages for the pieces he had made, the Vermont court allowed him to recover. The "entirety" doctrine was thereby reserved in Vermont only for agreements to serve for a definite time, but continued to be enforced in such cases for many more years.[41]

In England the courts at one point excluded workers engaged to perform a task or to make things (piece workers of a kind) from coverage of the Master and Servant acts. In the United States courts sometimes disallowed wage forfeiture in the case of similar kinds of workers. In both countries the courts were feeling their way toward a category of independent contractor, distinct and separate from wage worker. Two kinds of contract rules made it possible to treat such workers differently. First, the rule of substantial performance was sometimes applied to allow those who had contracted to build a house, for example, to recover the reasonable value both of their labor and of the materials they had supplied.[42] Second, the rule of express or implied acceptance was also used in cases where contracts called for a worker to make a certain number of things for an employer but the worker had only performed partially. If an em-

[38] *Booth v. Tyson*, 15 Vt. 515 (1843), 517–18.

[39] Ibid., 515.

[40] Ibid., 517–18.

[41] See, for example, *Winn v. Southgate*, 17 Vt. 355 (1845); and *Green v. Hulett*, 22 Vt. 188 (1850).

[42] *Hayward v. Leonard,* 24 Mass. (7 Pick.) 180 (1828).

ployer did not return the items that were produced, that act might constitute an acceptance and a waiver of the original contract, which would give the artificer a right to recover the reasonable value of his labor.[43]

These rules, however, had the potential for completely undermining entirety because they could also apply to wage workers hired for a term. As a term of service proceeded and an employer raised no objections to the labor supplied, it could be argued that he had implicitly accepted that portion of the contracted-for labor, waiving the original contract and creating in the worker an implied right to recover the reasonable value of his services. Lawyers arguing for workers who served under term contracts sometimes cited substantial performance and implied acceptance decisions to support their cases.[44] Indeed, implied acceptance of the labor was one of the principal grounds on which the decision in *Britton v. Turner* rested.[45] Nevertheless, aside from the New Hampshire court in *Britton*, no other court accepted these arguments in the case of workers hired to serve for a term until the 1850s. Of the three courts besides New Hampshire that adopted *Britton* in the years between 1850 and 1870,[46] two did so in cases that involved labor contracts to perform a task or to make things.[47] Only in Iowa during these decades was *Britton* adopted in the case of a worker hired to serve for a term.[48] Despite the considerable tensions in contract doctrine and principle, entirety continued to be applied to labor agreements, most especially to those involving service for a term, in the overwhelming majority of states until well after 1870.

CONTRACTUAL FORFEITURE PROVISIONS

As complicated as the story of entirety doctrine was, there was yet another basis on which employers commonly claimed wage forfeiture during the nineteenth century. Frequently, explicit forfeiture provisions were included in labor agreements. These provisions were distinct from contract provisions that declared a contract to be entire. They did not provide that wages would not be earned until a term or task had been completely fulfilled. Rather, they required a worker to give a certain amount of notice before leaving and to faithfully obey an employer's shop rules while employed. By the terms of the contract a worker who failed to fulfil these contractual obligations might forfeit all back wages withheld. These kinds

---

[43] *Booth v. Tyson,* 15 Vt. 515 (1843).

[44] See, for example, *Olmstead v. Beale,* 36 Mass. 528 (1837) (citing *Hayward v. Leonard*).

[45] 6 N.H. 481 (1834), 490–93.

[46] Karsten, "'Bottomed on Justice," 242. See also Holt, "Recovery by the Worker Who Quits."

[47] *Allen v. McKibbin,* 5 Mich. (1 Cooley) 450 (1858); *Coe v. Smith, Adm.,* 4 Ind. 79 (1853).

[48] *Pixler v. Nicholas,* 8 Iowa 106 (1859).

of provisions were commonly used in the industrial sector, generally requiring factory operatives to give two weeks' or sometimes a month's notice. They were part of a system of long pay periods in which wages were only paid quarterly[49] or monthly,[50] or at best fortnightly.[51] Long pay periods, together with either explicit contractual forfeiture or entirety, were designed to accomplish in the industrial sector in America the same things that short contracts and penal sanctions were meant to accomplish in England during the same period.

During the first half of the nineteenth century factory operatives in New England sometimes served under one-year contracts.[52] In these cases, the entirety doctrine would have applied to workers' rights to recover back wages. In many instances, however, operatives served under contracts of indefinite duration (no fixed term) determinable on a definite period of notice. In England the courts had had no difficulty in applying penal sanctions to such contracts when a worker failed to give the required notice. However, in the United States some courts balked at the idea of extending the entirety doctrine to contracts that did not contain fixed periods of service.[53] If there was to be wage forfeiture in such cases

---

[49] See, for example, *Thayer v. Wadsworth,* 36 Mass. 349 (1837) (contract for eleven months to do spinning at factory; wages paid "once in three months"); *Hunt v. The Otis Co.,* 45 Mass. 464 (1842). "[W]age settlements in the [Slater villages] by the early 1830s and perhaps even by the late 1820s, appear to have generally slipped into quarterly, monthly, and, in one instance, even bimonthly rhythms. . . . [M]ost post-1830 agreements in the Slater villages covered fewer than twelve months and contained clauses permitting 'either party [to] be released' by giving four weeks' notice." Jonathan Prude, *The Coming of Industrial Order: Town and Factory Life in Rural Massachusetts, 1810–1860* (Cambridge, 1983), 152.

[50] See *Rice v. The Dwight Manufacturing Co.,* 56 Mass. 80 (1848) (mill operative, monthly wage payments).

[51] *Stevens v. Reeves,* 26 Mass. (9 Pick.) 198 (1829).

[52] *Thayer v. Wadsworth,* 36 Mass. 349 (1837); *Wolfe v. Howes,* 20 N.Y. (6 Smith) 197 (1859) (glass works, one-year contract); *M'Millan v. Vanderlip,* 12 Johns. (N.Y.) 165 (1815); *Russell v. Slade,* 12 Conn. 455 (1838) (one-year contract, woolen manufactory). Jonathan Prude argues that in the mills he studied there was a general movement away from long contracts by the 1820s. Long contracts were not effective to stop worker mobility, he contends, both because the mills themselves often violated agreements by laying workers off during the term and because workers frequently left during the term in spite of the contract. Prude, *Coming of Industrial Order,* 153. But Prude did not find that short contracts and notice periods unraveled in a similar way.

[53] See, for example, *Hunt v. The Otis Co.,* 45 Mass. 464 (1842), 467. Reacting to the *Hunt* decision, some Massachusetts factories began to adopt contracts for a fixed term (a year, for example) to bring them within the entirety rule. These contracts, however, were frequently determinable at the will of the employer and on a certain period's notice (a fortnight, a month) by the employee. Structuring the contract in this way brought it within the entirety rule but preserved the monthly or fortnightly notice period for workers and the employer's total discretion to terminate the agreement at will. These contracts also commonly had provisions calling for wage forfeiture if the required notice was not given. Not infrequently wages were paid monthly. See *Rice v. The Dwight Manufacturing Co.,* 56 Mass. 80 (1848).

it would have to be on the basis of an explicit contractual provision calling for forfeiture.[54] If such a provision was included in a labor contract, however, the courts seem to have been willing to give it effect, allowing an employer to retain the accrued back wages of a breaching employee.[55]

Whether under entirety or under contractual forfeiture provisions, factory operatives in the first half of the nineteenth century frequently faced wage forfeiture for breach of conduct at work or for departure without notice, just as their English brethren faced penal sanctions for the same kinds of contract violations. It appears that by the 1840s and 1850s, factory operatives were often contractually obligated to give a fortnight's or a month's notice before leaving, and as in England these contracts, enforceable through wage forfeiture, helped employers to control turnover and agency costs.

Many American employers in the industrial sector firmly believed that the ability to enforce the performance of labor agreements was essential to the success of their operations.[56] In an 1842 Massachusetts case, for example, Elvira Hunt sued the Otis Company for back wages. She claimed "seven or eight months' work $121.84, and credited $61.90 as paid to her. Balance demanded, $59.94."[57] The employers answered by admitting that she had performed the work and agreed with her price for the work, but they said "that they had adopted a regulation [in their factory] which required all persons to give them four weeks' notice of an intention to quit their service, and that [Hunt] knowing that regulation, when she went into their employ, left their service without giving such notice . . . and was not entitled to recover for the services performed by her."[58] They argued

---

[54] *Hunt v. The Otis Co.*, 45 Mass. 464 (1842), 467.

[55] Ibid., 464; *Harmon v. Salmon Falls Manufacturing Co.*, 5 Me. 447 (1853). The issue of what formalities were required to bind the worker did arise in some of these cases because frequently the forfeiture clauses were part of the rules of the shop that were simply handed to a worker when he or she began work. In *Rice* and *Harmon* the Massachusetts and Maine high courts respectively held that under certain circumstances if a worker was given a "regulation paper" at the time he or she began work it would be enough to make the forfeiture clauses part of the contract between worker and company. In *Rice*, however, the court nevertheless allowed the worker to recover her wages on other grounds, preserving the general principle of wage forfeiture under such contract provisions but apparently feeling ambivalent enough to want to do justice in the individual case. Cf. James D. Schmidt, *Free to Work: Labor Law, Emancipation, and Reconstruction, 1815–1880* (Athens, Ga., 1998), ch. 1.

[56] In *Stevens v. Reeves*, 26 Mass. (9 Pick.) 197 (1829), an employer in a cotton factory tried to recover damages for contract breach from a weaver who had left without giving a fortnight's notice, as the shop rules required. This was a much more expensive and much less effective remedy than simply withholding wages and forcing a worker to sue, but the employer obviously felt that his fortnight's notice requirement was important enough to merit initiating a full-scale action for breach of contract.

[57] *Hunt v. The Otis Co.*, 45 Mass. 464 (1842), 465.

[58] Ibid.

to the court that an enforceable notice requirement was *"important to them in the due management of their business, not merely in regard to this case, but as to others"* (emphasis added).[59] Because she was not serving under a contract for a definite term and because the regulation paper she had received on taking up her job did not explicitly say that a worker would forfeit back wages if he or she failed to give the required notice, the Massachusetts court upheld a jury's verdict for the worker.

A number of judges also felt strongly that contracting and strict contract enforcement was essential in industrial employment. In a Maine case decided in 1853, Chief Justice Shepley laid out the principal arguments for enforcing wage forfeiture provisions in labor contracts. Enforcing such agreements, he wrote, made it possible for employers not only to control ordinary turnover costs but also to prevent large losses resulting from collective work stoppages:

> [T]he amount claimed [in this case] is small. The principles involved are alleged to be of importance. It is not difficult to perceive, that they may be so. A corporation or an individual employing several hundreds of persons, may have contracted to furnish large quantities of manufactured goods for sale or exportation, at certain times; and if the persons employed to perform the labor, may in violation of their agreements, and without loss of wages *leave the machinery at rest until other persons can be procured to take their places,* no confidence can be reposed in the manufacturer's ability to fulfil his contracts, and he can obtain no indemnity for losses occasioned by the fault of others. To offer such an employer the right to have a legal contest, and the chance therby to recover damages for the injury he may be able to prove that he has suffered by a violation of each laborer's contract, is little less to him than solemn mockery. The manufacturer and all his laborers would know, that the trouble and expense of such suits would prevent any attempt in that mode to obtain redress. The only valuable protection, which the manufacturer can provide against such liability to loss, and against, what are in these days denominated "strikes," is to make an agreement with his laborers, that if they willfully leave their machines and his employment without previous notice, all, or a certain amount of wages that may be due to them shall be forfeited. While courts of justice should not attempt by construction to make such agreements between the employer and those employed, they should not shrink from the duty of causing them, when fairly made, to be honestly and faithfully executed; or attempt by construction to aid a party to avoid the penalty to which

[59] Ibid., 467.

he has agreed to expose himself for a willful violation of his contract.[60] (emphasis added)

Similar arguments were part of the English discourse of labor contract enforcement during the same period.

Contractual provisions calling for wage forfeiture were used in the North well into the last quarter of the nineteenth century. In *Harrington v. Fall River Iron Works Company*,[61] for example, an employee sued to recover fifteen days' back wages. The company argued that under an agreement he had signed he forfeited all his back wages because he left work without giving the required notice. The agreement provided that "I, the undersigned, employee of the F.R.I. Works Co., agree that in case I intend to leave their employment I will give notice of such intention, and work ten full working days; in default of which I agree to forfeit all money which may be due me."[62]

In northern industry, when contracts for definite terms became less common, employers frequently incorporated into their employment agreements notice requirements together with forfeiture clauses and enforced them through long pay periods and wage forfeiture. They used labor contracts and labor contract enforcement in many of the same ways that English employers of the period did. Both sought to enforce the short contracts of their industrial wage workers strictly to make strikes more difficult, to make the departure of workers more orderly, and to punish breaches of conduct at work.

In northern agriculture, contracts for definite terms survived much longer. Typically such contracts called for three, four, five, or more months of labor, and in the case of these agreements failure to complete the term would often result in the loss of all wages. It was in these types of agreements that the traditional rule of entirety continued to play its most important role throughout the nineteenth century.[63] Clearly, strict contract enforcement was important in agriculture because it allowed farmers to lock in their labor supply for those critical moments when they simply had to have enough hands available and working.

An interesting New York case from the period makes clear why an action for damages could not serve agricultural employers nearly as well. In one of the relatively infrequent instances in which an employer sued an

---

[60] *Harmon v. Salmon Falls Manufacturing Co.*, 5 Me. 447 (1853), 452.

[61] 119 Mass. 82 (1875).

[62] Quoted in ibid., fn. on 82. The court permitted him to recover wages on the ground that his failure to give notice was due to illness and was therefore not willful, even though the contract did not make any distinction between intentional and unintentional failures to give notice.

[63] Schmidt, *Free to Work*, ch. 1.

ordinary manual worker for damages for contract breach (rather than withhold wages and place the burden on the worker to bring a suit for wages), the court found that the worker had indeed breached his agreement. The court, however, refused to allow the farmer to collect consequential damages. He was entitled only to the normal measure of damages, the excess cost involved in replacing the departing worker. "It is preposterous to say," the court declared,

> that the [worker] was at liberty, at any time, to leave the plaintiff's service without cause and on his mere fancy. . . . [H]e could not leave him before the season had expired, without violating his contract. . . . The [lower court], however, committed an error in admitting evidence of the damage to the plaintiff's crops, in consequence of the defendant leaving his service. The legal measure of damages in such cases is the difference between the contract price with the defendant and the price the plaintiff was obliged to pay for the labor to supply his place.[64]

Such a remedy made contracts largely unenforceable. It was hardly worthwhile in most cases for a farmer to bring suit to recover only the difference between the contracted-for wage and the wage he was forced to pay a replacement worker, and to recover nothing for what in some cases were his significant damages, that is, crop loss. Given the normal measure of damages, actions for breach of contract were not even a remotely close legal substitute for wage forfeiture. Wage forfeiture was not only an inexpensive remedy (employers had only to withhold wages), it also confronted workers with significant pecuniary disincentives, in many cases, to leaving their jobs before they had worked out their terms.

PECUNIARY VERSUS NONPECUNIARY REMEDIES

Today we would say that the nonpecuniary remedy of penal sanctions that the English used in the nineteenth century made English wage labor unfree, but that the pecuniary remedy of wage forfeiture that Americans used did not. These different characterizations, it should be clear, do not represent a natural line drawn between coerced and voluntary labor, but rather a societal judgment that employers must never be permitted to force workers to choose between performance of a labor agreement and certain disagreeable alternatives, because such choices transform labor contracts into contracts of slavery, but they may, if public policy permits,

---

[64] *Peters v. Whitney,* 23 Barbour (N.Y.) 24 (1856), 24–25.

force workers to choose between performance of a labor agreement and other very disagreeable alternatives. There is far from universal agreement, however, about how the remedy of wage forfeiture should be viewed. In the twentieth century, for example, the International Labour Organization took the position that "in certain circumstances conditions analogous to forced or compulsory labour may arise as a consequence of the method of payment to the worker whereby his employer defers payment to a given date or postpones payment after the agreed date, thereby depriving the worker of a genuine possibility of terminating his employment."[65] Earlier chapters demonstrated that on occasion twentieth-century courts declared that a kind of pecuniary alternative to performance of labor, starvation, could give rise to involuntary servitude.

However, one of the results of dividing labor into qualitatively different kinds, free and coerced, where coerced labor is associated with nonpecuniary forms of pressure and free labor with pecuniary forms of pressure, is to create the impression that the two types of coercion are not comparable. In fact, pecuniary and nonpecuniary contract remedies are comparable in the crucial sense that both create disagreeable alternatives to performance of labor, alternatives that are disagreeable enough so that a worker would frequently decide to perform the labor rather than suffer the alternative. It is entirely reasonable to compare the disagreeableness of the different alternatives.

Exactly how disagreeable any alternative is may well influence a judgment about whether it should be viewed as creating coerced labor. How disagreeable an alternative to performance is the pecuniary remedy of wage forfeiture? One difficulty is that the answer depends in good part on the circumstances of the case: How much labor is being forfeited and what does the value of that labor mean in the life of a particular worker? In two cases, for example, farm workers were confronted with losing ten and one-half months[66] and five months of back wages.[67] In another case, a factory operative faced the loss of three or four months of back wages.[68] The prospect of losing between a quarter of a year's and nearly a full year's labor must certainly have confronted those workers with a very disagreeable alternative to performance. Recall that in England some workers were prepared to submit to short prison terms to free themselves to take higher paying jobs, implicitly deciding that the pecuniary loss was more disagreeable than a short prison term.

---

[65] International Labour Conference, *Forced Labor*, Report IV(2) (Fortieth Session, Geneva, 1957), 28.

[66] *Lantry v. Parks*, 8 Cow. (N.Y.) 63 (1827).

[67] *Olmstead v. Beale*, 36 Mass. 528 (1837).

[68] *Hunt v. The Otis Co.*, 45 Mass. 464 (1842).

Large pecuniary losses in the case of wage workers living marginal lives might well mean that the disagreeable alternative to performance would involve physical suffering, such as insufficient food, inadequate heat, or insufficient shelter. Even the loss of two weeks' or a month's back wages, the prospect faced by many factory operatives, could represent a very disagreeable alternative if a worker was barely making ends meet with steady wages. Here too the alternative to performance might well involve physical suffering, either in the form of foregone necessities or in the form of mandatory labor if a worker was then forced to resort to the poor law.[69] Where a worker had resources to fall back on, however, forfeiting two weeks' wages might not have represented nearly as disagreeable an alternative as imprisonment at hard labor. The disagreeableness of the alternative that wage forfeiture created lay on a continuum from very disagreeable to hardly disagreeable, depending on circumstances. In many cases, however, it erected an alternative to the performance of a labor agreement that was nearly as disagreeable (coercive) as a short prison term. In these cases there is good reason for saying that the remedy produced coerced labor, and the failure to acknowledge this is the result of a deeply political judgment that pecuniary pressures, except in the most extreme case, should not be viewed as producing unfree labor.

We know less about the nineteenth-century American system of contract enforcement than we do about the English one because we lack the kind of comprehensive statistics that are available for certain periods in England. We do not know how many industrial employers used wage forfeiture provisions in their contracts or how many actually retained wages in the cases of workers who left. We also do not know how many farmers held onto the back wages of agricultural workers who failed to work out their terms of service.[70] However, there is reason to believe that this system of labor contracting and contract enforcement played an important role in nineteenth-century American northern wage labor, a role comparable to the one contracting played in nineteenth-century British wage labor.[71] For one thing, the supreme courts of many states repeatedly saw

---

[69] For labor requirements in the case of recipients of poor relief, see Robert Steinfeld, "Property and Suffrage in the Early American Republic," *Stanford Law Review* 41 (1989).

[70] There is fragmentary evidence that some farmers paid farm hands even when they failed to complete their terms of service. See Jack Larkin, "'Labor Is the Great Thing in Farming': The Farm Laborers of the Ward Family of Shrewsbury, Massachusetts, 1787–1860," *Proceedings of the American Antiquarian Society* 99, pt. I (1989): 197–98 (worker who left on account of sickness paid; payment of back wages to quitting worker delayed until the date of the end of the contract; quitting worker given twelve days' back wages "in justice he was not entitled to one cent").

[71] This view contravenes the conventional wisdom that American employers generally found it impossible to enforce contracts and early on abandoned all attempts to use contracts to control labor costs. See Prude, *Coming of Industrial Order,* 150–57, for a nuanced presentation of this view. It may be the case that outside of agriculture *long* contracts were

wage forfeiture cases throughout the nineteenth century. Given the significant burden that litigation must have represented for working people and how unlikely it must have been that any particular worker would undertake litigation, the frequency with which these cases arose suggests that the grievances on which they were based were common. Perhaps the best evidence we have is that beginning in the 1870s numerous state legislatures took up the issues of long pay periods and wages due on quitting, termination, or dismissal and enacted a variety of statutes to address them. If the practices of long pay periods and wage forfeiture had not been widespread, it is unlikely that so many state legislatures would have bothered to deal with these issues.

WAGE PAYMENT LAWS

In the years between 1834 (the year *Britton* was decided) and 1870 only three courts (besides New Hampshire's) adopted the *Britton* rule.[72] Moreover, even the *Britton* rule continued to allow entirety so long as an agreement explicitly called for it.[73] Between 1870 and 1915 the courts in only six additional states joined the ranks of the original four.[74] The real legal movement away from wage forfeiture did not originate with the common law courts but with state legislatures that began to enact wage payment statutes in the 1870s. The first of these was adopted in Massachusetts in 1879, and numerous other states followed suit over the next several decades. During the last quarter of the nineteenth century and into the twentieth century state legislatures enacted a range of pro-labor legislation, maximum hours laws, child and woman labor laws, anti-scrip laws, etc. Pay statutes were among these. Organized labor was partly responsible for the passage of these laws, but this legislative outpouring was also a product of broader populist and progressive reform movements.

Legislatures enacted wage payment statutes for a number of different reasons. Among the justifications offered were that these statutes would reduce the need for working people to seek credit between long pay periods and thereby help to eliminate widespread "money-lending activities

generally abandoned in the United States by 1840. However, quarterly, monthly, and bi-monthly notice periods supported by pay periods of similar lengths also created a form of binding contract; in this form binding contracts remained common in industrial employment throughout the nineteenth century. American employers would not have continued to insist on short binding agreements enforced through wage forfeiture if they had not found such contracts useful in helping them control labor costs.

[72] Karsten, "'Bottomed on Justice,'" 242. See also Holt, "Recovery by the Worker Who Quits."

[73] The Iowa high court made this clear when it adopted the rule of *Britton v. Turner* in 1859; see *Pixler v. Nichols*, 8 Iowa 106 (1859), 107.

[74] Karsten, "'Bottomed on Justice,'" 242.

tainted with usury [which] impos[ed] many hardships on the working classes." [75] Requiring regular pay periods would also reduce the power unscrupulous employers exercised to exploit their workers through company stores and the truck system. [76] Pay statutes also helped to eliminate the evil "of a forfeiture of compensation for time worked." [77] A number of wage statutes was passed in the strike-filled year 1919, and one writer has argued that legislatures passed these statutes "to deprive employers of too strong a weapon with which to combat a justifiable strike. The loss of compensation for labor already performed would be a serious deterrent from the use of that form of collective bargaining." [78] Although arguments were made that these reforms were necessary to reduce oppressive practices in wage labor, in no case was it suggested that they were necessary to eliminate practices that made wage labor unfree labor. In this respect the basis of the American reforms was different from the British reforms, in which in the final stages of debate over penal sanctions it was argued that reform was necessary if labor was to be free.

The American reforms were radically incomplete even by the 1930s. By 1935 only two-thirds of the states had enacted any form of pay statute. [79] The statutes themselves were of three basic kinds, and only in states that enacted all three kinds were wage workers completely protected against long pay periods and wage forfeiture if the courts of the state continued to adhere to traditional common law rules. The first kind of statute required employers to pay workers on a regular periodic basis. The trouble was that a large number of these statutes mandated that wages be paid either monthly or semi-monthly, leaving many workers in no better a position than before. [80] In 1935 only eight states required weekly payment of wages. [81] Moreover, under these statutes, if a worker left or was dismissed between pay periods he or she might lose back wages for the portion of the period already worked.

The second and third kinds of statute were aimed at remedying this defect. One required employers to pay a worker all back wages on discharge, the other required employers to pay all back wages whenever an employee quit. Some statutes of this kind covered both discharge and abandonment, but some only covered discharge and not abandonment,

<hr>

[75] Carl E. McGowan, "The Divisibility of Employment Contracts," *Iowa Law Review* 21 (1935): 71 (review of legislative histories of a number of these statutes, 69–72).

[76] Ibid., 70.

[77] Ibid.

[78] "Legislation," *Harv. Law Review* 43 (1930): 651 n. 41.

[79] McGowan, "Divisibility of Employment Contracts," 69.

[80] Only one state mandated monthly payments. A number of states, however, called for semi-monthly payments. See McGowan, "Divisibility of Employment Contracts," n. 57.

[81] Ibid.

whereas others covered abandonment but not discharge.[82] Where statutes of this kind had been enacted, but without a periodic wage payment statute having also been adopted, an employer could still rely on long pay periods to control his employees. Only where all three kinds of statutes were passed would employers legally lose the possibility of using wage withholding as a means of compelling the performance of labor agreements. Even in these cases that might not necessarily be true, given that in a number of states wage statutes did not cover all types of businesses. In some cases wage statutes covered only corporations or only a particular kind of corporation.[83] In other cases farm laborers and domestic workers were not covered.[84]

Even in these forms wage statutes met with considerable legal resistance. In a number of states employers challenged their constitutionality and succeeded in having the statutes struck down. There were successful constitutional challenges to these statutes from the 1890s into the 1920s. The two main grounds on which courts struck these statutes were that they infringed the right of freedom of contract and that they discriminated against certain classes of employers, but other constitutional grounds were also invoked for voiding laws.[85] Nevertheless, a number of statutes were rewritten and reenacted and thereafter successfully passed constitutional muster. Increasingly over the first few decades of the twentieth century state courts began to find pay statutes constitutional. By the 1930s employers had largely given up challenging wage payment legislation, apparently conceding in many states that there was no longer a real possibility that they would be legally permitted to use long pay periods and wage forfeiture to enforce labor agreements.[86]

This is a complicated, messy story. Only two-thirds of the states had adopted any wage statute by 1935, and the coverage of these statutes differed from state to state, producing what can only be described as a patchwork of different protections for workers against wage withholding and forfeiture, some more complete, others less complete, others largely nonexistent; in aggregate a radically incomplete reform. There can be little doubt, however, that these statutes played an important role in changing wage payment practices over time in many states and in eliminating in many places the enforcement of labor agreements through wage forfeiture. As in Britain, it was late-nineteenth- (and in the United States, also early twentieth-) century, pro-labor social legislation that pushed wage labor in the direction of modern free wage labor, in which contracts and pu-

[82] Ibid., n. 58–60.

[83] "Legislation," 649; see also McGowan, "Divisibility of Employment Contracts," n. 63.

[84] McGowan, "Divisibility of Employment Contracts," n. 63.

[85] Ibid., 75; "Legislation," 649, 651.

[86] McGowan, "The Divisibility of Employment Contracts," 74, 78.

nitive contract enforcement play no significant role. In the American North as well, modern free wage labor was not the product of the rise of free contract in free markets but of the social legislation and court decisions that restricted contract remedies over the half century between 1875 and 1925.

Conclusion

It is odd to think that the free wage labor of our imaginations, of no enforceable labor contracts, is a product of state regulation, but that is what a history of labor contract enforcement reveals. It is the product of a particular contracts policy that restricts both the remedies the law makes available to employers and the remedies it permits them to include in labor agreements. Before this restrictive contracts policy was adopted in England and the United States beginning in the last quarter of the nineteenth century, employers had available and were permitted to write into labor agreements a broader range of remedies. These made it possible to enforce labor contracts, compelling workers in many cases to perform the work they had promised to do. Employers regularly used these legal remedies to keep workers from leaving jobs without first giving notice and to punish them for misdemeanors at work.

I say it is odd to think of the free wage labor of our imaginations as a kind of regulatory constraint on contracts because we have become so accustomed to thinking of it as a kind of freedom from regulation. If pressed we might almost say that free wage labor arose spontaneously in free markets wherever a large population of the propertyless was available to work. We can believe these things because of several assumptions we continue to make about the history and development of wage labor.

The first is an economic assumption. It holds that the compulsion of the market, economic compulsion, worked well to supply employers with willing labor at low prices. They had no need to resort to physical or legal coercion and did not want to. Indeed, physical and legal coercion was costly and inefficient. It frequently meant having to carry workers through trade downturns. Because the compulsion of the market guaranteed that employers would always be able to secure enough workers at economic prices whenever they needed them, it was simply unnecessary to undertake these added expenses. Physical and legal coercion, moreover, produced workers who were sullen and performed their jobs poorly, raising real labor costs.

The second assumption was about contracts in Anglo-American law. Oliver Wendell Holmes Jr. articulated this assumption perhaps better than any one else more than a hundred years ago:

The only universal consequence of a legally binding promise is, that the law makes the promisor pay damages if the promised event does not come to pass. In every case it leaves him free from interference until the time for fulfillment has gone by, and therefore free to break his contract if he chooses. . . .[1]

If, when a man promised to labor for another, the law made him do it, his relation to his promisee might be called a servitude *ad hoc* with some truth. But that is what the law never does.[2]

Together, these assumptions created a compelling logic for the narrative of free wage labor. Labor contracts were useless, and in any case the compulsion of the market guaranteed that employers would have a productive labor force at the lowest possible cost. When employers in fully developed markets were left free to do as they wished they spontaneously adopted free wage labor because it served their economic interests better than any other form of labor, and where necessary they even imposed it on workers.

This account has withstood attacks on either assumption separately. Over the last few decades, for example, historians of both English and American labor have discredited the notion that the only natural consequence of breaching a binding labor agreement in the nineteenth century was that the promisor had to pay damages. A number of articles has been written about "entirety" and wage forfeiture in the United States. Others have been written about the use of penal sanctions to enforce labor agreements in England.[3] It has become apparent that English and American employers possessed or could incorporate into contracts remedies that made it possible for them strictly to enforce labor agreements, and that they often did so.

However, as long as the economic logic underlying the account of wage labor continued to be accepted, it was difficult to explain why employers would have engaged in this kind of behavior. They might have been indulging in a kind of atavistic ritual, or have been shamelessly abusing the system, or have been engaging in unnecessary piling on, but whatever the reason, it was not central to the nature of wage labor in the nineteenth century. Because there was no good economic reason for employers to have used contracts and contract enforcement in wage labor, the practice didn't seem to make sense and couldn't be connected coherently with any

---

[1] Oliver Wendell Holmes, Jr., *The Common Law* (Boston, 1881), 301. Cf. "RETURN of the Number of Persons Summarily Convicted and Committed to Prison, in the Several Counties of *England* and *Ireland*, for BREACH of CONTRACT in Neglecting Work or Leaving Service During Each of the Years 1854 and 1855," *Parl. Papers* (1856), L:633–37. ("Total in England (1854) 2, 42, (1855) 1,541.")

[2] Holmes, *Common Law*, 300.

[3] For citations, consult the notes in the Introduction.

larger story that could be told about the nature and development of wage labor. Indeed, because the practice made so little sense it has sometimes been ignored altogether by legal historians in the United States.[4]

Over the same period, but separately, historians writing about slavery discredited the other assumption. They demonstrated that physical and legal coercion did not invariably produce labor that was more expensive and less efficient than free wage labor.[5] Physical and legal coercion could be used to drive workers harder to produce more at lower cost. Indeed, these forms of coercion, alone or in conjunction with pecuniary inducements, might be more effective at addressing effort problems than market pressures. At the same time an economic approach to labor history became more common, making it clearer that even employers of wage labor often confronted sullen workers and had to deal with effort problems.[6] If there were costs associated with maintaining workers through downturns in the trade cycle, there were also costs associated with not binding workers to jobs during upturns in the trade cycle. It was simply not true that employers in developed markets could always find enough skilled workers at prices they were willing to pay whenever they happened to need them. The literature on the economic effectiveness of nonpecuniary pressures in slavery remained a separate literature, however. This was only natural while nonpecuniary pressures were viewed as fundamentally incompatible with wage labor.

Bringing the two literatures together makes it possible to understand what employers were up to when they required and strictly enforced labor agreements in wage labor. They were using forms of legal compulsion to tie workers to jobs for longer or shorter periods and to address effort problems because they hoped to reduce labor costs by taking these steps. Strict labor contract enforcement has seemed like an anomaly in wage labor because our understanding has been shaped by the assumptions of an older narrative tradition. That anomaly holds the key to a

[4] Benno Schmidt, Jr., "Principle and Prejudice: The Supreme Court and Race in the Progressive Era. Part 2: The Peonage Cases," *Columbia Law Review* 82 (1982): 705. Indeed, it seems that in the twentieth century even some English legal academics were unaware of the earlier history of crime and labor contracts. See Carleton Kemp Allen, *Legal Duties and Other Essays in Jurisprudence* (Oxford, 1931), 221 ("It is wrongful to break a contract: but there are only two or three cases in English law in which breach of contract is a crime. They are all modern. They occur in connexion with the contract of service and industrial disputes, and they contemplate circumstances in which the wilful and malicious breach of a contract of service would involve serious danger to life of property"), citing statutes only enacted in 1875 or later, Conspiracy and Protection of Property Act, 1875, and Trade Disputes Act, 1927.

[5] See in particular Robert Fogel and Stanley Engerman, *Time on the Cross: The Economics of American Negro Slavery* (Boston, 1974).

[6] Michael Huberman, *Escape from the Market: Negotiating Work in Lancashire* (Cambridge, 1996).

different understanding of the nature of wage labor in the nineteenth century.

During the early nineteenth century, as freer markets based on personal agreements were brought into being, the law made a broad range of contract remedies available to employers to enforce labor agreements as part of this first blossoming of freedom of contract. Where they had the choice, many employers of wage labor enthusiastically embraced these remedies. They used labor contracts and tried to enforce them strictly. They sought to punish wage workers for misdemeanors at work and to make it more difficult for them to leave their jobs. Although their interests didn't all coincide with respect to contracts and contract enforcement, many nineteenth-century employers believed that the freer labor markets that had recently been created would not work properly unless they were able to hold workers to agreements. In addition, as they embraced contracts and contract enforcement they strove to limit the costs to which contracts sometimes exposed them by limiting their obligations under contracts and, where desirable, by adopting shorter contracts, which gave them greater flexibility but which also continued to allow them to enforce agreements strictly.

Strict contract remedies expanded the options employers possessed for disciplining their workforce, placing them in a position to decide whether contracts and contract enforcement would work to their advantage. Many of them decided that contracts and their enforcement did, but they didn't think that they had to choose between market pressures and legal pressures once and for all, and they didn't want to. They preferred to have the option of using one or the other or both together, depending on circumstances. There were situations in which market pressures didn't work well and could be profitably supplemented by pressures derived from the strict enforcement of contracts. Many employers were quite happy to use nonpecuniary pressures to compel work where the state and culture permitted it. There was no strict line in their minds confining the use of nonpecuniary pressures to slavery or imported contract labor. Where they did not possess a remedy like penal sanctions, that has to be seen as a kind of regulatory constraint under which they were forced to operate.

The case of contract labor in the northern United States makes it easier to appreciate this point. The legal system in the North did not provide importers of contract workers with penal sanctions or orders of performance to enforce their agreements after the 1830s. This was a highly unusual state of affairs in the contract labor of the period. Employers of imported contract workers had powerful economic reasons for wanting to be able to hold workers to their agreements strictly. American employers were not different in this respect from importers of contract labor elsewhere. Why did they not possess nonpecuniary remedies to enforce labor agreements in the American North after the 1830s? The answer is to be found in the contracts policies of northern states, which limited the legal remedies that would be available to employers to enforce labor agreements, primarily on the ground that nonpecuniary contractual compulsion produced a kind of slavery. It is easiest to see the absence of nonpecuniary remedies as a kind of regulatory constraint in the case of American contract labor, but learning more about the position of English wage labor during the same period makes it apparent that it also constituted a regulatory constraint in American wage labor. When we consider that many American employers of this period seem to have been eager to use and enforce labor agreements in wage labor, we have to ask ourselves whether, all things being equal, they might not have liked to possess the kinds of remedies that English employers did. The legal system in the North, however, only authorized pecuniary remedies, although some of these could create quite harsh choices for workers.

The contracts policy of a state or nation determines how broad or narrow the range of remedies will be to enforce labor agreements. What were the political, legal, social, or economic conditions that led to the adoption of a more or less restrictive set of contract remedies? In the United States a number of factors contributed to making northern contracts policy.[7] The American Revolution was undoubtedly important, placing personal liberty at the heart of American values. However, two other more specific factors were of great importance. During the Revolution northern states began to wrestle with the question of whether black slavery should continue to be permitted. Over several decades these states either abolished slavery outright or adopted gradual emancipation schemes. As they did so it became apparent that other forms of servitude, including those arising from contract, would also have to be eliminated if abolition was eventually to succeed in the North. During the Revolution American states also began to reexamine the question of who should be entitled to vote in the newly declared republic. Over the next several decades, state constitutional conventions extended the right to vote to many people who had previously been excluded from the suffrage. A broadened suffrage, in conjunction with the popular rejection of servitude, seemed to place limits on the kinds of contract remedies most state legislatures felt free to consider. American workers also seem to have made a difference, at least in certain port cities into which European indentured servants continued to be brought. In certain cases, they agitated against the nonpecuniary enforcement of the labor agreements of imported workers, making enforce-

[7] I have described this process more fully elsewhere. See Robert Steinfeld, *The Invention of Free Labor: The Employment Relation in Anglo-American Law and Culture* (Chapel Hill, N.C., 1991).

ment of those agreements nearly impossible.[8] A few northern courts ruled that nonpecuniary remedies to enforce labor agreements contravened constitutional prohibitions on slavery and involuntary servitude.[9]

However, even if these political, constitutional, and social conditions led to a contracts policy that generally foreclosed the use of nonpecuniary legal pressures to enforce labor agreements, they did not produce a contracts policy that restricted contractual remedies as severely as modern law does. American employers could still avail themselves of or write into labor agreements a variety of harsh *pecuniary* remedies to enforce labor agreements. Perhaps because American common law courts were more insulated from electoral pressures[10] than legislatures and could invoke precedent and the timeless reasoning of the common law, it was to common law courts that employers primarily looked for effective remedies to enforce labor agreements in the northern United States. Although they were limited to pecuniary remedies, these could sometimes create highly disagreeable alternatives for workers to continued performance of their agreements. Indeed, it was because they could create such disagreeable alternatives that these pecuniary remedies could be used in place of nonpecuniary remedies in labor contract enforcement. A broad suffrage and the popular rejection of servitude were apparently not enough in the northern United States to restrict contract remedies further. Only when American labor became better organized after the Civil War and gained sympathetic allies in state legislatures was legislation passed that cut back contract remedies even further.

The English case seems easier to understand. The English did not confront slavery domestically and were not forced to think hard about whether the penal enforcement of labor contracts created slave-like conditions in their homeland. When the Master and Servant acts were being reconsidered in Parliament in 1823, no group had developed political or moral arguments against penal sanctions that were based on widely accepted English values. That only began to happen over the period from the 1840s to the 1860s. Without arguments that were capable of galvanizing large numbers of people and without the vote, abolition of penal sanctions did not seem like a live option. Until 1867 a large portion of the English working classes were excluded from the suffrage. However, once substantial numbers of working people gained the vote, Parliament became more responsive to their appeals. In addition to gaining the vote, by the 1870s the English working classes had become better organized, devel-

---

[8]   Ibid., 167–68.

[9]   *The Case of Mary Clark, a Woman of Color,* 1 Blackf. 122 (Ind., 1821); *Parsons v. Trask, and Others,* 73 Mass. (7 Gray) 473 (1856).

[10] Lawrence M. Friedman, *A History of American Law* (New York, 1985), 126–27, 371–73.

oped an aggressive legislative agenda, and generated powerful arguments against the continued use of penal sanctions. Parliament began to feel the pressing need to repudiate penal sanctions. In 1875 it moved to restrict significantly the range of contract remedies to enforce labor agreements that employers would henceforth possess.

In both England and the United States a broad suffrage, together with a well-organized labor movement and a set of arguments that resonated widely because they drew on fundamental values, seem to have been crucial for establishing a contracts policy that imposed strict limitations on the remedies employers would possess at law or be permitted to create contractually to enforce labor agreements.[11] In places where a distinct segment of the laboring population continued to be excluded from the suffrage and value continued to be placed on the faithful performance of contracts, there continued to be the possibility that legislatures would establish nonpecuniary remedies for the enforcement of labor agreements. Something like this seems to have happened in the American South during the final decades of the nineteenth century, when southern legislatures created a variety of nonpecuniary contract remedies to enforce the labor agreements of (largely black) agricultural workers.

The importance of the suffrage, however, goes well beyond the power it gave laboring people to place limits on the scope of contract remedies. It operated as a mark of inclusion in the political community, of citizenship. As one southern federal judge noted, penal sanctions for contract breaches subjected one person to the dominion of another in ways that were deeply incompatible with the exercise of political rights of self-government. Rights of citizenship seemed to demand that the law prohibit the complete commodification of labor.[12] Under the restrictive contracts policies of modern free wage labor, workers can only sell their personal energies on certain terms. In effect they are restrained from conveying irrevocable control over their persons to those for whom they work. We owe modern free wage labor to the contracts policies that place limits on the extent to which labor legally can be commodified. These contract restrictions were only put into place as a result of judicial decisions and the pro-labor legislation that was enacted in the half century between 1875 and 1925. Modern free wage labor is a product of this restrictive state regulation.

---

[11] David Montgomery makes a similar argument in *Citizen Worker: The Experience of Workers in the United States with Democracy and the Free Market during the Nineteenth Century* (Cambridge, 1993).

[12] On incomplete commodification, see Margaret Jane Radin, *Contested Commodities* (Cambridge, Mass., 1996), ch. 7.

Index